CONTINUITY & CHANGE IN THE AMERICAN FAMILY

To Larry Long and Martin O'Connell,
our Census Bureau mentors and longtime colleagues,
who showed us how to discern and write about demographic trends

Lynne M. Casper • Suzanne M. Bianchi

CONTINUITY & CHANGE IN THE AMERICAN FAMILY

Sage Publications
International Educational and Professional Publisher
Thousand Oaks ▪ London ▪ New Delhi

For information:

Sage Publications, Inc.
2455 Teller Road
Thousand Oaks, California 91320
E-mail: order@sagepub.com

Sage Publications Ltd.
6 Bonhill Street
London EC2A 4PU
United Kingdom

Sage Publications India Pvt. Ltd.
M-32 Market
Greater Kailash I
New Delhi 110 048 India

Printed in the United States of America

Library of Congress Cataloging-in-Publication Data

Casper, Lynne M.
  Continuity and change in the American family / by Lynne M. Casper and
Suzanne M. Bianchi.
       p. cm.
Includes bibliographical references and index.
  ISBN 0-7619-2008-0 (cloth: alk. paper)
  ISBN 0-7619-2009-9 (pbk.: alk. paper)
  1. Family—United States. 2. Social change—United States. I.
Bianchi, Suzanne M. II. Title.
  HQ536 .C386 2002
  306.85'0973—dc21

                                    2001003377

01   02   03   04   05   06   10   9   8   7   6   5   4   3   2   1

Acquiring Editor:	Jim Brace-Thompson
Editorial Assistant:	Karen Ehrmann
Production Editor:	Denise Santoyo
Copy Editor:	Judy Selhorst
Typesetter:	Marion Warren
Indexer:	Teri Greenberg
Cover Designer:	Michelle Lee

CONTENTS

3. Childbearing   67
By Martin O'Connell

4. Single-Mother Families   95

5. Fathering   123

ACKNOWLEDGMENTS

This project was conceived in 1997, when David Klein and Bert Adams, editors of Sage's Understanding Families book series, approached Lynne Casper about the need for a demographically focused book on the family. Lynne enticed Suzanne into collaborating on a proposal and enlisted Martin O'Connell to write Chapter 3, on childbearing. The project would never have been undertaken without the substantial commitment of resources by the Population Division of the U.S. Bureau of the Census. John Long, Robert Kominski, and Martin O'Connell deserve special thanks for their support.

During the 1998-99 academic year, we team-taught a graduate seminar in family demography at the University of Maryland, an endeavor that proved to be a lot of fun and also helped us to formulate many of the questions that most intrigued us about demographic changes in the family. After we completed a first-draft manuscript for this book, we wrote a *Population Bulletin* titled "American Families" (Bianchi and Casper 2000) at the invitation of the Population Reference Bureau. Our work for PRB gave us the perspective we needed to rework the introduction, Chapter 1, and the conclusion of the book. The insightful questions and suggestions of PRB editor Mary Kent not only improved our *Population Bulletin* but contributed to this book.

Thanks are due to John Haaga and Peter Donaldson of PRB, who provided a congenial sabbatical getaway for Suzanne that greatly assisted her in finishing work on the manuscript. This book also could not have been completed without the resources and encouragement provided by Christine Bachrach at the National Institute of Child Health and Human Development (NICHD), and we are both deeply grateful for her support.

Many people contribute to an undertaking such as this. We are especially indebted to our students and colleagues at the Census Bureau, the University of Maryland, and the National Institute of Child Health and Human Development. Special thanks go to Philip Cohen, who generated many of the tabulations that underlie the tables and figures in this volume. Philip also contributed to Chapter 1 through his collaboration with Lynne on a paper dealing with multigenerational households (Cohen and Casper forthcoming from *Sociological Perspectives*), to Chapter 2 through his collaboration with Lynne on the measurement of cohabitation (which appeared in *Demography;* Casper and Cohen 2000), and to Chapter 10 through his collaboration with Suzanne on trends in mothers' labor force participation (published in *Monthly Labor Review;* Cohen and Bianchi 1999). Liana Sayer, in collaboration with Lynne, produced the estimates of types and outcomes of cohabitation from the National Survey of Families and Households reported in Chapter 2. Liana also collaborated with Suzanne on the analysis of time diary data on time with children and time spent on housework (published in *Social Forces;* Bianchi et al. 2000) that appear here. Kristin Smith contributed to Chapter 7 through her collaboration with Lynne on a paper concerning children in self-care (*Journal of Family Issues;* Casper and Smith forthcoming).

Two individuals provided yeoman's service in putting the manuscript together, making editing changes, and correcting figures and tables: Beth Mattingly of the University of Maryland and Elizabeth Mumford of NICHD, both whizzes at MS Word, MS Excel, and working with good humor under pressure. Chris Morett generated some of the data for Chapter 9 while an intern at the Census Bureau in the summer of 1999, and David Cort and Liana Sayer provided invaluable service in tracking down references. We owe special thanks to Census Bureau colleagues Jason Fields and Kristin Smith for their assistance with analysis of the Survey of Income and Program Participation (SIPP) data. Jason assisted with the analysis of children's well-being (Chapter 8), and Kristin collaborated with Lynne on the analysis of child-care arrangements (Chapter 7). Thanks are also due to Cathy O'Brien, Jane Dye, and Joan Kidwell at the Census Bureau who assisted us in tracking down historical data and verifying numbers.

The final manuscript benefits from the thoughtful reviewer comments of two leading family demographers, Pamela Smock and Linda Waite. The project was launched and nurtured by David Klein and Bert Adams, with David providing extensive comments at various points. We also greatly benefited from the good humor and gentle prodding of our editor at Sage Publications, Jim Brace-Thompson.

Finally, our spouses contributed in two different but equally important ways. Matt, Lynne's husband, an aerospace engineer and ever a whiz on the computer, worked 24-hour shifts at some points, guiding Lynne through pesky tables and figures (better than that MS paper clip) and helping make sure deadlines were met (or missed by a little rather than a lot!). Matt also shopped, cooked, and did laundry so Lynne could have more time to devote to the project. Mark, Suzanne's husband, as always did extra parenting duty (almost without complaint!) when she inevitably allowed work on chapter drafts and manuscript revisions to spill over into "family time." In the end, it is their support, day in and day out, that most contributes to our successes. The insights we have into how families are changing reflect their collaboration with us in the "big adventure"—crafting our own balance in work and family life.

INTRODUCTION

Recently, one of us had the opportunity to attend the wedding of a close friend's daughter. As with most weddings, the event came off beautifully, despite the complexity of the seating arrangements required to accommodate all of the bride's and groom's various family members. The bride, age 29, was conceived outside marriage at a time when nonmarital births were less common than today. Her biological parents married shortly before her birth but did not feel financially able to care for her and therefore placed her for adoption. She was adopted as an infant and raised by two adoptive parents, who were present at the wedding.

In her mid-20s, the bride sought out her birth parents and discovered that subsequent to her adoption, they had two other daughters who were now of college age. The bride's two full biological sisters, whom she met as adults, were bridesmaids in the wedding. When the bride sought her birth parents, she found two biological parents no longer married to each other but open to a relationship with the daughter they had long ago placed for adoption. Thus her biological mother and her mother's cohabiting partner attended the wedding. Her biological father, who had subsequently married again, also attended the wedding, along with his second wife and their adopted 10-year-old daughter, who was the flower girl in the wedding.

Indeed, it is difficult to describe all the relatives of the bride who were present to witness her marriage. By some counts, the bride might be said to have had three mothers present at her wedding—an adoptive mother, a biological mother, and a stepmother (her biological father's current wife). When she established connections with her biological parents, she also found two biological siblings and another sibling not biologically related to her (the adopted daughter of her biological father).

Needless to say, the groom's relatives had their hands full just trying to figure out how all the bride's guests were related to each other. Yet the groom's family was only somewhat less complicated. The groom's parents were divorced, and the groom's mother attended with her same-sex cohabiting partner. His father also attended the wedding, with his second wife and their 13-year-old son, the groom's half brother.

We begin our book with this example of family complexity, first, because it is a real-life example, not one we made up. More important, our rendition of the array of relatives at this wedding allows us to comment on the demographic perspective and illustrate several of the themes that will emerge as we track change and continuity in American family life.

The foregoing account provides a descriptive skeleton of the bride's family life in which the first order of business is merely to understand how the bride is embedded in various family relationships and how she came to be connected to so many different people that she could have a wedding at which the guests would include her three mothers, two (or three, if we count cohabiting relationships) fathers, and three siblings (two full, one adopted). Our example illustrates where family demographers first concentrate their efforts—on detailed description of family relationships—in order to anchor speculation, hypotheses, and theorizing about family change.

The demographic events experienced by the bride's and groom's parents and their connections to kin also point to several important transitions in family life, some of which have changed greatly in recent years. The story contains a transition to marriage; a nonmarital pregnancy; two adoptions; child rearing by biological parents, stepparents, and adoptive parents; two marital disruptions; remarriages; and both same-sex and heterosexual cohabitation. Trends in many of these behaviors form the core of what we describe about American families in this volume. During her childhood and young adult years, the bride experienced changes in living arrangements and connections to various kin. She was born to one set of parents but then lived throughout her childhood with another set of parents. Presumably, she spent time on her own before marrying at age 29 and now was moving into her own married-couple family. She developed connections in recent years of her life to kin not available to her earlier in life. The dynamism of family life is apparent in this example, as well as the complexity of U.S. family relationships and the nuances involved in studying them properly.

Absent from our discussion of the bride's wedding is an exploration of the emotional attachment the bride felt for each of her "mothers" and "fathers," although one might presume some bond of affection between the bride and each of her kin, given that all were in attendance at the wedding. Demographic description of the family tends not to focus on meanings or emotions; rather, it leaves that to the purview of the social psychologist. Yet family demographer Frances Goldscheider (1995) argues that documenting and understanding family demographic behavior can help us to connect individuals and their societies and to forge the link between the micro behaviors of individuals and the macro structures of societies. Present in any demographic description of family events, including our example of a wedding, is plenty of grist for further research at both individual and societal levels. For example, would the bride's biological parents have been more, less, or equally as likely to place her for adoption if her birth had occurred today, when births outside marriage are far more common and presumably less stigmatized in U.S. society? And which parents will the bride feel obligation toward should they require assistance in their old age—all equally, her adoptive parents who raised her, or, perhaps, her biological mother, who may be the most needy if she ends up without a partner in old age? Conversely, will the bride be as likely as her biological father's other children, whom he raised, to receive a financial bequest from him upon his death?

After we describe U.S. family trends, how do we interpret them? What are their causes? What are the consequences, positive and negative, of recent changes in American families? As we shall discuss below, it is far easier to gain agreement on what family demographic changes have taken place in the United States than it is to achieve consensus on what those trends mean.

Is the American Family in Decline? ●

Many of the trends in family formation and dissolution in the United States in the past few decades are not disputed, but discussion of the meanings of these trends has often taken the form of acrimonious debate about family life and the future viability of the family. David Popenoe (1988, 1993, 1996) has been one of the most outspoken proponents of the view that the American family is in crisis. He argues that the family as an institution in U.S. society is in unprecedented decline. Americans are in the process of rejecting the bedrock of family functioning, the nuclear family. Increasingly, the family is becoming ill suited to serve its two most important functions: rearing children and providing sustained emotional sustenance to its members. Although not as outspoken as Popenoe, many family demographers have also voiced concern about the effects on children of some of the trends that so disturb him (Bumpass 1990; Cherlin 1999; McLanahan and Sandefur 1994; Preston 1984).

Others, particularly feminist scholars such as Judith Stacey (1990, 1993, 1996), argue that what is in decline is our normative idea of what a family is, or rather a particular historical ideological picture of the American family. This idealized conception, often referred to as the "Ozzie and Harriet" family, depicts a family as one in which parents marry for life, children are born inside the marriage, and the mother cares for the children in the home while the father works outside the home to provide for the family. This image, Stacey argues, is undergoing metamorphosis as we come to realize that the 1950s version of "ideal" family life is no longer viable, or even desirable. Those who offer this interpretation of family change are far more sanguine than Popenoe about the future of the American family. Although also concerned about negative consequences for children (see Cowan 1993; Stacey 1993), they are more likely to see the changing economy rather than the family as the culprit and are more likely to emphasize the positive aspects of changes in women's opportunities that have accompanied changes in their roles within the family.

Those on both sides of the "family decline" debate seem to accept the view that the 1950s version of the family was historically rooted in unusual times—bolstered by a vibrant economy and by the lack of opportunity afforded to women. That is, in the 1950s, discrimination against women in the labor market was widespread, and most women had few opportunities outside the home. At the same time, the post-World War II economy was expanding rapidly, creating many opportunities for even low-skilled male wage earners to command wages that could support a family (Levy 1998).

Along with economic conditions, family demographic behaviors were also unique in the mid-20th century (Cherlin 1992). Certain family behaviors today resemble behaviors of the 1930s more closely than those of the 1950s, for example. Family demographer Paul Glick (1975) has labeled the family demographic picture of the late 1930s as "gloomy"; he provides this description:

Many marriages had been delayed, so that the average age at marriage had risen, and a near-record nine percent of the women 50 years old had never married. Birth rates had lingered at a low level. . . . Lifetime childlessness was edging up toward 20 percent and many of the children whom some leading demographers thought were merely being postponed were never born. (Pp. 15-16)

Why was the picture of delayed marriage and forgone childbearing gloomy? The implicit assumption of observers of marriage and fertility patterns in the 1930s was that delayed marriage and forgone childbearing were not what women wanted, but rather a result of the Great Depression and the dire economic constraints faced by young adults during that decade.

As Glick notes, the picture changed dramatically with the post-World War II Baby Boom, when marriage occurred at early ages, a very high proportion of women married, and fertility increased. But the description he offers of the 1930s is quite similar to what a demographer today might write about recent trends in marriage and fertility. However, in the early part of the 21st century, it is less clear that these trends would be described as gloomy. If current marriage and family changes are largely viewed as consequences of poor employment opportunities for young men, as some argue (Oppenheimer, Kalmijn, and Lim 1997), they might indeed be termed gloomy. But to the extent that delayed marriage and fewer children result from greater educational and labor market opportunities for women in the 1980s and 1990s, recent trends might be considered anything but gloomy.

Two tendencies often impede observers' understanding of family change and cloud the current debate about the meaning of family change. One is the tendency to forget history and instead project the present into the future. That is, it is often assumed, at least implicitly, that changes in the family have been linear over time and that they will continue, unabated, indefinitely. Often this is not the case, as the above comparison of the 1930s, the 1950s, and the present illustrates. The other tendency that limits consensus on the "disappearing" American family is the tendency of commentators to choose particular starting points to use in their assessments of change that will support the arguments they wish to make. For example, changes in certain family behaviors can be exaggerated or minimized depending on whether one charts the trends from midcentury, when a unique set of demographic and economic circumstances prevailed (early marriage, early childbearing, unprecedented economic expansion), or from some other time point. In this volume, we try to be cognizant of the facts that trends are not always linear and that many of our data series begin with the usual post-World War II period.

The family demographic perspective guides our selection of topics and interpretation of trends. We are sociologists with training and research careers in family demography, and both of us have spent a number of years analyzing family patterns at the U.S. Bureau of the Census. Below, to orient the reader, we provide an overview of the demographic perspective and outline some of the theoretical traditions that have been most influential for demographers' understanding of family change. We also explain some of the terminology used throughout this volume and conclude with brief descriptions of the chapters that follow.

● A Note on the Demographic Approach to Studying Families

Family demographers study the changing composition of families, the ever-changing nature of intergenerational and gender ties that bind individuals together into familial and household units. The study of household formation, dissolution, and living arrangements that forms the core of family demography is ultimately the study of individual and societal well-being, for it is through these family ties and household groupings that resources are exchanged and less able members are cared for by more able members (Sweet and Bumpass 1987). Indeed, much of the family demographic work of the past few decades has examined the interrelationships of family change and socioeconomic outcomes for various segments of the population. Thus family demographers focus on marriage, divorce, childbearing, and living arrangements in order to understand both why individuals behave as they do toward each other and why, when those individual behaviors are aggregated into nations, societies look similar or dissimilar, not only in their family configurations but also in their economic, political, and cultural institutions (Goldscheider 1995).

Family demography focuses on structure and process: family composition at points in time and transitions between different family statuses (Teachman 1993). Family demographers describe who lives together and how this changes over time. But also of major concern is how people come to be joined in families—transitions into and out of first marriages, into parenthood, into and out of cohabiting relationships, into and out of remarriages, and so forth.

Like most demographers, family demographers tend to think in terms of rates and "at-risk" populations; they tend to want to separate family change into components such as change in population composition versus what reflects change in the propensity or likelihood that some family event, such as marriage, occurs. Demographers also tend to categorize change as reflecting age, period, or cohort effects—that is, they tend to separate explanations of change into those that emphasize aging of the population (or life-course change of individuals); those that focus on broad, sweeping societal or time-period effects; and those that result as successively younger birth cohorts with different life experiences replace older cohorts. Demographers also think about life stages or life-course events in terms of duration of time (or person-years or -months) spent in certain states, such as married and living with a spouse or living in a single-parent family. This represents a unique way of thinking about the world that begins with careful description and then moves on to causal interpretation.

At the heart of careful description lies the concept of a "universe" (the denominator in a percentage) and the time period under consideration. Let us try to illustrate. In November 1999, the Fertility and Family Statistics Branch of the U.S. Bureau of the Census received a phone call from Senator Daniel Patrick Moynihan's office about a disturbing news article regarding the decline of the American family. An Associated Press (1999) story heralded the results of a study by the University of Chicago's National Opinion Research Center (NORC) that found that just 26 percent of households were made up of married couples with children in 1998, down from 45 percent in the 1970s. The article also stated that NORC's results painted an even bleaker picture of marriage than recent Census Bureau figures, which reported that 36 percent of families were made up of married couples with children in 1997. A little more than a year earlier, an article had appeared in the *Washington Post* (Vobejda 1998) based on a Census Bureau report (Bryson and Casper 1998) declaring that the composition of the American family was stabilizing. The senator's office was calling to get the story straight. How could one article report the stabilization of the American family and then, just a little more than a year later, another decry its demise? And how could the two estimates (26 percent versus 36 percent) of the proportion of households with married couples and children be so different? Could the percentage of married-couple households with children really have declined by 10 points in a year?

The discrepancy, it turned out, was the result of a reporter's failure to take into account the difference in the denominators, or universes, for the two statistics. The 26 percent figure referred to the proportion of *all households* that included a two-parent family with children, but not all households include families. Persons living alone, for example, are not classified as families. The 36 percent figure actually referred to the proportion of all *family households* that contained married couples with children. When the focus is narrowed to only housing units that contain families, the percentage headed by married couples with children is higher than when all households—family plus nonfamily households—are considered. The Census Bureau report actually noted that 25 percent of all households were maintained by two parents with children, a figure very close to NORC's estimate of 26 percent. In addition, the Census Bureau report (and the *Washington Post* article) highlighted changes in the 1990s, whereas the NORC report (and the Associated Press story) focused on longer-term changes occurring after 1970. Thus when 1970 was used as a point of comparison, the two-parent family was seen to have declined substantially, but when the mid-1990s were the point of comparison, no change was noted.

The demographic perspective embodies a tendency to think in terms of rates and composition and a desire to separate these two components in explanations of change. What do we mean by that? Demographers often standardize for age composition in order to isolate "true" or "real" rates of behavioral change. For example, suppose the number of marriages decreases in the United States between two time points. A question that might arise is, Does this change represent a decline in the popularity of marriage? The demographer's first instinct is to ask the question, Has the population eligible for, or "at risk" of, first entering marriage shrunk in size or changed in some important way, causing the number of marriages to decline? For example, we know that first marriage is most likely to occur in young adulthood. What happens if the number of adults in the population between the ages of 20 and 29 declines, as was the case after the Baby Boomers passed through these ages? Marriages might decline just because there are fewer people in the age range in which first marriage is most likely to occur. For this reason, rather than examining merely the number of marriages, the demographer examines a rate, such as the first marriage rate of never-married females ages 20 to 29. If this rate of first marriage declines between two time points, we move closer to the interpretation that perhaps the popularity of marriage has declined.

But the inferential leap is still great, because most demographic behaviors, marriage included, are closely related to age and sensitive to shifts in the timing of events in individuals' lives. Hence family demographers have always been quite attentive to the age patterning of behaviors and to the importance of understanding the effects of shifts in age structure. Let's consider another example. The rate of first marriage for women in their 20s could decline either because more women remain single throughout their lifetime and there is more "nonmarriage" in the population or because a greater proportion of women are postponing marriage, perhaps in favor of doing other things, such as finishing school and getting established in the labor market before they marry. One might be more comfortable drawing the conclusion that marriage is becoming less popular if the former behavior, more lifetime singlehood, seems to be what is happening rather than if the latter behavior, marrying at later ages, is reducing the marriage rate for young women (Oppenheimer 1997). That is, the timing of family demographic events in people's lives is important and influences how we interpret change.

Theoretical Frameworks ● in Family Demography

Demography in general, and family demography in particular, is often accused of being merely descriptive. Demographers, it is claimed, have no theory. Like us, most family demographers claim homes in other disciplines, such as sociology, economics, anthropology, and social psychology, and frequently incorporate theories from these disciplines into their demographic studies. Family demographers, then, like most social scientists, have many theories about what causes individuals to behave as they do or what factors, demographic and nondemographic, impinge on historical and societal settings. Like other social scientists, demographers share the basic premise that good, sound, empirical description is the bedrock of theorizing. Without it, theories can often be spun to explain things that don't exist. To return to the above example, we must be sure that the likelihood of marrying is indeed declining before we can begin to theorize about why marriage is becoming less popular. If the declining number of marriages can be explained by a smaller population at risk or eligible to marry or by a shift in the age when marriage typically occurs, then a grand theory explaining why marriage is no longer valued is pointless. Much of the value of family demography, and indeed of this volume, is that it emphasizes making sure that there is a sound empirical basis from which to make claims about family change. Once we are certain about the nature and magnitude of family change, we can begin to theorize about the mechanisms causing that change.

This is not to suggest that all family demography has to contribute is description. Indeed, several theoretical strands that meld the demographic perspective with theories from other disciplines have been influential in explaining family change on the population level, and researchers often employ them to interpret changes in family behavior at the micro level. Below, we discuss three of these theoretical perspectives: demographic transition theory, the life-course perspective, and family economic theory.

Researchers have long used demographic transition theory to explain family and fertility change on the population level. Recently, some scholars have suggested that the United States and Europe are engaged in a "second demographic transition" and have made modifications to the original theory to explain more recent family change (Lesthaeghe 1995).

Probably the most frequently invoked perspective for thinking about family change in the family demographic literature in the United States today is the life-course perspective. This perspective seems less a theory than an overarching framework for thinking about family change in the lives of individuals. The perspective jibes well with how demographers think: The life-course perspective's focus on transitions and trajectories and the importance of attention to historical settings and places parallel nicely the demographer's toolbox emphasizing rates, person-years of experience, and age, period, and cohort effects.

Finally, the microeconomic theory of the family offered by economists such as Gary Becker (1974, 1991; Becker, Landes, and Michael 1977) has become influential among family demographers in their assessment of family behavior in the past few decades and coincides with a growing interest in family behaviors within economics. Although this perspective has increasingly been criticized and modified by both economists (especially feminist economists) and family demographers outside economics, aspects of Becker's theory concerning why family members act as they do continue to undergird the choices of topics that family demographers study and interpretations of the behaviors of individual family members. Hence we also sketch the tenets of this perspective below.

Demographic Transition Theory

Perhaps the main theory in demography is that of the demographic transition—the notion that a society moves from a high-mortality, high-fertility regime through a transitional phase in which mortality declines, first creating large population growth. Fertility ultimately follows suit until the society arrives at a situation in which mortality and fertility reach low levels and are again more or less in balance, as they were before the transition. Some family theorists, most notably Lesthaeghe (1995) and van de Kaa (1987), argue that Western countries such as the United States and European nations are experiencing a second demographic transition, motivated by some of the same factors that influenced the first transition from high- to low-fertility regimes but also with some marked differences in the causal mechanisms. Lesthaeghe (1995) argues that ideational change, in particular the increased value placed on individual autonomy, and to a lesser extent the goal of female emancipation or gender equality motivate family changes in the second demographic transition, changes that are unlikely to be reversed.

What characterizes the second demographic transition? Lesthaeghe charts three phases. The first, characterizing the 1960s and 1970s, witnessed an accelerated upswing in divorce, fertility decline, and delayed marriage. This was followed by the spread of premarital cohabitation and an increase in nonmarital births. Finally, in the last phase, reached only by some European countries (and the United States), there has been a plateau in divorce rates, more postmarital cohabitation replacing remarriage to some extent, some recuperation in fertility, especially at later ages, and an end to the decline in teen fertility. The results of these changes are an increase in single-parent families, with increased risk of poverty for children; more one-person households; and life-cycle transitions that are less strictly (or normatively) patterned and more complex.

Whereas the first demographic transition was motivated by a "quiet increase" in the importance of individual autonomy and a desire for improved child well-being, the second transition is much more adult focused. The emphasis on individual autonomy is more public, and increased "quality" is demanded of adult relationships (which makes it harder for individuals to sustain lasting commitments such as marriage). Individuals are also increasingly unwilling to accept the institutional control of the state or the church that characterized earlier periods. Finally, Lesthaeghe (1995) points to advanced consumerism and an increased market orientation as factors affecting the second demographic transition.

The Life-Course Perspective and Family Demography

As early as 1906, with the work of Roundtree on poverty, "the family life cycle has been associated with family demography" (Teachman, Polonko, and Scanzoni 1987). The family demographer most influential in developing the family life-cycle approach in the United States was longtime U.S. Census Bureau demographer Paul Glick (1979:Fig. 5), who tracked the "typical" ages at which women of different birth cohorts made transitions between family life-cycle stages—for example, the average age at which women first married, had a first birth and entered the family-building stage of the life cycle, or experienced the departure of the last child from the household, signaling the beginning of the "empty nest" stage of family life. Glick's work was ahead of its time in focusing attention on important family transitions, but the family life-cycle approach was ultimately discarded as a conceptual model by demographers who found the focus on stages too constraining theoretically (Teachman et al. 1987). As families changed, many individuals' lives did not follow orderly sets of life stages, families were often broken by divorce long before one spouse died, children left home but returned again with some frequency, and increased cohabitation made transitions between "family" stages uncertain.

Family demographers have increasingly turned to a life-course perspective of the family that focuses more on transitions than on stages. Researchers who take the life-course perspective do not assume predetermined stages and are more interested in studying family behaviors by focusing on the number, timing, and sequencing of important family-related transitions that occur during individuals' lives. As Glen Elder (1985), a leading proponent of the life-course perspective, has noted, the concepts of trajectory and transition are central in the contemporary study of the life course. Individuals are viewed as following, over the course of their lives, life trajectories. Components of a life trajectory include work and family decisions. Individuals' family trajectories are marked by transitions (or what a demographer would more commonly call *events*). People make transitions from being unmarried to being married, from being childless to being parents, from being married to being divorced or widowed, and so forth. Researchers who invoke a family life-course perspective are interested in many of the same events that Glick studied to define family life-cycle stages. But life-course analysts prefer the trajectory concept—the notion that as we age, we all make pathways, and that individual pathways take different directions.

Trajectories are marked by sequences of life events or transitions, and individual trajectories are intertwined bundles of decisions about family and work. Any individual's life trajectory is also interlocked with the trajectories of others, especially significant others such as parents, spouses, and children. Interlocking trajectories connect persons across generations (consanguineal connections) and gender (conjugal connections). Because age, sex, and the notion of cohorts figure prominently in demographic rates, the focus on ties that bind across generations and across gender forms an affinity between family demographic analysis and a life-course perspective.

The life-course perspective fits conceptually with certain methodological advancements in the study of the family—the increase in longitudinal studies of individuals and modeling techniques that share conceptual properties with the standard life table, a mainstay of demographic analysis. The focus on transitions, timing of transitions in terms of age, and durations between transitions converges with techniques demographers use to study population change. Demographers typically use life tables to study mortality, fertility, and nuptiality regimes. A life table focuses on how long a population "lasts" in a certain state (life in the case of mortality, marriage in the case of nuptiality) and the rate at which the population surviving in a state makes transitions between states. In life tables, duration in (and sequencing of) states as well as transition probabilities are important, just as they are conceptually to life-course analysis (Moen, Dempster-McClain, and Williams 1992). Increasingly, these are subject to modeling with a set of tools known variously as event-history models, survival analysis, and hazards models.

One final way in which the life-course perspective articulates well with an interest in family demographic change is in the focus on time and space, on the fact that family change or family life trajectories that are typical in one time period or historical setting may not be typical in another time or place. The family life cycle conceptualized by Glick, for example, was well suited to the analysis of mid-20th-century U.S. family behavior, with its low rates of divorce, relatively high rates of marriage and childbearing, and increasing life expectancy. It is not necessarily so fitting for analysis of family trends after 1965, as divorce and cohabitation rates rose, or earlier in the century, when premature death often broke a conjugal partnering before children left the household to form their own families.

The focus on the contexts in which work and family trajectories unfold allows life-course analysts to contemplate the different consequences that may attend family transitions in different historical settings. For example, the timing of childbearing that is optimal, or at least considered optimal, may vary between settings where child and maternal mortality is high and settings where such mortality is low. The focus on context fits well with the demographer's traditional focus on cohort—the notion that individuals born in a certain time (and place) may encounter unique experiences that carry through their lives and shape later behaviors.

Demographers have long paid attention to the "demographic metabolisms" of different populations—how rapidly they are replacing themselves or growing and the components of that growth (Ryder 1992), often with a somewhat deterministic, biological model as a frame. The life-course perspective offers a more probabilistic conceptual frame; individuals can take varying pathways, with different consequences attending their different choices.

Economic Theories of the Family

The development of family economics in the 1960s was linked to several theoretical streams within economics: life-cycle theories of consumption, theories of human capital development and labor supply, and work on household production and time allocation (Willis 1987). A whole new literature sprang up that examined marriage and fertility behaviors and decisions about the use of time and the consumption of goods within the home.

Gary Becker's (1974) theory of marriage formalized the notion of a marriage market and introduced concepts such as the "gains to marriage" and a specialized division of labor in the household. Mincer and Polachek (1974) developed a theory that connected the family behaviors of women to their earnings position in the labor market. Easterlin (1973) explained fertility swings as resulting from changes in preferences for children caused by changing income aspirations and labor market conditions of birth cohorts. Becker et al. (1977) discussed divorce in terms of costs and benefits, expected gains to partnerships, and the role of uncertainty and imperfect information.

In this literature, marriage and divorce behavior was connected to changes in women's allocation of time between the market and the home. Concepts such as "comparative advantage" were invoked to explain gender differences in time allocation between home and market. The rise in women's labor force participation and the decline in fertility within marriage were discussed in terms of opportunity costs for women. Children were discussed as "consumer" or "producer" durables, requiring investment to realize current and future utility. Much of the legacy of this theoretical development remains in the lexicon of terms used to discuss family demographic change.

Economic theory was particularly influential in the analysis and interpretation of the rise in female employment and its possible connection to marriage and fertility behavior. Women's increased education and rising employment were seen as increasing the likelihood of divorce and reducing fertility. Labor market experience raised the value of women's time spent in the labor market and hence the cost (in terms of forgone wages) of spending time outside the labor market raising children. It also contributed to divorce because it eroded the complementarity of what men and women brought to marriage (Becker et al. 1997). Marriages, it was argued, were most likely to be formed and least likely to be dissolved when each partner saw an advantage to being married over remaining single. When a woman's comparative advantage in the home relative to the market was greater than her husband's, the couple would allocate more of her time to the home and his to the market, and both would have much to gain in marriage and much to lose upon divorce.

The economic theory of labor market search was also suggested as a theory for understanding delayed marriage (Oppenheimer 1988). With increased investment in schooling and poor prospects for labor market entrants, more recent cohorts of young men were taking longer to get established in the labor market, thereby increasing the uncertainty as to what kinds of economic providers they would eventually be. This extended the period between reaching adulthood and entering a first marriage.

As Lundberg and Pollak (1996) note, the common preference model served as the basis for economic theorizing about the family in economics at least until the model began to be challenged in the 1980s. The notion was that family members acted as though they were maximizing a single, shared utility function. Although the theorists acknowledged that family members might have divergent preferences, they minimized the problems this assumption afforded by postulating that a family had an altruistic head who allocated resources to members in such a way as to achieve their cooperation in maximizing a single utility function (Becker 1991). Income was pooled and then allocated to maximize family well-being. What happened within families was more or less a black box: Income flowed in and then families efficiently allocated resources to the purchase of goods and services, the consumption of leisure, and the production of children, all in accord with a common, shared preference for optimal family output.

Economic theories of the family were influential because they seemed to provide a conceptually elegant way of thinking about family behaviors, especially expenditure patterns and labor supply. However, like the family life-cycle concept, many aspects of the theory ultimately proved too limited theoretically and too tautologous to be useful for the analysis of family behavior (Lundberg and Pollak 1996). Hence this abstraction of family functioning has come under increased scrutiny for failing to theorize adequately situations in which adults within families have different and conflicting preferences. Empirical evidence showing that money is spent differently depending on who controls it, with more allocated to children's needs when women control a greater share, casts doubt on the income-pooling and single-utility-function framework. Empirical work has also raised questions about the strength of the causal role of women's economic independence in the movement away from marriage (Oppenheimer 1997; Sayer and Bianchi 2000). Bargaining models arising out of game-theoretic approaches to economic behavior are increasingly favored by some economists who analyze family behaviors (Lundberg and Pollak 1996).

However, many of the concepts and other aspects of Becker's (1981) framework remain firmly ingrained in the study of family economic behavior. For example, part of the calculus involved in selecting a mate no doubt does include the weighing of costs and benefits of a particular marriage, just as a cost-benefit calculus must also figure into decisions about exiting marriage. The notion of opportunity costs connected to the expenditure of time remains useful. Women (and men) who allocate time to the labor market have less time to allocate to the home. Although perhaps too narrowly economic, the notion that actors behave in certain ways to realize their preferences, within a budget constraint, helps to conceptualize family decisions as purposive, rational behavior of actors operating within conditions of uncertainty and constraint. The economic perspective thus has introduced a rigor of thinking into the family demographic literature, as well as attention to measurement issues such as sampling selectivity and unmeasured variables, that has enhanced empirical analysis and thinking about family demographic change.

● A Note on Data and Family Terminology

In developing the empirical examination of trends in family behaviors we present in this volume, the data sources we have relied upon most heavily are the family data collected annually in the March supplements to the Current Population Survey (CPS). The CPS is conducted monthly by the U.S. Bureau of the Census, and in March of each year detailed family composition and family economic data are ascertained. The data gathered in this unbroken series of collection periods, dating from the late 1940s, have become, along with the data in the decennial U.S. Census of Population, the main data used by demographers who chart family living arrangements in the United States.

U.S. households and families comprise a wide variety of living arrangements, and to discuss them, we need to establish some standard definitions of key concepts. Given our reliance on data collected by the U.S. Census

Bureau, it would be useful to begin with an introduction to the specific ways in which that agency uses family terminology (see Bryson and Casper 1998). A *household* can contain one or more people—everyone living in a housing unit makes up a household. In most cases, the person who owns or rents the residence is known as the *householder*. For the purposes of examining family and household composition, the Census Bureau defines two broad types of households: family and nonfamily. A *family household* has at least two members related by blood, marriage, or adoption, one of whom is the householder. A *family* consists of all related people in a family household. The term *nonfamily household* is used to describe either a person living alone or a household in which the householder lives only with nonrelatives.

A family household can be maintained by a married couple or by a man or woman with no spouse in the home and may or may not include children. In contrast, a nonfamily household can be maintained only by a man or woman with no relatives at home. Prior to 1980, Census Bureau terminology referred to household members as primary individuals (if they were householders or related to the householder) and secondary individuals (if they lived in the household of someone to whom they were not related by marriage, blood, or adoption). *Children* include sons and daughters by birth, stepchildren, and adopted children of the householder regardless of the children's ages or marital statuses.

When we want to assess the different types of families and households and how they have changed, we look at the composition of households and families. When we want to know about the relationships and characteristics of persons in households, we examine the living arrangements of individuals. For example, if we wanted to know about children and families, we could ask the question, How many families have children? But we could also ask, How many children live in families? In the first case we are interested in family composition; in the second, we are interested in living arrangements.

If one reads the literature, one finds many suggestions about how families should be defined and what living arrangements should be classified as families. For example, Popenoe (1993), who is so concerned about family decline, argues for defining the family as "a relatively small domestic group of kin (or people in a kinlike relationship) consisting of at least one adult and one dependent person" (p. 529). He notes that many would not agree with his definition because it excludes married childless couples. Ryder (1987:117) argues for defining the family as two or more persons, each of whom is married to, a parent of, or a child of another member of the coresident group. This is actually quite close to the Census Bureau's working definition of a *family group,* which is a count of family households plus related subfamilies (i.e., families within families, either married couples or parent-child units living in a family household) and unrelated subfamilies who live in someone else's household. However, this definition still leaves out some potential family members, such as married partners.

Cohabitation presents the biggest challenge to Census Bureau definitions of households and families because, by definition, those cohabiting have not entered into legal marriage. If parents are not married to each other, one will be classified as a nonrelative under Census Bureau definitions even when both live with their biological children in the same household. As we discuss in Chapter 2, cohabitation obscures the distinction between one- and two-parent families as well as the dichotomy between family and nonfamily households.

In the family history literature, there is also a somewhat different classification of family that emphasizes whether household groups are nuclear or extended. A *nuclear family* consists of a conjugal couple and their children. More complex living arrangements are variously named and described. For example, Steven Ruggles (1994) classifies households that include kin other than spouses or children as *extended* households. He also uses the term *fragmentary* to include nonfamily households and single-parent households with no other kin. We include data on multigenerational households in Chapter 1 but restrict our examination of extended families to those that contain two or more generations of adults.

Demographic data have strengths and weaknesses. On the one hand, large data sets allow researchers to monitor family change on both national and state levels and to estimate the characteristics of even very small populations (e.g., cohabitors, single fathers) with a high degree of accuracy. The quality of federal data is also generally highly regarded. On the other hand, such large surveys are expensive, and cost constraints often prohibit collection of the more detailed information that researchers need to conduct in-depth research investigating causal mechanisms. Public funds allow agencies such as the Census Bureau, the Bureau of Labor Statistics, and the National Center for Health Statistics to undertake massive data collection efforts. When budgets are lean, agencies are sometimes forced to cut back on the numbers or types of questions they ask. Entire data collection efforts, most notably vital statistics data collection on marriage and divorce, have fallen prey to budget cuts.

Another consideration for statistical agencies is the maintenance of the comparability of data over time. As time passes, some concepts become outdated, and although it might seem to make sense to change the way a question is asked, the need to maintain a consistent series of estimates may take precedence. If a survey is altered, one cannot be certain whether any observed change in the data is due to a change in the population or to a change in the survey. Many such surveys are used to monitor trends that have significant and far-reaching impacts, such as the unemployment rate. Wall Street routinely relies on the accuracy of this information to conduct business. Just imagine the problems that could be caused if a multimillion-dollar decision were made based on a change in the unemployment rate that occurred solely because someone changed the wording of a question.

From time to time, surveys also become politicized because Congress mandates the inclusion or deletion of questions on specific topics. For example, the 2000 Census long form included three new questions on grandparents raising grandchildren due to requirements of welfare reform legislation. The marital status question was deleted from the short form because there is no existing law or regulation that depends for its enforcement on the gathering of this information.

In this book we focus primarily on trends in the past two decades because recent trends are less well-known, trends for earlier periods are documented elsewhere (e.g., in the 1980 Census monograph on the family by Sweet and Bumpass [1987], and in Cherlin's 1992 book on trends in marriage and divorce), and comparable data on a variety of family behaviors are plentiful. However, we shift our focus when it seems necessary to examine a longer or shorter time frame in order to understand and interpret recent change. The trends we document have different starting and ending points because the limited availability of some data and the lack of comparability of other data dictate the comparisons we can make. At times we would have preferred to use earlier or more recent data to extend our trends, but that wasn't always possible. The Current Population Survey is not readily available for original analyses before the mid-1970s;[1] many of our comparisons use data from 1978, 1988, and 1998.

Whenever possible, we have used printed historical data from the Census Bureau supplemented with data from other surveys or other researchers to fill in the gaps. We use different sources of data collected by the Census Bureau, such as the Survey of Income and Program Participation, and the decennial census as well as supplemental vital statistics (information on marriages, divorces, birthrates, and death rates) to document family demographic trends, changes in family structure and living arrangements, and the growing diversity of families.

● Choices of Topics and Organization of This Volume

Our main purpose in this book is to provide an overview of the social demography of families and households in the United States. We seek to paint a comprehensive picture of U.S. families and households and the family-related behaviors of individuals. In doing so, we attempt to document how and why families have changed over the years. We also strive to place family change within the larger context of other social, demographic, and economic changes. Finally, we seek to demonstrate how changes in family behaviors give rise to new social issues and family-related social problems.

In Chapter 1 we discuss the sweeping changes in demographic, social, and economic events that have been linked to changes in family structure and living arrangements, highlighting how these changes are associated with increasing diversity among American families. We address how changes in family composition and demographic trends may be related to other cultural, economic, and sociological shifts in society, such as the sexual revolution, the women's movement, and the emergence of the aging of the population. In each of the subsequent chapters, we focus in more detail on subjects of particular interest to family demographers in the past two decades.

Chapter 2 focuses on cohabitation. Increases in cohabitation have been noted by the Census Bureau since it began tabulating the relevant data in 1960. The measures used to document this trend are outdated, however. In Chapter 2 we use data from the Current Population Survey to provide new and improved estimates of the increases in cohabitation in the 1980s and 1990s and discuss the meaning of cohabitation within a family context. Drawing on the findings of other research and analysis of the National Survey of Families and Households, we also investigate the relationships among marriage, divorce, fertility, and cohabitation.

Chapter 3, authored by Martin O'Connell, chief of the Fertility and Family Statistics Branch of the U.S. Bureau of the Census, is devoted to trends in childbearing. The fertility level of American women in the past two decades has remained at an unusually low and unusually stable level, slightly below replacement fertility compared with the cyclical patterns exhibited during most of the 20th century. This lull in fertility swings belies some important transformations in the character of the American family and in the experiences of children who are born into families of widely differing household compositions. Identifying the concerns of women in different socioeconomic groups toward childbearing offers a prospective view of the future of the family that can highlight the current diversity of American households.

In Chapter 4 we turn to the topic of single-mother families. In this chapter we use data from the Current Population Survey to document the rapid growth in mother-child families in the 1960s and 1970s, the continued but slower growth from the 1980s through the mid-1990s, and the stabilization that has occurred since then. We describe how entry into single parenting has changed over time, with widowhood being the primary cause of entry into single parenting early in the 20th century; the dramatic increase in divorce accounting for the rapid growth of single parenting in the 1960s and 1970s; and the delay in marriage and shift toward childbearing outside marriage creating more never-married mothers among single parents of the 1980s and 1990s. We document the economic well-being of single mothers and discuss how welfare reform has affected single mothers and their children.

Chapter 5 focuses on fathering, a topic that is increasingly engaging the interest of family scholars. In searching for ways to strengthen the American family, researchers and policy makers have turned their attention to fathers and fathering. In this chapter we use CPS (Current Population Survey) and SIPP (Survey of Income and Program Participation) data to examine three types of fathers: single, noncustodial, and married. We begin with a discussion of the increase in single-father families based on the Current Population Survey, but go on to describe what we know about absent, nonresident fathers. We also provide new data on married fathers' time with children and mothers' and fathers' views about father involvement with children.

In Chapter 6 we address grandparenting. Many more grandchildren are living with grandparents today than was the case a quarter of a century ago. We open this chapter with a discussion of how changes in mortality, fertility, and immigration changed grandparenthood over the course of the 20th century. Then we use data from the Current Population Survey to document the composition of households that included grandparents in 1997 to describe who seems to be supporting whom in these families and how they fare economically. We also discuss differences in grandparenting styles and the amount and quality of contact between generations.

In Chapter 7 we take up the important topic of child care. The demand for child care has increased dramatically in recent decades, due in part to the increase in labor force participation of mothers with young children and in part to Americans' growing desire to educate children at younger ages. In this chapter we use data from the Census of Service Industries and the Survey of Income and Program Participation to document trends such as increases in the number of child-care centers, changes in the child-care arrangements parents choose for their children, and increases in the costs of child care since the 1980s. We also address such issues as what types of families use which types of care, how many "latchkey kids" there are, and how work schedules and other factors such as family income and family size affect the types of child care families choose. We draw on the research literature to discuss what is known about the quality, accessibility, and affordability of child care. We close the chapter with a discussion of how child care affects the well-being of children and their families.

In Chapter 8 we focus on child well-being, the issue that has sparked more heated debate about family change than any other. We use children as the unit of analysis and examine indicators of child well-being. We discuss the changing family living arrangements of children in the United States and also examine trends in children's economic security, educational performance, and health and risk-taking behaviors. We also include information on how children spend their time and the activities in which they engage. We present new data collected in the Survey of Income and Program Participation on children's participation in extracurricular activities, TV viewing and family rules about TV, and activities that parents do with children, such as reading to them.

Chapter 9 addresses the economic causes and consequences of changing family structure. American families are much more diverse than in the past, and some changes have resulted in increasing economic inequality among families. In this chapter we examine income differences among different household types, assessing the relative income advantage of dual-earning, two-parent families and the disadvantage of single-parent families. We use unique SIPP data on couples to document the changes in income for men, women, and children who experience marital disruption and provide a review of the literature on the economic consequences of divorce.

Finally, in Chapter 10 we focus on how men and women, especially parents, combine paid work and family responsibilities. Increases in women's labor force participation have meant that many more families today are being confronted with the challenge of combining work and family than was the case in the past. We explore trends in the labor force participation of married and single mothers, showing convergence between the two groups as married mothers' rates have increased rapidly. We also draw on time-use data to show trends in housework, documenting the decline in hours spent on housework by women, especially employed women, and the modest increase among men. Finally, we review the growing literature on how parents with jobs and children balance competing time demands.

Our goal in this volume is to provide enough detailed data to answer the "who," "what," and "where" questions about family change. We then attempt to place the discussion of family diversity and family change in the context of social, demographic, and economic change to begin to suggest answers to the "why" and "how" questions. As families change, societies are transformed. Taking stock of the family transformations of the latter part of the 20th century seems particularly useful as we try to assess family well-being and gauge the likely future of family behaviors in the 21st century.

Note

1. Data for earlier years are not comparable for family measures.

CHAPTER 1

CHANGING FAMILIES
IN A CHANGING SOCIETY

F
amily life in the United States underwent tremendous change in the latter half of the 20th century. Today, no institution elicits more contentious debate than "the American family." On one side are those who argue that "the family" has been seriously degraded by the movement away from marriage and traditional gender roles (e.g., Popenoe 1993, 1996; Waite and Gallagher 2000; Whitehead 1993). On the other side are those who view family life as amazingly diverse, resilient, and adaptive to new circumstances (e.g., Stacey 1993, 1996). In the United States the latter half of the 20th century was characterized by tumultuous changes in the economy, in civil rights, in sexual freedom, and in health and longevity. It is not surprising that marriage and family life felt the reverberations of these societal changes.

The rhetoric about the dramatically changing family may be a step behind where family life actually is, however. Recent trends suggest a "quieting" of family change, or at least the pace of change. Between 1995 and 2000, there was no change in the proportion of families that were maintained by married couples or single mothers. The household living arrangements of children, young adults, and the elderly stabilized. The divorce rate had been stable or declining for more than two decades, and newer forms of coupling, such as cohabitation, showed signs of a decreased rate of increase. The ratio of premarital births to marital births ceased increasing, and fertility levels remained constant. The major area of continued change involved fathers and families, with the number of father-only families increasing, a shift toward shared custody by fathers and mothers after divorce, and increased father involvement with children in two-parent families.

Whether this slowing, and in some cases cessation, of change in the family is a temporary lull or part of a new, more sustained equilibrium will be revealed only in the first decades of the 21st century. Family change certainly has not ended: Age at marriage continues its climb, as more young adults experiment with other living arrangements in their 20s; cohabitation continues to rise; and the number of grandparents raising grandchildren grew in the 1990s. Yet the interpretation of these trends is not always straightforward. For example, an increasing age at marriage can mean two quite different things: It may signal that young people are delaying marriage until they are older, or it may indicate that they are forgoing marriage altogether. And the quieting of change certainly does not signal a reversal of trends back toward what they were in the 1950s: A large proportion of families are still maintained by single mothers, cohabitation is very common, and the proportion of births to unmarried women remains high.

The pace and extent of family change have not been uniform among all race and ethnic groups. For example, the numbers of single-mother families began to increase much earlier among blacks than among whites, and today many more black families are mother-only families. Similarly, marriage is more common among whites and Hispanics than among blacks, and this difference has consequences for many of the family trends we describe in this chapter. We discuss many trends in the aggregate, but it is important to remember that the societal changes we outline may have differential effects on families of different racial groups who vary with regard to their position in the overall class structure of U.S. society.

In this chapter, we document changes in family configurations and try to provide some perspective on what they might mean. In order to begin the discussion, we present an overview of the broader social and economic transformations that constitute the context for family change. An understanding of this societal context will help the reader to interpret the family statistics we present in the second half of the chapter.

● A Changing Society

Enormous social and economic changes radically altered life for Americans during the second half of the 20th century, in part because conditions were so unique at midcentury. Consider the life of a young woman reaching adulthood in the 1950s or early 1960s. Such a woman was likely to marry straight out of high school or might take a job as a secretary or retail sales-clerk until she married. She would then move out of her parents' home to form a new household with her husband. This young woman was likely to be married by the age of 20, to give birth to her first child shortly thereafter, and to bear at least two more children. More likely than not, she would quit her job and stay at home to care for her children while her husband went to work at a steady job that paid enough to support the entire family.

Fast forward to the last few years of the 20th century. A young woman reaching adulthood in the late 1990s is not likely to marry before her 25th birthday. She will probably attend college and is likely to live by herself, with a boyfriend, or with roommates before marrying. She might move in and out of her parents' house several times before getting married. Like her counterpart reaching adulthood in the 1950s, she is likely to marry eventu-ally and have at least one child, but the sequence of those events may be re-versed. She probably will not drop out of the labor force after she has chil-dren, although she might curtail the number of hours she works outside the home in order to try to balance work and family. She is also much more likely to experience a divorce and possibly even a remarriage compared with a young woman in the 1950s or 1960s.

A Changing Economy

Many of the changes in women's (and men's) timing of marriage, chil-dren, and paid work reflect changed economic circumstances between the 1950s and the 1990s. (We discuss this topic in more detail in Chapter 9.) After World War II, the United States experienced an economic boom char-acterized by rapid growth and expansion of the economy, full employ-ment, rising productivity, higher wages, low rates of inflation, and increas-ing earnings. This meant that a man with a high school education in the 1950s and 1960s could secure a good-paying job that would allow him to purchase a house, support a family, and join the swelling ranks of the mid-dle class. The 1970s and 1980s were quite different. The two decades fol-lowing the oil crisis in 1973 were decades of economic change and uncer-tainty marked by a shift away from manufacturing and toward services; stagnating or declining wages, especially for less educated workers; high inflation; and a slowdown in productivity growth (Farley 1996; Levy 1998). The 1990s were just as remarkable for an economic turnaround: sustained prosperity; low unemployment, albeit with increased inequality in wages;

and economic growth that seemed to reach even the poorest segments of society.

Not surprisingly, when the economy is on such a roller coaster, family life often takes a similar ride. Marriage was early and nearly universal in the decades after World War II, most mothers remained in the home to rear children, and the Baby Boom generation was born and nurtured.[1] When those Baby Boomers hit labor market age in the 1970s, the economy was not nearly so hospitable to them as it had been to their parents. They postponed entry into marriage, delayed childbearing, and had difficulty getting established in the labor market. Many of the Baby Boomers' own children began reaching labor force age in the 1990s. This was a time when the differences in economic fortunes of individuals who stop schooling with high school compared with those who continue on to college made for widely differing abilities to attain independence and self-sufficiency.

For those with only high school education today, good jobs with high pay and benefits are in relatively short supply, and those lucky enough to land such jobs will receive pay that is about 25 percent less than comparable jobs would have paid just 20 years ago (Farley 1996). Young men and women are therefore more likely to remain in school to pursue college degrees. Both men and women experience extended years of independence, or quasi-independence, because they remain single longer, leave home in pursuit of a college education, cohabit with partners, and take time to launch careers before taking on the responsibility of having families of their own.

One of the most spectacular changes that is occurring today is the transformation of gender roles within the family. Women's increased participation in the labor force, the postponement of marriage, and the increase in single-parent families challenges the "separate spheres" organization of home life that dominated the post-World War II period. The gender-differentiated division of labor in the home has not disappeared, but it is fading in favor of much more egalitarian work and family roles among men and women (Goldscheider and Waite 1991). Women today expect to be employed outside the home, and men are more likely to be called upon to share in household tasks. More women and men are single parents. Many single mothers are the sole earners in their families, and more single fathers are taking the majority of the responsibility for raising their children. We return to these important topics in Chapters 4, 5, and 10.

Children are also affected by mothers' increased participation in the labor force and by the changing marital behavior of parents. More children are in day care than ever before, and the time they spend with their mothers and fathers has also changed. We discuss these topics in more detail in Chapters 7 and 8.

Changing Norms of Family Life

In 1950, there was a dominant and socially acceptable way for adults to live their lives, a well-understood road map for successful family life. Parents married for life and bore and raised children within marriage. The "ideal" family was composed of a homemaker-wife, a breadwinner-father, and two or more children. Americans shared a common image of what a family should look like and how mothers, fathers, and children should behave, and these shared values reinforced the importance of the family and the institution of marriage (McLanahan and Casper 1995). This vision of family life turned out to have amazing staying power, even as the underpinnings that allowed it to exist eroded.

For this "ideal" family to exist, Americans had to support distinct gender roles and the economy had to be vibrant enough for a man to be able to support a family on one wage earner's income. Government policies and business practices reserved the best jobs for men and blatantly discriminated against women when they married or had babies. After 1960, with the gaining strength of the civil rights movement and the renewed women's rights movement, women and minorities gained legal protections in the workplace, and discriminatory practices began to erode.

Bolstered by the revolution in contraceptive technology and other means of controlling fertility, a transformation in attitudes toward family behaviors also occurred. The movement of women into the labor force was accompanied by changing attitudes and values regarding work and family roles. People became more accepting of women's labor force participation, particularly among mothers. The views that women should not work if their husbands are capable of supporting them and that preschool children suffer when their mothers work outside of the home were replaced by more gender-egalitarian views of women's roles and much less concern about negative outcomes for children of working mothers (Axinn and Thornton 2000; Farley 1996; for a review, see Chapter 10). People became more accepting of divorce, cohabitation, and sex outside of marriage and less sure about the universality and permanence of marriage (Axinn and Thornton 2000; Bumpass and Sweet 1989b; Cherlin 1992; Thornton 1989). In short, society became more accepting of a variety of living arrangements, family configurations, and lifestyles.

Although the transformation of many of these attitudes occurred throughout the 20th century, the pace of change accelerated in the 1960s and 1970s—the years in which the "second" women's movement was in full swing, the attempt to pass the Equal Rights Amendment took center stage, more effective means of contraception were developed, abortion was legalized, and the sexual revolution and era of "free love" were ushered in.[2] Increasingly, American values shifted from those favoring family commitment and self-sacrifice to those favoring self-fulfillment, individual growth, and personal freedom (Lesthaeghe 1995; McLanahan and Casper 1995). People began to expect more out of marriage and to leave bad marriages if their expectations were not fulfilled. Although changes in norms and values may have followed rather than preceded increases in divorce and delays in marriage, cultural change has important feedback effects once it begins.

An Older Society

Another important change, one sometimes overlooked, was also altering family life: the "graying" of America. In 1900, average life expectancy in the United States was about age 50 at birth. Tremendous advances were made in the early decades of the 20th century in the control of communicable diseases of childhood, so that by 1960 life expectancy at birth had increased to 70 years. After 1960, reduction in mortality was concentrated in areas that enhance life expectancy at older ages. During the 1970s and 1980s, rapid declines in mortality from heart disease—the leading cause of death—significantly lengthened the life span (Crimmins 1981). In addition, the introduction of Medicare encouraged greater use of preventive health care services among older Americans. The development of new drugs to treat hypertension and other illnesses and the trend toward healthier lifestyles also contributed to increased longevity (Preston 1993; Treas and Torrecilha 1995). The reduction in mortality meant that a person born in 1998 could expect to live to be 77, and an individual who reached age 65, especially if female, could often expect an additional 20 years of life (National Center for Health Statistics 1999a, 2000b).

Throughout the 20th century, women outlived men. From 1900 to 1975, the difference in life expectancy between the sexes increased from 2.8 years to 7.8 years (National Center for Health Statistics 1999a). This gap widened mainly because of men's earlier and larger increase in rates of smoking compared with women, behaviors that increased men's smoking-related mortality rates vis-à-vis women. The gender gap in life expectancy narrowed after 1975 (to 5.8 years currently), reflecting relatively greater increases in lung cancer mortality for women than for men and relatively larger decreases in heart disease mortality for men (National Center for Health Statistics 1999a:Tables 7, 8).

Increased life expectancy translates into extended length of family relationships. Married couples today have many more years to spend together, assuming they remain married. In fact, the increased expectation of life may be implicated in the high incidence of divorce; sustaining one lifetime relationship, "till death do us part," may be more difficult as death comes at older ages. Family members today also have many more years together as adults: nearly two-thirds of the time mothers and daughters spend together is as adults (Goldscheider 1997). Siblings spend a greater proportion of their overlapping years as adults than was true in the past, when life expectancy was shorter.

Longer lives also mean that people spend smaller portions of their lives parenting young children. On the one hand, more parents live long enough to be part of their grandchildren's and even their great-grandchildren's lives. On the other hand, adult children more often see their parents become very old, and the caregiving their parents may require can come relatively late in life, when adult children may be experiencing the beginnings of their own health difficulties. Given the continued gender differential in mortality, adult children will more often have relationships with and responsibilities toward their very elderly mothers than their fathers.

In sum, an aging society alters the context for family relationships and intergenerational ties. Lengthening expectation of life combines with shifts in the economy and changing norms, values, and laws to influence life-course trajectories of individuals. When aggregated to the societal level, modifications in individual decisions are manifested in changes in household and family composition.

Changing Households and Families ●

Demographers have long been asking what is happening to the family, and their perspectives have been both historical and dynamic (Bumpass 1990). Five key demographic trends are relevant to an understanding of family change (DaVanzo and Rahman, 1993; McLanahan and Casper 1995):

1. The delay in forming marriages, increasing the time adults spend outside marriage, often living in their parents' homes, with friends, or with unmarried partners

2. The increase in heterosexual cohabitation, either as a precursor or alternative to marriage or as an alternative to living alone, combined with the growing acknowledgment of same-sex cohabitation and concerns of gay and lesbian families

3. The growth in single parenting due to widespread divorce (and, more recently, a growing tendency for births to occur outside marriage as marriages are postponed) and the increasing number of years adults and children spend outside of married-couple families

4. The steady increase in women's labor force participation, especially among married women, in the second half of the 20th century and the accompanying decline in the one-wage-earner, two-parent family (what some refer to as the "traditional" family)

5. Delayed and declining fertility and declining mortality resulting in fewer children, smaller families, and also a lengthening of life, adding to the time adults spend "postchildren," which has fueled the growth in married couples without children and elderly who increasingly live independently, apart from their children or extended kin

The changes in household structure that result from these five trends are evident in Figure 1.1. Traditionally, families have accounted for the large majority of households, but the "family" share of households has been declining. (Recall from our introduction that, according to Census Bureau definitions, households are separated into *family* and *nonfamily* designations [see Bryson and Casper 1998]. Family households include members who are related by blood, marriage, or adoption; nonfamily households include those who live alone or with nonrelatives.) Whereas in 1960, 85 percent of households included families, the proportion of family households had declined to 69 percent by 1998.

A large component of the decline in family households was the decrease in the proportion of married-couple households with children, reflecting fertility declines within marriage between 1960 and 1975, increased divorce rates in the 1960s and 1970s, and the postponement of marriage and children after 1975. These households dropped dramatically, from 44 percent of the total in 1960 to 25 percent in 1998. Overall, all households—not just married-couple households—were much less likely to include children under 18 in 1998 (34 percent) than in 1960 (49 percent), when U.S. fertility was high, with families averaging more than three children (see Chapter 3 on childbearing). The proportion of households made up of married couples without children remained relatively stable over this 40-year period, as did the proportion of other families without children (e.g., two adult sisters

● **Figure 1.1.** Households by Type: 1960-1998

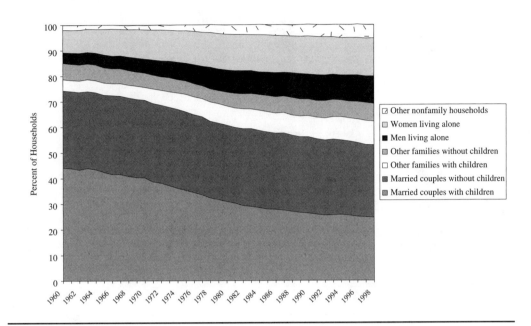

SOURCE: Current Population Survey, March supplements, 1960-1998.

living together, a mother living with her adult daughter, an uncle living with his adult nephew).

Another factor contributing to the decreased share of households that included children was the growth in nonfamily households, especially persons living alone. The proportion of households with one person doubled, from 13 percent to 26 percent, between 1960 and 1998. Those who live only with nonrelatives make up the other type of nonfamily household. The proportion of such households has also grown substantially since the 1960s, although these account for a much smaller component of the growth in nonfamily households. Cohabiting households are included in this category; we discuss their tremendous growth in more detail in Chapter 2.

Changes in fertility, marriage, divorce, and mortality and growth in the numbers of persons living alone have resulted in smaller households, on average. Figure 1.2 shows that the most profound differences have occurred at the two extremes—the largest and smallest households. Between 1960 and 1998, the share of households with five or more people decreased from 23 percent to 10 percent. During the same period, the share of households with only one or two people increased from 41 percent to 58 percent. Between 1960 and 1998 the average number of people per house-

● **Figure 1.2.** Households by Size: 1960-1998

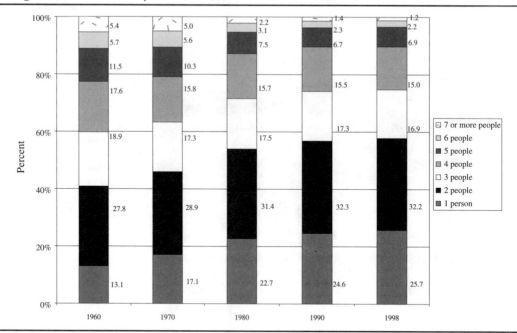

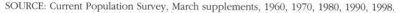

SOURCE: Current Population Survey, March supplements, 1960, 1970, 1980, 1990, 1998.

hold declined from 3.3 to 2.6, as did the average number of children under age 18 per family household.

Change in household composition in the United States began slowly in the 1960s, just as the nation was embarking on some of the most radical social changes in its history. The steepest decline in family households was experienced in the 1970s, as the Baby Boomers reached adulthood and aged through their 20s. By the 1980s, change was still occurring, but at a much less rapid pace. By the mid-1990s, household composition reached relative equilibrium, where it has been since.

What Is Happening to the Two-Parent Family?

Many regard the decline in the proportion of households made up of two-parent families with children as a sign of family disintegration. But is it? Or is it just that two-parent family living is occupying a smaller portion of our adult lives, especially as life expectancy increases and families average no more than two children? The vast majority of American adults could spend time parenting children in two-parent families and this household type could still decline as a percentage of U.S. households or families. Increased life expectancy and the delay in marriage until older ages mean that a growing share of households include individuals who either have not yet begun or have already finished rearing children.

Much of the concern about the "disappearing" two-parent family centers on the well-being of children—the worry that children are less adequately nurtured and supported when they do not live with both parents. To round out the picture of what is happening to the two-parent family, therefore, we need to narrow the focus to households that include children and ask how many of these are two-parent families and what the trends have been over time. Table 1.1 shows estimates of the number of family households with children under age 18 by whether there were one or two parents present for the period 1960 to 1998.

The share of family households with children that were two-parent families declined substantially over this period, from 91 percent to 73 percent.

TABLE 1.1   Family Households With Children Under Age 18 by Type: 1960-1998

	Total	Married Couple	Single Mother	Single Father
Number (in thousands)				
1960	25,689	23,358	2,099	232
1970	28,857	25,541	2,971	345
1980	31,022	24,961	5,445	616
1990	32,289	24,537	6,599	1,153
1998	34,760	25,269	7,693	1,798
Percentage distribution				
1960	100.0	90.9	8.2	0.9
1970	100.0	88.5	10.3	1.2
1980	100.0	80.5	17.6	2.0
1990	100.0	76.0	20.4	3.6
1998	100.0	72.7	22.1	5.2
Average annual rate of growth				
1960-69	1.2	0.9	4.2	4.9
1970-79	0.8	−0.2	8.3	7.9
1980-89	0.4	−0.2	2.1	8.7
1990-98	0.8	0.3	1.7	5.6

SOURCE: Casper and Bryson (1998b:Table FM-1).

The proportion of households headed by married couples with children declined most dramatically in the 1970s, as the number of single-mother households grew rapidly (at an average annual rate of more than 8 percent). (The figures for single-mother households presented in Table 1.1 include some single mothers who are cohabiting. See Chapters 4 and 5 for discussion of changes in single-parent families when cohabitation is taken into account.) This shift continued in the 1980s and into the 1990s, but at a much less rapid pace. In fact, by the mid-1990s, the shifting composition of families, for the most part, gradually came to a halt—no more growth in single-mother families, and no more decline in families consisting of married couples with children after 1994 (Casper and Bryson 1998b). The only area of continued rapid change was the increase in single-father families with children present.

Not all of the 73 percent of family households with children that included two parents in 1998 had two biological parents in the household. Using data that allow identification of biological relationships, Fields (2001) estimates that 12 percent of children who live in two-parent families are actually not living with both biological parents. If we apply Field's estimate and consider that perhaps only 88 percent of the two-parent family households with children include both biological parents, we estimate that 64 percent of family households with children are "intact," two-parent families. On the one hand, this *trend* suggests sizable erosion of the two-parent family. On the other hand, the *level* at the end of the 1990s—64 percent of children living with two biological parents—is much harder to reconcile with the notion that the two-parent family is disappearing.

One other important change in families is the increased likelihood that all parents in the home are employed. Figure 1.3 shows the change during the past two decades in the distribution of families with children by the parents' labor force status. There has been a substantial decline in what some consider the "traditional" family—two parents with only the father employed. The proportion accounted for by these families dropped from 31 percent of the total in 1978 to 16 percent in 1998. Meanwhile, two-parent families in which both parents worked outside the home increased slightly as a percentage of all families with children (from 45 percent to 49 percent).

Among the general public and in the mass media, as well as among policy makers and even academics, perceptions persist that the numbers of single-mother families are still increasing at breakneck speed and that most single mothers are not gainfully employed. Current Population Survey (CPS) data demonstrate that these perceptions are false. Between 1978 and 1998, the proportion of families with single mothers increased from 19 percent to 26 percent, and most of these mothers were employed. Although

● **Figure 1.3.** Families With Own Children by Type and Employment Status of Parents: 1978-1998

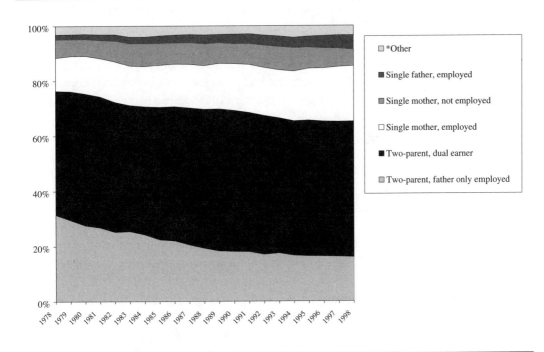

SOURCE: Current Population Survey, March supplements, 1960-1998.
NOTE: Families are family groups.
*Includes two-parent, mother-only-earner families; two-parent, neither-earner families; and single-father, nonearner families. The proportions of these families are small and have not changed substantially over the past 20 years.

this is an appreciable increase in single-mother families over the 20-year period, the proportion reached 26 percent in 1993 and has remained there since. Moreover, about two-thirds of single mothers were employed over the entire 20 years. Beginning around 1994, this proportion began to increase, so that by 1998 more than three-quarters of single mothers were employed. We discuss these changes in more detail in Chapter 4.

Racial Differences in ●
Household and Family Structure

Variations in household structure constitute some of the most significant differences among black, Hispanic, and white families in the United States (McLanahan and Casper 1995; Ruggles 1994; Spain and Bianchi 1996).[3] The

CPS does not have a large enough sample to make possible an examination of family change for Asians or Native Americans, or for Hispanics broken down by their different countries of origin (e.g., Mexico, Cuba, Puerto Rico). Despite differences in levels of single parenting, the patterns of family change have been similar for all of these groups over the past four decades. Since the 1960s, white, black, and Hispanic household composition has followed the same general pattern of declining married-couple and rising one-parent households, with the majority of the change occurring in the 1960s and 1970s (Spain and Bianchi 1996).

Table 1.2 shows that in 1978 almost two-thirds of white and Hispanic households and 41 percent of black households were maintained by married couples (with or without children). By 1998, just over half of white and Hispanic households and about a third of black households were maintained by married couples. For all three racial groups, the majority of this decline can be accounted for by the decrease in married couples with children. The percentage of households with mother-only families did not change dramatically in the past two decades, although percentages remain much higher for blacks (around 20 percent of total households) and Hispanics (13 percent of households) than for whites (5 percent of households).

During the 1980s and 1990s, the proportion of single-father households nearly tripled for whites and Hispanics and increased by 42 percent for blacks. Yet these households constituted a small percentage of all households, accounting for less than 2 percent of all white and black households and less than 3 percent of Hispanic households in 1998. All racial groups experienced an increase in persons living alone, but the percentage of all households of this type was about half as large among Hispanics (15 percent) as among either whites (27 percent) or blacks (29 percent).

Restricting attention to all families rather than all households, we can see that the most dramatic racial difference in family groups with children (hereafter referred to as families) is the contrast in the proportion that include a married couple versus those with a single mother. This difference has sparked controversy dating back to the infamous Moynihan Report (1965), which argued that the high rate of unemployment among black males was propelling "family disintegration" within the black community. Although many took issue with Moynihan's characterization of the black family, the likely causal relationship between lack of labor force opportunity and family formation decisions continues to be a theme in theory and research on poor and minority families to this day (Wilson 1987, 1996).

TABLE 1.2   Types of Households and Family Groups With Children Under Age 18 by Race: 1978-1998

	White			Black			Hispanic		
	1978	1988	1998	1978	1988	1998	1978	1988	1998
Total households (%)	100	100	100	100	100	100	100	100	100
Married couples	64.9	59.7	55.7	40.8	36.2	31.3	63.7	56.3	55.9
- With children	32.6	27.0	24.2	23.8	19.8	16.4	45.6	37.3	36.3
- No children	32.3	32.7	31.5	17.0	16.4	14.9	18.1	19.0	19.6
Female householders	23.3	25.5	26.9	42.7	45.6	49.1	24.3	27.6	27.6
- With children	4.6	4.6	5.0	20.0	19.7	20.5	12.7	13.3	13.1
- Living alone	14.1	15.2	15.9	13.2	14.2	16.0	6.7	7.5	7.2
- Other	4.6	5.7	6.0	9.5	11.7	12.6	4.9	6.8	7.3
Male householders	11.8	14.9	17.4	16.4	18.2	19.5	12.1	16.2	16.6
- With children	0.6	1.0	1.7	1.2	1.6	1.7	1.0	2.0	2.7
- Living alone	8.1	9.6	10.8	10.9	11.7	12.9	7.0	7.3	7.3
- Other	3.1	4.3	4.9	4.3	4.9	4.9	4.1	6.9	6.6
Total family groups with children under 18 (%)	100	100	100	100	100	100	100	100	100
Two parents, dual earners	47.8	56.6	55.9	31.0	29.6	28.6	37.3	36.5	36.9
Two parents, only father employed	34.2	20.8	16.2	13.1	7.9	6.0	33.3	25.5	23.7
Single mother, employed	9.9	12.9	15.8	27.4	32.2	44.3	10.5	15.1	19.4
Single mother, not employed	3.8	3.9	3.6	21.5	23.4	13.1	13.3	14.3	10.4
Single father, employed	1.6	3.2	5.4	2.6	3.0	4.2	1.9	3.6	5.2
Other[a]	2.8	2.7	3.1	4.4	4.0	3.8	3.6	5.1	4.5

SOURCE: Current Population Survey, March supplements, 1978, 1988, 1998.
NOTE: Race/ethnicity categories are white, non-Hispanic; black, non-Hispanic; and Hispanic.
a. Includes two-parent, mother-only-earner families; two-parent, neither-earner families; and single-father, nonearner families. The proportions of these families are small and have not changed substantially over the past 20 years.

Historically, men's and women's work patterns have varied by race, with higher labor force participation among black women than among white women and lower labor force participation among black men than among white men (Spain and Bianchi 1996). The bottom panel of Table 1.2 shows the distribution of families with children by whether they live with one or two parents and the labor force status of the parents. A declining proportion of children live with two parents, but the likelihood of having both parents employed has increased. Similarly, the type of single-parent family that is increasing is one in which the single mother (or, in a smaller proportion of cases, the single father) is employed. Single-mother, nonearner families experienced minimal growth between 1978 and 1988 and then declined as a percentage of families with children between 1988 and 1998. The decrease was relatively small among white families, but quite substantial for black and Hispanic families.

Figure 1.4 graphs the ratio of black and Hispanic percentages in each family type to the white percentages. A dramatic difference among the three race groups is found in the prevalence of the two-parent, father-earner family. Black families were about 40 percent less likely than whites to be in this group in all three periods. In contrast, Hispanic families were relatively similar to whites in 1978, but as time went on, they were increasingly more likely than whites to be in this group. By 1998, Hispanic families were 50 percent more likely than whites to be two-parent families with the father as the only earner in the family.

Compared with whites, the most dramatic difference in family structure for both blacks and Hispanics is in the proportion of single-mother, nonearner families. In 1978, black families were almost six times more likely and Hispanic families were three and one-half times more likely to be of this type. For both blacks and Hispanics, however, this gap declined in the 1990s so that by 1998, the ratio was 3.7 for blacks and 2.9 for Hispanics. Black and Hispanic families were also more likely to be single-mother, earner families. Black families were more than twice as likely as white families to have single-mother, earner families in all three periods. In contrast, the proportion of Hispanic families of this type was similar to white families in 1978, but increased over time. By 1998, Hispanic families were 23 percent more likely than white families to be single-mother, earner families. Single-father, earner families were more common among black and Hispanic families than among white families in 1978. But by 1998, this pattern was reversed, with single-father, earner families as, or more, common among white families.

Thus far, we have provided an overview of families and households and racial differences in family structure. But one can also assess family change from the point of view of the individual and examine how individuals' living arrangements and family-related behaviors have changed. For example, how are marriage and living arrangements changing in young adulthood? How stable are couples' marriages once formed, and is this changing? Who decides to become parents and when? And finally, how are

● **Figure 1.4.** Changes in the Ratios of Family Structure Proportions of Black and Hispanic Families to White Families: 1978, 1988, and 1998 (logarithmic scale)

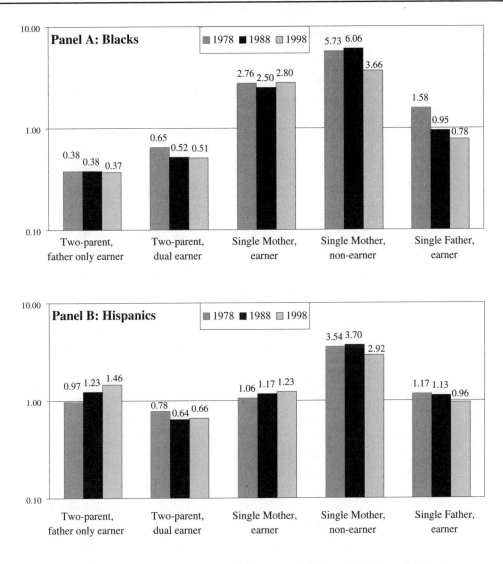

SOURCE: Current Population Survey, March supplements, 1978, 1988, 1998.
NOTE: Race/ethnicity categories are white, non-Hispanic; black, non-Hispanic; and Hispanic. Families are family groups with own children under age 18. Bars are the correct height, labels have been rounded to the nearest tenth.

living arrangements changing later in life, after children are grown and leave the nest?

● Delayed Marriage and Living Arrangements of Young Adults

In 1890, one-half of women first married by age 22 and one-half of men were married by age 26. Those ages of entry into marriage dipped to an all-time low during the post-World War II Baby Boom years, when in 1956 median age at first marriage dropped to 20.1 years for women and 22.5 years for men. We have already discussed how the family of the 1950s was anomalous: Women and men married younger in the 1950s and 1960s than in any other decade before or since. After 1956, age at first marriage began to ascend, reaching 25 years for women and 26.7 years for men by the end of the 1990s.

The proportion of women in their early 20s who had never married increased from 28 percent to 70 percent between 1960 and 1998 (see Table 1.3). In 1960, a woman who reached age 25 without marrying was unusual. Only 10 percent of women ages 25 to 29 had never married. A woman in her late 20s who had not married was still not typical in 1998, but she had far more friends like herself when nearly 40 percent of women ages 25 to 29 were not yet married. Among women in their early 30s, the proportion who had not yet married tripled over this period, from 7 percent to 22 percent.

Changes were similarly dramatic for men—the proportion of men in their early 20s who had never married increased from 53 percent in 1960 to 83 percent in 1998. And in 1998, the majority (51 percent) of men in their late 20s were still unmarried. Men in their early 30s who had not married for the first time increased from 12 percent to 29 percent. Thus by 1998, more than one in five women and almost one in three men ages 30 to 34 had never been married.

Despite its postponement, marriage is still very much a part of American life, with the vast majority of men (89 percent) and women (92 percent) age 35 and over in 1998 having married. Based on their use of life table techniques and an examination of marital history data collected in 1996, Fields and Kreider (2000) suggest that such high percentages ever marrying will continue into the future. They estimate, for example, that 87 percent of males and 89 percent of females who were age 15 in 1996 will eventually marry. Using different data but similar techniques, Raley (2000) also arrives at an estimate that 88 percent of recent cohorts will eventually marry.

Hence, at least among whites, what seems to be happening among young adults is a delay but not a forgoing of marriage. The evidence of de-

into a marital union amo| Ages 18 to 24: 1970-1998
in two important ways: It
same time it increases t
more often unintended)

The young adult yea
dense" because these ye
tions (Rindfuss 1991). Be
ally finish school, leave th
gin families, but these ev
marriage extends the peri
ternative living arrangem
may experience any num
they marry, as they chang
of intimate relationships.
ing school breaks, when
break up.

Many demographic, s
adults' decisions about w
transitions are influenced
by changing ideas about a
1980s, the transition to ad
sions, slow wage growth,
roles and behavior sparke
Goldscheider 1994). Even
dependently, they may no
today do not pay well, and
living out of reach for mar
necessary in today's labor
college-student children li
on expenses. Even when
they are still frequently de
may return home during t
find suitable jobs.

Current Population Sur
rangements of young adul|70, 1980, 1990, 1998.
creasing age of marriage, y| s and people living with unrelated roommates or
and more likely to live with| stitutions are excluded.
arrangements in their 20s.
to 1998, and this was true fo|t in 1998. While married life
ample, 31 percent of men |uasi-)independent living ar-
compared with only 9 p

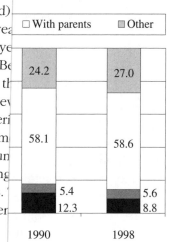

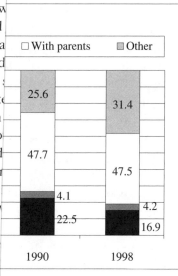

Differences in young men's and young women's living arrangements have declined over time. Traditionally, 18- to 24-year-old men were much more likely to reside with their parents than were young women, and young women were much more likely to marry and live with their spouses than were young men, reflecting, in part, the older age of marriage for men. Although this is still the case, these differences have diminished somewhat over time.

Evidence from the National Survey of Families and Households indicates that adults were leaving their parental homes at increasingly younger ages throughout most of the 20th century. Recently, this trend has reversed, however, so that young adult children currently are leaving home later than their parents did. Not only are recent cohorts leaving home later, they are also more likely to return home—a "backward" transition out of the adult role and back into the role of dependent. Today, about 40 percent of young adults who leave home eventually return. This proportion has increased from less than one-fourth of those reaching adulthood before World War II (Goldscheider and Goldscheider 1994).

Since World War II, those leaving home to attend school, to serve in the military, or to take jobs have had high rates of returning to the nest. Those who leave home to live with partners or to form other types of nonmarital families have almost as great a likelihood of returning home. In contrast, those who leave to get married have the lowest likelihood of returning home, but even among this group returns to the nest have increased over time. Historically, moving away to gain independence was associated with very low rates of returning home—less than 20 percent prior to World War II. This pattern has changed over time so that currently about 40 percent of those who first leave for independence return to the nest.

Since World War II, it has been acceptable for parents to take their children in after they return from the military, from school, or from a job. However, in the 1940s, parents were apparently much more reluctant to take children back after they left to become independent. Goldscheider and Goldscheider (1994) attribute this trend to a change in the meaning of independence over time. In the past, leaving home for simple independence was probably the result of friction, whereas today, leaving and returning home seems to be part of the process of making a successful transition to adulthood. It could also be that, in the 1940s, a young adult may have been reluctant to move back in with parents because a return home would imply failure; these days, there may be less stigma attached to returning home. Changes in the economy that have made it increasingly difficult for young adults to sustain independent residences have also contributed to this trend.

Cohabitation ●

Few trends in the family have been as dramatic as the increase in the prevalence of cohabitation (see Figure 1.6). The number of cohabiting households increased from about 440,000 in 1960 to 4.9 million in 1998. Thus by 1998 almost 10 million adults were living in cohabiting households. Unmarried-couple households made up less than 1 percent of all households in 1960 and 1970, with no significant increase occurring within the decade. However, by 1980, the proportion of such households had more than doubled, to 2.2 percent, and by 1990 it reached 3.5 percent. In 1998, almost 5 percent of households were maintained by unmarried couples. This trend represents a fivefold increase over the preceding 20 years. One of the biggest compositional shifts has been the increase in cohabitor households with children: In 1978, only 28 percent of cohabitor households had children under age 18 in them; by 1998, the proportion had increased to 37 percent (see Chapter 2 for more discussion of this topic).

Although a prevalence rate of 5 percent of households with cohabitors may seem quite low—especially considering the concern some researchers have about the impact of cohabitation on marriage and family life—a much larger percentage of people have ever cohabited. More than half of the marriages now occurring have been preceded by cohabitation (Bumpass 1990; Bumpass and Lu 2000; Bumpass and Sweet 1989b).

Although many researchers assume that cohabitation continues to grow at an ever-increasing rate, CPS estimates suggest otherwise. The number of cohabitor households increased 67 percent in the years between 1978 and 1983 (see Figure 1.7), but since then the rate of increase has been steadily declining, so that between 1993 and 1998 it was 23 percent, only a third of what it had been 15 or so years earlier. Although the growth rate from 1983 to 1988 for Hispanics was almost triple the rate for whites, both whites and Hispanics experienced substantial declines in the rate of growth for each successive 5-year period. The story for blacks is a bit different. Although the rates for blacks also declined consistently from 1978 to 1993, more recently, between 1993 to 1998, the rate of increase was higher than during the preceding 10 years.

● **Figure 1.6.** Unmarried-Couple Households by Presence of Children Under Age 18: 1978-1998

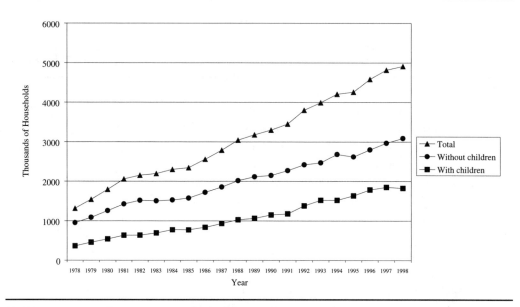

SOURCE: Current Population Survey, March supplements, 1978-1998.
NOTE: Unmarried-couple households estimated with adjusted POSSLQ measure (see Casper and Cohen 2000).

● Marriage, Divorce, and Remarriage

After 1970, the rate of entry into first marriage plummeted, from a rate of 93 to 49 per 1,000 unmarried women ages 15 to 44. Although punctuated by peaks and valleys, the annual divorce rate—the number of divorces per 1,000 married women age 15 and over—rose steadily during the first half of the 20th century, increased dramatically after 1967, peaked around 1980, and has decreased slightly since then (see Figure 1.8). Increasing divorce altered the marital status of the population. In 1960, there were only 35 divorced people for every 1,000 married people, compared with 176 in 1998.

Although it is still too early to tell for sure how many people who married in the 1980s will eventually divorce, estimates based on 1985 data indicate that the likelihood of divorce for these people would be lower than for those marrying in the 1960s and 1970s (Cherlin 1992). The most recent data indicate that the divorce rate has continued to decline in very small increments (from 21.7 in 1985 to 19.8 in 1997), providing 12 more years of data in support of the notion that we may have come to the end of more than a century of exponential increases in divorce.

● **Figure 1.7.** Change in Cohabitor Households: 1978-1998

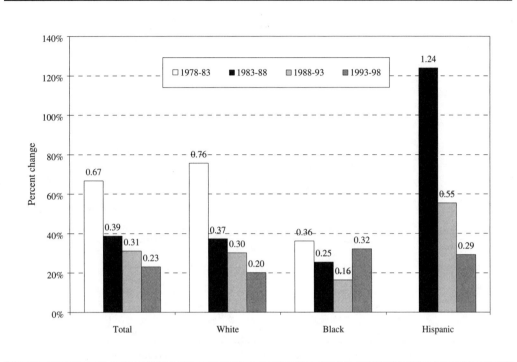

SOURCE: Current Population Survey, March supplements, 1978-1998.
NOTE: Race/ethnicity categories are white, non-Hispanic; black, non-Hispanic; and Hispanic. Hispanic 1978-83 change is not shown because the base is less than 100,000. Unmarried couple households estimated with adjusted POSSLQ measure (see Casper and Cohen 2000).

However, lest we feel the urge to pop a champagne cork in celebration of marriage, let's not forget that the likelihood of divorce is still extremely high. Fields and Kreider (2000) estimate that about 50 percent of first marriages for men currently under age 45 and between 45 and 50 percent of first marriages for women of this age may eventually end in divorce. These estimates are a little but not a lot lower than those for men and women born between 1946 and 1951 (the leading edge of the Baby Boom), many of whom married for the first time in the 1970s, when divorce rates were at their peak, and who appear to be the cohort that will have the highest lifetime rates of divorce.

Not surprisingly, given the changes in first marriage and divorce, the face of remarriage has changed dramatically as well. Although remarriage has always been commonplace, at the beginning of the 20th century it almost always followed the death of a spouse. By the 1930s, however, more remarriages involved divorcees than widows and widowers. Divorce and

● **Figure 1.8.** Rates of First Marriage, Divorce, and Remarriage: 1960-1997

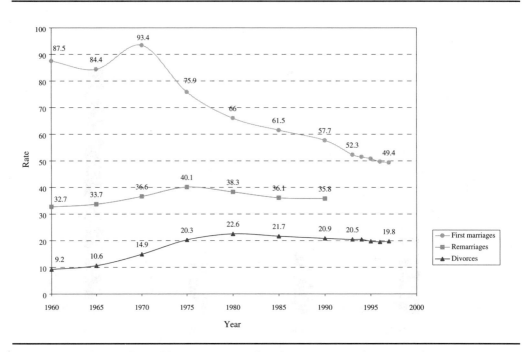

SOURCE: National Center for Health Statistics, *National Vital Statistics Reports* (various years).
NOTE: The rate of first marriage is the number of first marriages per 1,000 women ages 15 and older (ages 14 and older in 1960 and 1965). The rate of remarriage is the number of remarriages per 1,000 divorced and widowed women ages 15 and older (ages 14 and older in 1960 and 1965). Marriages of women under age 15 are included in the numerator. The rate of divorce is the number of divorces per 1,000 married women ages 15 and older. Remarriage rates from virtual statistics data are not available after 1990.

remarriage rates rose in tandem until the mid-1970s, when their trajectories diverged and the remarriage rate declined as the divorce rate continued to climb (see Figure 1.8). After 1980, both rates were again declining, and by 1990, the last year for which remarriage estimates were tabulated, the remarriage rate had dipped below what it had been in 1970.

Researchers have shown that rising cohabitation played a role in the declining remarriage rates during the past two decades. As cohabitation became more acceptable, divorced men and women began to forestall reentry into marriage in favor of the less formal arrangement of cohabitation. Thus, while the rate of remarriage was declining, the rate of union formation—the sum of remarriages plus cohabitations—was increasing such that union formation after marital separation was occurring at the same rate or perhaps even faster than it had been 20 years earlier (Bumpass, Sweet, and Cherlin 1991; Cherlin 1992; Spain and Bianchi 1996). For many people, cohabitation was a step on the way toward remarriage, as nearly half of those who remarried had lived with their partners prior to marriage (Bumpass and Sweet 1989b). Thus even more remarriages than first marriages begin as cohabitation.

The experience of a failed marriage has not permanently turned most Americans against marriage; about two-thirds of divorced women and three-fourths of divorced men eventually remarry (Sweet and Bumpass 1987). But increased cohabitation extends the number of years between divorce and remarriage. Following divorce, men are more likely to remarry than are women, in part because women are more likely to retain custody of children and children deter reentry into marriage. Women who are raising children may not have the time required to cultivate new social lives, and men may be reluctant to take on the responsibility of raising children who are not theirs (Spain and Bianchi 1996). Older men are also more likely to remarry than are older women, as their "remarriage pool" of second partners is greater, both because older women outnumber older men and because men tend to marry women who are younger.

Divorce rates in the initial years of marriage are higher for remarriages than they are for first marriages (Cherlin 1992). Family relationships surrounding remarriage can be quite complex, including children of either or both spouses, noncustodial parents, and a wide array of grandparents and other relatives. These complexities may contribute to (remarried) families' early demise. The multiple emotional, financial, and organizational demands placed on these families, often in the face of one or two adversarial parties, and the sheer number of quasi-kin relationships may strain parental-child and spousal relationships (Cherlin 1978). Another reason for higher divorce rates may be that people in remarriages differ from those in first marriages. For example, remarried individuals might hold less traditional views regarding the sanctity of marriage and thus may be more willing to throw in the towel at the first sign of trouble.

Although we do not devote a separate chapter to changes in marriage, divorce, and remarriage, we discuss the causes, consequences, and implications of these changes in every chapter in this volume.

Childbearing ●

The most dramatic demographic differences between the generation who parented the Baby Boom and had their children in the 1950s and early 1960s and the parents of today are that the parents of the Baby Boomers had more children, had them earlier, and were much more likely to be mar-

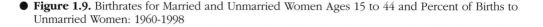
Figure 1.9. Birthrates for Married and Unmarried Women Ages 15 to 44 and Percent of Births to Unmarried Women: 1960-1998

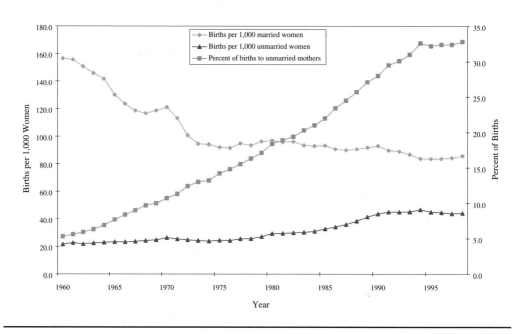

SOURCE: National Center for Health Statistics (1999b:Table 1).

ried when they had them. As Martin O'Connell describes in more detail in Chapter 3, between 1960 and 1975, marital fertility—births per 1,000 married women ages 15 to 44—declined sharply. Nonmarital fertility rates—births per 1,000 unmarried women ages 15 to 44—increased gradually from 22 in 1960 to a peak of 47 in 1994 (see Figure 1.9). In 1994, the long-standing decline in the marital birthrate stalled out at 84 births per 1,000, and the nonmarital birthrate actually began to decline.

From 1960 to 1994, these trends in marital and nonmarital fertility meant that more and more births were occurring outside of marriage. In 1960, only 5 percent of all births occurred outside of marriage; by 1994 this proportion had increased to 33 percent, where it has remained. The point that is often missed, however, is that much of the increase in the proportion of births to unmarried women has not been the result of an increased likelihood of unmarried mothers giving birth; rather, it is the result of the decreased likelihood of women marrying and the lower fertility rates of married women. That is, the postponement of marriage and the decline of fertility within marriage pushes the proportion of births outside marriage

upward, even during periods when nonmarital fertility rates are not changing much.

Although unmarried fertility rates are higher for black and Hispanic
women than for white women, historically these rates have risen much
more rapidly for white women (Spain and Bianchi 1996). More recently
(since 1994), the unmarried birthrates for black and Hispanic women have
fallen, and the rate for white women has remained relatively constant
(Ventura et al. 2000). One of the most striking racial differences in fertility is
that a far higher proportion of black and Hispanic children are born to unmarried teenage mothers than are white children. In 1998, 1 in 5 black children was born to an unmarried teenager compared with 1 in 8 Hispanic
children and just 1 in 15 white children. Similar differentials exist when we
consider the proportion of births to unmarried mothers in their early 20s.
The proportion of children born to unmarried women of any age also varies tremendously by race: In 1998, the portion of births to unmarried
women was 22 percent for whites, 69 percent for blacks, and 42 percent for
Hispanics (Ventura et al. 2000). However, we must keep in mind that
nonmarital childbearing today is *not* an isolated phenomenon occurring
primarily among teenagers or other select groups; birthrates for unmarried
women have increased among women of all ages, all races, and all sociodemographic groups (Bachu 1999).

Living Arrangements of the Elderly ●

We have summarized the changes in marriage and childbearing that have
altered the living arrangements of young and middle-aged adults and children. Changes among the elderly constitute an additional major component of growth in families without children and nonfamily living, especially
living alone. Extended lives mean more postretirement years and a greater
likelihood of spending those years with a spouse. This has added to the
number of married couples who do not have children under age 18 in the
household. But it also means more years living alone after a spouse dies,
especially for women, who continue to live longer than men.

Decennial census data from 1880 to 1980 demonstrate that the proportion of older Americans (age 65 and over) living in multigenerational
households declined throughout the 100-year period. At the beginning of
the 20th century, more than 70 percent of people age 65 or over resided
with extended kin. By 1980, only 23 percent did so (Ruggles 1994). Using

data from the March supplements to the Current Population Survey, we find that extended living arrangements among older people continued to decline slightly, to 20 percent in 1998. Meanwhile, living alone among the elderly increased dramatically in the latter half of the 20th century (Bianchi and Casper 2000; McGarry and Schoeni 2000; Ruggles 1995).

Both men and women age 65 and over were more likely to be living with a spouse in 1998 than in 1960, reflecting improvements in health and longevity that enable more joint survivorship of couples (see Figure 1.10). Men and women over age 65 were also more likely to be living alone and much less likely to be living with other relatives or nonrelatives in 1998 than in 1960. The majority of these changes occurred between 1960 and 1980. After 1980, change slowed and the patterns differed somewhat for men and women. Men experienced a slight decline in the proportion living with a spouse after 1980, whereas women continued to experience a slight increase. From 1980 to 1998, the proportion living alone continued to grow slightly for men, while for women it remained relatively stable. The proportion living in other arrangements has remained stable for both men and women since 1990.

Women are more likely to be widowed than are men, and this difference has important implications for gender differences in living arrangements and the quality of life of the elderly. In 1998, 45 percent of women age 65 and over were widowed compared with only 15 percent of men. And for those 85 and over, 77 percent of women and 42 percent of men were widowed. This stark gender contrast in widowhood is due to the fact that not only do women live longer than men, they also tend to marry men who are older; furthermore, women are less likely to remarry following the death of a spouse (Treas and Torrecilha 1995).

Widowhood has declined somewhat since 1960 as life expectancies for men and women have risen dramatically. For example, the proportion of men age 65 and over who were widowed decreased slightly from 19 percent in 1960 to 15 percent in 1998. For women the decline was similar—from 52 percent to 45 percent. Meanwhile, the average life expectancy for men increased from 67 in 1970 to 73 in 1995, and for women it increased from 75 to 79.

Gender differences in life expectancy and widowhood result in very different living arrangements for older women and men. In 1998, men age 65 and over were nearly twice as likely as women to be living with their spouses (72 percent versus 40 percent). In sharp contrast, women were more than twice as likely as men to be living alone (41 percent versus 17 percent). And women were also almost twice as likely as men to be living with others (19 percent versus 11 percent), in part because they tend to live

● **Figure 1.10.** Living Arrangements of Men and Women 65 and Over: 1970-1998

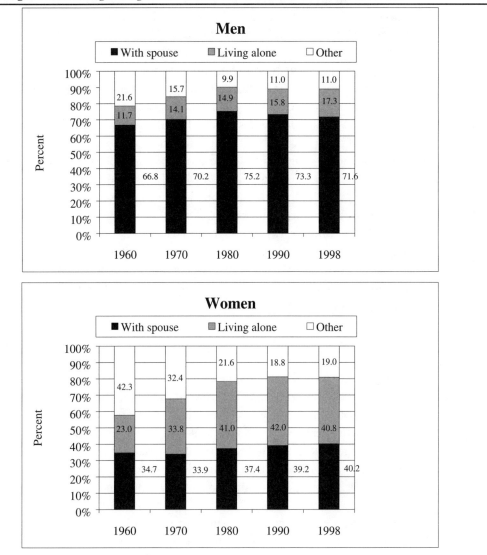

SOURCE: Current Population Survey, March supplements, 1970, 1980, 1990, 1998; decennial census, 1960.
NOTE: Other living arrangements include people living with unrelated roommates or other relatives and unmarried couples. People living in nursing homes or other institutions are excluded.

longer and are therefore more likely to be in frail health and in need of the physical care and financial help others can provide. Whereas men generally receive companionship and care from their wives in the latter stages of life, women are more likely to live alone and depend on themselves, rely on grown children, live with other family members, or enter nursing homes (Kramarow 1995; Silverstein 1995; Weinick 1995).

Why are the elderly living independently? Early sociological theories predicted a decline in extended family living among the elderly. Structural functionalists argued that industrialization rendered the extended family obsolete when production shifted from family to factory and the family economy was subsequently destroyed. The extended family vanished and the nuclear family evolved because it functioned more efficiently under this new economy (Parsons 1943). As a part of this process, the elderly had no productive function and became isolated from the family. Modernization theorists argued that urbanization, the rise of individualism, increasing economic and geographic mobility, technological advancements, and the weakening of community ties all worked to reduce the utility of the older generation, leading to the disappearance of the extended family (Inkeles and Smith 1974). Exchange theorists believed that relatives provide assistance, including coresidence, when family members experience "critical life situations" such as illness or unemployment. Further, they maintained that the need for extended families eroded in the 20th century as the incidence of such critical life situations ebbed (Anderson 1971; Ruggles 1987).

However, there is relatively little empirical support for any of these explanations. Industrialization, urbanization, mobility, and critical life situations were not closely related to living alone among those 65 and over. Instead, shifts in residential preferences and the loosening of bonds of obligation among kin had more to do with changes in living arrangements of older Americans prior to 1960 (Ruggles 1995).

To explain recent trends in living arrangements among the elderly, researchers have focused on a variety of constraints and preferences that shape people's decisions about such arrangements (Angel and Tienda 1982; Kobrin 1981; Mutchler and Frisbie 1987; Pampel 1983; Wister and Burch 1987). Goldscheider and Jones (1989) group these factors into a set of three determinants: availability and accessibility of relatives, feasibility, and preferences. Availability and accessibility have to do with the existence and proximity of kin with whom an elder can coreside. It is more costly to move in with an adult child if the child lives at a distance, for example, and impossible to do so if one has no living adult children. Health status and economic resources are two of the most salient factors affecting the feasibility of an elder's living alone rather than in an extended household. For example, can the older individual afford to live alone? Does he or she require daily care and assistance? Preferences have to do with the values that individuals place on particular arrangements—does the older person prefer to live alone or with others? Goldscheider and Jones argue that feasibility and preferences are linked to the power and status of the elderly within the extended family.

Empirical research has shown that all of these determinants play roles in the living arrangements of older Americans. Availability of kin as indicated by the number and composition of children is related to whether or not an older person lives with adult children (Crimmins and Ingegneri 1990; Goldscheider and Jones 1989; Spitze and Logan 1990). Crimmins and Ingegneri (1990) suggest that geographic distance from an adult child is an important element in whether an older person lives with adult children; having children who live nearby is an important factor producing coresidence.

Research also shows that feasibility is an important contributing factor; one of the most important determining factors is economic resources in the form of income. Older Americans with more money are more likely to live independently (Crimmins and Ingegneri 1990; Holden 1988; Mutchler 1992; Wolf and Soldo 1988). Similarly, financial need has been linked to extended living (Speare and Avery 1993). Ruggles and Goeken (1992) estimate that just under half of the shift in living arrangements among older people from 1960 to 1980 can be attributed to rising incomes, and McGarry and Schoeni (2000) confirm the importance of the Social Security program in the rise in the ability of the elderly to live independently of kin. Other research shows that poor health and the need for assistance with activities of daily living are negatively related to elderly persons' living alone (Mutchler 1992; Woroby and Angel 1990).

Numerous studies also show that normative and preference factors are strong determinants of living arrangements (Wister 1984; Wister and Burch 1987). A widespread preference for privacy and independence has been linked to minimalist living arrangements (Wister and Burch 1987). Social norms involving family obligations and ties also have an effect (Wister 1984).

Intergenerational Ties ●
and Multigenerational Living

Kin support comes in many forms. Research has focused on intergenerational support in the form of exchanges of money and other tangible goods, assistance with tasks and activities of daily living, and social and emotional support. Early studies on intergenerational exchanges assumed that support flows from adult children to their parents (Mancini and Bleiszner 1989). This is because most of these were gerontological studies, examining kin support among the frail elderly (Hogan, Eggebeen, and Clogg 1993). More recent research suggests that the flow often goes the other way. Kin assist family members in need over the entire life course (Eggebeen and Hogan 1990; Rossi and Rossi 1990), and although older adults sometimes receive assistance from their children, assistance from parents to adult children is the more common pattern for routine exchanges (Eggebeen and Hogan 1990). Although intergenerational transfers of assistance are a routine feature of American family life, half of all adults are not involved in such transfers on a consistent basis (Hogan et al. 1993).

Perhaps the strongest ties of intergenerational support occur when multiple generations of adults live together. Although extended families are less common today than in the past (Ruggles 1994), multigenerational families have not disappeared (Cohen and Casdper forthcoming). Table 1.4 provides a profile of when during adulthood multigenerational living is most common and highlights large differences by race. Multigenerational households are defined as households that include two or more generations of adults. (Laterally extended households—e.g., two brothers living together—are not included.) All adults within these households are identified as "hosts" (persons who own or rent the homes and their spouses) or "guests" (everyone else in the households). These households may be hosted (maintained) by the parents of adult children or by the adult children of older parents. (See Cohen and Casper forthcoming for a more thorough description of these households.)

The first three columns of Table 1.4 show the percentages of adults of each racial group who live in multigenerational homes. The next three columns provide ratios of the percentages who are the owner/renters (the hosts of the multigenerational homes in which they live) to the percentages living in other persons' homes (the guests in the multigenerational households). For example, about 12 percent of white male adults live in multigenerational households; hosts and guests are almost evenly split among white men, with about 0.7 hosts for every man who is a guest in someone else's home.

Around one-fifth of Hispanics and blacks live in multigenerational households, compared with 12 percent of whites. Age patterns suggest relatively high rates at younger ages, with rates "bottoming out" for men in their 40s and women in their 30s, when less than 10 percent of whites, 20 percent of blacks, and 16 percent of Hispanics live in households that contain more than one generation of adults. Rates rise to their highest level for

TABLE 1.4 Percentages of Adults Ages 15 and Older in Multigenerational Households and Ratios of Hosts to Guests: 1997-1999 (combined)

	% Living in Multigenerational Households			Ratio of Hosts to Guests		
	White	Black	Hispanic	White	Black	Hispanic
Men	11.8	23.2	20.7	0.73	0.35	0.51
Age						
15-29	12.2	23.6	19.3	0.10	0.09	0.12
30-39	11.0	24.3	16.4	0.19	0.10	0.39
40-49	9.8	20.3	16.4	0.63	0.37	0.94
50-59	13.8	22.7	33.3	3.60	1.60	1.44
60-69	13.7	25.9	33.5	6.00	2.08	3.49
70-79	11.9	24.7	34.0	2.37	2.16	0.92
Education						
Less than high school	13.6	24.9	20.0	0.63	0.39	0.57
High school only	12.8	24.1	22.2	0.67	0.30	0.43
College graduate	8.3	13.9	17.8	1.08	0.70	0.71
Marital status						
Married	7.7	13.4	15.1	6.39	6.27	3.11
Was married	17.7	26.9	29.6	0.35	0.24	0.24
Never married	17.7	29.6	24.3	0.09	0.07	0.11
Women	11.5	22.0	21.2	1.15	0.89	0.80
Age						
15-29	10.8	20.3	18.8	0.11	0.11	0.16
30-39	5.9	14.2	10.8	0.36	0.30	0.75
40-49	9.3	19.9	20.1	1.52	1.65	1.80
50-59	16.9	31.5	35.3	4.54	4.07	2.42
60-69	16.2	33.1	39.0	4.19	4.13	1.91
70-79	14.4	30.7	36.8	1.55	1.96	0.60
Education						
Less than high school	14.5	24.4	22.7	0.97	1.00	0.85
High school only	12.2	22.0	20.5	1.25	0.81	0.70
College graduate	7.1	16.5	16.9	1.01	1.05	1.08
Marital status						
Married	7.7	13.8	14.7	6.20	6.26	3.33
Was married	18.1	29.3	32.0	1.08	1.56	0.64
Never married	13.9	22.4	24.2	0.09	0.21	0.21

SOURCE: Cohen and Casper (2000).
NOTE: Race/ethnicity categories are white, non-Hispanic; black, non-Hispanic; and Hispanic.

those over age 50, and rates are higher for women than for men of these ages. What is most interesting is that, more often than not, the elderly individual in these settings is the host to the adults of other generations. Among white men in their 60s, for every man living in another generation's home, there are six men hosting another generation, usually an adult child. Among white women in their 60s, hosts outnumber guests four to one. Similar age patterns and host-versus-guest relationships characterize blacks and Hispanics as well.

Consistent with our earlier discussion about the difficulties that less educated male workers have had in the labor market in recent years, the likelihood of multigenerational living and of being a guest in someone else's home is much higher for men with a high school education or less than for college graduates. However, only among white male college graduates who live in multigenerational settings do the rates of hosting exceed the likelihood of being a guest in another's home. Women of all educational levels have ratios of hosting (versus being a guest) that hover much closer to one.

Rates of multigenerational living vary by marital status, with the married of each racial group less likely to live in a multigenerational household and the formerly or never married much more likely to share a residence with multiple adult generations. Additionally, the married are much more likely to be hosting others in their households, whereas those who have never married or were formerly married are much more likely to be living in someone else's homes than to be hosting more than one generation of adults in their homes. Within all marital statuses, rates of multigenerational living are much greater for blacks and Hispanics than for whites.

● Conclusion

Since the 1960s, changes in the economy and norms about family life have coincided with increases in divorce, cohabitation, and nonmarital births; marriages occurring at later ages; declines and postponements in fertility; more young adults living independently; and declines in mortality, lengthening the amount of time adults spend in families and increasing the propensity of the elderly to live alone. But since the mid-1990s, and even earlier in some cases, many of these trends have stabilized.

Changes in individual behaviors of family formation and dissolution result in changes in household and family structure. Since the 1960s, the two-parent family has been shrinking as a percentage of households, as nonfamily living and single-mother and single-father families have been increasing among all racial groups. All races continued to experience a decline in married-couple families with children and an increase in single-mother and single-father families in the 1980s and early 1990s. Yet by 1994 the growth in single-mother families had stabilized, although the numbers of single-father families continued to grow throughout the decade for whites and Hispanics, but not for blacks. White children were more likely to live with two parents than were Hispanic children, who in turn were more likely than black children to reside with both parents. The reverse order was true for single-mother families. But the difference between whites and Hispanics is less striking if we take cohabitation into account. Single-father families were the least common (but fastest-growing) type of family with children for all races.

Living arrangements and family formation change in response to economic conditions, cultural changes, and demographic shifts, such as the aging of the population. The United States may have been through a particularly tumultuous period in the latter half of the 20th century, resulting in rapid changes in family behaviors. Families have emerged from these changes more diverse, with the boundaries separating different family types less rigid than in the past.

Changes in marriage, cohabitation, and nonmarital childbearing have made it increasingly hard to distinguish between two- and one-parent families. Marriage can no longer be used to determine definitively when children live with both parents, just as a nonmarital birth does not automatically signify that a child is born into a single-parent family. More children today are born to mothers who are not currently married, but some of those children are born to cohabiting parents and begin life in households that include both parents. Cohabitation has also become almost normative as a mode of entry into remarriage, and this makes it hard to determine when many mothers and their children end periods of single-parent living. Thus cohabitation may effectively bring "stepfathers" into the picture before there is formal remarriage.

Whether U.S. families have now adjusted to the dramatic social changes that occurred in the latter half of the 20th century and have reached a new equilibrium, only time will tell. Economic fortunes and family relationships remain intertwined. The economy was quite robust during the latter half of the 1990s, perhaps encouraging the stability and "quieting" of family change that is observable across a variety of indicators. Norms, beliefs, and values about the family also affect family behavior, but norms change slowly, especially in comparison to the state of the economy. It is too soon to tell for sure how economic and normative forces will interact to affect family change. Whether rates of family change will quicken if and when economic conditions deteriorate remains to be seen.

Issues of growing importance that we take up in the subsequent chapters include the following: What does the growth in cohabitation mean for marriage? How has the decline in fertility within marriage and the growth in the proportion of births outside marriage altered how we think about the connections between marriage and child rearing? How do families balance paid work and child rearing, especially in single-parent families? Are fathers' roles within families changing? How and when do grandparents step in to assist their children and grandchildren? How is family change intertwined in both caregiving for children and adequate income provision for children? What will growing income inequality among families do to the fortunes of the next generation? What have been the consequences of changing family configurations for economic well-being, and how has the economy affected family formation and dissolution behaviors? In this chapter, we have used a broad brush to provide an overview of changes in family behaviors. In the chapters that follow, we turn to those topics that emerge as important from this overview.

Notes

1. This was more true in white middle- and upper-class families than in poor families or black families.

2. The Equal Rights Amendment was first introduced in Congress in 1923; the proposed amendment stated that "equality or rights under the law shall not be denied or abridged by the United States or by any State on account of sex." After nearly a half century, the ERA was passed by Congress in 1972. The first campaign to ratify the proposed 27th Amendment to the U.S. Constitution ended on June 30, 1982; ratification by the states fell 3 states shy of the 38 required (National Women's Conference Committee 1986).

3. The race categories are white, non-Hispanic; black, non-Hispanic; and Hispanic. The Census Bureau defines *white* and *black* as racial categories. The term *Hispanic* refers to ethnicity. For this reason, in most published U.S. Census reports, whites and blacks can be Hispanic and Hispanics can be of any race. In our analyses we define mutually exclusive categories.

CHAPTER **2**

COHABITATION

S hacking up. Living in sin. Living together. Persons of the opposite sex sharing living quarters. Doubling up. Sleeping together. All of these expressions have been used to describe the living arrangement that demographers refer to as cohabitation. Some of these terms are more value laden than others, and the one an individual chooses to describe this living arrangement can say a great deal about how he or she views unmarried sexual partners. Although *cohabitation* can refer to same-sex couples, most of the demographic research conducted to date has been concerned with opposite-sex partners.

The increase in heterosexual cohabitation that has accompanied the delay in marriage and increase in divorce is one of the most significant changes in family life to take place in the latter half of the 20th century (Seltzer 2000; Smock 2000). Some observers believe that the increase in cohabitation has eroded commitment to marriage and "traditional" family life (e.g., Waite and Gallagher 2000). One of the best examples of this view is presented in a report titled *Should We Live Together? What Young Adults Need to Know About Cohabitation Before Marriage,* published by the National Marriage Project (Popenoe and Whitehead 1999). This controversial report paints an overwhelmingly negative picture of cohabitation, asserting that "cohabiting unions tend to weaken the institution of marriage and pose clear and present dangers to women and children."

Most adults in the United States eventually marry: 91 percent of women ages 45 to 54 in 1998 had been married at least once (Bianchi and Casper 2000:15), and an estimated 88 percent of women in younger cohorts are likely to marry eventually (Raley 2000). But the meaning and permanence of marriage may be changing as cohabitation increases.

Marriage used to be the demographic event that almost exclusively marked the formation of a new household, the beginning of sexual relations, and the birth of a child. Marriage also typically implied that each partner had one sexual partner and identified the two individuals who would parent any child born of the union. The increasing social acceptance of cohabitation outside marriage has meant that these linkages can no longer be assumed. Also, what it means to be "married" or "single" is changing as the personal lives of unmarried couples come to resemble those of their married counterparts in some ways but not in others (Seltzer 2000; Smock 2000).

Cohabiting and marital relationships have much in common: coresidence; emotional, psychological, and sexual intimacy; and some degree of economic interdependence. But the two relationships differ in other important ways. Marriage is a relationship between two people of opposite sexes that adheres to legal, moral, and social rules, a social institution that rests upon common values and shared expectations for appropriate behavior within the partnership (Nock 1998b). Society upholds and enforces appropriate marital behavior both formally and informally. In contrast, there is no widely recognized social blueprint or script for the appropriate behavior of cohabitors, or for the behavior of the friends, families, and other individuals and institutions with whom they interact. There is no common term in use for referring to one's nonmarital live-in lover, whereas the terms *spouse, husband,* and *wife* are institutionalized. Most important, there is far greater societal acceptance of marriage—and far more ambivalence about cohabitation—as a desirable adult relationship for the rearing of children.

We begin this chapter with the intriguing story of the growth in cohabitation in the latter decades of the 20th century. Tracking trends in cohabitation has been difficult because until recently there was no direct measurement of the numbers of unmarried partners living together. Until the late 1980s, when national surveys began the routine collection of information on cohabitation, researchers relied on indirect estimates to document the increase in cohabitation. The 1987-88 National Survey of Families and Households (NSFH) collected the first cohabitation histories. The 1990 Census was the first census enumeration that included "unmarried partner" among a list of categories from which a respondent could choose in identifying his or her household relationship. Beginning in 1995, the Current Population Survey (CPS) also included the category "unmarried partner" as a possible response to the household relationship question, and the National Survey of Family Growth began to obtain detailed data on cohabitation.

In the discussion that follows, we use CPS data and indirect estimates to examine the growth in cohabitation since the late 1970s. In an effort to understand more about the meaning of cohabitation, we review relevant research on this topic, compare cohabitors with married and single people, and examine how cohabitors view themselves. We also investigate whether cohabitors are becoming more like married people over time as cohabitation becomes a more common experience and gains wider social acceptance. We describe the linkages between cohabitation and other demographic events and the potential positive and negative consequences they engender. We conclude the chapter with a discussion of what demographers know about cohabitation and what this implies for the future of marriage and family life in the United States.

Who Cohabits and How Has ● This Changed Over Time?

Unmarried heterosexual cohabitation began to capture national attention during and after the period of well-publicized student unrest on college campuses in the late 1960s and early 1970s. The image of the time was of sexually promiscuous college students experimenting with new family forms by living with their boyfriends or girlfriends rather than marrying, often trying to keep their arrangements secret from their disapproving parents. In the 1970s, Paul Glick and Arthur Norton (1977) of the U.S. Census Bureau were the first to use information on household composition from the decennial census and CPS to define cohabitors as "persons of the opposite sex sharing living quarters," or POSSLQs for short.

Figure 2.1 shows changes in cohabitation using a modified version of the indirect POSSLQ measure (Casper and Cohen 2000). The proportion of unmarried women who were cohabiting tripled, from 3 percent to 9 percent, between 1978 and 1998. Increases were similar among unmarried men—from 5 percent to nearly 12 percent—with men more likely than women to cohabit, both in 1978 and in 1998.

These estimates of cohabitation may seem low, especially considering the heightened concern of some observers that cohabitation is eroding commitment to marriage and family life. The rates are low, in part, because they represent only those who are cohabiting at a given point in time. A

● **Figure 2.1.** Percentages of Unmarried Men and Women Cohabiting, by Race and Gender: 1978-1998

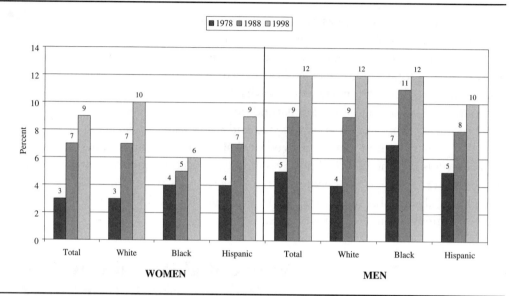

SOURCE: Current Population Survey, March supplements, 1978, 1988, 1998.
NOTE: Race/ethnicity categories are white, non-Hispanic; black, non-Hispanic; and Hispanic.

much larger proportion of people have ever cohabited, and the likelihood of cohabiting appears to be increasing over time. Only 8 percent of first marriages in the late 1960s were preceded by cohabitation, compared with 49 percent in 1985-86 (Bumpass 1990) and 56 percent by the early to mid-1990s (Bumpass and Lu 2000). Thus, young couples today are more likely to begin their coresidential relationships in cohabitation than in marriage.

Why has cohabitation increased so much? A number of factors, including increased uncertainty about the stability of marriage, the erosion of norms against cohabitation and sexual relations outside of marriage, the availability of reliable birth control, and the weakening of religious and other normative constraints on individuals' family decisions, seem to be ending the taboo against living together without marrying. For example, by the mid-1990s, a majority of high school seniors thought that living together prior to marriage was a good idea (Axinn and Thornton 2000).

Some argue that cohabitation reduces the costs of partnering, especially if one is uncertain about a potential mate, and allows a couple to experience the benefits of an intimate relationship without committing to marriage (Willis and Michael 1994). If a cohabiting relationship is not success-ful, one can simply move out; if a marriage is not successful, one suffers through a sometimes lengthy and messy divorce.

Meanwhile, the development of effective contraceptives has given childbearing-age couples greater freedom to engage in sexual intercourse without the risk of unwanted pregnancy. The availability of reliable birth control has increased the prevalence of premarital sex. As premarital sex has become more common, it has become more widely accepted, and so has living with a partner before marriage (Bumpass and Sweet 1989a). Widespread availability of contraception also makes it easier to avoid un-wanted pregnancy if one chooses to live with a partner after separation or divorce from a previous marriage.

Shifting norms mean that adults today are more likely to believe that co-habitation and divorce are acceptable and less likely to believe that mar-riage is a lifelong commitment than was true in the past (Thornton 1989; Thornton and Freedman 1983). Thus the normative barrier that once dis-couraged cohabitation has begun to wither away. Increasingly, American values have shifted from those favoring family commitment and self-sacri-fice to those favoring self-fulfillment, individual growth, and personal free-dom (Lasch 1979; Lesthaeghe 1995; McLanahan and Casper 1995).

Early estimates suggested that college students were in the vanguard of attitudinal and behavior changes that fostered the growth in cohabitation. Glick and Norton (1977:34), for example, highlighted the fact that a greater proportion of unmarried than married couples (8 percent versus 5 percent) included two partners who were college students and that, in 1970, one-fourth of unmarried couples had at least one partner who was enrolled in college. Subsequent research, however, has documented that cohabita-tion is a behavior that is prevalent among less educated individuals. Larry Bumpass and James Sweet (1989b), in discussing the first direct estimates of cohabitation, note: "Contrary to a common view of cohabitation as col-lege student behavior, education is strongly and negatively related to rates of cohabitation before first marriage. The highest rates are found among the least educated" (p. 622).

CPS trends, based on indirect estimates, indicate that about 16 percent of men who cohabit are college graduates; this figure has remained quite sta-ble over time (see Table 2.1). Among women, the estimate in 1998 was 17 percent, up from 13 percent in 1978 and 1988. Other estimates of the likeli-hood that an individual will ever cohabit suggest that increases in the rates of cohabitation continue to be greater for those with only a high school ed-ucation than for those with a college education (Bumpass and Lu 2000).

TABLE 2.1 Presence of Children, Age, and Marital Status Among Unmarried Couples: 1978-1998 (in percentages)

	All Couples		
	1978	*1988*	*1998*
Age			
Men			
Total	100.0	100.0	100.0
15-24	21.2	18.2	15.1
25-34	40.3	40.5	37.2
35+	38.5	41.3	47.7
Women			
Total	100.0	100.0	100.0
15-24	35.5	25.8	21.8
25-34	29.9	39.4	34.4
35+	34.6	34.8	43.8
Marital status			
Men			
Total	100.0	100.0	100.0
Separated/divorced	46.9	45.3	42.2
Widowed	6.5	3.3	3.2
Never married	46.7	51.4	54.6
Women			
Total	100.0	100.0	100.0
Separated/divorced	39.3	44.2	44.9
Widowed	15.1	8.0	5.7
Never married	45.7	47.9	49.4
Children in the household	27.6	33.8	37.1
College graduates			
Men	15.8	16.0	16.3
Women	13.4	13.3	17.1

SOURCE: Current Population Survey, March supplements, 1978, 1988, 1998.
NOTE: Unmarried partners estimated with adjusted POSSLQ measure (see Casper and Cohen 2000).

Who cohabits defies stereotypes in other ways as well. For example, increasingly, cohabitation is not a phenomenon confined to early adulthood. Although more than 60 percent of cohabiting men and almost two-thirds of women in unmarried partnerships were under age 35 in 1978, these proportions have declined. In 1998, a relatively high percentage of cohabitors were in their mid-30s or older (almost 50 percent of men and more than 40 percent of women in 1998). As age at first marriage increases, the average age of cohabitors also appears to be increasing. In addition, living together without marrying is common after first marriages end as well as before they begin. In 1998, 45 percent of the men and 51 percent of the women in heterosexual unmarried couples had been previously married, with the vast majority either separated or divorced.

One of the biggest compositional shifts that is occurring among unmarried couples is the increase in the presence of children in these households, either children born to the couple or those that one of the partners has from a prior relationship. In 1978, about 28 percent of cohabitor households included children under age 18 (see Table 2.1). By 1998, the proportion had increased to 37 percent. About two-fifths of all children spend at least some years during their childhoods living with a parent and the parent's unmarried partner, according to recent estimates by Bumpass and Lu (2000:35). This percentage is high both because of the popularity of cohabitation after separation and divorce, where children from a prior marriage may be present, and because more births outside marriage are to mothers who are living with their partners.

The proportion of births to unmarried mothers who are actually living with their partners (often their children's fathers) increased from 29 percent in the mid-1980s to near 40 percent in the mid-1990s (Bumpass and Lu 2000:35). In some European countries, most notably Scandinavian countries, cohabitation increasingly seems to function as a substitute for marriage, with couples unlikely to marry before the birth of their children. In the United States, the likelihood of marriage with the birth of a child is declining but seems to be a far smaller component of the increase in children in cohabiting unions than in Europe.

As more women spend time in cohabiting relationships, the time "at risk" of a pregnancy while a women is living with an unmarried partner goes up. Most of the increase in births to cohabitors (as much as 70 percent) is due to this factor (Raley 2001). Cohabiting women who become pregnant have become a little less likely to marry before the birth, and single women who become pregnant have become more likely to move in with the father of the child rather than remain single or marry. Yet these two changes in behavior—staying in a cohabiting arrangement rather than marrying if one becomes pregnant or moving in with a partner rather than marrying if one becomes pregnant while single—account for only about 10 percent of the increase in births to cohabiting women (Raley 2001:66).

The increased recognition that many unmarried couples are raising children is leading to greater attention to the ways in which children's lives may be affected by the marital status of their parents. For example, children born to unmarried couples have a higher risk of experiencing their parents' separation than do children born to married couples (Bumpass, Raley, and Sweet 1995). The ties that bind fathers to their children may also be weaker in cohabiting than in marital relationships: After parents separate, children whose parents never married see their fathers less often and are less likely to be financially supported by their fathers than are children born to married parents (Cooksey and Craig 1998; Seltzer 2000).

● A Note on Gay and Lesbian Cohabiting Households

Gay and lesbian family rights and responsibilities have emerged in recent years as among the most hotly contested social and political issues. Topics of discussion include the extension of family benefits, such as health insurance, life insurance, and family leave, to gay and lesbian couples; the parental rights of gays and lesbians and their suitability as adoptive parents; and the legalization of same-sex marriage. The importance of these issues and the need for accurate information to inform policy have prompted demographers and social scientists to develop national estimates for the gay and lesbian population.

Accurate measurement of cohabitation among the gay and lesbian population is even more difficult than accurate measurement of heterosexual cohabitation (Bianchi and Casper 2000). First, defining who is gay or lesbian is not straightforward, and estimates vary depending on the time frame and criterion used to identify sexual orientation. For example, among women, 3.5 percent have had a same-sex partner since turning age 18, but only 1.9 percent report that their sexual relationships have been exclusively with partners of the same sex during the past year. The comparable percentages for men are 4.7 percent with any same-sex partner since age 18 and 2.5 percent with *only* same-sex partners during the past year (Black et al. 2000:Table 1).

Although there appears to be increased societal acceptance of opposite-sex partners living together, people are much less accepting of homosexual relationships in general, let alone cohabiting same-sex relationships. Lack of social acceptance may lead more gay and lesbian than heterosexual couples to misreport their relationship status in surveys. In addition, most nationally based surveys with questions regarding sexual orientation are not large enough to provide reliable estimates of the numbers of cohabiting same-sex couples. Only the decennial census has enough information to provide reliable national estimates of gay and lesbian couple households.

In a recent study based on the 1990 Census, Black et al. (2000:147) estimate that about 7 out of 1,000 adult males were in gay-partnered households and 6 out of a 1,000 adult females were members of lesbian-partnered households in 1990. They further estimate that about 2 out of every 1,000 couples (married plus unmarried) was a gay or lesbian couple (see Black et al. 2000:Fig. 1). Restricting the universe to cohabiting couples (opposite-sex plus same-sex cohabitors), a little more than 4 percent of unmarried couples were in same-sex partnerships in 1990.

Gay and lesbian cohabitors tend to be urban dwellers: About 60 percent of gay cohabiting couples and 45 percent of lesbian cohabiting couples were concentrated in only 20 cities in the United States in 1990, with the greatest proportions residing in San Francisco, Washington, D.C., Los Angeles, Atlanta, and New York (Black 2000 et al.:Table 4). In contrast, about 25 percent of the population as a whole resided in these same 20 cities.

Cohabiting gays and lesbians have higher educational attainment than either heterosexual unmarried partners or married couples (Black et al. 2000:Table 8). Gay cohabitors generally earn less than other men, whereas cohabiting lesbians earn more than other women. The rate of home ownership is lower for gay and lesbian cohabiting couples than for married-couple families, but among those who own homes, gay and lesbian couples' homes tend to be more expensive. The difference in housing values might reflect the higher education levels of cohabiting gays and lesbians compared with married couples (Black et al. 2000) or the fact that a much higher proportion of gays and lesbians live in large cities with high housing costs (Bianchi and Casper 2000).

As with heterosexual cohabiting couples, a number of same-sex cohabiting households, especially lesbian-partnered households, include children; 22 percent of lesbian and 5 percent of gay households included children (any age) of at least one of the partners in 1990. Comparable figures for opposite-sex couples were 36 percent of heterosexual cohabiting couples and 59 percent of married-couple families in 1990. Many children in same-sex couple households were probably born of previous marriages: 17 percent of gays and 29 percent of lesbians previously had been in heterosexual marriages (Black et al. 2000:Tables 6, 7).

How do people feel about homosexuality? Over time, U.S. society has become more accepting of gay and lesbian rights. According to a data review published by the Roper Center, in 1977, 33 percent of adults thought that homosexuals should not have equal rights in terms of job opportunities, compared with only 13 percent in 1999 ("Considering Alternative Lifestyles" 2000:29). In general, Americans tend to view homosexuality as a moral issue, yet they express a certain degree of tolerance toward homosexual behavior. Whereas the majority of adults (59 percent) in 1998 believed that homosexual behavior is morally wrong, less than a third (28 percent) believed it to be unacceptable behavior that should not be tolerated ("Considering Alternative Lifestyles" 2000:26). And people who said they personally knew gays or lesbians tended to be more accepting of gay rights.

The public's view of homosexuality seems to be at odds with the views gays and lesbians hold themselves. For example, the same data review shows that whereas a third of all Americans thought that homosexuality is something you are born with, three-quarters of lesbian and gay adults believed this to be true. Similarly, a majority of Americans (56 percent) thought that homosexuals *can* change their sexual orientation, whereas nearly 9 out of 10 gay and lesbian adults believed they *cannot* change ("Considering Alternative Lifestyles" 2000:27). Gays and lesbians consistently reported that they thought higher percentages of straight people were bothered by their behavior in public (e.g., kissing or holding hands with someone of the same sex in public; presenting a gay or lesbian appearance in public through clothing, hairstyle, and so forth) than the percentages of all adults who reported that they actually were bothered. For example, 64 percent of gays and lesbians thought straight people were very much bothered when gays kiss in public, compared with only 51 percent of all adults who reported that this behavior bothered them ("Considering Alternative Lifestyles" 2000:28). About twice as many (60 percent) gay and lesbian adults compared with all adults nationally (33 percent) reported that they thought there was a lot of discrimination against gays and lesbians ("Considering Alternative Lifestyles" 2000:29).

Research on family relationships in gay and lesbian households is relatively limited, but reviews of the literature point to more similarities than differences in the family functioning of same-sex and heterosexual relationships (see, e.g., Patterson 1992, 2000). For example, gay and lesbian relationships seem to be as supportive as heterosexual relationships (Patterson 2000), and the home environments of gay and lesbian couples are as conducive to psychosocial growth among family members, including children, as are those of heterosexual couples (Patterson 1992).

Cohabitation and Marriage •

Much of the demographic research on cohabitation has been oriented around one question: How similar is (heterosexual) cohabitation to marriage? Economic theorists often view marriage as an institution in which individual goals are replaced by altruism and the subordination of self-interest in favor of goals that benefit the family (e.g., Becker 1991). Married couples supposedly maximize benefits for their families by specializing in different activities—wives tend to specialize in homemaking and husbands tend to specialize in breadwinning. This gender role difference has meant that women tend to seek spouses with higher education and earnings than themselves—men who would be good breadwinners. Men, by contrast, tend to look for women who will be good mothers and homemakers.

Evidence suggests that cohabitation may attract individuals who value more egalitarian, less specialized, gender roles. Gender-differentiated roles are not absent from cohabiting unions; for example, cohabiting couples with higher-earning male (but not female) partners are the ones that proceed more quickly to marriage (Sanchez, Manning, and Smock 1998). Yet research has found that cohabiting relationships endure longer when partners' employment patterns and earnings are more similar than different (Brines and Joyner 1999). Cohabiting couples also tend to divide housework in a more egalitarian fashion than do married couples (South and Spitze 1994), and cohabitors are less likely to espouse traditional gender roles (Clarkberg, Stolzenberg, and Waite 1995; Lesthaeghe and Surkyn 1988).

Cohabitation may also be especially attractive to those with more individualistic, more materialistic, and less family-oriented outlooks on life. Cohabitors are more likely than others to believe that individual freedom is important in a marriage (Thomson and Colella 1992). Men and women are more likely to choose cohabitation as their first union if it is important to them to have "lots of money" in life (Clarkberg et al. 1995). Women who value their careers are more likely than other women to cohabit for their first union, whereas those who think that finding the right person to marry and having a happy family life is important are more likely than others to begin their first union with marriage (Clarkberg et al. 1995).

Cohabitors are also more accepting of divorce. They are less likely than married persons to disapprove of divorce (Lesthaeghe and Surkyn 1988), with those who disapprove of divorce more likely to begin their first union with marriage (Axinn and Thornton 1992). Children of divorced parents are more likely to cohabit than are children of married parents (Cherlin, Kiernan, and Chase-Lansdale 1995), in part because people whose mothers divorced tend to hold attitudes that are more approving of cohabitation (Axinn and Thornton 1996).

To the extent that cohabitation is an "incomplete institution" lacking clear normative standards (Nock 1995), it may provide a more comfortable setting than marriage for less conventional couples. Perhaps the strongest indicator of this is the higher percentage of cohabiting than married couples who cross the racial divide in their partnerships (see Table 2.2). Cohabiting couples are more than twice as likely to be of different races than married couples—13 percent compared with 5 percent. About half of interracial cohabiting couples are made up of a white woman and a man of another race (data not shown).

Schoen and Weinick (1993) argue that because cohabiting relationships tend to be short-term relationships, cohabiting partners are less concerned with the ascribed characteristics of their partners than are the partners in married couples. Half of all cohabitations last a year or less; only about one-sixth of cohabitations last at least 3 years, and only one-tenth last 5 years or more (Bumpass and Lu 2000). Thus an individual's choosing a partner of the same age, race, and religion as him- or herself is not as important in cohabitation as it is in marriage, because cohabitation does not necessarily entail a long-term commitment or the accompanying normative standards such a relationship implies.

It is much more common in cohabiting than in marital relationships for the female partner to be older and better educated than her male partner (see Table 2.2). Women are more than 2 years older than their partners in 24 percent of unmarried couples but in only 12 percent of married couples, and women have a higher educational level in 21 percent of cohabiting couples compared with only 16 percent of married couples.

The data displayed in Table 2.2 support the notion that cohabiting couples are more egalitarian in terms of their labor force participation and earnings. Almost four out of five cohabiting couples have both partners employed, compared with only three in five married couples. Men tend to work more hours than their partners in cohabiting and marital relation-

TABLE 2.2   Characteristics of Cohabiting and Married Couples: 1998

	Cohabiting	Married
Total number of couples (thousands)	3,142	54,317
% of couples in which		
Woman is of different race/ethnicity than man	13	5
Woman is at least 2 years older than man	24	12
Woman has more education than man	21	16
Both man and woman worked for pay	77	60
Woman worked more hours[a]	24	16
Woman's contribution to couple's 1997 income (% of total income)[b]	41	37

SOURCE: Current Population Survey, March supplement, 1998.
NOTE: A cohabiting couple is defined as an unmarried couple who maintains a household together. Race/ethnicity categories are white, non-Hispanic; black, non-Hispanic; and Hispanic.
a. Woman worked more hours than her partner in the preceding year.
b. Calculated for couples in which both partners were employed.

ships, but women's hours of employment exceed their partners' hours in a greater percentage of cohabiting (24 percent) than married (16 percent) couples. When employed, women and men have earnings that are closer to equality in cohabiting than in married couples; women in cohabiting couples contribute 41 percent of the couple's annual earnings, compared with 37 percent, on average, for married women.

Some of the differences shown in Table 2.2 reflect the fact that unmarried couples tend to be younger, on average, than married couples, and younger generations have more egalitarian attitudes toward the labor force roles of men and women and are more likely to choose partners with different racial backgrounds. However, the evidence in Table 2.2, combined with the attitudinal and family background differences between unmarried and married couples noted in other research, suggests that cohabitation provides a living arrangement that suits couples who may be somewhat uncertain about whether their partnerships can be sustained over the long term. These may be couples who must work out issues that surround partnering across racial lines, couples who defy patterns that are considered "normal" in the larger society (such as when an "older" woman partners with a "younger" man or a more educated woman partners with a less educated mate), or couples for whom an equal economic partnership is a priority and who may be concerned that marriage will propel them into a gendered division of labor that will make it difficult to sustain their egalitarianism.

● Are Cohabiting and Married Individuals Becoming More Alike?

Cohabitors are more likely to value individualism, have higher career aspirations for women, and have more egalitarian views, but the gender-based division of labor within marriage is also breaking down. If cohabitation has become a more pervasive, socially acceptable behavior, and marriages are also becoming more egalitarian, at least with respect to market work, we might expect cohabitors to be more like married people today than they were 20 years ago.

With respect to personal income and labor force participation, cohabiting and married women have begun to resemble each other more closely. For example, in 1978 white cohabiting women's own income was more than three times that of white married women, on average (see Table 2.3). But by 1998, this difference was substantially reduced—a white cohabiting woman's income was only 15 percent greater than a white married woman's. A similar pattern occurred among Hispanic women. In contrast, black cohabiting women, who in 1978 had incomes 62 percent higher than their married counterparts, were actually earning less than married black women by 1998. Cohabiting white men also became more similar to white married men in terms of labor force participation and income, although they continued to have less income than married men. Patterns were less consistent for black and Hispanic men.

Convergence is less clear when the indicator is educational attainment. Cohabiting black and Hispanic women were substantially less likely than black and Hispanic married women to be college graduates in 1978. This gap was closed completely for Hispanic women by 1998, whereas for black women it was reduced greatly. Among white women, however, those who were cohabiting were about 30 percent more likely than married women to be college graduates in 1978. By 1998, they were actually about 30 percent *less* likely to be college graduates.

The education levels of cohabiting and married men also did not converge over the period. White and black cohabiting men actually lost ground compared with white and black married men. The gap increased

TABLE 2.3 Changing Economic Characteristics of Married and Cohabiting Men and Women by Race/Ethnicity: 1978-1998

	White				Black				Hispanic			
	Men		Women		Men		Women		Men		Women	
	Married	Cohabiting	Married	Cohabiting	Married	Cohabiting	Married	Cohabiting	Married	Cohabiting	Married	Cohabiting
College graduate (%)												
1978	20.0	18.8	12.3	16.1	7.4	4.3	8.5	1.9	7.9	7.0	5.4	3.5
1988	25.7	19.1	17.7	15.2	12.2	6.6	13.5	5.0	10.8	5.8	7.5	8.0
1998	30.6	17.9	25.3	18.3	16.9	8.5	19.7	9.2	10.7	10.3	10.8	11.6
% of married												
1978		0.94		1.32		0.58		0.22		0.90		0.65
1988		0.74		0.86		0.54		0.37		0.54		1.08
1998		0.58		0.72		0.51		0.47		0.96		1.07
Full-time, full-year worker (%)[a]												
1978	65.7	44.0	22.5	36.9	58.9	52.2	30.5	28.2	63.3	46.6	19.6	32.2
1988	64.2	58.9	30.9	49.4	59.1	47.7	41.6	36.3	63.9	60.1	27.9	42.9
1998	64.7	64.5	37.2	50.3	64.5	56.4	47.6	51.0	67.4	62.6	31.9	39.0
% of married												
1978		0.67		1.64		0.89		0.92		0.74		1.64
1988		0.92		1.60		0.81		0.87		0.94		1.54
1998		1.00		1.35		0.87		1.07		0.93		1.22
Median own income ($)												
1978	34,683	20,317	4,071	13,206	22,450	15,237	6,095	9,884	24,380	19,875	2,255	8,888
1988	34,395	24,019	9,962	16,002	22,185	14,129	10,596	8,449	21,369	15,541	5,052	9,890
1998	34,107	24,000	13,346	15,385	25,000	18,000	15,000	12,440	20,000	15,000	6,492	10,000
% of married												
1978		0.59		3.24		0.68		1.62		0.82		3.94
1988		0.70		1.61		0.64		0.80		0.73		1.96
1998		0.70		1.15		0.72		0.83		0.75		1.54

SOURCE: Current Population Survey, March supplements, 1978, 1988, 1998.

NOTE: Race/ethnicity categories are white, non-Hispanic; black, non-Hispanic; and Hispanic. Cohabiting partners estimated with adjusted POSSLQ measure (see Casper and Cohen 2000).

a. Worked full-time and for the full previous year. Full-time, full-year workers are those employed 35 or more hours per week and 48 or more weeks in the previous year.

only slightly for blacks, but almost doubled for white men. For Hispanic men, estimates are rather unstable: The gap in educational attainment of married and cohabiting Hispanic men increased from 1978 to 1988 and then decreased to become almost nonexistent by 1998.

Many of the comparisons displayed in Table 2.3 indicate that the lines demarcating cohabiting and married women are indeed blurring as cohabitation becomes more common. A closer examination of the data indicates that it may be the behavior of married women more than that of cohabiting women that has changed, as women became less traditional and more career oriented over this period. Although the evidence is not quite as strong for men, we see several areas of convergence, particularly with regard to income and labor force attachment. As cohabitation becomes more prevalent and more of the currently married have at some point in their lives cohabited, we would expect married people and cohabitors to look more alike. Thus, as time goes on, the cohabiting and married are increasingly likely to be the same groups of people, perhaps just at different stages in their relationships.

If gender roles are changing and men and women are becoming more egalitarian, we should be able to track these changes within married and unmarried couples. One way to do this is to compare the relative earnings of men and women in married and cohabiting couples. Increasing egalitarianism should translate over time into higher earnings for women relative to their partners. For all couples this is indeed the case—women were earning a larger share of the couple's total earnings in 1997 than they were in 1977 (see Figure 2.2). The increases are particularly large among married couples. However, within each racial group, cohabiting women contribute more than married women to the couple's earnings. Have these differences between unmarried and married couples in the ratio of partners' earnings narrowed over time? For white and black couples the answer is yes—the space between the cohabiting and married lines on the graph gets smaller as one moves from 1979 to 1997. In contrast, the gap between married and cohabiting Hispanic couples has been relatively stable over time, although it appears to have been decreasing somewhat since 1994.

● Cohabitation and Single Life

Although the bulk of research on cohabitation has been motivated by attempts to compare and differentiate cohabitation and marriage, there have been those who have argued that cohabitation is more similar to remaining

Figure 2.2. Women's Shares of Couple Earnings: 1978-1998 (dual-earner couples, 3-year moving averages)

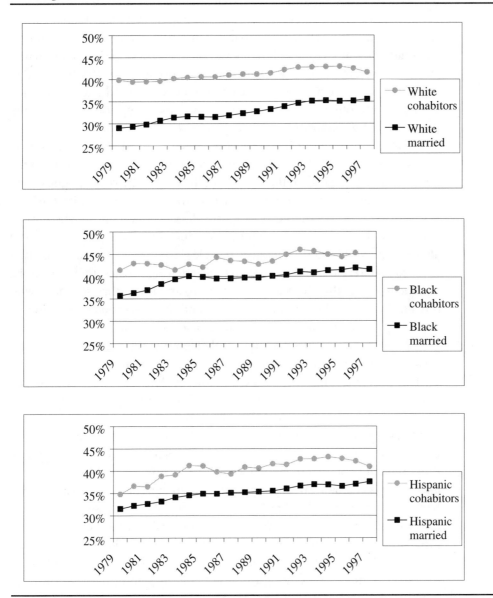

SOURCE: Current Population Survey, March supplements, 1978-1998.
NOTE: Women's earnings are represented as a percentage of couple earnings. Race/ethnicity categories are white, non-Hispanic; black, non-Hispanic; and Hispanic. Cohabiting partners estimated with adjusted POSSLQ measure (see Casper and Cohen 2000).

single than to marrying. Basing their argument on data that are now some-what dated, Rindfuss and VandenHeuvel (1990) have asserted that the growth in cohabiting relationships that began in the 1960s was the result of historical changes in dating and sexual relationships among unmarried individuals. They endeavored to show that cohabitors are substantially more similar to the never married than to married couples. For instance, cohabitors' fertility expectations, nonfamilial activities, and home ownership rates resembled those of the never married. They also found that cohabitors were intermediate between the never married and the married with regard to other factors, such as the amount of support received from parents and the proportion attending school.

Rindfuss and VandenHeuvel's comparisons relied on one relatively young cohort, and the researchers compared cohabitors only with never-married singles. On the one hand, the data in Table 2.4 suggest that, as cohabitation becomes more normative, those who cohabit before they first marry (i.e., never-married cohabitors) look like both those who remain single *and* those who marry in terms of education and employment. And although never-married cohabitors have less household income than their married counterparts and more than their single age-mates, their per capita income is higher than for the married group and lower than for those who remain single. On the other hand, what tend not to happen until marriage are "big" commitments—children and home ownership.

Cohabitors, even those who are relatively young, are not a homogeneous group; rather, they are a mix of people who are cohabiting before ever marrying and those who are cohabiting after a first marriage has already failed. On some dimensions, the distinctions between these two groups of cohabitors are greater than any differences between cohabitors and the married or the single. On the other hand, those who marry and experience divorce at young ages and then cohabit—almost one-third of those who are cohabiting in their late 20s and early 30s—are less educated and have less income and higher food stamp recipiency than do those who have never married (whether they cohabit or not) and those who are currently in marriages. On the other hand, previously married cohabitors are most similar to those who are married in terms of their likelihood of having children. Only one-third do not live in households with children, a far lower proportion than among those cohabiting before marriage or those who are currently not in relationships.

The comparisons in Table 2.4 highlight a conclusion that is becoming apparent in the cohabitation literature. What cohabitation is and what it means are far more complicated issues than simply whether cohabitation is like marriage or like being single. It is both and yet neither. A far more productive line of research is developing that delves into the variations among

TABLE 2.4   Characteristics of Adults Ages 25-34 by Combined Marital Status: 1998

	Never Married[a]		Married	Ever Married	
	Cohabiting	Single		Cohabiting	Single
Total (thousands)	1,648	12,022	21,267	731	3,687
Percentage[b]	100.0	100.0	100.0	100.0	100.0
Education					
Less than high school	15.5	11.9	10.9	15.1	17.2
High school graduate	29.9	29.3	32.0	45.9	38.5
Some college	27.4	28.1	28.4	31.4	30.6
College graduate	27.3	30.7	28.7	7.7	13.6
Employment last year					
Full-time, full year	62.2	60.4	61.8	60.0	59.8
Part-time or part year	29.4	27.0	24.8	28.9	26.4
Nonworker	8.4	12.6	13.4	11.1	13.8
Household income	42,100	40,056	49,010	40,912	30,000
Per capita income	16,071	17,794	14,000	12,279	11,931
% who receive food stamps	10.7	10.7	5.2	17.8	17.3
% who own home	39.6	43.4	63.7	41.5	42.7
% without children	61.1	80.4	27.2	33.2	55.2

SOURCE: Current Population Survey, March supplement, 1998.
a. The five marital status categories are mutually exclusive.
b. Except for income (medians).

cohabitors and attempts to elicit the meanings that cohabiting relationships have for those who engage in these living arrangements at various points during their lives.

Different Purposes, Different Cohabitors ●

Part of the reason researchers have been so caught up in the debate about whether cohabitation functions more like marriage or more like being single is that the likely future of family change varies under different scenarios. On the one hand, if cohabitation closely resembles marriage, family life as we know it is not likely to be altered much as a consequence of cohabitation, because cohabitors will either eventually marry or stay in relationships that function like marriages. On the other hand, if cohabitation is merely an enjoyable relationship of convenience that provides intimacy, its growth could signal a retreat from committed relationships like marriage in favor of relationships to which little responsibility is attached and that are easily terminated and temporary in nature.

Researchers have long argued that heterogeneity among cohabitors exists, despite the lack of solid evidence. Questions asked of cohabitors in the 1987-88 NSFH allow one to assess the heterogeneity among cohabitors and to distinguish those for whom the relationship likely entails more commitment from those for whom the relationship is likely one more of convenience (Bianchi and Casper 2000; Casper and Sayer 2000). Almost half of all cohabitors (46 percent) fall into the "precursor to marriage" category (Table 2.5): They say they have definite plans to marry their partners, they are certain about the quality of their relationship and their compatibility with their partner, and they believe in the institution of marriage. Brown and Booth (1996) suggest that plans to marry are an important factor in differentiating cohabiting relationships. On average, cohabitors report poorer-quality relationships than do those who are married, but cohabitors with plans to marry report similar-quality relationships to those of who are married. And cohabitors with plans to marry actually spend more time together than do married people.

The second-largest group of cohabitors consists of those for whom cohabitation is likely to be a coresidential-dating type of relationship (29 percent). Such cohabitors are uncertain about everything: the quality of their relationship, their compatibility with their partner, and the value of marriage. Another substantial minority (15 percent) of couples who are living together say they are cohabiting to evaluate the compatibility of a prospective spouse. "Trial cohabitors" are uncertain about their relationship and their partner but believe in the institution of marriage and believe that they will get married someday, even if not to their current partner.

The remaining 10 percent of cohabitors are living together instead of marrying; they see their relationships as functioning as a substitute for marriage. They claim to be certain about their relationship and about their partner, but uncertain about the institution of marriage. They have no intention of getting married, but they do intend to stay with their current partner.

Not surprisingly, how cohabitors feel about their relationship, their current partner, and the institution of marriage affects the eventual outcomes of their relationship. More than half of those cohabitors who considered

TABLE 2.5 Unmarried Couples by Relationship Type in 1987-1988 and After 5-7 Years (in percentages)

Type of Relationship in 1987-88	All Couples	Outcome of Relationship after 5-7 years		
		Still Live Together[a]	Married[b]	Separated[c]
All unmarried couples	100	21	40	39
Substitute for marriage	10	39	25	35
Precursor to marriage	46	17	52	31
Trial marriage	15	21	28	51
Coresidential dating	29	21	33	46

SOURCE: Casper and Sayer (2000).
a. Couple was still cohabiting at the time of the second survey.
b. Got married at some time between the two surveys (may or may not be currently married).
c. No longer cohabiting.

their relationship to be a precursor to marriage in the mid-1980s were married within 5 to 7 years, compared with only 25 percent of those who saw living together as a substitute for marriage, 28 percent of trial cohabitors, and 33 percent of dating cohabitors. Nearly 4 in 10 cohabitors who regarded living together as a substitute for marriage continued to cohabit, compared with only 17 percent of those who said living together was merely a precursor to marriage and 21 percent of both trial and dating cohabitors. Trial and dating cohabitors—those with the lowest level of commitment—were significantly more likely to split up than were precursor or substitute cohabitors. These relationships remain even after controls for age, race, education, income, employment status, relationship duration, and other factors (Casper and Sayer 2000).

Cohabitors' attitudes and behaviors also differ depending on their purpose for cohabiting. When cohabitation is a precursor to marriage, cohabitors indicate a higher level of commitment. Cohabitors in the dating group are more likely to have egalitarian gender role attitudes than are those in the substitute marriage or precursor to marriage group. Cohabitors in trial marriages have less traditional beliefs regarding home and family than do those in the substitute or precursor to marriage categories. And as one might expect, a relationship that is viewed as a substitute for marriage lasts the longest as a cohabitation.

Of course, how couples view their relationships may change over time as their life circumstances change, their attitudes and beliefs are transformed, and societal norms evolve. And both members of a couple do not necessarily always agree on the quality of the relationship. For example, in about one in five cohabiting relationships, one partner reports plans to marry but the other does not; in one in three cohabiting relationships, only one partner feels the couple spends a lot of time together; and in 40 percent of couples, one partner but not the other reports a high degree of happiness with the relationship (Brown 2000:838).

Just as poor marital quality increases the likelihood of divorce, poor-quality cohabiting relationships face increased odds of dissolution. When both individuals are unhappy in a cohabiting relationship, it tends to dissolve. Interestingly, when the female partner is not happy in a cohabiting relationship but the male partner is, the relationship tends to dissolve. By contrast, when it is the male partner who is unhappy in the relationship and the female partner who is satisfied, the relationship tends to continue, but the couple is less likely to marry than if both partners are happy (Brown 2000).

● Race and the Meaning of Cohabitation

Previous research has shown that black women are only half as likely as white women to marry the first man with whom they live (Raley 1996). Further, white cohabitors are more likely to marry than are black cohabitors: about 40 percent of cohabiting black women, compared with about two-thirds of cohabiting white women, go on to marry within a few years (Manning and Smock 1995). A pregnancy occurring during cohabitation is also a much stronger impetus to marriage for white couples than for black couples (Manning 1993). Economic determinants of marriage differ for black and white cohabiting couples as well. Among black couples, full employment of both partners is associated with an increased chance of marriage, whereas for white couples, women's employment level is not associated with a transition to marriage (Manning and Smock 1995).

These findings led Manning and Smock (1995) to conclude that cohabitation is more often viewed as a transition leading to marriage among whites, whereas among blacks cohabitation functions more as a substitute for marriage. Similarly, variation exists among Hispanic subgroups. Cohabitation appears to function as a substitute for marriage among mainland Puerto Rican women (Manning and Landale 1996), whereas Mexican American women are more pronuptial than whites and when they cohabit, they view the arrangement as a path to marriage (Oropesa 1996).

Given the behavioral differences between whites and blacks, it is somewhat surprising that blacks are more likely than whites to express the feeling that cohabitation is morally wrong and less likely than whites to want or expect to cohabit (Sweet and Bumpass 1990b). Apparently, although blacks favor marriage over cohabitation, black women are more likely to find themselves in situations that are not conducive to marriage. Blacks are more likely than whites to express the view that cohabitation is acceptable if there is no chance of marriage.

Because marriage rates differ so dramatically between blacks and whites, determining prevalence rates of cohabitation is highly sensitive to the way the cohabitation rate is calculated. Figure 2.3 shows three cohabitation estimates: the percentage of all adults who are cohabiting, the percentage of all unmarried persons who are cohabiting, and the percentage of all persons in unions who are unmarried. Compared with white and Hispanic women, black women have a similar likelihood of living with unmarried partners when all adults are the base for the percentage, the lowest likelihood of being in unmarried partnerships when only unmarried persons are the base of the rate, and the highest likelihood of being in unmarried unions when persons in unions (married plus unmarried) form the base of the percentage. Why is there so much variation? So many black women are unmarried, compared with white and Hispanic women, that any rate based on the unmarried population tends to be low for blacks. Conversely, so many unions are unmarried partnerships among blacks that a rate based on those in unions tends to be quite high relative to other groups.

Black men's rates of cohabitation tend to be as high as or higher than those of other groups of men no matter which estimate is used. In addition, the gender gap in the percentage cohabiting is much more pronounced for blacks than for other racial groups: Twice as many black unmarried men (12 percent) as black unmarried women (6 percent) were estimated to be cohabiting in 1998, for example. The lack of employment opportunities for black men is frequently cited as a reason for the retreat from marriage among black women (McLanahan and Casper 1995; Wilson 1996; Wilson and Neckerman 1986), and a similar phenomenon may occur with regard to cohabitation. In addition, sex ratios are often more skewed among the black population than among whites, with a surplus of women to men. Kiecolt and Fossett (1995) show that skewed sex ratios depress the marriage rate of black women (but not that of black men), and this effect may

● **Figure 2.3.** Percentages Cohabiting by Race and Universe Type: 1998

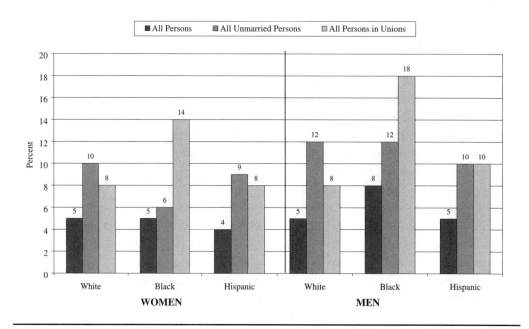

SOURCE: Current Population Survey, March supplement, 1998.
NOTE: Race/ethnicity categories are white, non-Hispanic; black, non-Hispanic; and Hispanic.

extend to unmarried partnering as well. A recent report from the National Research Council highlights the very high incarceration rates among black males, especially in the wake of changes in drug policy in the 1980s and 1990s, and the high rates of homicide among young black males, both of which contribute to the highly skewed sex ratios in lower-income black communities (Smelser, Wilson, and Mitchell 2001).

● Premarital Cohabitation and Risk of Divorce

One might argue that cohabitation provides a couple with the opportunity to assess their compatibility before getting married. In this period, incompatible mates can easily end the relationship without formally divorcing. Thus marriage and family life might actually be strengthened, because unhappy couples are weeded out before they ever marry. Contrary to such a scenario, the accumulated research shows that those who cohabit before marriage are more likely to divorce than are those who do not live together before marrying. The debate is about whether there is actually something about cohabiting that increases the odds of divorce or whether the explanation is that more "divorce-prone" individuals—those who have lower levels of commitment, are less religious, and so on—choose to cohabit before they marry and, because of their characteristics, are more likely to divorce.

In the 1970s, cohabitation and divorce both increased rapidly, leading some to conclude that cohabitation was linked to the rise in divorce, even though the rise in divorce began much earlier (Sweet and Bumpass 1990a). Opponents of cohabitation have argued strenuously that the practice of living together outside of marriage threatens the institution of marriage in modern society (e.g., Popenoe and Whitehead 1999). Although these opponents often offer evidence that cohabitors and their children are less well-off in various ways than are married couples and their children, their principal concern is that the practice of living together may lower commitment and increase the risk of divorce.

On the one hand, couples who cohabit before marriage are more likely to end up in divorce, but because these individuals differ in many other ways from those who marry without first cohabiting, most researchers believe that the relationship is not causal (e.g., DeMaris and Rao 1992). People who cohabit have demographic characteristics that make them more prone to divorce in the first place; for example, they more often have grown up in families where their parents divorced (Lillard, Brien, and Waite 1995). Cohabiting before marriage does not automatically increase the risk of divorce, but it also does not protect couples from entering into marriages that eventually fail. Thus claims about negative and positive effects of cohabitation on marriage are refuted by recent evidence.

The answer to the question of how cohabitation and divorce are related is closely tied to the way the question is asked and the time period analyzed. Although people who cohabit before marriage continue to be more likely to get divorced, this is less apparent in more recent cohorts of couples. Differences between those who cohabit and those who do not also appear to have diminished over time (Schoen 1992).

On the other hand, there is evidence not only that cohabitors begin their relationships with attitudes that are more accepting of divorce but that the cohabitation experience itself appears to increase the acceptance of divorce (Axinn and Thornton 1992). Here again, the effect of cohabitation may depend on the type of cohabiting relationship involved. DeMaris and MacDonald (1993) found that serial cohabitation is more strongly associated with marital instability than is one-time cohabitation. Perhaps people prone to fragile relationships are more likely to cohabit, and when they marry, they increase the divorce rate.

Ironically, it is possible that people who cohabit before marriage are more likely to divorce after a given period of marriage because their relationships have already lasted longer than most marriages by that point. That is, the odds of a marriage breaking up after 3 years may be higher for couples who started out cohabiting because their relationships are already 5 or more years old (Teachman and Polonko 1990).

● Conclusion

Cohabitation has increased dramatically over a relatively short period of time, raising concerns about the effects of this new family form on the institutions of marriage and the family in the United States. Currently, the majority of individuals live with partners before they marry. Hence the lines that differentiate marriage from being single have faded over time. The effects of cohabitation on the institution of marriage are likely to vary according to how cohabitors view their relationships. Some cohabitors have definite plans to marry their partners and end up doing so, whereas others live together in relationships of convenience with low levels of commitment—these couples often separate.

Not only is cohabitation increasing among people who have not entered a first marriage, it is also slowing the rate of remarriage after divorce or separation. Almost one-half of those cohabiting at any given point in time are doing so after rather than before a first marriage. In part due to the role cohabitation is playing after marriages end, the characteristics of cohabitors are changing. Compared with 20 years ago, more of them are older than age 35 and more cohabiting households include children. And, although cohabitation was initially linked to experimentation among college students, its increase has been widespread and its popularity today is as great or greater among those with less education.

As cohabitation continues to increase and to become more normative, will it replace marriage as the preferred living arrangement for raising children in the United States, as it seems to have done in some countries, most notably Sweden? The answer still seems to be no. Although unmarried partners do not necessarily rush to marry if the woman becomes pregnant, and single women who become pregnant may move in with their partners rather than marry them, these behaviors are still not widespread in the

United States, at least not among the majority white population. And only 1 in 10 cohabitors believes that the cohabiting relationship is a substitute for marriage. The largest factor explaining why more births occur in cohabiting relationships today than two decades ago is merely that so many more people cohabit before and after marriage. What this means, however, is that a significant percentage of the babies born to unmarried mothers—perhaps as large a proportion as 40 percent—actually begin life residing with both parents, who live together but are not married.

Demographers are only beginning to study the heterogeneity of cohabiting relationships. New estimates suggest that about 4 percent of cohabiting couples are in same-sex relationships. One-fifth of lesbian-couple and about 5 percent of gay-couple households include children, often from one partner's previous heterosexual union. Heterosexual cohabitation is on the rise among all racial groups, although estimates of the prevalence among different groups vary by whether the percentages are calculated for all adults, unmarried adults, or all unions. Blacks have a high portion of all unions that are unmarried partnerships, but black unmarried women have relatively low rates of living with partners. The gender gap in rates of cohabitation is greatest for blacks because black unmarried men have rates of partnering as great as or greater than other racial groups. Also, more unmarried than married heterosexual couples are mixed-race couples.

Cohabiting couples defy gender stereotypes more often than do married couples: Women's and men's labor force roles are more similar and the woman's age, education, and hours of market work more often exceed the man's in cohabiting than in marital unions. Partly this is because cohabitors are younger than married couples and younger cohorts have more gender-egalitarian attitudes. Yet cohabitation also seems to be chosen as a first relationship more often by women who value career goals than by other women and by couples who either value an equal economic partnership or defy gender stereotypes in other ways (such as having a female partner who is older than the male partner).

Although researchers have been preoccupied with comparisons of cohabitation to marriage (or, in some cases, to singlehood), the reality is that cohabitation is serving a diverse set of couples with an array of reasons for living together rather than marrying. About one-half of cohabitors indicate strong intentions to marry their partners, and 1 in 10 claims that the unmarried partnership is a substitute for marrying. The remainder seem uncertain about their compatibility with their current partners, their future plans, and/or marriage as an institution. Not surprisingly, whether cohabitors marry, break up, or continue living together as unmarried couples varies by how they see their relationships. And partners often disagree on the quality of the relationship, with the partnership more likely to dissolve if the woman is unhappy and more likely to continue as a cohabitation but not proceed to marriage if the man is unhappy.

Finally, although one might think that couples' living together before or instead of marrying should make marriages more stable, because partners can discover irreconcilable differences before they tie the knot, one of the strongest findings is that those who cohabit prior to marriage divorce more often than those who do not. The debate is over whether living together makes such couples more "irreverent" toward the institution of marriage or whether they have characteristics and attitudes that are more accepting of divorce in the first place. The evidence to date suggests it is more the latter than the former, and the question is whether cohabitation will become less selective of certain types of individuals. If living together is increasingly "what one does" before marrying or remarrying, and as marital partnerships change as well, those who cohabit may become less distinct from those who marry. On economic dimensions such as labor force participation and earnings, married and unmarried partners seem less differentiated today than they were 20 years ago. Still, among whites, educational attainment may be diverging between the two groups. How cohabitation alters the future of marriage will ultimately rest on whether unmarried cohabiting couples are increasingly a distinct group of persons who doubt the possibility of long-term commitment or are merely couples captured at different points in their relationships than those who have married, but who nonetheless continue to aspire to the goal of committed family life.

CHAPTER **3**

CHILDBEARING

Martin O'Connell

The variations in American childbearing patterns over the 20th century have been extreme and unpredictable. First, there were fears of overpopulation in the 1920s (East 1923; Ross 1927), followed by dire cries of depopulation during the Great Depression (Charles 1934; Myrdal and Myrdal 1934). The demographic euphoria of a brighter world after World War II gave way to the great American postwar Baby Boom, a period characterized by women having more than three children each (compared with an average of two children each today) by the end of their childbearing years.[1] Fears of overpopulation both in the United States and abroad, especially in the developing nations of Africa, Asia, and Latin America, again prompted more speculations of a Malthusian world by the end of the century and popularized Paul Ehrlich's *The Population Bomb* (1968), perhaps the most widely read book about population growth in history.

These warnings prompted Congress in 1970 to establish the Commission on Population Growth and the American Future in recognition of "a broad range of problems associated with population growth and their implications for America's future" (Commission on Population Growth and the American Future 1972:184). The roller coaster of American fertility then promptly, and unexpectedly, began to plummet by the late 1960s, requiring the government to revise population projections downward (U.S.

Bureau of the Census 1970, 1972) almost as rapidly as fertility was falling. By the mid-1970s, annual fertility fell below two children per woman, or the level needed for the natural replacement of the population.[2] Thus the "Baby Bust" was born in the throes of the Vietnam War, the contraceptive revolution, the women's movement, Woodstock, and just about all the other cataclysmic events that seemed to mark the late 1960s and early 1970s with day-to-day uncertainties. The up-and-down movements of fertility as a response to both historical events and individual choices caught demographers off guard and only reinforced the old adage penned by Norman Himes in 1936: "The whole history of population thought shows that populations adjust to conditions more promptly than do writers on population" (p. 417).

Various theories of fertility behavior attempted to explain these transitions during the 1960s and 1970s. Economists put forth arguments about the value and benefits of children as economic goods and the competition between a woman's time as a homemaker and her time in the labor market (Becker 1960, 1981; Mincer and Polachek 1974; Willis 1973). Counterarguments then followed by sociologists (e.g., Blake 1968) who challenged economic theories of fertility behavior. Norman Ryder (1982, 1990), with the aid of information from new surveys on fertility and contraceptive behavior, suggested that the Baby Boom resulted more from poor contraceptive techniques than from genuine desires to raise large families. He based this claim on what fertility levels would have been had women had the numbers of children they intended.

Another economist, Richard Easterlin (1973, 1980), synthesized common themes prevalent in both economic and sociological literature. He explained the cyclical variations in fertility among alternating generations as a function of whether children were born during high-fertility or low-fertility regimes. In effect, the prosperous large families of the 1950s unwittingly created problems for their offspring when these children came of working age in the 1970s and were forced to compete for jobs among themselves. Easterlin hypothesized that this excess supply of labor would lower wages, thus leading to poorer economic lives and resulting in economic obstacles to starting and raising families.

Butz and Ward (1979a, 1979b) sought to examine the timing component of postwar fertility trends. They hypothesized that couples faced with an economic recession would increase their fertility during periods when the cost of dropping out of the labor force was low (i.e., times of high female unemployment and relatively low wages). That is, their theory predicted that annual fluctuations in fertility should be countercyclical to business cycles. Although their model is principally concerned with the loss of income by the woman during pregnancy and the ensuing months of child rearing, high child-care costs would also have a negative effect on fertility and keep levels well below those recorded during the Baby Boom years. An increasing proportion of women securing college degrees and the opening of opportunities for women in the labor market—which makes women's time more economically valuable—should also have the effect of maintaining low levels of completed fertility.

And while these theoretical arguments were being conducted in the pages of scholarly journals, more alarmed observers revived the fears of the 1930s with a gloomy prognosis for the United States (e.g., Wattenberg 1987). These writers asserted that continued low fertility levels, especially among the more highly educated and wealthy couples who could most afford to raise families, could deprive future America of a more enlightened generation. This apocalyptic "birth dearth" would leave in its wake "tens of millions of unhappy adults who, through no real choice of their own, will end up with no children at all," or worse, "because of the changing ethnic and racial balances that come along with the Birth Dearth (i.e., fertility differences by race), we may face some increased divisiveness and turmoil in America" (Wattenberg 1987:8).

While these arguments were raging back and forth, the annual numbers of births began to rise, slowly but consistently, during the 1980s, finally reaching the seemingly magic level of 4 million again in 1989, exactly 25 years after the end of the Baby Boom (see Figure 3.1). Terms such as Echo Boom sprang up to refer to the large numbers of children being born to Baby Boomers. Magic or mathematics? There were 58 million women in their childbearing years (15 to 44 years old) in 1990 compared with only 36 million women in the same age group in 1960. The number of births in 1990 (4,158,000) was still 100,000 fewer than the number in 1960, despite the fact that there were two-thirds more women by 1990 in the childbearing ages.

The nature of the rise in annual fertility of the 1980s was very different from that of the 1950s. The leading edge of women responsible for the fertility rise of the 1980s were women 30 to 39 years old, an age group traditionally past the peak reproductive years. The press was quick to trumpet a new "Baby Boomlet" as the runaway trend for the remainder of the century (e.g., Vobejda 1991). However, this brief foray into the 4-million-births level ended in 1994, leaving us by 1999 with 3.9 million annual births—a number still lower than that recorded for most of the 1950s, when there were 20 to 25 million fewer women in the childbearing age groups.

● **Figure 3.1.** Total Fertility Rate and Annual Numbers of Births: 1930-1998

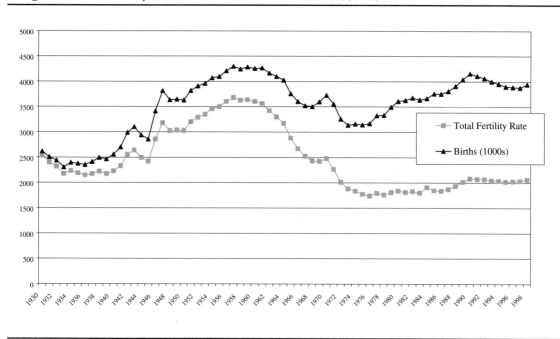

SOURCE: Heuser (1976) and National Center for Health Statistics, *Vital Statistics of the United States* (annual issues).
NOTE: The total fertility rate (the sum of age-specific fertility rates per 1,000) is the average number of births a cohort of women would have over their lifetimes. Rates of 2,000, or approximately 2 births per woman, indicate a cohort is near replacement-level fertility.

Most of the increase in the annual numbers of births since the 1980s has not been the result of a new baby boom of rising birth expectations among younger women. Rather, it resulted from a shift in the pattern of childbearing to older ages coincident with large increases in the numbers of women in these age groups as the Baby Boomers of the 1950s grew older. And are birthrates now so low that there is nothing left to explain, only to observe? This chapter examines some of the changes in the timing or tempo of childbearing that have interested demographers in recent years (Chen and Morgan 1991). We address how rapidly recent birth cohorts of women enter motherhood and their marital situations at the time of their first births.[3] And because much of American fertility, either directly or indirectly, has been the result of the Baby Boom, we also look at how the childbearing patterns of the mothers of the Baby Boom of the 1950s compare with those of their children who are now completing their childbearing years.

In addition, we present new data on the employment patterns of women during and after their first births and the implications of these trends for future childbearing and child-care issues. We also take a look at birth expectations of women and, finally, comment on fertility in men's lives, a topic that has received relatively little research attention.

Entering Motherhood: ●
Childbearing Among Cohorts of Women

The post-World War II Baby Boom caught demographers by surprise—not the beginning of the boom, but its longevity. Most European nations experienced short-term increases in fertility following the end of World War II; in contrast, the United States experienced almost 20 years of uninterrupted high fertility levels, with total fertility rates reaching three births per woman in 1947 and staying at or above this level until 1964.[4]

Several demographers in the 1950s recognized that a better way both to examine and possibly to predict the direction of fertility was to look not at the annual changes in the birthrate but rather at the changes experienced by different birth cohorts of women as they grow older (Grabill, Kiser, and Whelpton 1958; Whelpton 1954). After all, what better way of predicting the proportion of women who will ever have a child by age 30 than to see what proportion had a child by age 29? The idea was both simple and brilliant in its inception and created a new realm of analysis appropriately called *cohort fertility analysis*. It led to the development of surveys that asked women about their expectations for future births, based on the recognition that past experiences form the basis for future behavior (Freedman, Whelpton, and Campbell 1959; Ryder and Westoff 1971; Whelpton, Campbell, and Patterson 1966).

Let us put ourselves in the place of demographers in the mid-1970s, when the total fertility rate had fallen to less than 1.8 births per woman, the lowest level ever recorded in U.S. history (Coale and Zelnik 1963). What did demographers see for the future of American fertility using cohort fertility analysis? Table 3.1 shows two fertility indicators displayed by the year or cohort of a woman's birth. The first indicator measures how rapidly women enter childbearing by charting the proportion ever having a birth at three stages in their lives: by the end of their teenage years (age 20), at the traditional peak ages of first-birth childbearing (age 25), and near the end of their childbearing years (age 40). The second indicator shows the cumulative number of births per 1,000 women at each of these three ages. These indicators show the two critical components of a cohort's childbearing career: the proportion who become mothers and the average number of chil-

TABLE 3.1   Cumulative Fertility Patterns to Ages 20, 25, and 40 by Year of Woman's Birth: 1918-1973

	% With a Birth by Age			Cumulative Births per 1,000 Women by Age		
Year	20	25	40	20	25	40
1918	19.6	52.8	83.9	254	939	2,468
1923	21.5	61.0	88.7	287	1,086	2,776
1928	24.8	66.6	88.9	325	1,306	3,024
1933	29.7	73.0	91.3	425	1,591	3,193
1938	32.6	74.3	**90.8**	476	1,691	**2,930**
1943	30.1	68.5	88.2	446	1,414	2,438
1948	26.2	62.3	86.2	357	1,126	2,091
1953	24.9	**52.6**	82.9	322	**898**	1,948
1958	**22.2**	50.1	83.2	**285**	852	1,957
1963	21.0	47.4	—	271	809	—
1968	20.3	47.2	—	266	835	—
1973	23.0	49.7	—	311	874	—

SOURCE: Heuser (1976) and National Center for Health Statistics, *Vital Statistics of the United States,* vol. 1, *Natality* (annual issues 1977, 1982, 1987, 1992, 1997).

dren born to the cohort, the latter number identifying those cohorts that will not replace themselves naturally by childbearing alone.

Tracking the proportions of women ever having a first birth by age 20 shows how rapidly the Baby Boom mothers entered childbearing compared with previous birth cohorts. Women who were born in 1918 turned age 20 by 1938, during the Great Depression; less than 20 percent of these women gave birth as teenagers. In comparison, women born in 1938 turned 20 in 1958; they were the mothers of the Baby Boom, and one-third had a child by age 20.

Not only did women born in 1938 enter motherhood more rapidly as teenagers, but 74 percent of them had become mothers by age 25, compared with only 53 percent of the 1918 cohort. Following the 1918 and 1938 birth cohorts to age 40, the older cohort neared the end of their childbearing years with 84 percent ever having a child (or 16 percent remaining childless), compared with 91 percent for the 1938 birth cohort. Obviously, there was considerable "catch-up" childbearing between ages 25 and 40 that enabled the older group of women to narrow the 21-percentage-point deficit they had at age 25 to a 7-percentage-point difference by age 40.

Cohort analysis portrays the timing or tempo of childbearing of a birth cohort as the women in that cohort grow older. The only problem is that one must wait 30 years for a cohort to pass through its childbearing years and reveal completed fertility patterns. Hence demographers often use partial information and the behavior of past cohorts to project the completed family sizes of women still in their childbearing years.

Let us imagine now that we are demographers in 1978. Returning to Table 3.1, the only statistics available to us are those shown above the boldfaced numbers: those below the boldfaced numbers will not be available for many years. In 1978, the statistics showed that the Baby Boom children who were born during the 1950s had also delayed their childbearing by ages 20 and 25 to levels similar to those of women born in 1918. In 1978, projections based on incomplete data suggested that large proportions of women growing up in the 1970s would remain childless, with childlessness perhaps even reaching 25-30 percent among cohorts born in the 1950s (Bloom 1982: Bloom and Trussell 1984). Modern birth control practices available at the time and the legalization of abortion in the United States in 1973 made it seem inevitable that successive birth cohorts would experience very high levels of childlessness (Westoff 1978).[5] Rindfuss and Bumpass (1976) suggested that the longer women postponed childbearing, the more likely it was that they would participate in other activities that consume time and energy, be out of step with their age peers who had children earlier, and decide against having children. In other words, childbearing would not be fashionable at older ages, and these 30-something mothers would be alone or at least "different."

How times changed by the end of the 20th century! When we leap to the late 1990s with 20 more years of data to examine, we can see that the Baby Boom children born in the 1950s have almost completed their childbearing years and several important trends are apparent. First, the high anticipated levels of childlessness were never realized. Childbearing was delayed through age 25, but these Baby Boomers will apparently end their reproductive careers with about 17 percent being childless, comparable to the levels of the 1918 cohort and considerably lower than historical high levels of 22 percent recorded by women born in the last quarter of the 19th century (Heuser 1976:Table 6A). Late-19th-century women had a high incidence of fecundity problems, and a high proportion never married (McFalls and McFalls 1984).

● Number of Children and Childlessness

Using cohort analysis as a descriptive tool, Figure 3.2 shows the percentages of women by numbers of births for three cohorts of women. The 1906-10 birth cohort passed their principal childbearing years during the Great Depression—as a result, as many women ended up being childless as had either one or two children (22 percent each). By contrast, the 1926-30 cohort, who were the mothers of the Baby Boom of the 1950s, had childlessness levels only one-half those of the previous generation (11 percent) but significantly higher proportions at parity levels of three children or more.[6]

The final cohort of women born in 1946-50, representing the first of the postwar Baby Boomers, show a marked departure from the two previous cohorts. Reversing the trend of declining proportions of childlessness and one-child families, their completed levels indicated smaller family sizes than those of their mothers. Only a small proportion will have five or more children (5 percent), compared with 20 percent for the 1926-30 cohort.

● **Figure 3.2.** Percentages of Women by Number of Children in Selected Birth Cohorts: 1906-1910 to 1946-1950

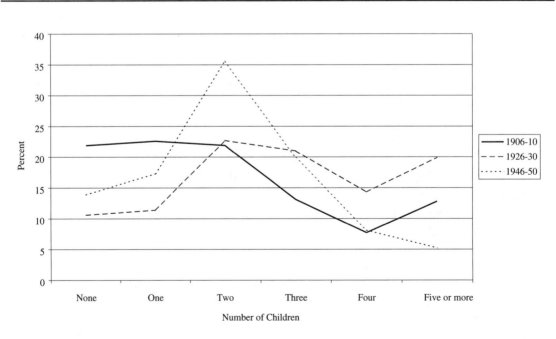

SOURCE: National Center for Health Statistics, *Vital Statistics of the United States,* vol. 1, *Natality* (1992).

● **Figure 3.3.** First-Birth Probabilities for Childless Women: 1932-1997

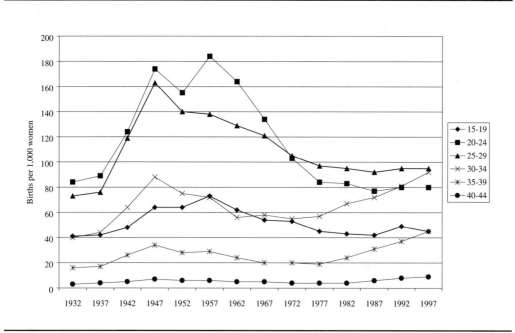

SOURCE: Heuser (1976) and National Center for Health Statistics, *Vital Statistics of the United States* (various issues).

Most noticeable is the large peak around two births (36 percent). In other words, the variation in the number of children born to more recent cohorts has narrowed—a much larger proportion has two children. The average number of children born to the 1946-50 cohort will be about 2.1 children, slightly less than the 1906-10 cohort (2.2 births per woman), however, the reduction has been accomplished not through increases in childlessness but through decreases in the proportions of women having large numbers of children.

High levels of childlessness were averted by the Baby Boom cohorts through a shift in their timing of first birth to older ages. One way of looking at the likelihood that a childless woman will have a birth in a given year is to examine first-birth probabilities. The first-birth probability for a given year is simply the likelihood (usually expressed as a rate per 1,000 women) that a childless woman will have her first birth over the course of that year.

Figure 3.3 shows the trend in first-birth probabilities for women in different age groups. Increases in first-birth probabilities occurred during and after World War II. There was a noticeable spike in the graph in 1947 immediately following the end of the war and another high point in 1957 for the younger age groups of women. A downward spiral then occurred, so by

1977, first-birth probabilities for teenagers and women in their early 20s were about the same level as they were by the end of the Great Depression—this initially suggested that childlessness levels may be headed for all-time highs.

Twenty years later, in 1997, we can better understand the major transformation that has occurred in the timing of the first birth for American women. Although the pace of entry into motherhood among teenagers and women in their 20s has not changed much since the 1970s, sharp increases in first-birth probabilities have occurred for women 30 to 39 years old. Until the early 1970s, first-birth probabilities were higher for childless 20- to 24-year-olds than for childless women in any other age group. In fact, from the early 1930s through the early 1970s, childless women 20 to 24 years old were twice as likely as childless women 30 to 34 years old to have a first birth.

After the early 1970s, first-birth probabilities were highest for women 25 to 29 years old, and by 1997 this distinction was almost equaled by women 30 to 34 years old. Since 1992, rates of first births were higher for women 30 to 34 years old than among women 10 years younger. Even more amazing is that by 1997 first-birth probabilities were just as high for women 35 to 39 years old as for teenagers (each about 45 births per 1,000 childless women). Nowadays, it is common for women to become first-time mothers in their 30s.

How much of contemporary childlessness is the result of voluntary decisions to forgo parenthood? Data collected by the National Survey of Family Growth for ever-married women 15 to 44 years old indicate that only a very small percentage of ever-married women deliberately decided not to have children—about 2 percent in the 1970s, rising to 4 percent by 1990 (Abma and Peterson 1995; Mosher and Bachrach 1982). However, about 8 of 10 never-married women who expect never to have a child say that they chose to be childless. Although almost 90 percent of women will eventually marry, as marriage is delayed more childbearing years are spent in the "never-married" status. Hence the preferences and fertility plans of never-married women become a bigger component in projections of childlessness and completed family size.

● Generational Differences in Childbearing

How can the changes in the timing and levels of childbearing of past generations be summarized? Using a set of cohort-based statistics, we can compare how women today completing their childbearing years have fared relative to a previous generation of women who represent their mothers. Table 3.2 displays retrospective fertility and marital history data from the Survey of Income and Program Participation conducted in 1996 to make these comparisons possible. Two age groups of women have been selected: women who were having their principal childbearing years during the Baby Boom and their offspring who entered their childbearing years during the low-fertility period of the 1970s.

The "mothers" generation in Table 3.2 consists of women 60 to 64 years old in 1996 (women born during the Great Depression); the "children" generation consists of women 40 to 44 years old in 1996 (women born during the Baby Boom). The most noticeable generational difference is in their level of completed fertility: Baby Boom mothers had an average of 3.2 children each (3,161 per 1,000 women), compared with 1.9 children each (1,944 per 1,000 women) for their children's generation. Especially significant is the reduction in the proportion of women having families of 4 or more children between the two generations (36 percent and 11 percent, respectively). This fertility decline has long-term repercussions: If the "children" generation of women had completed their childbearing years with the same average number of children as the "mothers" generation (3.2 children), there would have been 12.9 million more children born who would be entering their childbearing ages throughout the first decade of the 21st century.

Table 3.2 also presents these statistics for white and black, non-Hispanic women. Similar patterns of fertility decline between the generations are evident for both groups in the average numbers of children ever born and in the proportion of women with four or more children. Especially noticeable is a reduction in the fertility differential between the two groups of women for the younger cohort. Black non-Hispanic women completing their childbearing years today will have only an average of 0.3 children more than white non-Hispanic women. Comparable figures for the older cohort of women show a difference of slightly more than 0.7 children per woman.

Although in recent decades considerable research and political concern have focused on teenage childbearing (Furstenberg, Lincoln, and Menken 1981; Nathan and Gais 1999; National Research Council 1987; U.S. House of Representatives 1986; Ventura, Mathews, and Curtin 1999) and the long-term repercussions of early childbearing (Furstenberg, Brooks-Gunn, and Morgan 1987), it is interesting to note that, as a group, Baby Boom mothers were more likely to begin their childbearing as teenagers than more recent cohorts have been. About one-fourth of the Baby Boom mothers had their first births as teenagers, compared with 20 percent of the chil-

TABLE 3.2 Fertility Indicators for Baby Boom Mothers and Their Children by Race: 1996

Characteristics	All Women Mothers	All Women Children	White Mothers	White Children	Black Mothers	Black Children
Number of women (thousands)	5,176	10,587	4,088	7,867	545	1,295
Children ever born						
Per 1,000 women	3,161	1,944	2,990	1,819	3,727	2,109
Childless (%)	10.6	17.9	10.9	19.7	10.6	14.8
1 birth (%)	9.9	17.6	9.3	17.1	14.7	22.1
2 births (%)	19.8	36.0	20.7	37.8	17.6	30.1
3 births (%)	23.4	17.1	25.4	16.8	13.0	17.4
4 or more births (%)	36.3	11.3	33.7	8.6	44.0	15.6
Had a teenage first birth (%)	25.3	20.1	22.9	17.1	40.4	33.8
Marital characteristics (%)						
Never married by age 30	9.1	19.9	6.8	16.7	18.2	37.8
Marital disruption by age 40	22.8	34.7	23.0	36.5	28.8	32.0
Characteristics of first birth[a] (%)						
Premaritally conceived	19.0	26.8	14.3	20.5	50.5	58.0
Premaritally born	10.3	16.5	5.7	10.0	38.2	48.8
Postmaritally born	8.7	10.3	8.6	10.5	12.3	9.2

SOURCE: Survey of Income and Program Participation, 1996, Wave 2.
NOTE: Baby Boom mothers are women 60 to 64 years old in 1996 and Baby Boom children are women 40 to 44 years old in 1996. Race/ethnicity categories shown are white, non-Hispanic, and black, non-Hispanic.
a. Distributions based on women who had a birth.

dren of Baby Boomers. Regardless of race, cohorts of women completing their childbearing today were less likely to become mothers as teenagers than the previous generation of women. Among both generations, however, black women were twice as likely to become teenage mothers as were their white counterparts. Data series for Hispanic and Asian subgroups of the U.S. population do not extend as far back as those available for non-Hispanic whites and blacks. The fertility levels of these groups are also greatly influenced by immigration, as relatively large shares of these groups were born outside the United States. Also, there is great variation among Hispanic and Asian subgroups. In general, Hispanic fertility is higher than that of whites or blacks and occurs at younger ages than among whites (Bachu and O'Connell 2000). Many Asian subgroups, especially Chinese Americans, are characterized by very low fertility and more delayed childbearing even than among non-Hispanic whites (He 2000).

The marital history of these two generations during the course of their childbearing years was also characterized by several radical changes. First, we see a noticeable postponement in first marriage: Twice as many women had never been married by age 30 among the children generation of women (20 percent) than among the mothers of the Baby Boom (9 percent). Despite these delays in marriage, a larger proportion of Baby Boom children (35 percent) had experienced at least one marital disruption (widowhood or divorce) by age 40 than did the mothers of the Baby Boom (23 percent). Again, marital delays and disruptions increased for both race groups between the generations.

These statistics document that more recent cohorts have spent more of their principal childbearing years unmarried (although more often cohabiting). Two predictable results emerge. First, there has been a general decline in the average number of children borne by women accompanied by a relatively smaller proportion of women with large families. This, of course, is a function of a lower degree of sexual activity among unmarried women and an aversion among many to starting a family deliberately while unmarried. Second, although postponements in marriage and disruptions of married life have the general effect of reducing overall fertility, these trends also result in a larger number of potentially sexually active and fecund years when a woman can have a child born out of wedlock.[7]

Among Baby Boom mothers, about one in five had first births that were premaritally conceived, whereas slightly more than one-fourth of Baby Boom children had first births that were premaritally conceived. The children resulting from premarital conceptions can be categorized as either premaritally born (born before first marriage) or postmaritally born (conceived before first marriage but born within 7 months of the first marriage date). In previous times, these latter births were often thought to precipitate forced or "shotgun" marriages—marriages that were quickly entered into to avoid out-of-wedlock births. Aside from larger proportions of births resulting from premarital conceptions in the more recent cohort, we can also see from the data in Table 3.2 that fewer women are marrying before these children are born. Among women with premaritally conceived first births, slightly less than half of Baby Boom mothers had married before their children were born, compared with 38 percent of Baby Boom children. Black women were more likely to have premaritally conceived first births and less likely to marry before their children were born than were white women. In both generations, the majority of first births to black women were the result of premarital conceptions.

In the span of only one generation, remarkable changes have occurred in the course of American fertility. We have seen the modal completed family size shift from four or more births to two births, resulting in the fall of completed fertility below replacement level (of 2.1 births per woman). Delays in marriage and childbearing have occurred, but more women when married are likely to experience marital disruption during their childbearing years. Fewer women become mothers as teenagers, but more women have their first births conceived and born before they marry.

All of these changes have occurred during a period when contraceptive techniques have improved to a level of virtually 100 percent effectiveness. In addition, the legalization of abortion services in the early 1970s increased the likelihood that the United States could become the "perfect contraceptive society." Yet one of the most perplexing trends to have emerged in the past few decades has been the rise in the proportion of children born outside marriage. In the next section, we examine this aspect of fertility and its components since the steady rise in nonmarital childbearing began in the 1960s.

● Nonmarital Childbearing

Contraceptive effectiveness and the availability of abortion services have greatly increased during the past three decades—theoretically, these developments should have formed the basis for declines in nonmarital childbearing in the United States. However, changes in sexual activity among unmarried women and declines in the proportion of women marrying before the birth of a premaritally conceived child may work in opposition to the previous trend of increasing contraceptive effectiveness. Overall, rates of childbearing among unmarried women have increased steadily since the 1970s for all ages of women, only recently leveling off in the mid-1990s (Alan Guttmacher Institute 1999). Recent trends also indicate a simultaneous stabilization in the proportions of teenagers who are currently sexually active (Singh and Darroch 1999) and an increase in the proportion of teenagers using condoms (Warren et al. 1998).

Placing these changes in perspective, Table 3.3 displays data on trends in the marital status of women at the time of their first birth. First births are the focus in this table because their timing sets the tempo for future child-

TABLE 3.3 Marital Status of Women at First Birth: 1960-1964 to 1990-1994

Age and Year		% Premaritally Conceived		% Marrying before the Birth[a]
	Total	Premaritally Born	Postmaritally Born	
15 to 19 years old				
1960-64	45.0	18.3	26.7	59.3
1965-69	56.7	29.2	27.5	48.6
1970-74	65.4	34.8	30.6	46.8
1975-79	69.9	47.9	22.0	31.5
1980-84	75.7	56.5	19.2	25.4
1985-89	83.8	65.7	18.1	21.6
1990-94	89.0	75.2	13.8	15.5
20 to 29 years old				
1960-64	15.8	6.1	9.7	61.2
1965-69	20.9	7.8	13.1	62.6
1970-74	19.1	9.1	10.0	52.2
1975-79	22.3	15.1	7.2	32.4
1980-84	27.5	18.1	9.4	34.0
1985-89	28.1	20.2	7.9	28.1
1990-94	37.6	25.9	11.7	31.1

SOURCE: Bachu (1999:Tables 1, 2).
a. Percentage as a proportion of women who had a first birth conceived premaritally.

bearing and also marks a fundamental change in the lives of women as they transition to the role of parent. Currently, about 75 percent of all first births occur to women under 30 years of age. The age and marital status of the mother at the time of her first birth are important determinants of the social and health circumstances of both mother and child. Data from the 1980 and 1995 June supplements to the Census Bureau's Current Population Survey (CPS) have been used to develop the marital status distributions displayed in the table for women having their first birth between the ages of 15 and 29 for the period 1960-64 to 1990-94. (Because these data are from surveys, they are subject to recall errors and reflect only the experiences of women who were living at the time of the surveys.)

About 9 out of 10 first births among teenagers in 1990-94 were pre-maritally conceived, double the level recorded in 1960-64. The principal

TABLE 3.4 Employment Before and After First Birth Among Women by Year of First Child's Birth: 1961-1965 to 1991-1995

Child's Birth Year	Worked 6+ Months Continuously	% Working During Pregnancy		% Employed After First Birth	
		Total	Worked Until Birth	3 Months After First Birth	12 Months After First Birth
1961-65	60.0	44.4	10.1	9.9	16.8
1966-70	66.4	49.4	12.9	12.7	23.9
1971-75	68.9	53.5	14.5	15.6	27.9
1976-80	73.1	61.4	25.1	22.4	38.8
1981-85	73.4	62.0	32.6	35.9	56.2
1986-90	75.5	67.2	36.8	41.5	60.8
1991-95	73.8	66.7	35.1	40.9	60.9

SOURCE: Data for 1961 through 1980 are from O'Connell (1990:Tables B-2, B-5); data for 1981 through 1995 are from the Survey of Income and Program Participation, 1996, Wave 2.

component of the increase was in the proportion premaritally born: 18 percent of first births to teenagers in 1960-64 occurred premaritally; by 1990-94, the proportion had increased fourfold. A similar pattern was found among women 20 to 29 years old, but at a much lower level of premarital childbearing.

What is the overall effect of these changing statistics on the likelihood that a premaritally pregnant woman—who decides to have the child—will marry before the birth of the child? The last column in Table 3.3 tracks the propensity of couples to marry before the birth of a premaritally conceived child. It shows that during the 1960s, more than one-half of either teenagers or women in their 20s with premaritally conceived births married before their children were born. Research on periods going back to the 1930s also indicates that the majority of women who conceived premaritally married before their children were born (Bachu 1999). A sharp decline in this measure occurred after the mid-1970s, and by 1990-94 only 16 percent of teenagers and 31 percent of 20- to 29-year-olds with premaritally conceived births married before their children were born. During these decades, the availability of very effective birth control measures increased, family planning programs became more widespread, and abortion laws were relaxed.

● **Figure 3.4.** Premaritally Pregnant Women Ages 15 to 29 Who Marry Before the Birth of First Child: 1960-1964 to 1990-1994

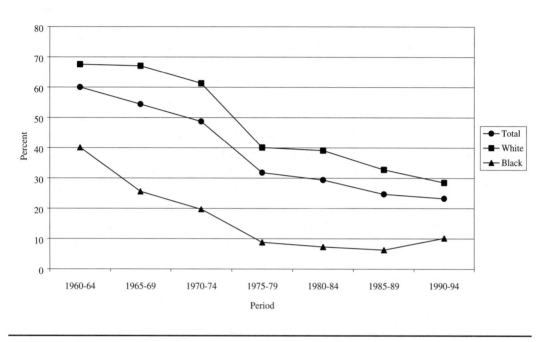

SOURCE: Bachu (1999:Table 1).

But, as previously mentioned, these were also decades characterized by delays in marriage and increases in cohabitation among unmarried couples.

Declines in the propensity to marry among women who have conceived premaritally may reflect decisions by recent generations of women to question the stability and long-term benefits of forced early marriage, especially if the father is young or financially unable to provide a secure home environment. Other research has shown that mothers who are teenagers, who have low levels of education, and are minorities are less likely to marry when faced with premarital conception (Bachu 1999). Figure 3.4 shows the large difference between white women and black women in their likelihood of marrying before the birth of a first child. The delay in marriage among young men and women, particularly blacks—much more so than any change in nonmarital fertility rates—was the major factor increasing the proportion of births outside marriage in the 1980s (Smith, Morgan, and Koropeckyj-Cox 1996).

The likelihood of marrying before the birth of a premaritally conceived child has always been lower for black women than for white women. In the early 1960s, 40 percent of black women married before their first child's birth, compared with 68 percent for white women. Sharp declines have occurred since the 1960s for both races, so that by 1990-94 only 10 percent of black women married before their child's birth, compared with 29 percent of white women. Although the CPS data sets that produced these estimates do not include cohabitation histories, other researchers suggest that cohabitation hastened the transition to marriage among premaritally pregnant white women but not among black women (Manning and Landale 1996). In any event, these statistics suggest that the familial and social pressures that may have induced forced marriages in prior decades have significantly diminished. As discussed in Chapter 2, Raley (2001) shows that a large fraction of births to unmarried mothers occur to cohabiting couples. Over time, these couples have become somewhat less likely to marry before the birth. Additionally, unmarried mothers not living with their partners have become somewhat more likely to move in with those partners rather than marry them when they become pregnant. Some demographers have proposed that the connections between marriage and family formation have disintegrated to the level that the two may indeed move on independent paths for large segments of the population in future generations (Rindfuss and Parnell 1989).

The data clearly show that nonmarital childbearing constitutes the majority of childbearing among many population groups—as of 1998, births to unmarried women still made up one out of every three births (1.3 million) occurring in the United States (Martin et al. 1999). If the number of unmarried women in the population increases due to delays in marriage or marital disruptions, nonmarital childbearing will likely continue to represent a major component of all childbearing in the United States.

● Employment Patterns Before and After Pregnancy

The labor force experiences that women have around the time of their first births can test their ability to juggle both family and working life (O'Connell and Bloom 1987)—this, in turn, can influence their likelihood of returning to work and their desire for subsequent children. The recent shift in childbearing to older ages has produced cohorts of women who, on average, have potentially more years of labor force experience before their first births than did their predecessors. Work history data from various fertility and maternity leave supplements to the Survey of Income and Program Participation show that since the 1960s, the majority of women have had at least 6 months of continuous employment experience before the birth of their first child. Among women who had their first births in 1961-65, 60 percent had 6 or more months of continuous employment; the proportion had risen to 73 percent by 1976-80 and has remained at about this level since then (Table 3.4).

These early attachments to the labor force result in increasing proportions of women who work during their pregnancies and who work longer into their pregnancies. Women's working during pregnancy and their rapid return to work after childbirth may reflect more than economic needs. Research has suggested that the work attachments women develop before pregnancy may produce greater commitment or psychological need for work after childbirth to establish a sense of continuity in their social lives after the birth of their children (McLaughlin 1982; Mott and Shapiro 1983; Presser 1989a).

Paralleling these increases in work experience are increases in the proportion of women who work during pregnancy. Slightly less than one-half (44 percent) of all women who had their first births in 1961-65 worked during their pregnancies; the proportion had increased to about two-thirds by the mid-1980s and has since remained at that level. Even more remarkable has been the increase in the proportion of women who continue to work during a first pregnancy up to within a month of the child's birth. Only 10 percent of pregnant women who had their first births in 1961-65 worked until that late in their pregnancies, compared with 35 percent of women who had first births in 1991-95.

These trends point to a fundamental shift in work and family life by women during first pregnancy. Women in recent years may be working longer into their pregnancies for reasons other than immediate financial needs. Perhaps childbearing today is viewed from a long-term perspective that is planned to dovetail with career plans instead of acting as a competitor. Reduction in time lost during pregnancy, in addition to minimizing lost wages, also increases the likelihood of job retention after childbirth (O'Connell 1990).

Certainly, commitment to the labor force is most evident in the increasing proportions of women returning to the labor force shortly after giving birth. Table 3.4 shows that it was a fairly rare occurrence for women to work soon after childbirth in the early 1960s. Only 10 percent of mothers had returned to work by the third month, increasing to only 17 percent by month 12. These proportions almost doubled by 1971-75 and doubled again by 1981-85. Only small increases have occurred since the 1980s. In any event, childbearing has become a less time-disruptive event in the course of a woman's working life than ever before.

Work experience during pregnancy strongly influences how rapidly women return to work. Among women having their first births in 1991-95, 78 percent had returned to work by the 12th month after the birth if they had worked during pregnancy, compared with only 27 percent among women who had not worked during pregnancy. Figure 3.5 shows that very large differences between these two groups of mothers are found for all time periods since the 1960s. Research has also shown that women who work full-time during pregnancy are more likely to return to work than are women who work part-time during pregnancy (Klerman and Leibowitz 1999; O'Connell 1990).

Looking at the pace of mothers' entry into the workforce within a year of a first birth, two very distinct patterns emerge based on work history during pregnancy. Women who worked during pregnancy, if they go back to work at all within the first 12 months after birth, go back relatively soon. Between 60 percent and 75 percent of the women who return to work within a year after giving birth are back at work within 3 months. Only about one-third of women who did not work during pregnancy enter the labor force as rapidly; their entry is more evenly spaced out over the 12-month period. This pattern probably reflects the more random chances of securing employment among women who did not have jobs being held for them (i.e., they were not employed during pregnancy) compared with women who worked during pregnancy and had jobs to which they could return.

High levels of work activity among pregnant women both before and after childbirth send a strong signal to employers. Obviously, the trade-offs between work and family life are weakening: Long-term departures from the labor force are disappearing as fertility continues to increase among women over 30, who generally represent the more experienced and more highly educated segments of the labor force.

● Birth Expectations

The transitions noted in employment patterns around the first birth undoubtedly reflect attitudes toward childbearing and child rearing as well as the economic needs of the mother, her family, and her employer. How

● **Figure 3.5.** Interval Between First Birth and First Job After First Birth by Employment Status During Pregnancy: 1961-1965 to 1991-1995

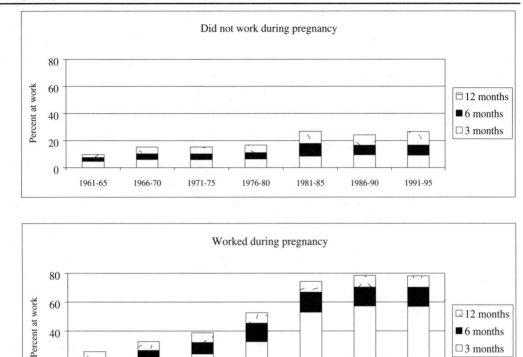

SOURCE: O'Connell (1990:Table B-5) and Survey of Income and Program Participation, 1996, Wave 2.

have women's attitudes toward childbearing and entry into motherhood changed over the past 25 years, since the explosion of labor force participation rates and the shifts in the timing of the first birth?

One way of tracking changing attitudes toward childbearing is to examine the birth expectations of women—asking them how many children, if any, they expect to have. Birth expectations data were first collected in the 1950s (Freedman et al. 1959), when it was anticipated that demographers could use such information to predict the future path of fertility. The success of these indicators to predict the future has been less than spectacular, as expectations data for many years in the 1950s through the 1970s have seemed to lag behind rather than foretell changes in fertility (Westoff 1981).

At first, birth expectations data were collected only for married women, as unmarried women were thought to have little basis for accurately answering this question. It was not until the mid-1970s that single (never-married) women were routinely included in the sample universe in fertility surveys (O'Connell 1977; O'Connell and Moore 1977). However, unpredictable changes in marital status, health and fecundity status, access to birth control, economic lifestyles, and job situations are almost insurmountable factors in attempting to foresee future births.

Although birth expectations are simple in concept, it was often thought that they mirrored current feelings and past experience rather than foretold future behavior. But attitudes and expectations, even for a short duration, are important for understanding how decisions are made about family formation. Recent analysis by Williams, Abma, and Piccinino (1999) shows that childless women who desire to remain childless are less likely to have unpredicted births than women who already have children and who also say that they want no more children. The researchers suggest that these findings are consistent with the idea that the transition from being childless to the first birth is the most important decision a woman makes about her fertility career.

Table 3.5 displays data regarding the birth expectations of childless women 18 to 34 years old between 1978 and 1998 based on a series of supplements to the Census Bureau's Current Population Survey.[8] Several important trends emerge that are consistent with the previously noted shifts to older ages at childbearing. First, since 1978, expectations for a future birth have been relatively stable for childless women 18 to 24 years old. Expectations for a future birth have consistently risen for childless women 25 to 29 years old and for all parities of women 30 to 34 years old.

Which groups of women are responsible for these rising expectations? Figure 3.6 graphs the changing expectation levels for women 30 to 34 years old by level of educational attainment. Clearly, the vanguard for this increase has been women who have graduated from college; between 1978 and 1998, expectations for a future birth have increased from 29 percent to 54 percent for these women. Relative increases of approximately 50 percent for a future birth are also noted among women who were high school graduates or who had some years of college. Virtually no change at all has occurred for women with less than a high school education.

The differences in expectations by educational attainment largely reflect the fact that at any given age, women with fewer years of schooling begin childbearing at earlier ages and hence have larger families than do women with more years of schooling. But even controlling for differences in parity,

TABLE 3.5 Percentages of Women Expecting a Future Birth by Number of Births to Date: 1978-1998 (limited to women reporting on birth expectations)

Age and Year	Total	Childless	One Birth to Date	Two Births to Date
18 to 24 years old				
1978	72.7	81.6	70.1	33.7
1983	74.5	84.1	70.6	30.4
1988	76.0	85.6	72.2	28.9
1992	86.3	86.3	69.6	35.9
1998	82.2	82.2	64.4	32.7
25 to 29 years old				
1978	45.5	65.2	61.5	21.9
1983	49.0	72.7	61.2	22.1
1988	53.2	76.3	64.2	25.3
1992	53.6	78.9	65.3	24.0
1998	54.2	79.1	64.4	23.0
30 to 34 years old				
1978	16.7	35.2	33.5	7.7
1983	20.8	45.2	31.1	9.5
1988	24.7	51.1	37.8	11.4
1992	27.2	53.9	44.7	12.3
1998	30.7	59.8	49.2	14.2

SOURCE: Current Population Survey, June supplements, 1978, 1983, 1988, 1992, 1998.

women with more years of schooling, at each age, are more likely to expect a future birth. For example, the 1998 CPS data suggest that the majority of college-educated childless women in their early 30s expect a child in the future, compared with 31 percent of childless women who failed to graduate high school (data not shown). Martin (2000) shows that over time, delayed fertility is much more likely to result in lifetime childlessness for less educated women, whereas college-educated women are increasingly likely to have one or even two births, usually within marriage. It is difficult to say what may account for these variations by level of education among childless women—all childless women are relatively inexperienced in an-

● **Figure 3.6.** Women 30 to 34 Years Old Expecting a Future Birth by Educational Attainment: 1978-98

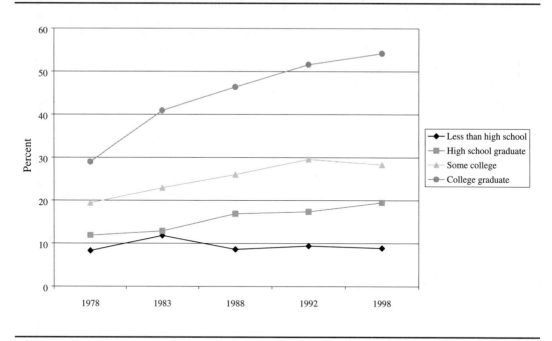

SOURCE: Current Population Survey, June supplements, 1978, 1983, 1992, 1998.

ticipating what it is like to raise a child and how motherhood may affect their daily lives. Perhaps the process of attaining a college degree helps a woman to develop a more planned and deliberate pacing of her life, and having a child at a later age is part of an overall plan.

● Fertility in Men's Lives

Because women experience pregnancy and childbirth, most of the demographic work on fertility has been based on data collected on women of childbearing age. Men's connections to their biological children are usually filtered through their relationships with the biological mothers of their children. Researchers have only recently begun to focus on how becoming a father affects a man's life. The increase in cohabitation and births outside marriage has heightened interest in fathers' involvement in the social role of parent, a topic to be discussed in Chapter 5.

Women's increased access to effective means of contraception and legal abortion has given them more control over reproduction. When a man and a woman agree about reproductive goals, this also gives the man greater control over whether or not he becomes a parent. When they disagree, the woman's reproductive rights may not align well with the man's goals. The bulk of fertility research on men has focused on contraceptive use, because contraceptive failure or nonuse can lead to unintended pregnancies. Especially when such pregnancies occur at young ages or outside marriage, they are often defined as a "social problem." Bachrach and Sonenstein (1998) note that there have been virtually no studies of unintended fertility among men, but anecdotal evidence suggests that when men articulate why they fail to pay child support, they often state that they did not want a child.

With the spread of sexually transmitted diseases such as AIDS, condom use and the incidence of unprotected sex have become public health issues of heightened concern. Researchers have examined men's motivation to contracept and the means they use, and have found that younger men are more likely than older men to use "male" methods of contraception, such as condoms, and that over the course of a relationship, couples are more likely to shift to effective "female" methods of contraception (Ku, Sonenstein, and Pleck 1994).

What is known about male contraception and fertility behavior suggests, not surprisingly, that trends that characterize women also pertain to men. For example, rates of nonmarital sexual activity have increased as marriage has been delayed (Bachrach and Sonenstein 1998). Parenthood occurs at older ages for men who successfully postpone fertility until marriage and increasingly occurs outside marriage for men who father their first children when they are relatively young.

One recent investigation of fathers who have had children before marriage confirms that early, nonmarital fatherhood tends to have many of the same negative economic consequences for men that early, nonmarital motherhood has for women. Men who have children before marriage leave school earlier, have lower earnings, work fewer weeks per year, and are more likely to live in poverty than are comparable young men who do not father children (Nock 1998a). Part of this disadvantage is due to the fact that less educated, less "able" men are the ones who tend to become fathers early, and these men may have completed less education and had low earnings even if they had not become fathers early in life. But Nock shows that selection is not the whole story—young fathers get less schooling and earn less income as a result of changes that accompany the birth of a child, often an unplanned birth.

The increase in nonmarital cohabitation is changing the nature of the relationships unmarried fathers have with their children and their children's mothers. Increasingly, men may live with the children they father even when they do not marry the children's mothers. Examination of the interrelationship among a man's fathering a child, his likelihood of living with the child and the child's mother, and his level of involvement with the child is beginning to receive attention, particularly among low-income populations. *Fragile families* is a term that has been applied to low-income, unmarried couples who may be able to coparent their children but who may need an array of supports if the biological fathers are to remain actively involved in their children's lives (Garfinkel and McLanahan 2000; Mincy 1994).

● Conclusion

Despite the stability in fertility rates at below replacement levels since the mid-1970s, major changes have occurred that have resulted in considerable policy debate in Congress and that have long-term effects on both mothers and children (U.S. Senate 1998). More than one-third of births today are to unmarried women, compared with 15 percent in the mid-1970s. Currently, half of all first births to women under age 30 are premaritally conceived, and most of these children will be born to women who will not marry by the time of their births. A rising portion of these nonmarital births are to cohabiting couples, but unmarried partners are more likely than married partners to separate before completing the task of child rearing.

Women today have more labor force experience before the birth of their children as they shift childbearing to older ages; they work longer into their pregnancies and return to work very quickly. Approximately 60 percent of mothers with infants are working before their children are a year old. This major change in family and work life has created significant needs for the child-care industry and has placed new and challenging demands on families; in the late 1990s, the demands on employers increased as well, as they tried to maintain their workforces in an economic climate that has produced the tightest labor market in decades.

Will the day of the four- or five-child family return? It seems unlikely, given both the current employment and educational trends of women and the ability of women today to control family size under the current level of contraceptive technology. The two-child family appears to be the modal family today and for the new century ahead.

Interestingly, whereas fertility has dropped well below replacement in most European countries, recent cohorts of U.S. women born in the 1960s and 1970s continue previous fertility levels, suggesting they will end their childbearing years with an average of two children per woman (Frejka and Calot 2001). In this regard, the U.S. patterns are quite exceptional among developed countries.

Finally, the increase in childbearing outside marriage and the rise of co-habitation, as well as changing gender roles within families, are leading to an expanded focus on what childbearing and child rearing mean for men's as well as women's lives. To date, much of the fertility research on men has focused on contraceptive use by young men, but a broader focus on child-rearing motivations and intentions and father involvement in children's lives is leading to expanded data collection and analysis of men, especially men in low-income populations.

Notes

1. The postwar Baby Boom encompasses the years 1946 to 1964. The first postwar year, 1946, represented the largest increase in births (553,000) ever recorded in U.S. history between two successive years. The final year of the Baby Boom, 1964, was the last year, of a succession of years that began in 1954, when there were more than 4 million births in the United States.

2. Replacement-level fertility represents the number of children a woman must have to replace herself with another woman surviving to the mean age of childbearing. Because there are generally more boy than girl babies born and not all children live to reach childbearing age, replacement-level fertility has usually been around 2.1 births per woman for the past 50 years.

3. Birth cohorts define a specific time period in which a group of women are born: a cohort may be a group of years (e.g., 1950-54) or a single year (e.g., 1970). It is often useful to analyze fertility by birth cohorts to examine the reproductive experience of women as they pass through the childbearing years, usually ending at age 40 or 44 for statistical purposes (less than 1 percent of all births annually are to women 45 years and over).

4. The total fertility rate for a given year is the hypothetical number of children women would have at the end of their childbearing years based on the prevailing age-specific fertility rates for that year. It is an estimate of the number of children women would have and not necessarily how many they actually have.

5. The number of abortions performed in the United States in 1973 was 745; since 1979, abortions have numbered between 1.3 and 1.6 million annually (Henshaw 1998).

6. *Parity* refers to the number of children born alive to a woman. The parity of a childless women is zero, a woman with one birth is of parity one, and so on.

7. *Fecundity* is generally used to indicate the biological ability to conceive a child and carry the pregnancy to term, whereas *fertility* refers to the statistical measures of childbearing. Frequently, European demographers reverse the use of these terms.

8. These figures and those presented in the subsequent tables are based only on those women answering yes or no to the question "Looking ahead, do you expect to have any [additional] births?" For a discussion of nonresponse rates to these items and the effect of these nonresponses on the validity of birth expectations questions, see O'Connell (1991).

CHAPTER 4

SINGLE-MOTHER FAMILIES

In August 1996, President Clinton signed into law the Personal Responsibility and Work Opportunity Reconciliation Act (PRWORA) amid the
resignations of high-level administrators in the Department of Health
and Human Services and claims that the act would "reform welfare as we
know it."[1] Some argued that this was the beginning of the end of support
for poor mothers and their children, whereas others heralded the act as the
first step toward helping poor women gain control of their lives and making fathers take responsibility for their children.

The debates over public support for poor women and children were not
new, but the changes embodied in PRWORA—time limits on welfare eligi-
bility, mandatory job training requirements, and so on—seemed far-reaching (Cherlin 2000). PRWORA formalized in federal legislation what had already begun to occur in selected states, such as Wisconsin (Greenberg
1999). Preliminary findings suggest that the act has had far less influence,
positive or negative, on poor women's lives than it was at first expected to
(Blank forthcoming). This may be due in part to the robust economy into
which the changes were introduced.

Why has welfare receipt become such a contentious issue? In part, it is
because of the dramatic growth in the second half of the 20th century in the
numbers of single mothers and the fact that the source of this growth has
changed in ways that many find troubling. As we document in this chapter,
when legislation to protect poor women and children was enacted with the
Social Security Act of 1935, most single mothers, poor as well as nonpoor,

were widows. That changed dramatically in the 1960s and 1970s, as the divorce rate soared in the United States. Since 1980, the delay in marriage and resulting increase in the proportion of births that occur to unmarried mothers has been an increasingly significant component of the growth in single-parent families. We document this shift below.

In recent decades, the rapid movement of married women into the paid labor force has altered our notions about the optimal combination of mothering and paid work. As more married women began to work outside the home, supporting poor women to remain out of the workforce to rear their children seemed increasingly out of step with what mothers more generally were doing. In this chapter, we often compare single to married mothers because this comparison is being made, implicitly if not explicitly, in public policy debates.

Why have mother-child families increased in number and as a proportion of American families? There are a number of explanations, and we return to some of these in Chapter 9, in our discussion of family economics. Some common explanations tend to include the argument that women's increased independence—owing to their own wages or to welfare—and men's poor and declining labor force prospects erode the incentive to marry or to stay married and lead to fathers' lack of involvement with their children. Other observers see a cultural shift toward more individualism as implicated in the general movement away from marriage.

One of the most striking facts about single parenting in the United States is that, although the trend toward single parenting characterizes women of all racial and ethnic groups, it is much more pronounced among some groups. So, for example, as we will show, births outside marriage are much higher than average among black and Puerto Rican women and much lower than average among Asian American and Cuban American women. Racial and ethnic differences in single parenting are sometimes of long duration—for example, U.S. Census data from the beginning of the 20th century show that single-mother families were far more prevalent among blacks than among whites as far back as 1910 (McDaniel and Morgan 1996).

In this chapter, we provide some perspective on single mothering. We address the incidence of single-mother families, the growth in numbers of single-mother families and the components and possible causes of that growth, and the characteristics of single mothers. We rely primarily on data from the Current Population Survey (CPS) but augment our discussion of single mothers by examining "lifetime" probabilities of a woman raising children on her own.

Who Is a Single Mother? ●

The question of who is a single mother and for how long turns out to be more difficult to answer than it would first appear. The U.S. Census Bureau has long charted family composition, both in the decennial censuses of the population and in the annual March supplements to the CPS. Yet there are at least three possible estimates of single mothers from these sources. The number that is easiest to track over time is the number of families in which an unmarried woman is the householder, the person who "heads" or "maintains" the household. In 1998, there were 7.7 million such "mother-child" families.

But there are also single mothers who do not have their own households; rather, they live in the homes of others. For example, a divorced mother and her child may move into the home of the woman's parents. When we include the sizable fraction of unmarried mothers who do not maintain their own homes, estimates of the number of single mothers increase by about 25 percent. In 1998, for example, the estimate of single mothers including those living in other persons' households was 9.6 million.

However, even this estimate may not be accurate, especially if we think that unmarried mothers who are cohabiting with their partners should be excluded from the count of single mothers. When we remove the estimated 12.7 percent of unmarried mothers who were living with partners in 1998, the estimate of single mothers decreases to about 8.6 million. Hence, depending on which of the above three methods of estimating is preferred, there were somewhere between 7.5 and 9.5 million mothers raising children without fathers present in their households in 1998.

In addition, there are other limitations of the trend estimates that decennial census and March CPS data provide. First, censuses and surveys give only cross-sectional snapshots. They can tell us how many women live with children without the children's fathers present at a point in time, but they must be supplemented with other data to provide a perspective on how many women (or children) will spend some years in a mother-only family over their lifetimes. Marital and fertility histories, collected periodically in the June CPS, the Survey of Income and Program Participation, the Panel Study of Income Dynamics, the National Survey of Families and Households, and the National Survey of Family Growth, have been used to calculate such lifetime estimates, and we review these estimates later in this chapter.

Second, the ways in which women enter and exit single parenting have changed in ways that cloud estimates of the number of women who are raising children without the day-to-day assistance of the children's fathers. Changes in marriage, cohabitation, and nonmarital childbearing, changes documented in Chapters 1, 2, and 3 of this volume, have tended to blur the distinction between two- and one-parent families. More children today are born to mothers who are not currently married, but some of these children are born to cohabiting parents and begin life in households that include both parents. Cohabitation has also become almost normative as a mode of entry into remarriage, and this makes it difficult to ascertain exactly when many mothers and their children end particular periods of single-parent living. Cohabitation may effectively bring a "stepfather" into the picture before there is a formal remarriage.

And finally, survey data that are household based do not readily capture surrogate parenting that occurs within households or parenting that occurs across households. Single mothers may live with their parents, with other relatives, or with friends who take an active role in parenting the children. Living arrangements of mothers and their children also cannot tell us how involved nonresident fathers are in rearing their children. Some mothers with physical custody of their children may share legal custody with the children's fathers and such families may have high levels of father involvement, whereas other single mothers may receive no assistance, even financial assistance, from their children's fathers. In sum, there may be degrees of single parenting, depending on how involved other household members and nonresident parents are in children's lives, that are not easily measured by standard, household-based surveys on the family.

● Trends in Single Motherhood

Over time, it is easiest to calculate the numbers of single mothers who have maintained their own independent residences. Sweet and Bumpass (1987: 362, 372) provide evidence that the number of one-parent family households changed little between 1940 and 1950: The number of mother-child family households increased by 6 percent, but this was more than counterbalanced by a decline in the number of father-child family households. Figure 4.1 shows that in 1950, a little more than 6 percent of family households with children under age 18 were mother-child families; this increased to 22 percent in 1998 as the percentage of families with two parents present in

● **Figure 4.1.** Family Households With Children Under Age 18 by Presence of Parents, 1950 and 1998

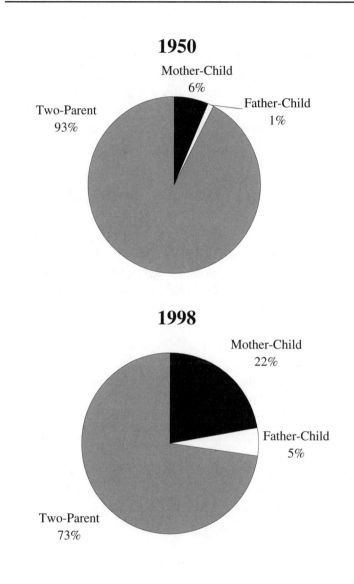

SOURCE: Casper and Bryson (1998b:Table FM-1).

the household declined. (Note that these estimates do not include single mothers living in other persons' households, but do include single mothers who are cohabiting.)

Recall from Table 1.1 (in Chapter 1) that the numbers of two-parent and single-parent family households and the average annual rate of growth increased in each of the past four decades, the 1960s through the 1990s. Between 1960 and 1980, the number of single-mother families increased dramatically, from 2.0 to 5.4 million, and more than doubled, from 8 percent to 18 percent of all family households with children. During the 1970s, the rate of increase was 8 percent per year. After 1980, the number of single-mother family households continued to increase, reaching 7.7 million by 1998, but the annual average rate of increase slowed to about 2 percent per year, and the growth rate actually neared zero after 1993.

Perhaps one of the most dramatic changes among single mothers in the past two decades has been the shift in marital status, with an increasing number who have never married. Sizable fractions of children experienced single-parent living around the turn of the 19th century because of high levels of parental mortality (Uhlenberg 1980). Over the first half of the 20th century, Hernandez (1993:69) estimates that roughly one-third of most cohorts of children experienced single-parent living because at least one of a child's parents would die before the child reached adulthood. When the Aid to Dependent Children (later called Aid to Families with Dependent Children) program was first enacted in the 1930s, most single mothers were widows. As mortality declined, reducing the number of widowed single parents, there was a counterbalancing increase in divorce as a source of single-parent living. Still, at the time of the 1960 Census almost one-third of single mothers were widows (Bianchi 1995a:Table 2).

As divorce rates rose precipitously in the 1960s and 1970s, the more common path to single parenting became for a woman to marry, have one or more children, experience divorce or separation, and then raise dependent children on her own. As mortality continued to decline, the proportion of single mothers who were widows continued to drop, so that by 1978 only about 11 percent of all unmarried mothers were widowed (see Table 4.1). In 1978, the vast majority of single mothers were either divorced or separated.[2]

During the past two decades, as marriages are delayed and cohabitation has increased, a different path to single motherhood has become more common, and that is for a woman who has never married to have a child and raise that child on her own. In 1978, about one in five single mothers had never married. By 1998, 42 percent of single mothers had not married, an increase of almost 20 percentage points. Already by 1978, the most common marital status for black single mothers was "never married," and the percentage of single mothers who had not married increased from 43 per-

TABLE 4.1 Marital Status of Unmarried Mothers Living Wi[th]... by Race: 1978, 1988, and 1998

	1978		1998	
All races (number in thousands)	6,194	8		
Total (%)	100.0			
Never married	22.4			
Separated/spouse absent	27.6			
Divorced	39.0			
Widowed	11.0			
Whites (number in thousands)	3,479	4,186	4,951	
Total (%)	100.0	100.0	100.0	
Never married	9.7	17.3	28.3	18.6
Separated/spouse absent	25.1	20.9	17.6	−7.5
Divorced	52.2	54.7	48.9	−3.3
Widowed	13.1	7.2	5.2	−7.9
Blacks (number in thousands)	2,114	2,766	3,124	
Total (%)	100.0	100.0	100.0	
Never married	42.6	57.2	63.9	21.3
Separated/spouse absent	29.7	20.5	15.5	−14.2
Divorced	19.8	16.9	17.9	−1.9
Widowed	8.0	5.4	2.7	−5.3
Hispanics (number in thousands)	512.0	978.0	1,499.0	
Total (%)	100.0	100.0	100.0	
Never married	26.7	35.9	44.2	17.5
Separated/spouse absent	36.3	28.9	25.7	−10.6
Divorced	28.2	29.3	24.7	−3.5
Widowed	8.9	5.9	5.4	−3.5

SOURCE: Current Population Survey, March supplements, 1978, 1988, 1998.
NOTE: Table includes all single mothers in family groups. Race/ethnicity categories are white, non-Hispanic; black, non-Hispanic; and Hispanic.

cent to 64 percent between 1978 and 1998. The marital status of white and Hispanic single mothers was also shifting toward never-married mothers during this period, but the proportion of single mothers who had never married was higher among Hispanics than among whites.

The percentages of births to unmarried mothers vary greatly by race and ethnicity. Figure 4.2 shows the percentage of nonmarital births for non-Hispanic whites, non-Hispanic blacks, American Indians, and various sub-groups of the Asian American and Hispanic populations. Whereas about 22 percent of white births are to unmarried mothers, 69 percent of black and 42 percent of Hispanic births are outside marriage. Among the American Indian population, the proportion is 59 percent. Rates are relatively low for Asian Americans (16 percent), with very low rates for Chinese Americans (6 percent). By contrast, rates are extremely high for certain Hispanic sub-groups: 60 percent of Puerto Rican births are to unmarried women. A much lower one-fourth of births are outside marriage among the Cuban American population.

Data on the proportion of births occurring outside marriage do not allow us to know how many of these births are to women who are cohabiting with the fathers of their children. In some sense, then, these estimates might be viewed as the uppermost boundary on the number of children who begin life in mother-child families. We turn now to a discussion of the role of cohabitation in defining the "beginnings" and "endings" of spells of single parenting for unmarried mothers.

● Cohabitation and Single Parenting

As we have noted above, one of the elements complicating our ability to estimate the number of single mothers is the increase in cohabitation. Although the Census Bureau now ascertains whether or not mothers are co-habiting, this change is fairly recent, and trend data on families include co-habiting mothers with other unmarried mothers. Bumpass and Raley (1995) argue that although childbirth to unmarried mothers is a major com-ponent of entry into a first "spell" of single motherhood, CPS data tend to overstate the growth in the numbers of single parents because some of those children are actually living with two biological parents who are co-habiting.

Table 4.2 shows the living arrangements of single mothers and how they have changed during the past two decades. Using indirect methods for the years when cohabitation was not ascertained in the CPS (see Casper and Cohen 2000), we estimate the percentages of women classified as single mothers in 1978, 1988, and 1998 who were actually living with partners.

● **Figure 4.2.** Percentage of Births to Unmarried Women: 1998

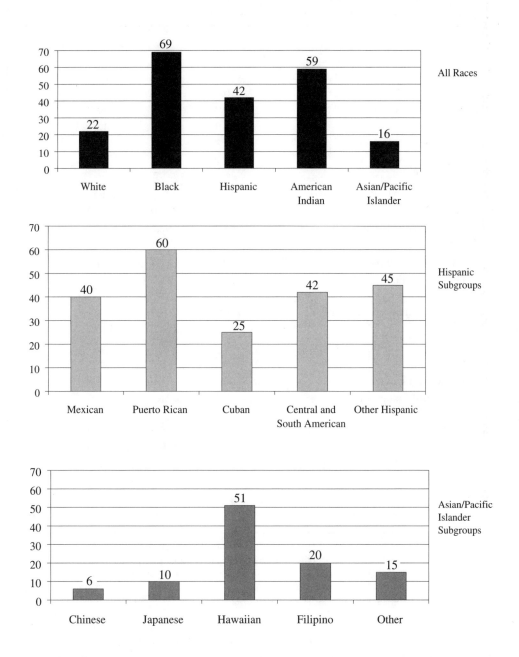

SOURCE: National Center for Health Statistics (2000a:Tables 13, 14).

TABLE 4.2 Living Arrangements of Unmarried Mothers Living With Children Under Age 18 by Race: 1978, 1988, and 1998

	1978	1988	1998	% Point Change
All races (number in thousands)	6,194	8,160	9,845	
Total (%)	100.0	100.0	100.0	
No other adults in household	59.8	56.4	54.0	−5.8
Cohabiting	4.7	9.6	12.7	8.0
Living with parent(s)	14.3	15.2	16.7	2.4
Living with other adults	21.2	18.8	16.6	−4.6
Whites (number in thousands)	3,479	4,186	4,951	
Total (%)	100.0	100.0	100.0	
No other adults in household	63.8	60.2	54.7	−9.1
Cohabiting	5.7	12.6	16.4	10.7
Living with parent(s)	10.5	11.4	14.5	4.0
Living with other adults	20.1	15.8	14.3	−5.8
Blacks (number in thousands)	2,114	2,766	3,124	
Total (%)	100.0	100.0	100.0	
No other adults in household	53.2	51.9	56.9	3.7
Cohabiting	3.3	5.7	8.1	4.8
Living with parent(s)	20.7	21.1	17.5	−3.2
Living with other adults	22.7	21.4	17.6	−5.1
Hispanics (number in thousands)	512	978	1,499	
Total (%)	100.0	100.0	100.0	
No other adults in household	59.4	53.7	46.3	−13.1
Cohabiting	3.9	8.4	9.8	5.9
Living with parent(s)	14.1	15.2	21.7	7.6
Living with other adults	22.6	22.7	22.2	−0.4

SOURCE: Current Population Survey, March supplements, 1978, 1988, 1998.
NOTE: Table includes all single mothers in family groups. Cohabiting single mothers estimated with adjusted POSSLQ measure (see Cohen and Casper 2000). Race/ethnicity categories are white, non-Hispanic; black, non-Hispanic; and Hispanic.

The proportion of unmarried mothers who were cohabiting grew from 5 percent to 13 percent between 1978 and 1998. Growth in cohabitation has characterized all racial and ethnic groups, but the trend has been greatest among whites. Cohabiting couples account for as much as 16 percent of the white mothers classified as unmarried mothers in the Current Population Survey in 1998, compared with 8 percent of black mothers and 10 percent of Hispanic mothers.

Using marital and fertility history data collected in the National Survey of Families and Households (NSFH) in 1987 to estimate how long mothers and children reside in single-parent families, Bumpass and Raley (1995) show a strong effect of cohabitation in reducing time in single-parent households, especially for blacks. That is, they estimate that when the number of years single mothers are living with partners are taken into account, a white woman who became a single mother in the early 1980s would spend only 2.5 years in her first spell as a single parent, compared with 4.5 years if her time cohabiting is counted as time being a single mother. For blacks the difference is even greater, from about 6 to 11 years. Although a partner may be living with the single mother and her children, it is important to keep in mind that the extent of that person's involvement with the mother's children is unknown. Some men may be very involved, acting as surrogate fathers, whereas others may have little involvement and still others may be abusive.

Table 4.2 also shows that about half of single mothers do not have other adults in the household they can rely on to help them with their children. The proportions are a little higher for blacks and a little lower for Hispanics than for whites. In contrast, a third of single mothers are living with their parents or other adults who are not their cohabiting partners. The percentages are highest for Hispanics, intermediate for blacks, and lowest for whites. We discuss the multigenerational living arrangements of single mothers— single mothers living with their parents—in more detail in Chapter 6.

Cohort Change in Lifetime ● Experience of Single Mothering

How many women will ever be single mothers, and how long will they spend as single mothers? Demographic and microsimulation techniques can be used with marital history data to generate estimates. Moffitt and Rendall (1995) have estimated how the likelihood of becoming a single mother has changed across birth cohorts. They have also estimated how the number of years as a single parent has changed and how the age pattern of single parenting may have changed. Their estimates are based on living arrangements observed in the Panel Study of Income Dynamics

TABLE 4.3 Lifetime Experience of Single Motherhood Across Birth Cohorts

	% Who Experience Single Motherhood		Duration (Years) of Single Mothering	
	One or More Spells	Two or More Spells	Per Spell	All Spells
1935	35	14	6.4	8.8
1940	39	16	6.2	8.8
1945	42	17	5.8	8.3
1950	45	19	5.6	8.2
1955	47	23	5.6	8.7
1960	49	25	5.5	8.8
1965	53	29	5.4	8.9
1970	53	30	5.4	9.1

SOURCE: Moffitt and Rendall (1995:Tables 3, 4).
NOTE: Spell lengths are for those experiencing a spell of single parenting.

(PSID) and the marital history data collected in the 1985 PSID. They remove years in a cohabiting union from the count of years as a single parent. Their calculations appear in Table 4.3.

The percentage of women who are projected to experience some years as single mothers has risen dramatically. For women born around 1935, about 35 percent became single mothers at some point before all their children were raised to age 18. The proportion is projected to increase to 53 percent among women born around 1970—women who were in the midst of their child-rearing years at the end of the 1990s.

Moffitt and Rendall (1995) have estimated a parallel increase in the proportion of women who will have more than one spell of single parenting. For example, a mother who experiences a divorce, raises children alone for a time, then enters a cohabiting union but that union dissolves before her children reach age 18 would experience two spells of single parenting: one after her divorce and one after the end of her cohabiting union. Among the 1935 birth cohort, 14 percent of women experienced two or more episodes of single parenting, but the proportion may increase to as much as 30 percent of women born around 1970.

The right side of Table 4.3 reports the average number of years that a woman who becomes a single mother is likely to raise children on her own. Interestingly, according to these estimates for birth cohorts, the average duration of an episode of single parenting has not changed much over time. Each episode is estimated to last 5 or 6 years, on average, and over a lifetime, a single mother spends a somewhat higher 8 or 9 years in total raising children without a partner present, due to multiple spells of single parenting for some mothers. The stability in these estimates suggests that women who become single mothers today do not spend any more of their lives as single mothers than did their grandmothers or mothers who became single parents. Rather, the big change is in the heightened likelihood that any given woman will have an episode of single parenting. But once they are single mothers, women in more recent cohorts are likely to have more spells (30 percent versus 14 percent) of single motherhood, suggesting more instability over their child-rearing years.

The age pattern of single parenting has also changed over time. As the source of single motherhood has shifted from widowhood (a transition that occurs later in life) to nonmarital childbearing (a transition that occurs relatively early in life for most women), women enter single motherhood at younger ages than in the past. The peak in single motherhood occurs around age 30 for recent cohorts, whereas for the 1935 birth cohort the peak would have come for women in their late 30s and 40s. This shift in the age of entry to single motherhood implies that younger children may now be involved in single-mother households than in the past.

The changing age profile and stability in the duration of single motherhood suggest that increased exits from single motherhood (via cohabitation, marriage, and remarriage or the aging of children out of childhood) have kept pace with increased entries. Younger women are more likely to remarry or cohabit than are older women, hence the shift toward younger single mothers curtails the length of single motherhood in more recent cohorts but also increases the number of transitions into and out of single parenthood. Women are also having fewer children, and smaller families mean there are fewer years in total that women spend mothering. For more recent cohorts, there are fewer years during which families have children under the age of 18 than for earlier cohorts of women with larger families. This cuts the length of time that women spend as single parents and counterbalances the opposing trend of single parenting occurring earlier in women's lives, but it exposes individual children to the possibility of more years in single-parent families.

Finally, Moffitt and Rendall (1995) illustrate the large racial differences in single parenting between black and white women. The trends are the same for both groups: increasing percentages experiencing single parenting, increasing proportions experiencing more than one episode of single mothering, and relative stability in the number of years spent as a single mother. However, among blacks, the likelihood of becoming a single parent increased from 65 percent of all women in the 1935 birth cohort to 80 percent for the 1970 birth cohort. The comparable estimates for whites were from 31 percent to 45 percent. And whereas a white woman who entered a period of single parenting could expect to spend 4 or 5 years as a single mother, a black woman's spell of single parenting was more likely to be 9 or 10 years, according to these estimates.

One caution about Moffitt and Rendall's estimates (based on the PSID data) and Bumpass and Raley's estimates discussed earlier (based on the NSFH data) is that both rely on data collected in the mid- to late 1980s. Incomplete cohort data can lead to erroneous projections, as Martin O'Connell notes in his discussion in Chapter 3 of the high and incorrect projections of lifetime childlessness that demographers made in the 1970s for Baby Boom women. If growth in single parenting is slowing, as suggested by CPS data, the high estimates of single parenting for younger cohorts may be leveling out and could possibly decline a bit, given the decrease in divorce since 1980 (Goldstein 1999; Heaton 1998). Rates of single parenting for the 1965 and 1970 birth cohorts in the Moffitt and Rendall (1995) calculations, for example, were level at 53 percent. Bumpass and Raley (1995) estimate declines in duration of single parenting between the 1970s and 1980s for white women when they include cohabitation. As women currently in their childbearing years age, we will be able to track changes for cohorts born after 1970 with more certainty and will be better able to assess changes that occurred in the 1990s.

● Changing Socioeconomic Characteristics of Single Mothers

An important question about single mothers concerns their ability to support themselves and their children financially. Increasingly, the U.S. economy seems to require that individuals attain higher skills and more education to secure employment that pays wages adequate to support a family. Table 4.4 shows that the educational attainment of single mothers has increased over time. (The universe of single mothers that we use for this table includes single mothers living in other persons' households but does not exclude those who are cohabiting.)

TABLE 4.4 Education, Employment, and Occupational Attainment of Single Mothers: 1978, 1988, and 1998 (numbers in thousands)

	1978	1988	1998
All races			
Education			
% high school dropouts	39.0	29.5	21.6
% college graduates	6.1	8.4	10.6
Employment			
% employed previous week	55.8	57.5	68.8
% employed full-time previous year	32.3	37.0	44.1
% in managerial, professional, or technical occupations	17.7	21.6	25.2
Whites			
Education			
% high school dropouts	29.4	19.3	13.3
% college graduates	8.3	11.1	13.9
Employment			
% employed previous week	64.3	67.3	73.8
% employed full-time previous year	37.8	44.1	47.0
% in managerial, professional, or technical occupations	20.6	26.4	32.0
Blacks			
Education			
% high school dropouts	48.0	35.3	21.7
% college graduates	3.2	5.8	7.3
Employment			
% employed previous week	46.5	47.8	65.7
% employed full-time previous year	26.7	29.5	43.8
% in managerial, professional, or technical occupations	13.3	14.1	18.4
Hispanics			
Education			
% high school dropouts	65.7	55.4	47.8
% college graduates	2.0	3.0	5.7
Employment			
% employed previous week	36.7	45.3	60.0
% employed full-time previous year	17.3	27.5	36.6
% in managerial, professional, or technical occupations	12.0	12.4	14.4

SOURCE: Current Population Survey, March supplements, 1978, 1988, 1998.
NOTE: Table includes all single mothers in family groups. Race/ethnicity categories are white, non-Hispanic; black, non-Hispanic; and Hispanic.

TABLE 4.5 Education, Employment, and Occupational Attainment of Mothers by Marital Status: 1998

	Never Married	Divorced	Separated	Widowed	Married
Education					
% high school dropouts	27.6	12.6	24.5	21.9	11.4
% college graduates	6.4	15.9	9.3	14.2	27.2
Employment					
% employed previous week	61.4	78.0	69.6	64.2	67.9
% employed full-time last year	34.8	56.9	42.5	39.7	40.0
% in managerial, professional, or technical occupations	17.7	33.5	21.7	38.3	39.6

SOURCE: Current Population Survey, March supplement, 1998.
NOTE: Table includes all single mothers in family groups.

In 1978, close to 40 percent of single mothers had not completed high school, but the proportion dropped precipitously thereafter, so that by 1998 about 22 percent were high school dropouts. At the same time, the proportions who were college graduates increased modestly, from 6 percent to 11 percent. Along with this increase in skills, there was a concomitant increase in employment rates; in full-time, year-round participation in employment; and in the percentage of employed single mothers who were in managerial, professional, or technical occupations. Racial differences in educational attainment and labor force participation remained in 1998, but these trends—upgrading of educational and occupational attainment and increased attachment to market work—characterized white, black, and Hispanic single mothers.

The upgrading in educational and occupational attainment of mothers is all the more noteworthy when we consider that the group of single mothers whose numbers have increased most, never-married mothers, tend to be disadvantaged relative to divorced mothers in terms of educational attainment and employment. For example, more than one-fourth of never-married mothers in 1998 had not graduated from high school, compared with 13 percent of divorced mothers and about 11 percent of married mothers (see Table 4.5). Conversely, whereas more than one-quarter of married mothers had college degrees, the proportion with college degrees was just 16 percent among divorced mothers and only 6 percent among never-married mothers.

● **Figure 4.3.** Percentage of Family Households With Children Under Age 18 in Poverty: 1978-1998

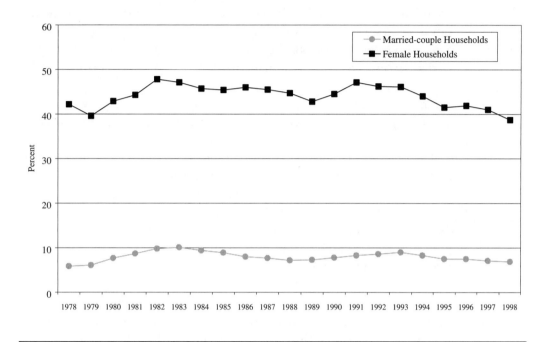

SOURCE: U.S. Census Bureau unpublished tabulations, Historical Income Tables, Table 4 (on-line at http://www.census.gov/income/histpov/hstpov04.txt).

Divorced mothers were similarly much better positioned to support children financially, with employment rates approaching 80 percent compared with much lower rates of around 60 percent among never-married mothers. And whereas 57 percent of divorced mothers worked full-time and year-round, only 35 percent of never-married mothers had this level of labor force attachment. Divorced mothers were also almost twice as likely as never-married mothers to hold jobs in the better-paying sector of the economy (professional, managerial, or technical occupations). Never-married mothers tend to be young (34 percent were under age 25 in 1998) and to be among those for whom it is exceedingly difficult to obtain and hold jobs that pay well enough to support a family.

The robust economy at the end of the 1990s, along with the reform in the welfare system, reduced the proportion of single mothers in poverty as well as the proportion reporting any public assistance income. Figure 4.3 shows the percentages in poverty in single-mother and married-couple households for the 1978-98 period; poverty figures are for the years shown.

Because the calculation of poverty estimates is based on the number of related persons who share a residence, mothers who reside with others are included in the calculation of poverty, but rates are shown for the restricted universe of single mothers who are householders.

Poverty rates stood at 38.7 percent in 1998, the lowest rate of the 20-year period. In only one other year in the 1978-88 period was the poverty rate of single-mother households below 40 percent (39.6 percent in 1979). Still, the rate for single-mother families was extraordinarily high when compared with that of two-parent families, whose poverty rate in 1998 stood at 6.9 percent.

The U.S. Census Bureau's published series of data on mean and median annual income for family households with female householders and children under age 18 suggests that income was higher at the end of the 1990s than in most of the preceding 20 years. Throughout the period between 1978 and 1998, median income in family households maintained by a single mother fluctuated between $15,000 and $18,000 ($19,000 and $24,000 if one uses mean family income). Income was lowest in the recession years of the early 1980s and 1990s.

Table 4.6 examines the sources of income of single mothers and contrasts them with those of married mothers. The means and medians reported for selected years in Table 4.6 are weighted by all single and married mothers and include those who maintain households on their own as well as those who live in the homes of other friends, partners, or relatives. Income amounts are for the previous year.

Mean family income for single mothers in 1998 was similar to 1978; median income was about $1,000 lower. More striking is the trend relative to married mothers. As family income rose for married mothers, the ratio of family income for single relative to married mothers declined. In 1978, single mothers had median family incomes only about one-third those of married mothers; this fraction was closer to one-fourth in 1998. This suggests a widening gap in average levels of well-being between single and married mothers over the period, consistent with the general increases in inequality during the period (discussed in Chapter 9).

Women's earnings tended to rise for both single and married mothers during the period, but the increase was sharper for married mothers. Most of this difference was due to the larger increase in the percentage of married mothers with their own earnings. The proportion with own earnings grew by 18 percentage points (from 56 percent to 74 percent) from 1978 to 1998 for married women, compared with 12 percentage points (66 percent to 78 percent) for single women. Whereas the composition of single moth-

TABLE 4.6 Sources of Income for Single and Married Mothers: 1978, 1988, and 1998 (1997 dollars)

	Single Mothers			Married Mothers			Ratio Single/Married Mothers		
	1978	1988	1998	1978	1988	1998	1978	1988	1998
Family income									
Mean	19,622	18,073	19,810	51,682	57,227	66,854	0.38	0.32	0.30
Median	15,425	12,255	14,448	46,972	50,863	54,050	0.33	0.24	0.27
Mother's earnings									
Mean	10,600	11,999	13,827	7,223	12,245	16,505	1.47	0.98	0.84
Median	5,587	6,358	9,600	1,067	7,064	11,000	5.24	0.90	0.87
% in households with									
Own earnings	65.5	66.8	77.1	55.9	70.6	74.2	1.2	0.9	1.0
Child support/alimony	27.9	32.9	29.2	3.1	7.4	4.9	9.0	4.4	6.0
Public assistance/welfare	36.3	32.1	21.1	1.7	1.8	1.5	21.4	17.8	14.1
Other income	47.0	47.8	54.3	99.2	99.0	98.9	0.47	0.48	0.55
Median for those receiving									
Own earnings	15,029	15,209	14,309	10,158	14,129	18,000	1.48	1.08	0.80
Child support/alimony	3,809	2,684	2,700	3,047	1,695	3,000	1.25	1.58	0.90
Public assistance/welfare	6,583	4,491	3,000	4,084	3,073	2,448	1.61	1.46	1.23
Other income	5,120	2,261	3,040	39,744	38,983	38,900	0.13	0.06	0.08

SOURCE: Current Population Survey, March supplements, 1978, 1988, 1998.
NOTE: Table includes all single and married mothers in family groups. Amounts received refer to income and earnings in the previous calendar year (1977, 1987, and 1997).

ers was shifting toward younger, less educated, never-married mothers during the period, the married mothers who increasingly entered paid work tended to be the better educated among the group of married mothers. Hence median earnings among those who earned an income in the past year decreased by about $1,000 for single mothers in the 1990s compared with an increase of about $4,000 for married mothers. Average earnings of all single mothers tended to be about 50 percent greater than for married mothers in 1978 but dropped to only 84 percent of average earnings of married mothers by 1998.

Table 4.6 also provides estimates of the proportions of single mothers who receive child support, rely on welfare, and live in households where they have access to earnings from others or other nonearnings income. Around 30 percent of single mothers who have children under age 18 living with them report receiving any child support income. Among those who receive child support, the amounts reported in 1988 and 1998 were about $1,100 lower than in 1978. Still, if the median child support of $2,700 that mothers received in 1998 was received by 100 percent rather than 29 percent of single mothers, median family income of single mothers would have been 13 percent higher, on average, in 1998.

Similarly, the proportion of mothers reporting any welfare receipt declined precipitously at the end of the 1990s. In 1978, 36 percent of single mothers reported receiving public assistance income in the preceding year. This figure stood at 32 percent in 1988 and was down to 21 percent in 1998. Among recipients of public assistance, the dollar amount received in 1998 also was less than half the amount reported in 1978 ($3,000 in 1998 compared with $6,583 in 1978).

Table 4.6 also highlights the major source of income difference between single and married mothers. Almost all married mothers have access to other income, typically their spouses' earnings, and that other income is the major source of married mothers' much higher living standards. In 1998, 54 percent of single mothers had income from sources other than their own earnings (and child support and public assistance). Those single mothers who had access to other income received about $3,000 from these sources, on average, whereas married mothers had almost $40,000 in other income (primarily their husbands' earnings). Obviously the two groups, married mothers and single mothers, are quite different, but it is interesting to note that when single mothers have access to income from their children's fathers, it tends to be in amounts of less than $3,000. Married mothers benefit from incomes provided by their husbands that approach $40,000. This provides some perspective on how large the income gap is, on average, between children who live with their fathers and those who do not and why diminishing the income disparities between children who grow up with one rather than both parents is so difficult.

Variation Among Single Mothers ●

In this chapter, we have noted the shift in the 1980s and 1990s toward single mothers who have never married. We have also just shown trends in economic indicators that suggest that single mothers may have lost ground economically vis-à-vis married mothers and that the income disparities between married and single mothers tend to be extremely large. Table 4.7 shows selected demographic and socioeconomic differences among single mothers and provides information on single fathers and two-parent families for comparison purposes. The table is weighted by the number of children residing in each family type. Characteristics for children with widowed mothers are not shown separately because only about 1 percent of children under age 18 lived with widowed mothers in 1998.

In 1998, about one-fourth of all children were currently living only with their mothers, about 5 percent were living only with their fathers, and the remaining 71 percent were residing with two parents. Because this characterization of living arrangements does not include cohabitation, some of the children categorized as living with only one parent actually reside with both, just as some of the children living with two parents no longer reside with both their biological parents but now live with a parent and stepparent.

The type of single-mother family that has increased most in the past two decades—one in which the mother has never married—is distinctive in several important ways. First, these mothers are young when compared with divorced or separated mothers, single fathers, or married parents. Never-married mothers are less well educated and less often fully employed than are divorced mothers. The family income of children who reside with never-married mothers is only 23 percent that of children in two-parent families, the lowest of any group of children living with single mothers. Almost three of every five children who live with never-married mothers reside in poverty. Child support receipt is also much lower for never-married than for other single mothers. Whereas 60 percent of divorced mothers with custody of children under age 21 receive some child support from their children's fathers, less than 20 percent of never-married

TABLE 4.7 Socioeconomic Characteristics of Children in Mother-Child, Father-Child, and Two-Parent Families: 1998

	Single Mothers				Single Fathers	Two Parents
	Total	Divorced	Separated	Never Married		
% children in this household type	24.3	8.3	5.2	9.8	4.6	71.1
Mean number of siblings	1.3	1.3	1.7	1.3	1.0	1.5
% with parent under age 25	13.5	3.1	5.3	28.0	9.9	2.7
% with adults other than parent(s) in household	41.4	42.4	36.5	43.3	59.5	17.0
% with parent who is high school graduate	75.0	85.4	70.5	68.3	77.4	86.2
% with parent employed full-time previous week	51.2	62.9	49.7	42.3	76.5	75.7
Median family income ($)	16,236	21,316	15,297	12,064	29,313	52,553
As % of two-parent family	30.9	40.6	29.1	23.0	55.8	100.0
% below poverty	47.5	35.6	51.0	57.8	19.9	9.3
% in owned housing unit	37.4	48.9	36.3	25.7	52.8	75.8

SOURCE: Current Population Survey, March supplement, 1998.
NOTE: Characteristics in this table are weighted by the number of children residing with parents of a given type.

mothers report receiving such support on a regular basis (Bianchi 1995a:Table 6).

Although the family income of divorced mothers is only about 40 percent that of two-parent families and the rates of poverty of divorced-mother families are much greater, children who live with divorced mothers live with mothers who are substantially better educated and more often employed than do children with either separated or never-married mothers. Home ownership is also significantly higher among those who have divorced, although it is much lower than for two-parent families.

Single Mothers and Welfare Reform ●

The Personal Responsibility and Work Opportunity Reconciliation Act of 1996 introduced the most dramatic and widespread reforms in the welfare system for single mothers since the inception of the Aid to Families with Dependent Children (AFDC) entitlement program in 1935. Under this act, AFDC was replaced by Temporary Assistance for Needy Families (TANF), ending entitlement to federal cash assistance. Under TANF, states receive a lump sum of federal money to run their own programs. They are free to develop these programs in any way they see fit, but they must require work and set time limits on the receipt of cash assistance.

TANF stresses work, responsibility, and self-sufficiency. With few exceptions, recipients of TANF must work after 2 years of receiving assistance. Under TANF, "work" can take the form of employment, looking for a job, on-the-job training, community service, or providing child care for children whose parents are participating in community service. Single parents were required to work 20 hours per week by 1999 and 30 hours per week by 2000. Another important component of TANF is time limits: The federal law states that families who have received assistance for 5 cumulative years are ineligible to receive additional cash aid. Individual states may set lower lifetime limits, however. Other goals of TANF are to provide assistance so that children can be cared for in their own homes; to reduce dependency by promoting job preparation, work, and marriage; to prevent nonmarital pregnancies; and to encourage the formation and maintenance of two-parent families (Administration for Children and Families 2001).

When PRWORA was first passed, many policy makers predicted that the new policies would have severely deleterious consequences for single mothers and their children. Thus far, these consequences have not come to pass. An experimental study was recently conducted to assess the effects of the new policies as part of the National Evaluation of Welfare-to-Work Strategies, and the results indicate that welfare-to-work programs have had few effects on mothers' psychological functioning, stress, or parenting practices (Hamilton and McGroder 2000). For the most part, children also appear to be unaffected; the study found few effects overall and most were small in magnitude. The one exception is in the area of children's cognitive development—children whose mothers worked and received other supplemental assistance did better in school than did children in poor families that received public assistance under the old welfare rules. The researchers conclude that welfare programs that combine work requirements with other policies (e.g., child-care subsidies, health insurance, cash supplements) that raise income improve children's school performance.

Have the goals of welfare reform been realized? The answer to this question is currently unclear. Some policy makers see welfare reform as an unqualified success. After all, caseloads have declined by about 50 percent since the peak in 1994, when many states began to implement the new rules. In addition, studies from several states indicate that between 50 percent and 70 percent of single mothers are employed after leaving welfare (Brauner and Loprest 1999).

These statistics appear to indicate the success of welfare reform, yet there are several reasons to believe otherwise. First, it is unclear if caseloads would have declined to such an extent if the economy had not been in good shape. Welfare reform occurred during a period of unprecedented economic expansion in which unemployment was low and jobs were plentiful. The U.S. Council of Economic Advisors (1999) estimates that 40 percent of the AFDC caseload decline from 1993 to 1996 and 10-15 percent of the TANF decline from 1996 to 1998 occurred because people who were looking for work (unemployed) found jobs in the booming economy, not because of welfare reform per se.

Second, one-fifth of welfare leavers were not working, had no partner working, and were not receiving government disability benefits (Loprest 1999). Exactly how these people make ends meet is unclear. In addition, many of the people who leave the welfare rolls are "cyclers" who cannot sustain a livable income and frequently move in and out of the system (Bane and Ellwood 1994). About a third of recent welfare leavers have subsequently returned (Loprest 1999). These people are likely to spend a great deal of time on welfare even though they are not enrolled for extended periods of time. One study estimates that only one-half of welfare leavers have actually moved from welfare dependency to independence from welfare (Moffitt and Roff 2000).

Third, many single-mother welfare leavers who are working find themselves in low-paying jobs with few benefits. Two-thirds of these mothers are in service, sales, or clerical/administrative jobs (Loprest 1999), and about three-quarters are in poverty (Moffitt and Roff 2000). The loss in benefits among the poorest mothers has meant that even though they are working, they have experienced substantial declines in their income. More than one-fourth work night shifts, and one-half report having trouble coordinating work and child care (Loprest 1999).

Fourth, many of the single-mother families that are entitled to receive food stamps, Medicaid, and child-care subsidies under PRWORA are not receiving them (Garrett and Holahan 2000; U.S. Department of Health and Human Services 2000b; Zedlewski and Brauner 1999). Many former welfare recipients report difficulty in providing sufficient food and shelter for their families (Loprest 1999). Clearly, these dismal circumstances would be tempered if more families received the benefits to which they are entitled.

Finally, few people have changed their fertility and marriage behaviors because of welfare reform rules (Cherlin et al. 2000; Hamilton and McGroder 2000). Only 5 percent of women report taking steps to avoid having children because of the rules, and less than 1 percent report marrying (Cherlin et al. 2000).

Thus, although some success can be claimed, there is still much room for improvement. Policy makers are beginning to discuss midcourse corrections in the new welfare strategy. Ripe for debate is how more families can be enrolled in food stamp and Medicaid programs. And as more and more single mothers leave the welfare rolls, those who remain are likely to be the most disadvantaged and the hardest to place in jobs. It is still unclear how many of these women and how many of the "cyclers" will be able to achieve economic independence. And finally, it is unclear how single mothers and their families will fare if there is a downturn in the economy. Will single mothers be successful in finding jobs in a more competitive job market? Welfare reform is still in its infancy. We will be able to answer the question of how successful it has been only after more time has passed.

Conclusion ●

Growth in single-mother families was very rapid during the 1970s but slowed in the 1980s and the first half of the 1990s, leveling off after 1994. Even though more women in recent cohorts have become single mothers and experience more than one spell of single mothering, the numbers of years they spend as single mothers have not increased. But defining exactly who is a single mother is not as easy as it would first appear. Some single mothers are cohabiting, whereas others live with their parents or other relatives who can help out with the children. And some nonresident fathers are very involved in parenting their children. Thus the extent to which single mothers are parenting solo can vary widely.

Since 1980, the divorce rate has declined but the percentage of children born to unmarried mothers has increased. The postponement of marriage and, to a lesser extent, the increase in birthrates to unmarried women have been the most significant components of growth in mother-child families in recent years. Given that the composition has shifted toward never-married single mothers, who have in the past been among the most disadvantaged socioeconomically, it is perhaps all the more remarkable that the educational, employment, and occupational attainment of single mothers increased as much as it did in the 1980s and 1990s. Single mothers, as a group, became more likely to be college graduates and to be employed in professional, managerial, and technical occupations despite the increase in the proportion of single mothers who were never-married mothers—mothers who tend, on average, to be young, less well educated, and less firmly attached to the labor market.

Whether these trends have run their course is not entirely clear. Whatever the future holds, an awareness of the diversity of paths to single parenting and of the likely economic differences that accompany those divergent paths is necessary if we are to meet the needs of children who will spend time living only with their mothers for at least part of their childhoods.

Several topics related to how well mothers and their children fare in single-mother homes have been debated in recent years. There have been ethnographic studies of how low-income mothers package work and welfare to try to support their families (Edin and Lein 1997a). There is a large and growing literature suggesting that single-parent families have negative outcomes for children, and these poorer outcomes for children are not only the result of poverty (McLanahan and Sandefur 1994). Yet most children who grow up in single-parent families turn out fine, even though, on average, their well-being is lower in childhood (Cherlin 1999).

An important issue, introduced more than two decades ago by Clair Vickery (1977), is the whole notion of a time deficit in single-parent families. Many low-income single-mother families not only lack income, they are time poor. Resources of time as well as money are stretched to the limit, and there is some indication that a bifurcated situation for mothers and children may be emerging. Women who have children late increasingly have their children in marriage and raise those children with a father present. They also have their children when they are financially better able to support them. Early childbearers, on the other hand, tend to have their children outside marriage and to raise their children without the help of the children's father. The ability of these mothers to support their families on their wages alone is quite limited. This type of inequality in life circumstances of two groups of children needs much greater scrutiny, especially given the compositional shift in single-mother families (toward never-married mothers) in recent years.

Never-married single mothers are also more likely not to be working and to be affected by the new TANF regulations. The new work requirements will further reduce the amount of time these mothers have to spend with their children. Young, never-married mothers are also the least qualified for the labor market. So even though many single mothers have left welfare and begun working, they often are no better off financially than they were when they were on welfare—many are still in poverty and are having trouble making ends meet. To the extent that states target their TANF funds toward ensuring that all who are eligible for food stamps, Medicaid, and child-care subsidies receive the benefits to which they are entitled, many of these single mothers and their children may be lifted out of poverty. However, if the economy worsens, many more single mothers may find themselves out of work and with only short-term, limited benefits on which to rely.

Notes

1. One of those officials, Peter Edelman, described his objections to the act in a piece that appeared in the March 1997 issue of the *Atlantic Monthly*.

2. The estimates in Table 4.1 and all subsequent tables include all single mothers, both those maintaining their own households and those living in other persons' households. Estimates do not remove cohabitors, but we follow London's (1998) lead and correct the 1978 estimates for the underreporting of single mothers living in other persons' households (i.e., in what the Census Bureau terms *subfamilies*).

CHAPTER **5**

FATHERING

The May 7, 2000, issue of the *Washington Post Magazine* featured a cover story on Dennis, age 41, a "stay-at-home" father of 4-year-old twin boys (Salmon 2000). A graduate of Harvard's master's degree program in architecture, Dennis has put his architectural career on hold in order to be a full-time parent to his preschoolers. He is supported in this choice by his wife, Patti, a highly paid Hewlett-Packard executive with a demanding travel schedule. If the couple's roles were reversed, the article's author would have found little to write about. "Stay-at-home" mothers, although less common today than in the past, still constituted almost one-third of married mothers of preschool-age children in 1998 (Cohen and Bianchi 1999). But for a father of young children to make this choice still strikes us as unusual.

Survey results reported earlier in the same week in the business section of the *Washington Post* suggest that younger fathers are increasingly questioning whether they want to work so many hours that they are effectively excluded from active involvement with their children (Grimsley 2000). Fathers report that they want to spend time raising their children, and time diary data from a variety of sources suggest that they are doing just that. In 1965, for example, married fathers reported spending an average of 2.8 hours per day with their children, compared with 3.8 hours in 1998 (Bianchi 2000). Parallel findings are emerging from data collected on children's activities and the people with whom children spend time (Sandberg and Hofferth 1999; Yeung, Duncan, and Hill 2000; Yeung et al. 2001) and from studies of trends in fathers' time with their children from other industrialized countries, such as Britain (Fischer, McCulloch, and Gershuny 1999) and Australia (Bittman 1999b).

Along with the increased participation of married fathers in their children's lives, there has also been an increase in the number of father-only families, a trend we discuss later in this chapter (Garasky and Meyer 1996). There also appears to be an increase in shared custody after divorce (Cancian and Meyer 1998), although fathers who have sole physical custody of their children remain relatively uncommon.

At the same time that there appears to be growing investment in children among married fathers and among a segment of divorced fathers, other trends may increasingly remove fathers from children's lives. For example, births to unmarried women often make for tenuous ties between fathers and their children. Furstenberg (1988) uses the label "good dads, bad dads" to describe the parallel trends of increased commitment to children and child rearing on the part of some fathers and lessened connection and responsibility for children on the part of others. He sees both phenomena as resulting from a decline in patriarchal attitudes and the increased economic independence of women. Furstenberg argues that as women's labor market participation and earnings have expanded, women have been able to demand greater father involvement in child rearing and domestic chores. Women's changing roles have in some sense helped to create "good dads." Men's own changing notions of what it means to be a father and what they want for themselves as fathers have no doubt also affected what fathers do and say they want to do for their children. The breaking down of rigid gender norms, combined with greater earnings capacity on the part of women, may have expanded the range of choices available not only to women but to men.

At the same time, women's increased access to their own earnings or to other sources of support for their children, such as welfare, Furstenberg argues, has allowed other dads to shirk their parenting responsibilities and to do so with relative impunity and little guilt. They can do this because they feel their children will be adequately cared for, at least at some minimum level, even without their financial assistance. Fathers with little education and poor labor force prospects have difficulty assuming the "provider" role that has typically characterized men's responsibility as fathers. This may also lead some men to abdicate their role as fathers (Oppenheimer, Kalmijn, and Lim 1997). However, "bad dads" are not found only among low-income men, and many less educated men fulfill child support obligations despite great financial hardship (Meyer 1998). A host of factors, including conflict between mothers and fathers, result in failed obligations of support and nurturance. An important focus of public policy efforts in recent years has been on how to ensure the flow of resources from fathers to their children (Garfinkel 1992; Garfinkel, McLanahan, et al. 1998).

In this chapter, we provide a broad overview of what we know about fathers and fathering in the United States. We begin with a discussion of changing cultural beliefs about father involvement, and then we examine men's living arrangements and trends in father-only families. We compare the demographic and socioeconomic characteristics of single and married fathers' households. We also address several questions about fathers' involvement with their children, whether or not they live with the children's mothers. For example, have child custody patterns changed among divorced couples? Does the type of custody that fathers have determine their involvement in their children's lives? How often do nonresident fathers pay child support and spend time with their children? How much time and what types of activities do fathers engage in with their children in two-parent families? How is this changing? Do fathers and mothers agree on the level of father involvement in child rearing?

Beliefs About Father Involvement: ● Ideals and Realities

Cultural ideals about fathering have changed over time, largely in relation to structural shifts in the location of work and due to mothers' increased labor force participation (LaRossa 1988). According to scholars such as Demos (1982), the key dimension of fatherhood in the 18th and early 19th centuries was that of the "moral overseer" of the family and children: Fathers were responsible for religious training and for raising their children to be moral adults. With industrialization and the relocation of (paid) work away from the home, this paternal role diminished. The father's contribution to the family came to be seen as primarily economic—the father was the "provider." There was also a shift in the early part of the 20th century toward viewing fathers and children as playmates and friends (LaRossa 1997; Mintz 1998). As the absence of fathers became more pronounced during and after World War II, attention was focused on the importance of the father as a "sex role model" for his children, especially his sons (Mintz 1998). With the feminist movement of the late 1960s and early 1970s, a new view of fatherhood emerged, one in which men were responsible for and significantly involved in all aspects of caring for children. The ideal father essentially became a coparent (Pleck and Pleck 1997).

Research on fathering beliefs in the current era provides evidence for social change in ideals: People today, compared with those in earlier times, believe that fathers should be more involved in caregiving. Items included in national surveys such as the General Social Survey have asked Americans to indicate the extent to which they agree with statements such as "It is much better for everyone involved if the man is the achiever outside the home and the woman takes care of the home and family." There has been notable change in how Americans respond to such questions, with a much lower percentage of respondents supporting this gender division of labor in the family in the latter part of the 20th century compared with the 1960s (Farley 1996; Thornton 1989).

LaRossa and Reitzes (1995), using parents' letters written to a nationally known educator in the 1920s and 1930s, have shown that there may exist a "her versus his" parenthood, with mothers presenting a traditional picture of the division of child care and fathers presenting themselves as more equally involved. Part of the difficulty in understanding how fathers see the work of parenting is related to methodological issues—fathers are often left out of studies, so that available information about fathers is based on mothers' reports about what fathers do (Marsiglio 1995). Not only may the picture of child care and parent-child relations be incomplete because of the historic exclusion of men from parenting research, but how men and women view child care remains unclear (Pleck 1997).

● Declining Fatherhood: Long-Term Trends in Men's Coresidential Parenting

It is difficult to get an exact estimate of "father involvement" in the United States. It has been customary to ask women how many children they have ever borne, providing an estimate for entry into motherhood (or, conversely, an estimate of childlessness) for women. For men, it is more difficult to arrive at such an estimate. Just as for women, any man who has contributed biologically to the conception of a child is a parent. Yet in the United States, at least in the past century, fathers' ties to their children are more often severed than are mothers' ties. If a father has not been or is not currently a presence in his child's life, some might not consider him much of a parent. By this definition, only those filling the role of "social parent," either to their own or to someone else's children, would be included in the definition of *father* (or *mother*, for that matter).

Many of the trends we have documented in the preceding chapters have complicated the connections between parents and children. The separation of men from their children tends to be greater than the separation of women from their children. On the one hand, divorce often separates men residentially from their own biological children because more mothers (85 percent) than fathers (15 percent) have physical custody of children after a marriage ends (Grall 2000). Unless a father is living with the mother of his child at the time of birth, a child born to an unmarried mother often begins life in a household that does not include the biological father. On the other hand, men often play a role in raising other men's children when they cohabit with or marry mothers who have children from previous relationships. And some men, such as grandfathers, may find themselves playing the role of "father surrogate" for related children who live in their households because of economic need or other extenuating circumstances.

Given the long-term decline in fertility, parenthood occupies an increasingly circumscribed period in adult men's and women's lives; both women and men spend fewer years and smaller proportions of their adult lives rearing children today than was true in the past. Hogan and Goldscheider (2000) note the relative paucity of research on men as parents and use census data from the late 1800s through 1990 to examine men's likelihood of sharing a residence with children under age 15—both their own children (including stepchildren) and other children. They show that the decline in the percentage of men living with an "own child" is of long duration: 42 percent of men between the ages of 18 and 75 lived with their own children (either biological or stepchildren) in 1880. The proportion declined to 33 percent in 1940 and dropped further to 28 percent in 1990. Hogan and Goldscheider also found a steep decline in the likelihood of men's living with children other than their own biological children or stepchildren.

The major interruption to this long-term trend is found in the years when the Baby Boom generation was being reared in U.S. households (captured in the 1950 through 1970 censuses). Almost one-half of adult men coresided with an "own child" in these years, a higher percentage than in 1880. Using 1950 or 1960 as a starting point suggests a very steep decline in men's coresidential involvement with children in the second half of the 20th century (Eggebeen 1999; Eggebeen and Uhlenberg 1985), a decline that looks more gradual when we consider the long-term decline in fertility over the entire 20th century. Given that the decline in coresidential fathering has been developing over a long period and similar declines in coresidential parenting have occurred among women, Hogan and Goldscheider (2000) conclude that there is no recent crisis in coresidential parenting among American men.

● Lifetime Estimates of Parenthood

How many years do men spend as parents? King (1999) has recently estimated the numbers of years men and women will spend as parents of children (either biological children or stepchildren) under age 18 if transition rates into and out of parenting that characterized the late 1980s and early 1990s continue into the future. She includes in her definition of parenting both years when an individual has a biological child under age 18 and years when a person is living with a child other than a biological child. Her estimates of the distribution of parenting years of men and women are shown in Figure 5.1. The figure shows the projected percentages of adult years (between ages 20 and 70) during which a person does not have responsibility for children under age 18 ("nonparent" years), during which a person has and lives with biological children ("custodial-biological" parenting years), during which a person has biological children under age 18 but is not living with them ("biological-nonresident only" parenting years), during which a person is raising children who are not his or her biological children ("stepparent only" years), and a residual that includes years with more than one type of parenting ("mixed"), as, for example, when a father has a biological child living elsewhere but is helping to raise stepchildren who are living with him.

King estimates that almost two-thirds of the adult years of women and men under age 70 will be "child-free" years—years when the individual does not have biological children under age 18 or responsibility for anyone else's children. Men will spend about 20 percent of their adulthood living with and raising their own biological children, compared with an estimate of more than 30 percent for women. The estimated number of years during which a man has biological children under age 18 but is not living with them is 3 years for white men, on average. The estimate for black men is twice that for whites: 6 years, on average. The comparable estimate for women of either race is less than a year, because most women raise their biological children to adulthood.

King (1999:384) notes that, whereas 86 percent of women's (white or black) parenting years are spent rearing their biological children, the com-

● **Figure 5.1.** Percentages of Adulthood Spent in Various Parental Statuses

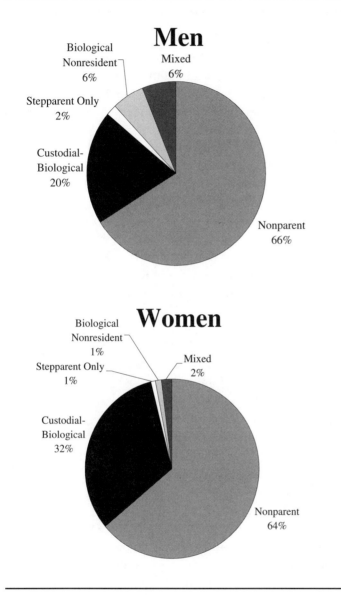

SOURCE: King (1999). Reprinted by permission.

parable proportion of men's parenting years that are spent as "custodial-biological" parents is only 62 percent for white men and 38 percent for black men. Men will spend more time than women as stepparents (of other men's biological children) or in some mixed parenting arrangement.

● Father-Only Families and Cohabitation

The statistical series providing annual estimates of the number of families with father present (either a married father or a single father), the Current Population Survey (CPS), only begins mid-20th century, with the Baby Boom years. Hence our starting point for charting family change is often 1950, even though we must keep in mind the uniqueness of the American family in the middle of the 20th century.

In 1950, at the beginning of the Baby Boom, there were 18.8 million married-couple family households with children under age 18 in the United States. This number increased to 25.3 million in 1998, at the same time as the proportion of all families with a married father present declined (from 93 percent to 73 percent; see Figure 4.1 in Chapter 4). Between 1950 and 1998, the number of households with children maintained by unmarried fathers increased from 229,000 to 1.9 million. The count of single fathers climbs to 2.1 million in 1998 if we include all unmarried fathers living with their children, not just those who maintain their own independent households.

As with the count of single-mother families, one of the questions about single-father families is, When is a father-only family a single-parent family and when is it effectively a two-parent family because the father is living with a cohabiting partner? Bumpass and Raley (1995) indicate that many unmarried fathers with children under age 18 are actually cohabiting. These families may be more like two-parent than one-parent families.

Garasky and Meyer (1996) have used 1960 through 1990 census data to track the increase in the percentage of families that are father-only households, removing cohabiting couples from the count. Before cohabitors are removed, they estimate that father-only families increased from 1.5 percent to 5.0 percent of family households with children between 1960 and 1990 and that the number of father-only family households increased by 240 percent in the 1980s. When fathers who are likely to be cohabiting are removed, the increase is from 1.5 percent to 3.2 percent of all family households with children, with an increase of 121 percent in the 1980s.

In 1990, if cohabitors are not excluded, about 18 percent of single-parent families were father-only families. Excluding cohabitors results in an estimate of 14 percent, because more unmarried fathers than unmarried mothers are living with partners. Father-only families declined as a percentage of all single-parent families in the 1970s (when the number of single-mother families increased rapidly) but then grew as a percentage of single-parent

TABLE 5.1 Living Arrangements of Single Fathers and Mothers With Children Under Age 18: 1978, 1988, and 1998

	1978	1988	1998	% Point Change
Fathers (number in thousands)	673	1,214	2,099	
Total (%)	100.0	100.0	100.0	
No other adults in household	42.4	46.8	38.2	-4.2
Cohabiting	13.5	26.8	33.3	19.8
Living with parent(s)	17.6	10.3	10.5	-7.1
Living with other adults	26.5	16.1	18.0	-8.5
Mothers (number in thousands)	6,194	8,160	9,845	
Total (%)	100.0	100.0	100.0	
No other adults in household	59.8	56.4	54.0	-5.8
Cohabiting	4.7	9.6	12.7	8.0
Living with parent(s)	14.3	15.2	16.7	2.4
Living with other adults	21.2	18.8	16.6	-4.6

SOURCE: Current Population Survey, March supplements, 1978, 1988, 1998.
NOTE: Table includes all single fathers and mothers in family groups.

families in the 1980s (as the rate of increase in father-only families outpaced that for mother-only families; Garasky and Meyer 1996:Table 1). Data for the 1990s suggest that father-only family households continued to grow as a percentage of all single-parent family households as the rate of increase in mother-only family households leveled (see Table 1.1 and the discussion in Chapter 1).

In Table 5.1, we include all unmarried men living with their children (stepchildren, adoptive children, or biological children) in the Current Population Survey in 1978, 1988, and 1998. Among the 2.1 million "single" fathers in 1998, about one-third were living with partners, up from 14 percent in 1978. If we were to remove those with cohabiting partners from the count of father-only families, we would estimate that about 1.4 million American men were raising their children on their own in 1998. Unmarried fathers living with children are much more likely than unmarried mothers to be living with partners—33 percent of single fathers compared with 13

TABLE 5.2 Marital Statuses of Single Fathers Living With Children Under Age 18: 1978, 1988, and 1998

	1978	1988	1998	% Point Change
Fathers (number in thousands)	673	1,214	2,099	
Marital status (%)	100.0	100.0	100.0	
Never married	14.9	20.6	34.6	+19.7
Divorced	41.4	48.8	44.4	+3.0
Separated	26.1	23.2	16.7	-9.4
Widowed	17.6	7.4	4.3	-13.3

SOURCE: Current Population Survey, March supplements, 1978, 1988, 1998.
NOTE: Table includes all single fathers in family groups.

percent of single mothers in 1998. A much smaller proportion of single fathers (38 percent) than single mothers (55 percent) are the only adults in their households, although the proportion of single fathers living with parents or other adults declined between 1978 and 1998.

As with single mothers, the postponement of marriage and the rise in unmarried fertility have resulted in more never-married single fathers. Between 1978 and 1998, the proportion of coresident single fathers who were never married grew rapidly, more than doubling, from 15 percent to more than one-third of single fathers (see Table 5.2). The most dramatic change occurred in the 1990s. As the proportion of single fathers who were never married rose, the proportion separated or widowed plummeted. This shift occurred for all single fathers regardless of race, but a higher proportion of black (53 percent) and Hispanic (59 percent) than white single fathers (31 percent) were never married in 1998 (data not shown). These changes parallel the increase in never-married mothers shown in Table 4.1 (in Chapter 4).

Because single parenting, especially as a result of a nonmarital birth, is so much more common among blacks and Hispanics than among whites, black men (and women) are at greater risk of becoming single parents. However, the likelihood that a single-parent family is maintained by a father rather than a mother is actually greater among whites. For example, among whites in 1998, 22 percent of the single-parent families formed were father-only families (Casper and Bryson 1998b:Table 11). The comparable estimates for blacks and Hispanics were 8 percent and 16 percent, respectively.

Characteristics of Single and Married Fathers ●

How do single fathers who live with their children compare with married fathers on demographic and socioeconomic dimensions? Table 5.3 compares never-married, divorced, and separated fathers living with children with married fathers in 1998. About one-third of single fathers were never married, 44 percent were divorced, and 17 percent were separated in 1998. A small proportion (4 percent) were widowed, but their characteristics are not reported separately because the sample size is exceedingly small.

Single men who are cohabiting are not shown separately but are included under the marital statuses they reported. More than half of never-married fathers, one-fourth of divorced fathers, and almost one-fifth of separated fathers reported that they were living with partners in 1998. Never-married single fathers were a much younger group of parents than the other three groups. Divorced custodial fathers tended to be older than married or separated fathers. All groups of single fathers were much more likely than married fathers to have only one child living with them.

In addition to their relatively young age, never-married single fathers were the most likely to have dropped out of high school (29 percent were not high school graduates). Less than 60 percent worked full-time and year-round, and fewer than 1 in 10 were employed in a managerial or professional job. Never-married fathers were economically far more disadvantaged than divorced or separated fathers. Their economic status, as indexed by earnings and household income, was also low. These differences by marital status of single fathers parallel the differences by marital status of single mothers discussed in Chapter 4.

Table 5.3 also shows that married fathers were much better-off than single fathers regardless of their marital status. Married fathers were better educated (30 percent were college graduates), more likely to be employed full-time and year-round, more often working in managerial or professional occupations, and more often home owners. Married fathers also had higher median earnings than single fathers—$35,000 for married fathers versus $24,000 for single fathers in 1998.

In 1998, single fathers had median family incomes of just under $27,000, compared with just over $54,000 for married fathers (see Table 5.4). The in-

TABLE 5.3 Selected Socioeconomic Characteristics of Never-Married, Divorced, Separated, and Married Fathers Living With Children Under Age 18: 1998

	Never Married	Divorced	Separated	Married
Fathers (number in thousands)	728	932	350	25,231
As % of all single fathers[a]	35	44	17	NA
% cohabiting	53.4	26.1	18.8	NA
Age (%)	100.0	100.0	100.0	100.0
Under 25	29.6	1.4	2.9	2.6
25-34	44.5	17.6	24.7	27.2
35 or older	25.9	81.0	72.4	70.2
Number of children (%)	100.0	100.0	100.0	100.0
One	66.8	63.0	56.1	38.0
Two	22.9	25.8	30.3	40.4
Three or more	10.3	11.2	13.7	21.7
Educational attainment (%)	100.0	100.0	100.0	100.0
Less than high school	29.3	15.3	18.0	13.2
High school/some college	65.9	68.5	69.7	56.7
College graduate	4.9	16.2	12.3	30.1
Employment status (%)	100.0	100.0	100.0	100.0
Employed	79.7	88.2	86.9	92.1
Unemployed	10.2	3.9	6.4	2.8
Not in the labor force	10.1	7.9	6.7	5.2
% employed full-time, year-round	58.5	76.4	71.1	82.6
% in managerial or professional occupations	8.7	20.9	21.9	32.1
% who are home owners	40.1	61.8	47.5	76.9

SOURCE: Current Population Survey, March supplement, 1998
NOTE: Table includes all single and married fathers in family groups.
a. Excludes widowers, who account for 4.2 percent of single fathers. Sample size is too small to show separately. NA = not applicable.

come gap is large, in part, because married men are much more likely to have other earners (their wives) in their families. For example, in 1998 single fathers earned on average 84 percent of the family income, compared

TABLE 5.4   Income and Earnings for Single and Married Fathers: 1978, 1988, and 1998 (1997 dollars)

	Single Fathers			Married Fathers			Ratio Single/ Married Fathers		
	1978	1988	1998	1978	1988	1998	1978	1988	1998
Family income									
Mean	35,839	32,935	33,931	51,969	57,641	67,224	0.69	0.57	0.50
Median	31,897	26,805	26,581	47,215	51,145	54,428	0.68	0.52	0.49
Father's earnings									
Mean	29,040	27,824	28,681	38,954	39,604	44,237	0.75	0.70	0.65
Median	26,919	24,019	24,000	36,270	35,321	35,000	0.74	0.68	0.69

SOURCE: Current Population Survey, March supplements, 1978, 1988, 1998.
NOTE: Table includes all single and married fathers in family groups.

with a much lower 66 percent of married fathers. Over time, single fathers have been losing ground relative to married fathers in large part because married fathers' wives' earnings have increased. Table 5.4 shows that in 1978, single fathers' average income was more than two-thirds that of married fathers, but by 1998, this differential had increased so that single fathers' incomes were only 50 percent of married fathers'. If we examine the ratio of single fathers' earnings to married fathers' earnings, we see that the decline is only from 75 percent to 65 percent, suggesting that part of the widening family income differential is due to wives' increased earnings rather than to a growing difference in single and married men's earnings.

Child Custody ●

One of the questions about the increase in father-only families in the 1990s is whether it has been associated with an increase in fathers' seeking custody of children after marriages are disrupted. Garasky and Meyer (1996) suggest this may be the case, although they do not provide direct evidence and national estimates are not readily available. Most of the research on custody decisions has focused on selected states. Cancian and Meyer

(1998) recently conducted one of the few trend analyses of how custody may be changing to date, using data from Wisconsin for the 1986-94 period.

Historical evidence suggests that during the 19th century, custody preferences shifted: At the founding of the republic, fathers were deemed to have the rights to custody of and responsibilities for children in the event of marital disruption. By the 20th century, opinion had shifted to a preference for mothers. Cancian and Meyer (1998) note that "a doctrine of 'tender years' developed, suggesting that mothers were better caretakers for children and should receive custody. . . . the explicit preference for mothers in custody determinations continued until the 1960s" (p. 148).

With the passage of civil rights legislation and antidiscrimination legislation, the courts acted to remove gender preferences in custody statutes, and the concept of "best interest of the child" came to be the standard used in custody disputes (Buehler and Gerard 1995). However, the reality was that mothers continued both to ask for and to receive sole custody rights in the vast majority of cases. Over time, however, there was a move toward granting (and indeed often encouraging) joint legal custody of children, such that by the second wave of the National Survey of Families and Households (NSFH) in 1992-94, about half of divorced couples with children reported having joint legal custody (Seltzer 1998:139). Joint legal custody is far less common among couples who have births outside marriage. Also, reports of joint legal custody are lower in the Survey of Income and Program Participation than in the NSFH (see Nord and Zill 1996; Seltzer 1998:n. 9).

The actual award of physical custody—who the child lives with—has changed much more slowly than the trend toward joint legal custody. Using information on divorce cases in Wisconsin for the 1986-94 period, Cancian and Meyer (1998) examined physical custody of children after divorce and distinguished among cases in which custody was awarded solely to the mother, those in which custody was awarded solely to the father, or those in which custody was shared or split (with some children in the family living with the father and some with the mother). They found little change over time in fathers' being awarded sole custody: In about 10 percent of divorce cases throughout the period, physical custody was awarded solely to the father. CPS data also suggest that little change occurred in child custody between 1994 and 1998, although the CPS does not distinguish between sole and joint custody (Grall 2000). However, Cancian and Meyer show that over time the proportion of cases in which sole custody was awarded to the mother diminished from 80 percent to 74 percent as the proportion of cases resulting in shared physical custody between the mother and father grew. Between 1986-87 and 1992-94, the proportion of shared custody cases doubled, from 7 percent to 14 percent. These trends, if generalizable beyond Wisconsin, suggest increased father involvement in the lives of their children after divorce, with fathers serving not as sole custodians of their children but as greater participants in legal decisions (joint legal custody) and shared physical custody arrangements.

Cancian and Meyer (1998) also analyze the factors that predispose parents to agree on or to be awarded shared physical custody and sole father custody. Shared custody is more common among higher-income families and among divorcing couples who own their homes. Fathers are more likely to get custody (either shared or sole) when there are older children and the children are boys, raising interesting questions about when fathers become most involved after marital disruption and how much their involvement is a result of their own preferences, those of their former spouses, or those of their children.

Even when mothers have sole physical custody of children, there may be important differences in father involvement with children depending on whether legal decision-making authority is shared by fathers and mothers. Seltzer (1998) has found that fathers with joint legal custody see their children more often and have more overnight visits than do fathers who do not. They also pay more child support, although this relationship can be explained by other factors (e.g., fathers with joint legal custody have more income). These findings, combined with those of Cancian and Meyer (1998), suggest that although mothers much more often than fathers remain the main caregivers for children after couples separate, changes may be under way that are slowly increasing the involvement and interaction that fathers have with their children after divorce.

Contact Between Nonresident ● Fathers and Their Children

Although single-father families are increasing in number, they account for only a small percentage of families with children. Shared custody arrangements may be on the rise, but children still live with their unmarried mothers far more often than with their fathers. Fathers, then, often take the role of nonresident parent, both after divorce and when children are born to unmarried parents who do not live together. An important issue, therefore, is how much contact fathers have with children with whom they do not reside.

Early research suggested that parenting tends to be serial: Once a father leaves the relationship with the mother, he tends to lose contact with children from that relationship, especially as he remarries and gains step children in a new relationship (Furstenberg et al. 1983; Seltzer and Bianchi 1988). The father's contact with his children was found to diminish greatly with the amount of time since the family disruption, and many fathers were found to have little or no contact with children from previous marriages. More recent research is calling those earlier findings into question and suggests that either the situation is changing or the picture is far more complex than was previously thought, involving men's value of family, fertility in second relationships, and commitment to new relationships and to parenting.

Reports of contact between children and their nonresident fathers tend to vary by who is doing the reporting. For example, Seltzer (1991b), using information from custodial mothers in the NSFH, found that 30 percent of children had not seen their nonresident fathers in the past 12 months. Reports by fathers suggest that the figure is only 16 percent. Three in five fathers surveyed in the NSFH who did not reside with their children reported that they saw their children at least once per month, and a little less than half reported regular (weekly) telephone or letter contact with their children (Cooksey and Craig 1998).

Seltzer (1991b) found that different types of contact tend to be complements, not substitutes. Fathers who visit their children regularly also tend to telephone or write their children often and to pay child support. Cooksey and Craig (1998) note that distance matters greatly—visiting decreases the farther away fathers live from their children. Poor relations with the mother and lack of authority over child-rearing decisions also decrease a father's contact (Furstenberg 1995; Seltzer 1991b). Arendell (1992) has observed that fathers may purposefully absent themselves from their nonresident children's lives, especially in situations of high parental conflict. Some fathers report that they are not involved with their children not because they do not want to be with their children, but because they wish to reduce the tension and stress associated with visitation. Some fathers feel that their ex-wives and the courts have taken away their right to "parent" and have relegated them to the status of "visiting father." For these fathers, the only way to exercise some control over the situation is to stop visiting their children. And still other fathers report that it is too painful emotionally to interact with their children in their new status as "visiting father."

Fathers who form new families do not necessarily swap old families for new. Manning and Smock (1999) found that nonresident fathers who remarry or cohabit see their children as often as do those who do not form new unions. They also found that it is not the simple presence of new bio-logical children per se that reduces nonresident father contact; rather, it is the number of new children (particularly new biological children) that makes a difference.

Child Support Among Nonresident Fathers ●

Perhaps the most important issue for children not living with their fathers is whether or not the fathers remain committed to their children's financial support. Trends in child support payments suggest that efforts to improve collection of child support are increasing the likelihood that it is paid. How-ever, the shift toward single-parent families formed as a result of births out-side marriage rather than after divorce or separation complicates the collec-tion of child support. Child support awards are less often established in the case of nonmarital births, and payment is less often forthcoming from the absent parents. The issue of child support enforcement has received re-newed attention in the wake of welfare reform.

At the end of the 1970s, the U.S. Census Bureau began collecting system-atic national data on the receipt of child support by custodial mothers. The first collection, in 1979, showed that only about one-third of women with children under age 21 received any support for those children. Estimates using data collected in the early 1980s suggest that the potential for in-creased child support collection from reform efforts was substantial: In-stead of the $7 billion that was actually being collected in child support ob-ligations, the potential for collection was near $30 billion (Garfinkel and Oellerich 1989). Data showed that the problem was one of both establish-ment of awards and collection of awards. That is, in 1997 only about 60 per-cent of single mothers had informal child support agreements or court-ordered child support awards (Grall 2000:Table A). Among those who had awards, a large fraction either did not receive any payments (31 percent) or did not receive the full amount owed (an additional 27 percent; Grall 2000:Fig. 5).

Garfinkel, Meyer, and McLanahan (1998) have reviewed the steps taken to improve child support collection since the mid-1970s. In 1975, child sup-port legislation and enforcement was almost entirely left up to the states; since then, a series of federal laws have been enacted that are aimed at set-ting up a national child support enforcement bureaucracy or infrastructure, eliminating judicial discretion in setting award amounts, moving toward standard guidelines for setting amounts, increasing paternity establish-ment, and otherwise increasing compliance (for example, via mandatory withholding of child support obligations from wages; Garfinkel and McLanahan 1995:213). Although considerable progress has been made in shoring up the private transfer system, the changes are taking place very gradually, requiring assessment of progress over relatively long intervals (e.g., 10 to 15 years).

Hanson et al. (1996) have assessed trends in child support for the 1979 to 1990 period. On the surface, the trends do not seem to support an assessment of progress. The rate of establishing awards dropped between 1978 and 1989, from 57 percent to 50 percent among custodial families recently eligible for child support (Hanson et al. 1996:Table 1). Award amounts declined by 21 percent, and there was a parallel decline in the proportion of award amounts actually received by custodial parents over the 1978-89 period.

Why has the decline in awards and payments occurred when child support enforcement has been strengthening? First, Hanson et al. estimate that the decline in award rates was due primarily to a demographic shift—the increase in the proportion of new child support cases stemming from nonmarital births rather than divorce. Second, award rates declined due to the decrease in earnings of nonresident fathers. These two changes went hand in hand: Nonmarital births tended to occur to mothers and fathers who were younger and had lower earnings than parents who divorce. If shifts in the marital status of parents and earnings of absent fathers had not occurred, Hanson et al. (1996:Table 3) suggest, award rates would actually have increased a percentage point (rather than declining by 7 percentage points). With regard to declining award amounts in the 1980s, nonresident fathers' lower average earnings, fewer children per award, and the failure of courts to adjust award amounts upward for inflation explain the decline.[1] More recent data from the Current Population Survey indicate that these demographic shifts may still be having an effect—the proportion of mothers awarded child support did not change between 1993 and 1997, nor did the average amount of the award received (Grall 2000). However, of those mothers receiving child support, the proportion receiving the full amount increased by 30 percent.

The major factors explaining the decline in child support in the 1970s and 1980s despite improvements in enforcement—less marriage and declining wages of fathers—may well be linked (Wilson 1987). Meyer (1998) demonstrates that the effect of child support enforcement falls disproportionately on low-income fathers, those least able to comply. Oppenheimer et al. (1997) report that young men's increased difficulty in becoming established in the labor market in a secure job over the 1979-90 period resulted in considerable delay in marriage. This likely also contributed to young men's inability (or unwillingness) to take financial responsibility for the children they father outside marriage.

What explains why fathers who do not have low incomes and can afford to pay child support often do not fulfill their obligations to their children? Men form new families after their earlier relationships dissolve, and scholars have argued that men shift allegiances from their nonresidential children to their coresidential children when these new families are formed (Furstenberg 1995). Manning and Smock (2000) note that fathers do swap support of their children, but only when the trade-off is between new biological children residing with their fathers and existing nonresident biological children.

Married Fathers' Time • and Activities With Children

Although much of the "fatherhood" literature in recent decades has focused on fathers who are single parents or nonresident fathers, there is growing interest in what fathers do for their children when they are present, when they are married and living in two-parent families. How much does father involvement matter—for fathers themselves, their wives or partners, and their children? Is the father's role primarily one of financial provider, as suggested by some previous research (Furstenberg, Morgan, and Allison 1987)? Or do fathers also provide important caregiving to children in two-parent families?

Evidence suggests that married fathers do spend time caring for their children while mothers are at work (Casper 1997a) and that they have significantly increased the time they spend with children (Bianchi 2000). Figure 5.2 shows three direct measures of fathers' time with children from roughly comparable time diary studies in the United States conducted in the mid-1960s and the late 1990s. The three measures—time spent in which the main activity was a child-care activity, time when the main activity was something other than child care (say, cooking dinner) but a child-care activity (e.g., helping with homework) was also mentioned, and time when a parent reported doing any activity (child care or other) in the company of children—all show an upward trend for married fathers. In 1998, married fathers reported spending 3.8 hours per day with their children compared, with 2.8 hours per day in 1965.

● **Figure 5.2.** Change in Married Fathers' Hours of Child Care and Time With Children: 1965 and 1998

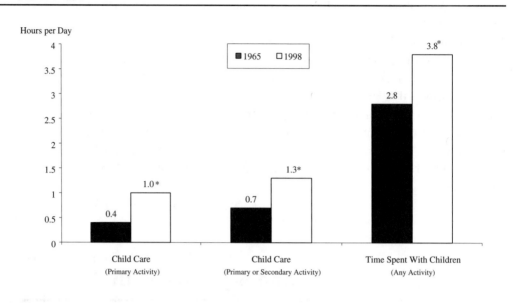

SOURCE: Bianchi (2000). Reprinted by permission.
NOTE: Estimates based on one-day, "yesterday" time diaries collected from 326 married fathers in 1965-1966 and 194 married fathers in 1998-1999, all with children under age 18 at the time of the interview. Child care includes child and baby care, helping/teaching children, talking/reading to children, indoor/outdoor play with children, and medical/travel/other child-related care.
*Test of 1965-1998 difference in means is statistically significant; $p < 0.05$.

Most interesting are the relative estimates of mothers' and fathers' time with children (see Figure 5.3). In 1965, the time fathers reported spending directly in child care (as a primary or secondary activity) was about one-fourth the time mothers estimated they spent with their children. By 1998, fathers' average child-care time was 55 percent of mothers' time. With respect to being in the company of children when they did activities, in 1965, married fathers had children with them about half the amount of time mothers did. By 1998, this figure had reached 65 percent of mothers' time. The change was not because mothers' time decreased—mothers' time held steady or increased, a topic we discuss in Chapter 8. Rather, fathers' reported time with children expanded faster than mothers' time, albeit from a low base in 1965.

The U.S. time diary data tend to be based on small samples, but the corroboration of these findings from several European countries is noteworthy (Joshi 1998; Niemi 1988). In addition, Sandberg and Hofferth (1999) have

● **Figure 5.3.** Ratio of Married Fathers' to Married Mothers' Hours With Children: 1965 and 1998

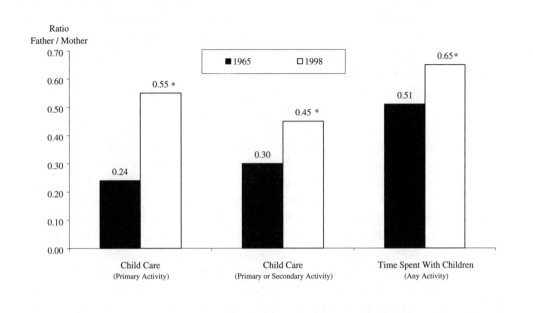

SOURCE: Bianchi (2000). Reprinted by permission.
NOTE: Estimates based on one-day, "yesterday" time diaries collected from 358 married mothers in 1965-66, 326 married fathers in 1965-66, 194 married mothers in 1998-99, and 141 married fathers in 1998-99. Ratios are averages across married men and women with children under age 18, not couples married to each other.
*Test of 1965-98 difference in means is statistically significant; $p < 0.05$.

reported parallel findings from time diaries with children: Despite changes in family structure (more single parenting) and maternal employment, the proportion of children's time spent with at least one parent changed little between 1981 and 1997. But in two-parent families, children's time with mothers and fathers rose sufficiently to more than counteract decreased time associated with increased maternal employment.

Fathers' and Mothers' Views ●
on Father Involvement

Much feminist research suggests that men's involvement in families is lacking and that more involvement is better for women (for a review, see Thompson and Walker 1989). For example, Kalmijn (1999) has found that involved fathers in the Netherlands have more stable marriages because their wives are happier. Similarly, Deutsch, Lozy, and Saxon (1993), using a convenience sample of dual-earner couples in Massachusetts and Connecticut, found that marital happiness was related to how satisfied people were with the parental division of child care and the level of fathers' involvement. Pleck (1997) has reviewed the literature on the consequences of father involvement with children for mothers and fathers and notes that, for mothers, father involvement affects satisfaction with marriage; the findings indicate both positive and negative effects, however, and Pleck argues that evidence in this area is mixed and incomplete. Some families also suggest a "credit-taking bias" in which both men and women report that they are more involved in child-care tasks than their spouses give them credit for.

Figure 5.4 shows the percentages of fathers and mothers who say that, ideally, both parents should be equally involved in disciplining children, playing with them, providing emotional support for them, monitoring their activities and friends, caring for them, and supporting them financially. In terms of ideal parental involvement, there is overwhelming consensus between men and women that parenting should be shared equally across most domains. More than 90 percent of men and women say the following four parenting domains should be shared equally: disciplining children, playing with them, providing emotional support for them, and monitoring their activities and friends. And about 70 percent of men and women say that caring for children's needs should be shared equally by mothers and fathers. The strongest gender difference to emerge concerns financial support of children: A higher proportion of mothers (about 66 percent) than fathers (61 percent) believe this parenting domain should be shared equally.

When we examine reports of actual parental involvement, however, mothers and fathers often disagree about fathers' contributions to child rearing (see Figure 5.5). Mothers are more likely than fathers to report that they, the mothers, are the main disciplinarians of their children (35 percent versus 4 percent), that it is mainly the mothers who play with the children (22 percent versus 10 percent), that the mothers provide the main emotional support to children (34 percent versus 19 percent), and that it is mainly the mothers who monitor their children's activities (32 percent versus 19 percent). More mothers than fathers believe that mothers are the main caretakers of children (63 percent versus 55 percent). Even with respect to the "male" domain of financial support, mothers see fathers as less involved than fathers see themselves: 54 percent of mothers see fathers as their families' main breadwinners, but 60 percent of fathers see themselves in this role. Overall, fathers are much more likely to hold the view that the

● **Figure 5.4.** Who Should Care for Children? Percentages Reporting Both Equally

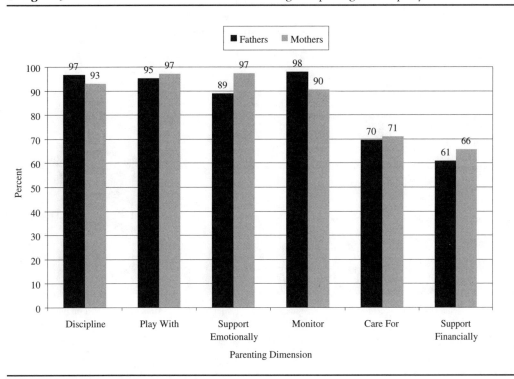

SOURCE: Milkie et al. (2000).

child-related domains mentioned above (other than financial support) are shared equally with their partners (data not shown). Mothers, on the other hand, are much more likely to hold the view that they are primarily the ones involved in rearing their children.

Milkie et al. (2000) show that the level of father involvement is correlated with other family functioning. Increased father involvement is significantly related to lower reported stress and feelings of success in balancing work and family among men and women. It also correlates with improvements in women's feelings of fairness in the household division of labor.

Conclusion ●

As American families have changed, so have the roles of fathers within their families. Increases in divorce and nonmarital births, the postponement of marriage, and increased life expectancy have increased the diversity of fa-

● **Figure 5.5.** Who Cares for Children, Mainly Moms or Mainly Dads?

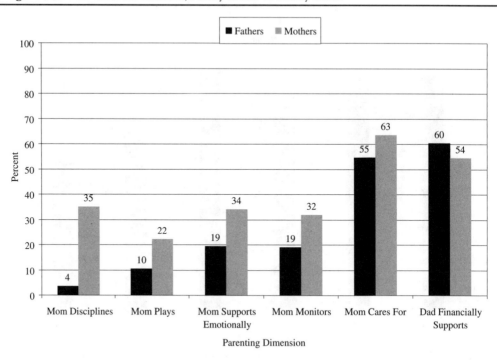

SOURCE: Milkie et al. (2000).

thers' roles. On the one hand, men now spend less of their adult lives as fathers of young children than in the past. On the other hand, they frequently live apart from their own biological children and help raise stepchildren. And even though single-father families are still a small proportion of all households in the United States, the numbers of such households increased rapidly in the 1990s, and they now account for about one in five single-parent families. Not only have the numbers of single-father families increased, but a growing share of divorced fathers have joint legal custody or shared physical custody of their children after divorce.

Fathers' interactions with their children depend in large part on whether or not they live with their children. Married fathers and fathers with sole custody are liable to have more interaction with their children than are nonresident fathers. However, some nonresident fathers are effectively coparenting with their children's mothers, just as some single fathers with sole custody receive parenting help from their unmarried partners and some married fathers play peripheral roles in their children's lives. Fathers' roles are further complicated by the fact that over their lifetimes, many fathers have more than one family, and they must juggle their time and resources among nonresident children, resident biological children, and stepchildren.

Mounting evidence suggests that even with the increased diversity of family circumstances, fathers are more involved and spending more time with their children than they did in the past. But the picture of increased father involvement must be tempered by the fact that more single-parent families involve biological parents who have never married. Unless they have physical or joint custody, never-married fathers often have tenuous connections to their children, and financial support from these fathers is often not forthcoming. When these fathers, many of whom have low earnings, do pay child support, it can exact a substantial toll on their economic well-being. The challenges these fathers face in trying to be "good fathers" have become increasingly apparent as efforts to enforce and increase child support collections and reform the welfare system have emerged on the national policy agenda.

Note

1. Interestingly, although the coefficient of mother's income on award rates and amounts is negative—suggesting that mother's increased earnings work against child support—these effects are small and nonsignificant. Although some researchers have reported that women's increased earnings may have hurt them in child support dispositions (Robins 1992), these findings have been disputed on methodological grounds (Graham 1995; Hanson et al. 1996). Consistent with past findings (Beller and Graham 1993), Hanson et al. (1996) report that women's increased labor force participation and earnings do not seem to be major factors in the decline in child support awards and amounts.

CHAPTER **6**

GRANDPARENTING

The most recent estimates indicate that there are 53 million grandparents in the United States and that about 70 percent of adults over age 50 are grandparents (Watson and Koblinsky 1997). Although the majority of Americans will experience the role of grandparent as they age, just how they carry out this role is likely to vary greatly. Grandparent-grandchild relations are embedded in societal, environmental, cultural, familial, and individual contexts that are interdependent and change over time (King, Russell, and Elder 1998). Because of differences in these contexts, grandparenting styles are diverse; they can range from extremely involved, as in the case of a grandparent raising a grandchild without the help of the child's parents, to very remote, as in the case of grandparents who live on the opposite coast from their grandchildren (Cherlin and Furstenberg 1985; Kivnick 1982; Neugarten and Weinstein 1964; Robertson 1977; Wood and Robertson 1976).

Since the 1940s, grandparents have often been portrayed as "rescuers" in family crises, stepping in to help out after wartime marriages dissolved due to death or divorce, or in times of economic crisis (Szinovacz 1998). More recently, increases in drug abuse, child abuse, teen and nonmarital births, divorce, the incidence of AIDS, and changes in welfare laws have presented families with new crises. The increased severity and prevalence of these crises has meant that more and more grandparents are raising their grandchildren on their own (Bryson and Casper 1999; Casper and Bryson 1998a). At the same time, increased longevity and continued preferences for noninstitutional living have meant that other grandparents are in need of care and assistance and may reside with their children and grandchildren for the help they can provide (Bryson and Casper 1999). These grandparents may be in need of assistance, but they may also be able to help out with child care, light household chores, and financial contributions, although they have much less responsibility in the rearing of their grandchildren than do grandparents who are raising their grandchildren alone.

A recent front-page feature in *USA Today* highlighted three families that included grandparents and described the circumstances through which each family came to be formed. Grandparents Tom and Pat Torkelson went to live with Tom's daughter and her husband after Pat was hospitalized for cardiac problems (Kasindorf 1999). The family is doing well financially and Mr. Torkelson works almost full-time to contribute. He enjoys a close relationship with his grandchildren, talking to them frequently and giving them advice. He also drives the youngest children to piano, dance, singing, and soccer practices. Mrs. Torkelson is home when the children get home from school and keeps an eye on them.

In contrast, Cora Stewart, a 63-year-old single grandmother in ill health, is raising her four grandchildren whose mothers could not raise them because of drug problems (Sharp 1999). The Stewart family survives on $250 a month in food stamps and $364 a month in welfare payments. For all intents and purposes, Mrs. Stewart acts as both mother and father to her grandchildren and is fully responsible for their upbringing.

The third family highlighted in the *USA Today* feature includes Mr. and Mrs. Gibson, their daughter, Amy, and their granddaughter, Nicole (El Nasser 1999). Amy Gibson got pregnant when she was 13 years old. Rather than give the baby up for adoption, the Gibsons raised their daughter and granddaughter together and say the two girls grew up more like sisters. The Gibsons are fairly well-off, and Mrs. Gibson quit her job to be home full-time with Nicole.

These stories not only illustrate the diversity of grandparent-grandchildren families and the different types of interactions grandparents and grandchildren can have, they highlight the unique processes through which each family was formed. These families were joined together by circumstances brought about by illness, drug abuse, and nonmarital childbearing, and they bear testimony to the resilience of the American family and its ability to cope with even the most severe crises. The diversity of these families also illustrates the blurring of the definition of family and of the traditional roles each member performs. In some of these families the parents are fulfilling their legal, moral, and social obligations to their children; in others, parents are sharing these responsibilities with the grandparents; and in still others, the grandparents have full responsibility.

Other demographic shifts, including improvements in life expectancy and declines in fertility and immigration, have altered opportunities for interaction between grandparents and grandchildren (Uhlenberg and Kirby 1998). Because more people are surviving to older ages, more children today will have the opportunity to establish relationships with several grandparents than was true in the past. And more grandparents will live long enough to have adult grandchildren.

We begin this chapter with a discussion of how basic demographic trends have changed the experience of grandparent-grandchild relationships over time. We then explore the different roles grandparents play in the lives of their grandchildren and the factors that lead to different grandparenting styles and grandparent-grandchild relationships. We also discuss the special role grandparents play in the lives of single mothers and fathers. Much of the current research on grandparenting has investigated families in which grandparents and grandchildren live together. The importance of examining the diversity of these families is underscored by the *USA Today* feature described above. In this chapter we use Current Population Survey (CPS) data to investigate the differences among these families and examine who they are and how they are doing.

How Has Grandparenthood ● Changed Over the Years?

Social and demographic shifts have altered the face of grandparenthood over the past century. Changes in mortality, fertility, and immigration can greatly affect how people experience the roles of grandparent and grandchild. In the past, when mortality was higher among adults, children and young adults were less likely than they are today to have living grandparents. Uhlenberg (1996) used life table techniques to estimate the proportion of people who, at various ages, would have had a living grandparent at the beginning and end of the 20th century. Less than one-fourth of infants born in 1900 would have had four living grandparents. By 2000, life expectancy among adults had improved to such an extent that more than two-thirds of newborns had all four grandparents alive. Only one-fifth of adults age 30 would have had any living grandparents in 1900, compared with more than three-fourths of those turning 30 in 2000. Many scholars have maintained that at the beginning of the 20th century very few grandparents were alive. Although it is true that children today are more likely to have living grandparents than were children in the past, even a century ago more than 90 percent of 10-year-old children had at least one living grandparent.

Throughout most of the century, the gender gap in mortality grew and the likelihood of having a living grandmother increased more rapidly than the probability of having a surviving grandfather, especially for young adults (Uhlenberg and Kirby 1998). These differences in mortality also mean that a larger proportion of living grandparents are grandmothers and that the vast majority of great-grandparents are female.

The number of grandchildren a grandparent can expect to have is affected by the level of fertility—higher fertility rates imply more grandchildren and lower fertility rates imply fewer grandchildren. The likelihood of being a grandparent is also affected by changes in childlessness and the timing of births within the population. Changing fertility patterns over the 20th century affected grandparenthood in three major ways (Uhlenberg and Kirby 1998). First, because of declining fertility, grandparents have fewer grandchildren today than they did in 1900. For example, it is estimated that a woman age 60 to 64 in 1900 would have had 12.1 grandchildren; a woman in the same age group in the 1990s would have had fewer than 6 grandchildren. Second, due to a decline in childlessness, a higher proportion of older Americans are grandparents than was true a century ago. Third, because of changes in the age at which women complete their childbearing, people today are less likely than they were in 1900 still to be raising their own children when they become grandparents. This is not to say that early childbearing today does not produce overlap in these roles for some people. For example, because childbearing occurs at younger ages for blacks and Hispanics, they are more likely than whites (or Asian Americans) to become grandparents while still raising their own children (Morgan 1996). Yet overall, as fertility declines for all groups, fewer people are likely to experience this overlap than in the past.

Record numbers of immigrants poured into the United States at the beginning of the 20th century before restrictive laws that limited immigration were passed in the 1920s. This meant that the children of immigrants typically lived in a different country than did their grandparents, and interaction between grandparents and grandchildren was infrequent. One-third of children under age 15 in 1900 had a parent who was born in another country, compared with one-fourth of children in that age group in the late 1990s (Uhlenberg and Kirby 1998).

Other social changes occurring throughout the 20th century were also important in transforming grandparenthood. The changing economic fortunes of the older population and improvements in health have meant that grandparents today have greater opportunities for more meaningful inter-action with their grandchildren. Today's grandparents are also likely to have more free time to spend with their grandchildren; they have more postretirement years and more years after they raise their own children to pursue relationships with their grandchildren. Prior to the 1960s, many documents portrayed grandparents interactions' with grandchildren in a negative light (Szinovacz 1998). Judging from the articles in *USA Today* de-scribed above, these views have diminished substantially.

Grandparenting •

Styles of grandparenting are defined in part by the extent of the con-nectedness between grandparents and their grandchildren. The degree of this connectedness is influenced by norms, roles, interactions, sentiments, and exchanges of support (Silverstein, Giarrusso, and Bengtson 1998). Bengtson and his colleagues suggest that intergenerational connectedness between grandparents and grandchildren must be measured along a num-ber of dimensions (Bengtson 2001; Bengtson and Schrader 1982; Mangen, Bengtson, and Landry 1988; Silverstein and Bengtson 1997). The degree of emotional closeness felt between grandparents and grandchildren and the degree to which they share beliefs and values affects connectedness. Closeness between the generations depends on structural factors that facili-tate interaction between the grandparents and grandchildren, such as geo-graphic distance and family structure. Grandparenting styles are affected by the number of activities grandparents and grandchildren share and how often they see each other. The extent to which grandparents and grandchil-dren receive assistance from each other is another important factor. And fi-nally, the degree to which grandparents and grandchildren have a sense of familial duty to each other and share family values affects grandparenting styles.

In general, very few normatively explicit expectations are placed on the role behavior of grandparents. However, American grandparents generally adhere to the norm of noninterference; that is, they believe that parents should be free to raise their children as they see fit (Cherlin and Furstenberg 1985, 1986). Yet most Americans also feel obligated to pro-vide assistance when close relatives are in need (Rossi and Rossi 1990). These two contrasting norms, along with variations in the six dimensions of grandparent-grandchild connectedness, help to explain why there is such broad diversity in grandparenting styles.

In one of the earliest studies on grandparenting, Neugarten and Weinstein (1964) used factors such as biologic continuity, emotional self-fulfillment, teaching, vicarious accomplishment, degree of formality, authority, contact, the transmission of family wisdom, and having fun to categorize the meaning of grandparenthood and the style of grandparenting. They identified the following types of grandparents: "formal," "funseeker," "surrogate parent," "reservoir of family wisdom," and "distant."

Cherlin and Furstenberg (1985, 1986), in one of the benchmark studies on grandparenthood, used nationally representative data to develop a typology of grandparenting styles based on the extent of exchange of services, the degree of parentlike behavior (authority), and frequency of contact. They labeled those who scored low on exchange of services, demonstrated little parentlike behavior, and had little contact with their grandchildren "detached" grandparents. "Passive" grandparents reported minimal exchange of services and little parentlike behavior, but had more frequent contact with their grandchildren. "Active" grandparents were those who exchanged services and/or had some parentlike influence in their grandchildren's lives. Cherlin and Furstenberg (1985) further categorized active grandparents as "supportive" (those scoring high only on exchange), "authoritative" (those scoring high only on authority), or "influential" (those scoring high in both areas). Using this typology, they found that 26 percent of the grandparents in their sample were detached, 29 percent were passive, 17 percent were supportive, 9 percent were authoritative, and 19 percent were influential. According to this typology, more than 70 percent of grandparents do not assume parentlike roles with their grandchildren. Thus, even though most grandparents have involvement with their grandchildren, the majority seem to adhere to the norm of noninterference.

In their study, Cherlin and Furstenberg (1985) also examined other differences across grandparenting styles. They found that detached and passive grandparents were much older than supportive and authoritative grandparents and that influential grandparents tended to be the youngest. They interpret this finding as evidence that grandparental activity levels are determined in part by the aging process. They also found that detached grandparents had less contact with and lived further away from their grandchildren than other grandparents. They suggest that because 63 percent of detached grandparents lived more than 100 miles from their grandchildren, geographic limitations may impede such grandparents from adopting more active roles. Cherlin and Furstenberg also found that about half of the passive, supportive, and authoritative grandparents saw their grandchildren at least once a week. Therefore, the degree of contact between grandparents and grandchildren was not necessarily indicative of whether grandparents had a passive or moderately active style of grandparenting. In contrast, influential grandparents lived very close to their grandchildren and had a very high degree of contact. In regard to this finding, Cherlin and Furstenberg note that near daily contact seems to be essential to a grandparent's maintaining an influential grandparenting style.

Although family rituals, such as special family recipes and dishes, jokes, common expressions, songs, and sharing special events, were common among all grandparents, detached grandparents were the least likely to acknowledge such rituals (Bengtson 2001; Cherlin and Furstenberg 1985). They were also the least likely to report that they had close or extremely close relationships with their grandchildren.

Styles of grandparenting are related to other factors as well, including gender, lineage (paternal or maternal relation), ages of grandparents and grandchildren and their relative ages, family structure, and race. (For a recent review of this literature, see Aldous 1995.) Studies have shown that grandmothers generally have closer relationships with their grandchildren than do grandfathers (Cherlin and Furstenberg 1986). Grandmothers also interact differently with grandchildren than do grandfathers; they are more likely to interact as caregivers, whereas grandfathers are more likely to interact as mentors (Eisenberg 1988).

Divorce and premarital fertility in the parental generation also affect grandparenting styles. Grandparents are more likely to assist the middle generation when daughters are single mothers (Aldous 1985; Eggebeen and Hogan 1990). In addition, when parents divorce, the mother usually retains custody and her parents tend to have greater access to the grandchild. Aldous (1995) suggests that one of the consequences of these customary custody arrangements is that grandparents are generally less important in the lives of their descendants in the male line. This may be particularly salient for black families, because single-mother families are more prevalent among blacks.

Yet even apart from single parenting, the intergenerational linkages between mothers and adult daughters tend to be somewhat stronger than those between mothers and sons (Silverstein and Bengtson 1997). This predisposes grandchildren to have more contact with maternal grandparents. Feelings of closeness are also stronger between adult children and mothers (Bengtson 2001; Silverstein and Bengtson 1997), further increasing the likelihood that grandmothers more than grandfathers will be influential in the lives of their grandchildren.

The ages of the grandparents and grandchildren also affect grandparenting styles. Younger grandparents are more likely to be involved with their grandchildren (Troll 1983), yet grandparents who are too young may not be prepared for the role of grandparent and may feel overburdened by the prospect of having to raise both their own children and their children's children (Burton and Bengtson 1985; Troll 1985). Older grandparents are more often detached or passive in their grandparenting styles. Research suggests that older grandparents often lack the energy to interact with their grandchildren (Burton and Dilworth-Anderson 1991). Grandchildren's ages also matter; grandparents tend to be more highly involved with young grandchildren and less involved with adolescent grandchildren (Troll 1983). In addition, whereas grandparents feel responsible for disciplining and advising younger grandchildren, they feel responsible for sharing wisdom with older grandchildren (Thomas 1989).

Research in the area of grandparent roles and grandparent-grandchild relationships has also focused on how historical and experiential events shape the way the grandparent role is enacted (Cherlin and Furstenberg 1986; Hagestad 1985). Children who grew up in cohesive families with affectionate parents exhibit stronger feelings of obligation as mature adults when they are enacting the grandparent role (Rossi and Rossi 1990). Childhood experiences with grandparents also influence how grandparents interact with their own grandchildren (King and Elder 1997). Also, relations between grandchildren and grandparents depend on current relations between grandchildren and their parents and, more important, on relations between their parents and grandparents (King and Elder 1995).

A few researchers have also investigated cultural differences in grandparenting styles. Young black adults tend to believe that grandparents should have a parental role in rearing grandchildren and that the boundary between parent and grandparent roles is malleable. In contrast, young white adults hold attitudes consistent with the norm of noninterference—grandparents should maintain contact, but leave the role of parenting to the parent (Kennedy 1990). Cherlin and Furstenberg (1985) report similar black-white differences with regard to the norm of noninterference. Sotomayor (1989) found that Mexican American grandparents believe they have an important function in helping to rear their grandchildren. Asian American families are more likely to reject the norm of noninterference; Kamo (1998) suggests that this may be explained in part by Confucian ethics, under which children belong to the entire extended family.

Grandparents and Single Parenting ●

The involvement of grandparents in the lives of their daughters (and sons) who become single parents is receiving increased attention with court cases over grandparents' visitation rights and welfare reform measures that highlight the responsibilities of (grand)parents whose teenage daughters become mothers. The 2000 Census even included a new set of questions, mandated as part of welfare reform, on grandparents' support of grandchildren to address this important issue.

Research suggests that grandparents increase the assistance they provide to their adult children after their children experience divorce (Hirshorn 1998). As in the case of the Gibsons in the *USA Today* article cited earlier, grandparents also frequently coparent or raise their grandchildren who are born into single-parent families. In these cases grandparents may provide child care, act as coparents or as surrogate parents, and help out with expenses.

Table 6.1 illustrates the importance of grandparents in mother-child families. In 1998, about 17 percent of unmarried mothers with children lived in the homes of their parents. These single mothers are likely to benefit from sharing residences with their parents; grandparents can help out by providing food and shelter, caring for their grandchildren, and providing parenting advice. The table also shows that the proportion of single mothers living with their parents is the highest for Hispanics (22 percent), followed by blacks (18 percent) and whites (15 percent). These findings provide further evidence that "distant grandparenting" and the norm of noninterference may be more prevalent among whites, perhaps in part because the higher economic status of white single-parent families, on average, means they less often require direct (grand)parental assistance. Grandparents also coreside with and provide support to sons who are single fathers. Data presented in Chapter 5 indicate that about 1 out of 10 single fathers lived with his children's grandparent(s) in 1998 (Table 5.1). Hagestad (1996) has used the expression "Family National Guard" to describe the ways in which elders, especially grandparents, provide assistance when necessary, and the living arrangement data are consistent with this notion of grandparents as a reserve to be called upon during times of need.

Living arrangements data such as those shown in Table 6.1 provide only a snapshot of grandparental assistance to single mothers and underestimate the proportion of single mothers who ever receive assistance from

TABLE 6.1 Coresidence With Parents and Receipt of Child Care in Single-Mother Families by Race (in percentages)

	Total	White	Black	Hispanic
Single mothers living with their parents	16.7	14.5	17.5	21.7
Preschoolers with grandparents as primary child-care providers[a]				
All preschoolers of employed mothers	16.3	14.1	22.1	22.4
With married mothers	13.5	12.1	18.0	19.5
With unmarried mothers	25.4	24.8	25.1	29.2

SOURCE: Data on single mothers living with parents are from the Current Population Survey, March supplement, 1998; data on preschoolers are from the Survey of Income and Program Participation, 1994.
NOTE: Race/ethnicity categories are white, non-Hispanic; black, non-Hispanic; and Hispanic.
a. Care provided while the mother was at work.

their parents during their years of single parenting. A much higher 36 percent of single mothers live at some point in their parents' homes (Bumpass and Raley 1995:Table 3). Coresidence with a parent is especially prevalent among black single mothers, 57 percent of whom have lived in their mothers' (and/or fathers') homes while raising children without their children's father present. Grandparent coresidence is especially likely in cases where there is a birth before marriage: 60 percent of white and 72 percent of black single mothers who had a child before marrying resided at some point with their parent(s).

Data from the Survey of Income and Program Participation give us an idea of another type of help grandparents provide to single parents: child care. In 1994, one-fourth of preschoolers with unmarried mothers had grandparents as primary child-care providers while their mothers worked, compared with only 14 percent of children with married mothers (see Table 6.1). Slightly more Hispanic preschoolers with unmarried mothers had grandparents as their primary care providers than did their black and white counterparts (29 percent, 25 percent, and 25 percent, respectively). Data also suggest that grandparents are more likely to provide primary care for their grandchildren when their children are never married than when they are divorced or separated (Casper 1997b:Table 2). Thus as single parenthood shifts toward women who have never married, grandparents may be providing financial and child-care assistance for increasing numbers of single mothers and their children (Ghosh, Easterlin, and Macunovich 1993).

Grandparent interaction with grandchildren in single-parent families blurs the boundaries of the traditional roles of parenthood and grandparenthood. To the extent that grandparent involvement substitutes for the nonresident parent's involvement or compensates for time and resources the single parent cannot give to children, single parents may experience different "degrees" of raising children alone and grandparents may experience different degrees of parenting and grandparenting.

Multigenerational Families ● With Grandparents

In the 1990s, amid the passage of the new welfare legislation and continued discussion of the decline of the family, grandparenting research shifted toward the examination of different kinds of households containing grandparents and grandchildren (Szinovacz 1998). The three types of grandparent-grandchild families depicted in the *USA Today* articles noted earlier provide a real-life example of the diversity of these families. The main structural difference among these families is that Mrs. Stewart and the Gibsons took their grandchildren into their homes and had primary responsibility for parenting them, whereas the Torkelsons moved in with their adult children and were supplemental caregivers for their grandchildren. These two household structures, with homes maintained by either the grandparents or the parents, imply different caregiving scenarios in which the roles of the grandparents vary enormously.

Researchers, public policy makers, and the media first began to notice the increases in grandparent-maintained households around 1990, prompting them to question why this was happening. An explosion of analytic research occurred in the early to mid-1990s that sought to answer this question and to examine further the area of grandparent caregiving in general (Burton 1992; Chalfie 1994; Dowdell 1995; Dressel and Barnhill 1994; Fuller-Thomson, Minkler, and Driver 1997; Jendrek 1994; Joslin and Brouard 1995; Minkler and Roe 1993; Rutrough and Ofstedal 1997; Shore and Hayslip 1994). These studies identified several explanations for the increase in the numbers of grandparents raising and helping to raise their grandchildren. Increasing drug abuse among parents, teen pregnancy, divorce, the rapid rise of single-parent households, mental and physical illnesses of parents, AIDS, crime, child abuse and neglect, and incarceration

● **Figure 6.1.** Grandchildren in Grandparents' Homes by Presence of Parents

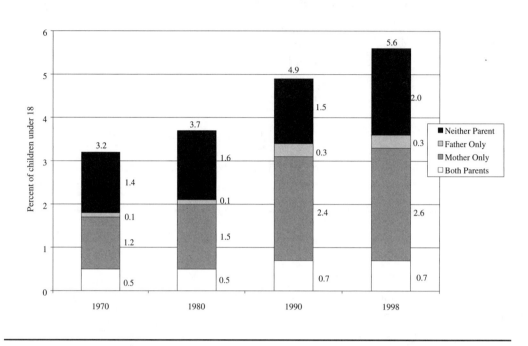

SOURCE: U.S. Census, 1970, 1980; Current Population Survey, March Supplements, 1990, 1998.

are a few of the most common explanations offered (for a review of these causes, see Minkler 1998).

CPS data for the 1990s confirm the researchers' impressions, showing that more grandparents were taking their children and grandchildren into their homes. In 1990, there were 2.1 million grandparent-maintained households in the United States, constituting 6.3 percent of all family households. By 1998, this number had increased to 2.6 million, representing 7.4 percent of all family households. The number of children residing with grandparents increased as well. Figure 6.1 shows that in 1970, 2.2 million or 3.2 percent of American children lived in households maintained by grandparents. By 1998, this number had risen to 4 million, or 5.6 percent. Thus the number of children living in their grandparents' homes increased by more than 80 percent over the 28-year period. Substantial increases occurred among all types of households maintained by grandparents, regardless of the presence or absence of the grandchildren's parents, but increases were greatest among children with only one parent in the household. The majority of change for most household types occurred in the decade of the 1980s. Although the proportion of children living *only* with their grandparents (i.e., no parent present) did not increase in the 1970s and 1980s, the greatest growth in the 1990s was registered in these skipped-generation living arrangements. This means that the 1990s was a decade marked by increasing numbers of grandparents with sole responsibility for raising their grandchildren.

Given the increase in this type of family, it is not surprising that the popular media began to focus attention on the growing number of children being raised by their grandparents (e.g., Culter 1991; Norris 1991). It wasn't long before federal lawmakers followed suit—both the Senate and the House of Representatives recognized that this trend constituted a pressing issue for public policy and held congressional hearings on the matter in 1992. The Senate hearings of the Special Committee on Aging focused on the causes of the trend (U.S. Senate 1992), whereas the House hearings, held by the Select Committee on Aging, examined the new roles and responsibilities of grandparents (U.S. House of Representatives 1992). Both sets of hearings also highlighted policy deficiencies in the areas of grandparents' rights and grandparents' access to public assistance. In January 1995, then-President Clinton signed a formal proclamation declaring 1995 the "Year of the Grandparent," recognizing the "extraordinary place that grandparents hold in our families and communities."

The recent increase in numbers of grandparents raising their grandchildren is particularly troubling because both these grandparents and their grandchildren often suffer significant health problems. Researchers have documented high rates of asthma, weakened immune systems, poor eating and sleeping patterns, physical disabilities, and hyperactivity among grandchildren being raised by their grandparents (Dowdell 1995; Minkler and Roe 1996; Shore and Hayslip 1994). Grandparents raising grandchildren also appear to be in poorer health than their counterparts; studies have noted high rates of depression, poor self-rated health, and multiple chronic health problems among grandparents raising their grandchildren (Dowdell 1995; Minkler and Roe 1993). For example, Minkler et al. (1997) found that grandparents raising grandchildren were twice as likely to be clinically depressed as were grandparents who play more traditional roles.

These families are also more likely than other kinds of families to experience economic hardship. A number of studies have focused on the economic well-being of grandparents and their grandchildren, documenting their disproportionately high poverty rates (Bryson and Casper 1999; Casper and

Bryson 1998a; Chalfie 1994; Fuller-Thomson et al. 1997; Rutrough and Ofstedal 1997).

At the other end of the spectrum are growing concerns for the well-being of adults who are taking their aging mothers and fathers into their homes and providing care for them, often at the same time they are raising children of their own. The demographic shifts discussed in Chapter 1—the extension of the life span, aging of the population, fewer children per family, increasing divorce and remarriage, and the delay in childbearing—have contributed to the sense of urgency in this matter. In this type of household, the flow of resources is usually from the parent to the grandparent. Grandparents in this situation may be more limited in the roles they can play in their grandchildren's lives. They are likely to be older and to have older grandchildren than grandparents who provide homes for their grandchildren. They are also more likely to have health problems (Bryson and Casper 1999).

Despite the trend toward independent living among older Americans, research has shown that many families who have older kin in frail health provide extraordinary care (Horowitz 1985; Stone, Cafferata, and Sangl 1987). Providing intensive care can have many negative consequences for caregivers, including increased stress and strained relationships (Semple 1992; Stommel et al. 1995). The level of stress in these households is also likely to affect how grandparents and grandchildren experience their relationships.

● Heterogeneity in Multigenerational Families With Grandparents

These two household structures—grandparent maintained and parent maintained—are but two broad examples of the types of multigenerational families that include grandparents. Allen, Bleiszner, and Roberto (2000), in a decade review article titled "Families in the Middle and Later Years: A Review and Critique of Research in the 1990s," emphasize the importance of researchers' taking into account detailed structural diversity in the study of families. All individuals do not follow the same life-course trajectories, nor do they experience all the possible life-course transitions. Differences in marriage, divorce, fertility, and cohabitation affect family structures, relationships, and processes in later life. Norms and culture also affect these processes and their outcomes. Different family structures imply very different caregiving scenarios. Although CPS data do not allow us to investigate caregiving behaviors directly, they document the diverse composition of families with grandparents and provide clues about the nature of relationships within them.

We distinguish nine family types spread across the two major types of multigenerational households: those in which the grandparent is the householder (owns or rents the home) and those in which a parent or parents of the grandchildren maintain the home. Characteristics of grandparents and grandchildren are likely to differ depending on whether the grandparent or parent maintains the home. Home ownership and the provision of shelter are indicative of the direction of the flow of support between the generations.

Other structural features are key to understanding the diversity of multigenerational grandparent households. For instance, in a grandparent-maintained household, is just one grandparent present, or are both present? If only one grandparent is present, is it the grandfather or the grandmother? Are both parents in the household as well? Similarly, does a given parent-maintained family include both parents or both grandparents? Family structure, including information on the number, marital statuses, and genders of the grandparents and parents, is key to understanding family relationships and processes and the types of problems different families are likely to encounter (Aldous 1995; Casper and Bryson 1998a; Cherlin and Furstenberg 1986; Hilton and Macari 1997). (For more detailed information regarding all of these multigenerational family types, see Bryson and Casper 1999.)

Which type of coresident grandparent family is most common? In the majority of these multigenerational families, the grandparents take in their children and grandchildren; three-fourths of households were of this type in 1997 (see Figure 6.2). The remaining families are maintained by a parent with a grandparent or grandparents living in the adult child's home. Approximately half of grandparent-maintained families have both a grandfather and a grandmother living with the grandchildren. Most of the others (43 percent of the total) are maintained by a single grandmother without a grandfather. Only 6 percent are maintained by a grandfather alone. In nearly one-third of the grandparent-maintained families, grandparents are living with their grandchildren without the children's parents. These families, in which grandparents are raising their grandchildren, are known as *skipped-generation families*.

In contrast, 70 percent of multigenerational parent-maintained families have only a grandmother, 17 percent only a grandfather, and 13 percent

● **Figure 6.2.** Families With Coresident Grandparents and Grandchildren: 1997

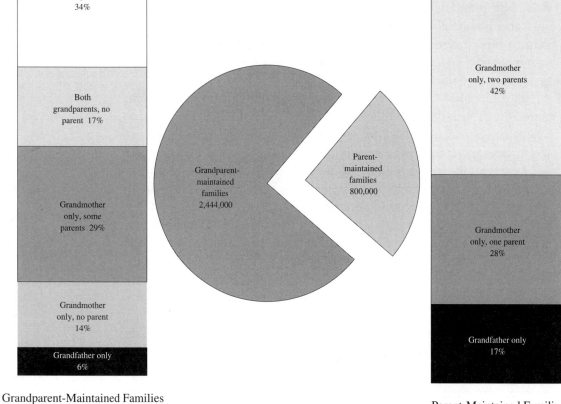

Grandparent-Maintained Families

Parent-Maintained Families

SOURCE: Bryson and Casper (1999).

have both a grandmother and a grandfather present. Of the parent-maintained families with grandmothers only, approximately three-fifths have both parents of the grandchildren present, whereas two-fifths have single parents present.

Characteristics of Grandparents ●
in Multigenerational Families

How many grandparents live with their grandchildren, and who are they? Nearly 4.7 million grandparents were living with their grandchildren in 1997. About four-fifths maintain the households in which the grandchildren live. The remainder live in households maintained by their children—the parents of the grandchildren. Almost two-thirds of coresident grandparents are grandmothers (Bryson and Casper 1999), and the proportions are similar for grandparents in grandparent-maintained (62 percent) and parent-maintained households (65 percent). One reason coresident grandmothers are more common than grandfathers in multigenerational families is the higher mortality of men. Because women live longer, they are more likely to reach ages where they have grandchildren.

There are more grandmothers in parent-maintained families because grandmothers often live long enough to be in frail health and have no surviving spouses to care for them. Thus some of these grandmothers may want to live with their children and grandchildren for the companionship or for the assistance they can provide. Women are more likely to be widowed and less likely to remarry after the death of a spouse. Older single women are also more likely to be poor than are older single men and may be more likely to live with their children to be able to pool economic resources.

Caregiving norms also come into play and help explain why there are so many more grandmothers than grandfathers maintaining multigenerational households. Studies have shown that a disproportionate share of caregiving responsibilities for grandchildren as well as for elderly parents are assumed by women (Dwyer and Coward 1991; Eisenberg 1988). Grandmothers who are divorced or may have never married are more likely to have raised their children and maintained close ties to them during adulthood; this, coupled with the fact that women are more likely to be caregivers, results in stronger links between grandmothers and their children and grandchildren. Bengtson (2001) shows that only 7 percent of mother-adult child bonds are "detached"—that is, characterized by low levels of closeness, contact, or exchange of help. By contrast, 27 percent of father-adult child bonds can be characterized as detached. Almost one-third of mother-adult child bonds can be characterized as close-knit, compared with only one-fifth of father-adult child bonds.

● **Figure 6.3.** Characteristics of Grandparents in Multigenerational Households: 1997

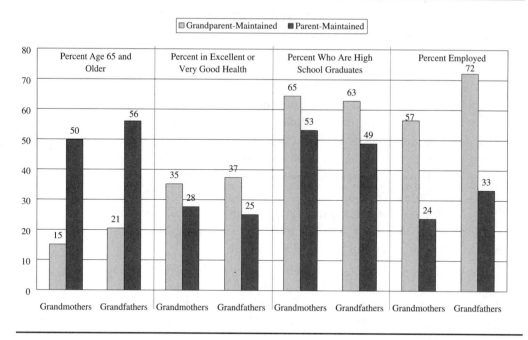

SOURCE: Current Population Survey, March supplement, 1997.

As one might expect, both grandmothers and grandfathers who maintain homes for their grandchildren are younger and in better health than those who live in their children's homes. For example, in grandparent-maintained households only 15 percent of the grandmothers and 21 percent of the grandfathers are age 65 or older (see Figure 6.3). This contrasts sharply with those in parent-maintained households, where roughly half of the grandmothers and grandfathers are age 65 or older (50 percent and 56 percent, respectively). Also, both grandmothers and grandfathers in grandparent-maintained families are more often reported to be in "excellent" or "very good" health than are those in parent-maintained households.

Given the large age differences between grandparents in the two types of households, it is remarkable that there is not a greater difference in their health status. However, a closer look indicates that grandparents in certain types of multigenerational families are not doing so well. More than 40 percent of single grandfathers are in fair or poor health (Bryson and Casper 1999). Similarly, single grandmothers raising their grandchildren and those living in the homes of their single children are often in poorer health—about half have fair or poor health.

Grandparents who maintain multigenerational homes are more likely than those who live in their children's homes to have at least a high school education. Levels of high school completion have risen continuously over the past decades, and grandparents who maintain their own households are younger, and hence better educated, than their older counterparts who are living in their children's homes. Similarly, about one-fourth of grandparents who maintain multigenerational homes have at least some college, compared with less than 15 percent of those living in their children's homes (data not shown).

Grandparents maintaining multigenerational households are also more likely to be in the labor force: 72 percent of grandfathers and 57 percent of grandmothers in grandparent-maintained households are employed, compared with only 33 percent of grandfathers and 24 percent of grandmothers in parent-maintained households. This again is in part because grandparents in grandparent-maintained families tend to be younger and therefore are less likely to have reached retirement age. Grandparents who maintain homes for their grandchildren are also about twice as likely as those living in their children's homes to be working full-time and year-round (data not shown).

Parent-maintained families with both dependent children and dependent grandparents have been referred to as "sandwich" families because the parents in these families provide economic support for both their children and their parents who live with them. If the grandparent is elderly or in poor health, the parent may also be providing physical care for both the grandparent and the children (Dressel 1996). Thus parents in this type of coresident grandparent family are sandwiched between the competing demands of their parents and their children. These findings indicate that although grandparents in parent-maintained households are older, in poorer health, and not as likely to be employed as grandparents in grandparent-maintained families, many are neither elderly nor in poor health, and a sizable minority are, in fact, working. Many of these grandparents are capable of playing an active role in the family, contributing to the family income, and perhaps providing child care for their grandchildren while the parents work. To be sure, some of these families find themselves juggling competing caregiving and financial demands, but the evidence suggests that the number of such families may be overstated.

● Economic Well-Being of Grandparents in Multigenerational Families

Family structure is especially important to any examination of the economic well-being of multigenerational families with grandparents. Two components of family structure help to determine a family's economic status: the total income of the family and the ratio of dependents to earners in the family. The number of adult members in the family and each member's age, gender, marital status, and labor force status influence both of these components. Each of these characteristics is related to family structure (Casper, McLanahan, and Garfinkel 1994; McLanahan, Casper, and Sørensen 1995). For example, the more adult earners in the family, the more income the family is likely to have, all else being equal. Also, the more dependent children or grandparents (nonearners) in the family, the more people there are to support. In general, men earn more than women. On average, then, households with grandfathers and/or fathers do better financially than those with only grandmothers and mothers.

A key indicator of economic well-being, particularly for families that include children, is the likelihood that the family resides in poverty. Single mothers more often find themselves getting the short end of the financial stick, and single grandmothers are no exception. All coresident grandmothers are about twice as likely to be poor as are all coresident grandfathers (21 percent compared with 12 percent). As Figure 6.4 shows, single coresident grandmothers are especially likely to suffer economic hardship, except when they are living in homes maintained by both parents of the grandchildren. Among single grandmothers who maintain households for their grandchildren, more than one-fourth are poor if one or both parents live there and almost 60 percent are poor if no parent lives in their home. Among single grandmothers living in homes maintained by their children, one-fourth are poor if only one parent (generally the mother) of the grandchildren is present. In contrast, only 5 percent of single grandmothers who live in homes maintained by both parents of the grandchildren live in poverty.

The three family types most likely to have incomes below the poverty level—single-grandmother-maintained households with and without parents present and households maintained by one parent with only the grandmother present—have in common that they do not have grandfathers present. They usually do not have the fathers of the grandchildren present, either. In 85 percent of parent-maintained, grandmother-only, one-parent-present families, the mother is that parent. Also in 78 percent of grand-

● **Figure 6.4.** Percentage of Grandparents in Multigenerational Families Who Are Poor: 1997

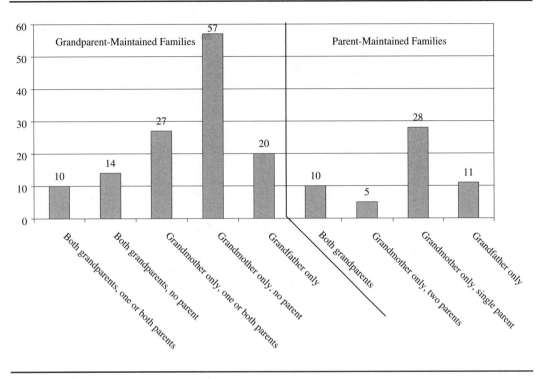

SOURCE: Current Population Survey, March supplements, 1997.

mother-maintained families with some parents present, the mother is the only parent present. Thus the vast majority of these families do not include fathers. Note that the grandmothers are even more likely to be poor if neither the parent of the grandchild nor a grandfather is present. Because men are more likely to be in the labor force and tend to earn more than women, the absence of grandfathers in all of these families, and of fathers in most of the families—that is, the absence of a male breadwinner—is reflected in the high percentage of grandmothers who are poor.

Racial Differences in Multigenerational ●
Families With Grandparents

Poverty among grandparents, particularly grandmothers, also varies by race. The three multigenerational family types that are most likely to be poor are also the most likely to have black grandmothers (data not shown).

Black grandmothers are more commonly found in living arrangements with no spouse present. This is due in part to differences in the union formation and dissolution patterns and fertility behavior of blacks as well as to the higher mortality and incarceration rates of black men.

Racial differences in family formation and mortality are also evident in the living arrangements of grandchildren in multigenerational families. The majority of children in multigenerational families live in their grandparents' homes (72 percent), with black grandchildren (86 percent) more likely than white (72 percent) or Hispanic (65 percent) grandchildren to be in grandparent-maintained rather than parent-maintained multigenerational homes. About one-fourth of the children living with grandparents do not have their parents living with them and are, in effect, being raised by their grandparents. A higher proportion of black grandchildren (about one-third) than white or Hispanic grandchildren (about one-fifth) are in this situation.

Table 6.2 displays the percentages of grandchildren in each of the nine types of multigenerational families. White and Hispanic grandchildren are much more likely to live in their grandparents' homes with both grandparents and at least one parent (about 27 percent each) than are black grandchildren (14 percent). In contrast, black grandchildren are much more likely to live in their grandmother's home with a parent (34 percent) than are white grandchildren (18 percent) or Hispanic grandchildren (15 percent). And black grandchildren are 2.5 times more likely than Hispanic grandchildren and 4 times more likely than white grandchildren to live in their grandmother's home without a parent. Within their parent's home, most white and Hispanic grandchildren live with a grandmother and both parents, whereas most black grandchildren live with a grandmother and a mother only.

● Economic Well-Being of Grandchildren in Multigenerational Families

Different family structures not only have implications for the poverty of grandparents, they also affect the economic well-being of the grandchildren living in them. How do grandchildren in different multigenerational families fare compared with the national average? Grandchildren in multigenerational families are more likely to be poor—one in five children in the United States lives in a poor family, compared with about one in four coresident grandchildren. Grandchildren in homes maintained by their

TABLE 6.2 Grandchildren Living With Grandparents by Type of Family and Race: 1997

	All Coresident Grandparent Families		Grandparent-Maintained Families						Parent-Maintained Families				
	No.	%	Total	Both Grandparents/ Some Parents	Both Grandparents/ No Parent	Grandmother Only/Some Parents	Grandmother Only/No Parent	Grandfather Only	Total	Both Grandparents	Grandmother Only/Two Parents	Grandmother Only/One Parent	Grandfather Only
Number of grandchildren	5,435		3,894	1,241	598	1,144	669	242	1,541	246	630	396	269
Percentages by race													
White	2,310	100.0	71.5	27.8	15.0	17.6	5.6	5.5	28.4	4.1	13.4	4.6	6.4
Black	1,636	100.0	85.5	14.3	8.2	34.0	25.6	3.5	14.3	0.5	3.0	9.9	1.0
Hispanic	989	100.0	65.0	26.3	9.2	14.5	9.9	5.0	35.2	5.0	13.6	9.5	7.2

SOURCE: Current Population Survey, March supplement, 1997.
NOTE: Numbers are in thousands. Race/ethnicity categories are white, non-Hispanic; black, non-Hispanic; and Hispanic.

171

● **Figure 6.5.** Percentages of Children in Different Living Arrangements Who Are in Poverty, Without Health Insurance, and Receiving Public Assistance: 1997

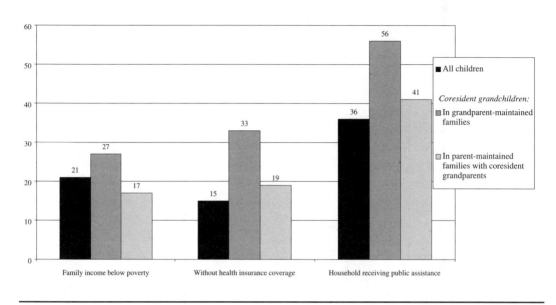

SOURCE: Bryson and Casper (1999).

parents are a little less likely than average to be poor, whereas grandchildren in homes maintained by their grandparents are much more likely to be poor (see Figure 6.5).

Children in multigenerational families that do not contain grandfathers and/or fathers fare the worst. Grandchildren being raised by their grandmothers, for example, are the most likely to be poor—63 percent live in families with incomes below the poverty line. In parent-maintained families, 39 percent of children living with a grandmother only and one parent (usually the mother) are poor (data not shown).

Why are grandmother-only and mother-only families so much more likely to be poor? One reason is that these families have fewer earners. For children in homes maintained by a single grandmother with no parent, 44 percent have no earners in the household, compared with only 14 percent in all other grandparent-maintained family types (Bryson and Casper 1999). Similarly, 15 percent of the grandchildren in single-parent homes with a grandmother only (and no grandfather) have no earners. But if the home is maintained by two parents with a lone grandmother present, almost all have at least one earner.

Figure 6.5 also shows that grandchildren who live in their grandparents' homes are more likely than other children to be without health insurance.

Overall, approximately one child in seven (15 percent) has no health insurance. Grandchildren in parent-maintained households fare better than those in grandparent-maintained households. In parent-maintained homes, 19 percent of grandchildren have no health insurance, but in grandparent-maintained homes, fully one-third (33 percent) have no health insurance. Grandchildren living in homes maintained by both grandparents without a parent are the most likely to be without health insurance—fully one-half are not covered (data not shown).

One of the reasons grandchildren in parent-maintained homes are more likely to have health insurance is that their families are better able to obtain private insurance (Bryson and Casper 1999). Because there are more earners in parent-maintained households, the likelihood of these families' having access to employer-based insurance is greater. Most private health insurance is purchased through group plans offered by employers, and policy holders may have difficulty obtaining coverage for family members other than spouses and children. Particularly in grandparent-maintained households without any parents present, grandparents may have problems securing private health insurance if they do not have legal custody of their grandchildren. In fact, in the absence of parents, grandchildren who live with their grandparents are more likely to have public health insurance (usually Medicaid) or no health insurance at all. In 1996, 40 percent had only public health insurance and 44 percent had no health insurance at all (Bryson and Casper 1999).

Figure 6.5 also shows that grandchildren in grandparent-maintained families are more likely than other children to live in households that receive public assistance. About 52 percent of coresident grandchildren lived in households that receive public assistance, compared with 36 percent of all children under 18 years of age. Grandchildren in parent-maintained households are less likely (41 percent) to receive public assistance than are grandchildren in grandparent-maintained homes (56 percent). As one would expect, the family type most likely to be getting public assistance is the same as the type that is most likely to be poor—grandmother-maintained homes without any parents present. In households of this family type, 84 percent of grandchildren are receiving some public assistance.[1]

Conclusion •

Demographic and social changes have radically altered the meaning of grandparenthood over the years. Compared with a century ago, more children have living grandparents, and more people live long enough to become grandparents. Increases in premarital births and divorce have created more single-parent families in need of assistance from grandparents. Increases in the incidence of AIDS, drug abuse, child abuse, and incarceration have led many grandparents to assume primary responsibility for the care of their grandchildren. At the same time, declining mortality has increased the numbers of grandparents who are likely to depend on their children and grandchildren for assistance.

All of these factors have contributed to immense heterogeneity in grandparenting styles and types of multigenerational households with grandparents. Some grandparents take very active roles in the lives of their grandchildren by raising them when the parents are unable or unwilling to do so. Other grandparents take a more hands-off approach but still interact frequently with their grandchildren. Still others live so far away from their grandchildren that maintaining involved relationships with them is nearly impossible. Some multigenerational homes are maintained by grandparents and some by parents. Some have a parent in the home and some do not. Differences in these household structures imply different caregiving scenarios. They also imply differential flows of resources that affect the economic well-being of the grandparents and grandchildren living in them.

As the number of multigenerational households with grandparents increases, the traditional roles of grandparent and parent become harder to define. Continued increases in the numbers of the elderly and high levels of premarital childbearing portend continued increases in multigenerational families with grandparents. As these events unfold, grandparents and parents will need to adapt to new, if somewhat ambiguous, roles.

Bengtson (2001) has recently hypothesized that for many Americans, as life expectancy increases and families undergo change, relationships across generations are becoming increasingly important, perhaps even more important than nuclear family ties. The increase in the numbers of grandparents raising children without parents present may be but one extreme manifestation of the private "safety net" that extended families continue to provide in U.S. society. Grandparents are an important part of the "latent matrix" of kin connections (Riley and Riley 1993) that often sustains grandchildren and their parents in times of need and helps weave the network that supports family members over the life course.

Note

1. In an earlier study that examined grandchildren's well-being in grandparent-maintained families, Casper and Bryson (1998a) used multivariate techniques to establish whether family type is significantly related to poverty status, health insurance coverage, and receipt of public assistance when other socioeconomic and demographic variables are taken into account. The relationship of family type to the three grandchildren's outcome variables persisted when the researchers controlled for these socioeconomic and demographic characteristics.

CHAPTER 7

CHILD CARE

In December 1992, Americans watched in disgust as David and Sharon Schoo were arrested when they returned home from a 10-day trip to sunny Acapulco. Their crime? Leaving their daughters, Diana, age 4, and Nicole, age 9, to spend Christmas in snowy Chicago alone, without adult supervision. Then in 1997, America was riveted to the "British nanny trial"—the case of Louise Woodward, an au pair accused of killing 8-month-old Matthew Eappen while he was under her care. These two cases and others like them have led mothers and fathers, researchers, policy makers, and concerned citizens to ask, Who is caring for America's children?

Many of the newspaper articles written about child care in the 1980s were also sensationalized accounts of the maltreatment of children. But something in the tone of such articles changed over the next two decades: the public perception of accountability and who is at fault. As people began pointing fingers at parents themselves, the ethics of parenting choices took center stage. Newspaper articles described the verbal battering Mrs. Eappen received and the way some observers called her morality into question because she left her child in the care of a 19-year-old au pair while she pursued her career as a doctor. Stay-at-home mothers began to criticize employed mothers for neglecting their children, and employed mothers disparaged stay-at-home mothers for getting "some sort of retro free ride" (Thompson 1998). Such exchanges came to be known in the media as the "mommy wars."

For many parents the choices are not as simple as the media image of the mommy wars would suggest. Families must take into consideration several factors when deciding who in the family should work for pay and what type of child care to use to substitute for parents' time with children. They must consider financial constraints, career aspirations, and the quality, cost, and availability of child care. Tracy Thompson (1998) has illustrated these complicated and sometimes agonizing decisions in a recent *Washington Post Magazine* article in which she describes the employment/child-care choices of several new mothers. As the families Thompson writes about took into account their own desires and constraints, their choices varied radically—one mother chose self-employment; another chose to return to her job and work different hours from those her husband works, so he could care for the children; yet another chose to put her career on hold and accept the consequential material sacrifices.

Some parents need other people to care for their children so that they can work or pursue other activities outside the home, whereas others place their children in child-care situations principally for the educational and developmental benefits these provide children. The growth in mothers' labor force participation over the past few decades has augmented the need for child care while parents are at work. Although the increase in employment among married mothers with young children has slowed recently, with the passage of the Personal Responsibility and Work Opportunity Reconciliation Act (PRWORA) of 1996 and the booming economy of the late 1990s, poor mothers, most of whom are single, increased their labor force participation. Low-income mothers will require care for their children as they transition from welfare to work, further increasing the demand for child care. Parents have also increasingly sought out "quality" child care for the purpose of promoting the social, emotional, and cognitive development of their children. As a consequence of these changing employment patterns and societal norms, today unprecedented numbers of children are being cared for by someone other than their mothers or fathers for at least some hours each week.

Children often have more than one regular child-care arrangement, spend many hours in nonparental care, and sometimes care for themselves when parents are not available. Changes in how American families care for their children arouse public concern for children's well-being, including their safety, education, and social, psychological, and emotional development. In the 1970s, debates about child care centered primarily on how child-care availability affects parental employment. In the early to mid-1980s, the focus shifted somewhat, to the consequences of nonparental care for children. Debates ensuing in the late 1980s more clearly defined the key issues, among which were the following: the inability of some families to obtain affordable child care when they needed it, which prevented them from working outside of the home and often curtailed labor force participation of parents, particularly mothers; the poor quality of some child-care programs; the difficulty of attracting and keeping good child-care providers in the field; and the roles federal, state, and local governments should play in resolving these issues. Thus the national policy debate on child care has identified three areas of concern: accessibility, affordability, and quality. In 1991, Hofferth and Phillips suggested that the crux of the issue is the conflict between price and quality:

> Employed mothers, whose salaries are generally modest, need care that is low enough in cost to make their employment profitable. Providers need to make enough money to remain economically viable and to attract people who are committed to providing high quality, stable care for children. Children need the highest quality of care possible. To promote maternal employment (particularly among low-income welfare mothers), the price of child care needs to be moderate. To promote the development of children, the quality of care needs to be improved, which is likely to raise its cost substantially. (p. 5)

The problem is not so much an inadequate supply of child care per se, but rather a mismatch between the availability of the type and quality of care that parents desire at a price they can afford.

In this chapter, we review the trends in the need for child care and in child-care usage. We then discuss the factors that are important in parents' choices among child-care options. For instance, a family with a homemaker parent may be more likely to choose a child-care arrangement with a strong educational component because the parents may use child care primarily as an enrichment activity, whereas the parents in a dual-earner, two-parent family must consider whether an arrangement fits their combined work schedules. Care arrangements also vary substantially by the age of the child, both because children's developmental needs change as they get older and because older children do not need care when they are in school. We use the most current data available to examine the child-care arrangements for all children, regardless of whether their parents work. We close the chapter with a discussion of how child care affects children's well-being.

● Growth in Nonparental Child Care

The numbers and ages of children, mothers' labor force participation, and parents' desire to enhance their children's development are key factors determining the demand or need for child care (Hofferth 1992). Between 1978 and 1988, the potential demand for child care grew steadily over time, as the total number of American children under age 15 grew by almost 17 percent, from 51 to 59 million. The growth rates were almost three times greater for preschool-age children than for grade school-age children—29 percent for children under 5 years old compared with 11 percent for children 5 to 14.

Much of the research on child care has used the increase in mothers' labor force participation as the backdrop, not because child care is solely a mother's responsibility, but because mothers more so than fathers take responsibility for care of children and because it is mothers' rather than fathers' labor force behavior that has changed dramatically in recent decades. Figure 7.1 shows the growth from 1978 to 1998 in the proportion of children whose mothers were employed. The largest increases were for children whose mothers worked full-time, although the proportion of children with mothers who worked part-time also increased over this period. By 1998, about 29 percent of all preschoolers had mothers employed full-time, up from 19 percent in 1978. Among school-age children, the proportion with mothers employed full-time increased from 27 percent to 38 percent. In addition, about one-fifth of each age group of children had mothers employed part-time in 1998.

PRWORA, the welfare reform legislation enacted into law in August 1996, incorporated more stringent guidelines for work participation and required a larger proportion of welfare parents, most of whom are single mothers, to obtain employment or participate in work-related activities than had its predecessor, the Family Support Act of 1988. Although growth in the labor force participation of children's mothers overall has slowed over the past decade, since 1995 the increase among children with poor mothers has accelerated. For example, 22 percent of poor preschoolers had employed mothers in 1995, compared with 26 percent in 1998 (see Figure 7.2). In contrast, no increase in employment occurred over this period for nonpoor mothers of preschoolers. Similarly, employment among poor elementary school-age children's mothers rose from 27 percent to 33 percent between 1995 to 1998, whereas among the nonpoor the rate was constant.

● Figure 7.1. Children Ages 0 to 14 by Age of Child and Labor Force Status of Mother: 1978-1998

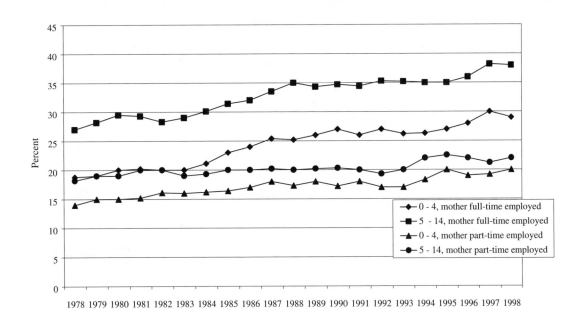

SOURCE: Current Population Survey, March supplements, 1978-1998.

Evidence suggests that the rapid rise in the proportion of children with employed mothers is only part of the story, as more and more parents, regardless of their labor force participation, enroll their children in child-care programs with educational components. Current Population Survey (CPS) data show that, overall, nursery school/preschool enrollment for children ages 3 and 4 increased from about 500,000 in 1965 to about 4.5 million by 1997. This represents a ninefold increase in the number of children enrolled over the period. The increased enrollment rate—from 5 percent in 1965 to 48 percent in 1997—reflected a shift in the societal norm toward early childhood education, with more parents desiring a "school-like" experience for their children before their children entered kindergarten (Bianchi 2000; Martinez and Day 1999).

Nursery school enrollment increased as rapidly among children with homemaker mothers as among those with working mothers. Between 1967 and 1998, the proportion of children ages 3 to 5 of homemaker mothers who were enrolled in nursery schools jumped from 5 percent to 43 percent (see Figure 7.3). The comparable increase for children of mothers who

● **Figure 7.2.** Children Ages 0 to 14 Whose Mothers Are in the Labor Force by Age and Poverty Status: 1978-1998

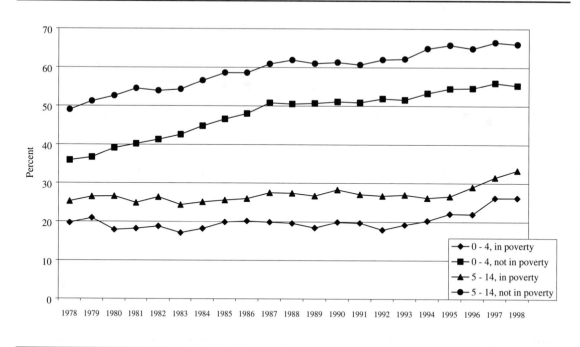

SOURCE: Current Population Survey, March supplements, 1978-1998.

were in the labor force was from 8 percent to 52 percent. The increased preprimary school enrollment rates for both groups of children suggest that the educational component of child care is an important consideration for all families regardless of the employment status of mothers.

Given the increase in the demand for child care, what has been the response in terms of the supply of child care? Using data from the Profile of Child Care Settings Study and the National Child Care Study, Hofferth (1992) has estimated that in total there were about 80,000 child-care programs serving preschool-age children in the United States in 1990, about three times as many as there were in the mid-1970s. Child-care programs may be federally funded, as is Head Start, or may be run as nonprofit businesses or for-profit businesses. Some programs are run by employers for employees who are parents, and some are run as part of community organizations, such as charities or churches. Data from the Census of Service Industries indicate that the number of incorporated child-care centers more than doubled, from fewer than 25,000 to more than 50,000, between 1977

● **Figure 7.3.** Preprimary Enrollment Status and Attendance for Children Ages 3 to 5 by Labor Force Status of Mother: Selected Years

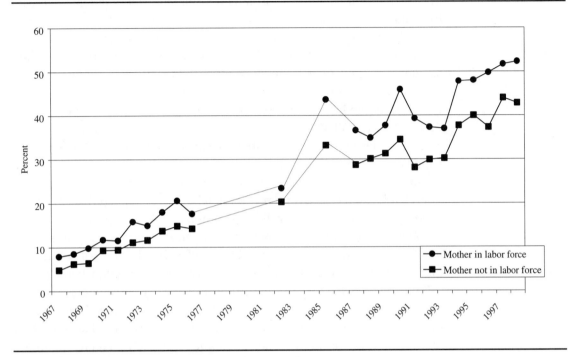

SOURCE: Current Population Survey, October supplements, 1967-1998.

and 1992 (Casper and O'Connell 1998a). The number of for-profit centers grew from 14,000 to more than 35,000, whereas the number of nonprofit centers grew from fewer than 11,000 to almost 16,000. In 1997, there were 17,000 Head Start centers; this number remained relatively constant through the 1990s (Head Start Bureau 1998).

Another source of child care is family day care, in which a provider cares for more than one child in the provider's home. In 1990, the number of family day-care providers in the United States was estimated to be between 668,000 and 1.2 million (Hofferth 1992). The number of regulated family day-care homes has increased since the mid-1970s, but not by as much as the number of day-care centers (Hofferth and Kisker 1994).

Relatives, including grandparents, aunts and uncles, and older siblings, are also an important source of child care (Casper 1996; Presser 1989a). In addition, when one parent cannot be with a child because of work obligations or other activities, the other parent frequently steps in (Casper 1997a; Presser 1988). Estimation at the national level of the number of relatives who could serve as care providers is difficult, because one needs to know the number of relatives as well as their availability and willingness to care for children. As the labor force participation of women has risen over time, fewer female relatives are available to care for other relatives' children because they are more often employed (Presser 1989a, 1989b). Families are smaller today and are more likely to move than in the past, further decreasing the number of potential caregivers who live nearby. Over time, the increase in mother-only families is likely to have decreased the supply of fathers who are available to provide care during the mother's working hours. Together, these factors suggest that the supply of care by relatives has declined over time.

Given the increase in the demand for child care and in the supply of nonrelative child care over time, one might expect that child-care choices have changed over time as well. For example, does the large increase in the number of day-care centers mean that parents are more likely to choose that form of child care for their children today than in the past? To answer this question, we can use Survey of Income and Program Participation (SIPP) and CPS data to examine how primary care arrangements have changed since 1965 for preschoolers of employed mothers. Here, we define a child's primary care arrangement as the type of care that is used for the most hours during the time the mother is working. Figure 7.4 shows that the general trend from 1965 to 1985 was an increase in the use of center care and family day-care homes, with a corresponding decline in the use of mothers (while they worked), other relatives, and baby-sitters.

As child-care centers and family day-care homes became more numerous, families became more likely to choose them. Likewise, as the supply of other relatives and baby-sitters declined, so did the propensity to use them. Care by mothers during their working hours may have declined because the amount of hours mothers worked increased over this period, making it harder for them to provide care over this longer time span.

The trend since 1985 is a bit more complicated, although like the earlier period, the general tendency has been one of increasing use of center care. Several aspects of this post-1985 trend merit discussion. First, there was an interruption of several long-standing trends in 1991. The increase in care by fathers and mothers and the decrease in the use of center care that abruptly occurred in 1991 was more than likely a rational response to the recession that began in July 1990 and reached its lowest point in March 1991 (Casper 1996, 1997a; Casper and O'Connell 1998b). During the recession, increases in unemployment occurred across the board, full-time workers who changed jobs often ended up as part-time workers, and for people chang-

● **Figure 7.4.** Trends in Child-Care Arrangements for Preschool Children Whose Mothers Are Employed: 1965-1994

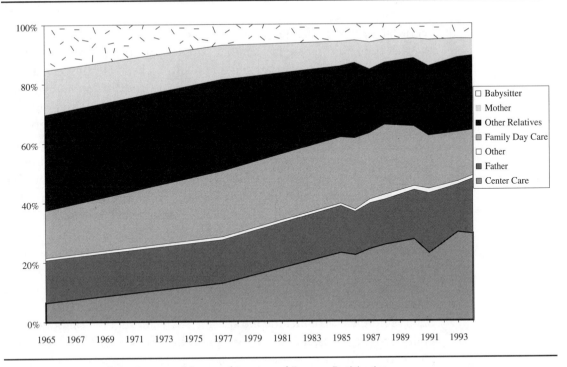

SOURCE: Current Population Survey and Survey of Income and Program Participation.
NOTE: Percentages have been interpolated for years in which data are unavailable.

ing jobs, the new jobs paid less than the old ones (Masumura and Ryscavage 1994). Consequently, real income declined by 5.1 percent. Furthermore, married fathers with preschoolers were more likely to be working part-time or to be unemployed and to have lower family incomes in the recession year of 1991 than in 1988 or 1993 (Casper 1997a). Thus more fathers were available for care and fewer families were able to afford nonrelative care in 1991. Care by the mother while working also increased during 1991 for the same reasons. Second, the declining popularity of family day care in the 1990s may in part reflect a growing uneasiness about the use of a minimally regulated arrangement where there is a single provider, as opposed to a heavily regulated arrangement—a child-care center—where there are more providers and presumably more oversight. The decline in the use of family day-care homes also occurred over a period in which media reports of child neglect and abuse at the hands of baby-sitters and family day-care providers were on the upswing.

● How Do Parents Choose Child Care?

A critical element in the design of child-care public policy and legislation is the determination of the factors that parents consider in choosing child-care providers. Many scholars have applied Becker's (1981) neoclassical economic model of household production to the study of employment and child-care choices. According to Becker's theory, parents derive satisfaction from consuming market- and home-produced goods and services, producing and rearing children, and leisure activities. Family members consider different combinations of time spent in employment and home production and the relative satisfaction each member derives from these alternatives. Parents simultaneously choose a child-care provider, a set of market goods and services, and particular amounts of nonwork time to maximize their satisfaction given their budget constraints (Blau 1991). The budget constraint is determined by the prices of goods and services and the income a family has with which to purchase them.

The desired quality of substitute care is key to the determination of child-care choices, but parents' preferences are also important (Blau 1991). Such preferences can include the specific characteristics or components of child-care programs; the desire for a provider who shares the parents' religious and cultural values; the convenience of the arrangement; and the reliability of the provider. Economic theory states that other preferences not directly related to child care, such as tastes for other consumer goods and the importance attached to leisure time are also important in parents' choices among child-care providers. Parents will make trade-offs among all of these factors based on the relative costs and perceived benefits attached to them. For example, a family may prefer a child-care program with a strong educational component, but if the only such program available is located so far away that it is inconvenient, the family may instead choose a family day-care home that is convenient but does not have a strong educational curriculum.

Social norms can also affect parents' choices in child care. Preferences may be shaped by gender ideologies that prescribe appropriate employment and family behaviors for women (Riley and Glass 2000; Van Dijk and Siegers 1996). Significant others may grant rewards or approval to parents who act in accordance with their beliefs and may inflict sanctions on parents who violate these norms (Coleman 1990). Thus one might expect that families whose social networks have liberal gender ideologies might be more likely to use father care and nonrelative care. Social networks not only define appropriate types of care, they are also valuable sources of information about the availability and quality of child-care providers.

Using the theories described above as a basis, researchers who study child-care choice have focused on a trilogy of policy concerns: accessibility, affordability, and quality.

Accessibility

Studies have found that the likelihood of a parent's choosing a particular type of child care depends upon its availability. For instance, when mothers are not available to care for their infants, they tend to prefer care by fathers (Mason and Kuhlthau 1989), but most fathers are employed and may not be available for care when it is needed (Casper 1997a). In fact, in 1994, only 21 percent of children age 1 year or younger had their fathers caring for them during most of their mothers' working hours (Casper 1997b). Family structure also affects availability: A single mother living only with her young children has no coresident relatives available to care for them, whereas a married mother or a single mother who is living with her adult relatives may be able to rely on another household member. Studies have shown that households with teenage siblings or other adult relatives are less likely to use paid child care (Connelly 1992). Similarly, the proximity of noncoresidential relatives and the compatibility of their schedules affect the choice of care.

Shortages of arrangements of a certain type or that service certain groups of children may also affect child-care choice. For example, it is more difficult to find center care for infants than for older children; only slightly more than half of center-based programs accept children who are not toilet trained (Hofferth 1992). Mothers who work nonstandard evening or weekend hours are more likely to choose informal or relative care than are those working standard day shifts, in part because few centers are open during evening and weekend hours (Casper 1996; Presser 1988; Presser and Cox 1997). Geographic mismatches also occur in certain areas—there are relatively more spaces than children in centers in the South and relatively fewer spaces than children in the West (Hofferth 1992). The accessibility of an arrangement is also related to child-care choice because it affects how convenient the arrangement is. If parents prefer center care but cannot find a center close to their home that cares for infants, or one that is open during the hours they need care, they may opt for the convenience of using a nearby family day-care provider.

Affordability

Research indicates that the cost of child care is another important consideration for parents. In 1993, slightly more than half (51 percent) of all child-care arrangements used for preschoolers while their mothers were working required cash payment (Casper 1995). Whether a family pays for care depends in part on the type of arrangement used; parents are more likely to have to pay for child care when nonrelatives are used. For example, more than 90 percent of center care, 92 percent of family day care, and 84 percent of in-home baby-sitter arrangements required cash payment. In contrast, when relatives were used, only one in six arrangements required cash payment. Expenditures for care also vary by arrangement type. In 1993, families with employed mothers using in-home baby-sitters or center care paid the most per arrangement (about $65 per week for each), followed by those using family day care ($52 per week) and those using relatives ($42).

The average amount of time children spend in care affects its overall cost, and this too depends on the arrangement. Children spend fewer hours in the care of sitters than in centers, family day care, or with relatives—23 hours per week on average with sitters compared with about 28 hours in each of the other three arrangements. Thus care by sitters is the most expensive on an hourly basis.

Several studies have examined the relationships among cost of care, economic resources, and choice of arrangement. Families who confront higher costs for out-of-home child care are more likely to use informal or unpaid care (Blau and Robins 1991; Connelly 1992; Hofferth and Wissoker 1992). Studies have generally found that the higher the mother's wage, the more likely a family is to choose paid care, but that the father's wage does not seem to matter (Blau and Robins 1988, 1991; Hofferth and Wissoker 1992). The age of children and the number of children also affect the cost of the arrangement. For example, costs are higher for infants and young children because they require more intensive care than older children, including feeding, diaper changing, and more constant monitoring (Casper 1995; Connelly 1992). Families with two preschoolers pay on average $43 more per week for child care than families with only one child (Casper 1995). How many hours a mother is employed and the time of day she works also affect cost. As one might expect, families with mothers who work full-time and/or day shifts spend more on child care (Casper 1995; Hofferth et al. 1991).

Child-care expenditures consume a substantial proportion of a family's budget. In fact, for working parents at all income levels, the cost of child care ranks as the single largest expense behind housing, food, and taxes (Committee for Economic Development 1993). SIPP data indicate that in 1993, families with working mothers spent almost 8 percent of their pretax monthly income on child care for their preschoolers (Casper 1995). Even though the dollar amounts paid for care may be similar for all families, they account for a much larger share of the family budget in certain types of families. For example, child-care costs consume 25 percent of the family income for families with monthly incomes of less than $1,200 per month, compared with a mere 6 percent for families with monthly incomes of $4,500 or more. And single working mothers spend about 12 percent of their income for child care, compared with 7 percent for married parents with working mothers (Casper 1995).

The amount of money families pay for child care has increased dramatically since 1985. After adjusting for inflation, families with employed mothers spent on average $59 per week on child care in 1985, compared with $85 per week in 1995. The proportion of families with employed mothers who paid for child care also increased from 34 percent in 1985 to 41 percent in 1995.

Quality

Another important factor that parents consider when selecting child care is the quality of the available arrangements. The quality of child care is directly related to various positive outcomes for children, such as the development of language and social skills. Parents want the best-quality care to promote these outcomes, but just what is high-quality child care? According to Hofferth and Chaplin (1994), the various components of high-quality child care can be grouped into three main categories: child-caregiver interaction, structural features, and caregiver turnover. Child-caregiver interaction encompasses the nature of the contact between caregiver and child. For example, is the caregiver sensitive, loving, warm, harsh, detached, and/or intellectually stimulating? And is the nature of the interaction appropriate for the situation and the age of the child? Structural features include child/staff ratios, the size of the group, the physical environment (cleanliness, safety features, organization and orderliness of the space, availability of toys and materials for crafts), program components (curriculum), and the education and training of teachers or care providers.

Much of the scholarly research has examined the structural features of high-quality child care, in part because these are the most easily measured and observed. Four of these features are commonly considered: child/staff ratios, group size, provider education and training, and provider turnover

(Hofferth and Wissoker 1992; Kisker and Maynard 1991; Leibowitz, Waite, and Witsberger 1988; Waite, Leibowitz, and Witsberger 1991). From a policy perspective, these features are also the most easily regulated. The Panel on Child Care Policy of the National Academy of Sciences has reported that these structural aspects of quality affect child-caregiver interactions, which in turn affect child development outcomes (Hayes, Palmer, and Zaslow 1990).

But do parents take these structural features into account when choosing care? For most of the features, the answer to this question appears to be no; there is not much evidence that the structural factors professionals consider important to the quality of child care affect parental decisions. For example, Hofferth and Chaplin (1994) found that parents are no more likely to select center care if a center has trained providers than if it does not, when price and convenience are controlled. And parents who have identified family day-care providers with formal training are actually less likely to choose this type of care. Hofferth and Chaplin also found that group size in centers and family day-care homes does not appear to be important in parents' decisions. Nor is the child/staff ratio important in determining the use of family day-care homes, although it plays an unexpected role for families who chose center care; when price and convenience are controlled for, parents are actually *less* likely to choose centers that have lower child/staff ratios. Hofferth and Chaplin speculate that this apparent paradox may result from the inadequacy of this measure to serve as a proxy for quality. Centers that have high child/staff ratios may actually attract greater numbers of children because the providers are especially loving and nurturing or because their programs are of excellent quality.

If structural qualities are not important for parents, what qualities are important? According to Hofferth and Chaplin (1994), most parents say that their primary consideration in choosing a child-care provider is quality of care. But for these parents, "quality" lies in caregiver-child interaction, not structural features. Parents report that they consider such caregiver qualities as warmth, nurturing, a high level of interaction, individualized attention, and the ability to make learning fun to be important, whereas they de-emphasize features such as child/staff ratio, group size, safety, and types of equipment available. For example, Hofferth and Chaplin report that the most important aspect of quality identified by parents was a warm and loving provider. Other researchers have found that parents also want child care to be provided in a safe and healthy environment, and many parents express concern about child abuse (Kisker and Maynard 1991). Few parents consider the availability of educational materials and recreational equipment as the most important factor when compared with other factors (Johansen, Leibowitz, and Waite 1996).

When asked, parents say that in deciding what type of care to use they consider convenience and cost factors to be less important than the quality of care (Willer et al. 1991). For example, data from the National Child Care Study indicate that 37 percent of all parents consider some aspect of quality to be the most important factor in choosing care. In contrast, only 10 percent report that convenience is the most important factor, and 9 percent consider cost to be most important (Hofferth et al. 1991). But other empirical evidence suggests that convenience and cost are important. Hofferth and Chaplin (1994) found that the farther parents live from a particular type of child care, the less likely they are to use that type of arrangement. Other studies provide evidence that parents may be more concerned about distance from home and available hours than they are about certain aspects of quality (Johansen et al. 1996; Sonenstein 1991).

In sum, research on the actual choices parents make has found fairly strong effects of price and convenience and only weak or inconsistent effects of quality characteristics. Yet when parents are asked which factors they consider to be important in their decision making about child care, they consistently downplay cost and convenience and emphasize quality. Given the seemingly contradictory evidence, how do researchers account for this discrepancy? One possible explanation is that parents do not really make their decisions based on quality, even though they say they do (Hofferth and Chaplin 1994). Another explanation is that there is a mismatch between how researchers conceptualize and measure quality and how parents define it (Moore 1982). Still others have concluded that many parents may not be able to weigh considerations of quality, cost, and convenience simultaneously because they have limited information about alternative care arrangements (Hayes et al. 1990). Another possibility is that different parents have different definitions of quality, making it difficult to assess an overall effect of quality. For example, Johansen et al. (1996) found that parents who value developmental aspects of child care are more likely to choose center care, whereas those who value their children's knowing their caregivers choose family day care, and those who value hours, location, and cost are more likely to choose care in the home. These findings seem to indicate that parents assess quality in different ways, which leads them to choose different types of care.

So how do parents choose child care? Hofferth and Chaplin (1994) suggest that parents go through a two- or three-step process in which they first determine the distance they are willing or able to travel and the amount they are willing or able to pay for care. Then, from among care providers that meet these two criteria, parents trade off aspects of quality and convenience until they find an available provider that most fulfills their other wants and needs. Thus parents can report honestly that quality factors are most important in their child-care choices because, at the outset, they rule out care that is too far away or too costly. By contrast, Kisker and Maynard (1991) maintain that parents select their child-care arrangements on the basis of quality, location, and cost considerations, in that order.

● Complexity of Child-Care Arrangements

Child-care arrangements can be quite complex, and parents choose different arrangements for different children at different times of their lives. The Survey of Income and Program Participation includes questions about the child-care arrangements families have made while the "designated" parent works. In the vast majority of cases, designated parents are mothers, but they can also be single fathers or guardians if there is no mother in the household (Smith 2000). We refer to the designated parent here as *the parent* and the spouse of the designated parent as the *other parent*. The other parent is most often the child's father. SIPP data show that almost all preschool children (98 percent) had at least one arrangement during the time the designated parent was at work or school in 1995 (Smith 2000). A substantial proportion of these children also had regular arrangements when the parent was not at work or in school (45 percent). In sharp contrast, less than half of the preschoolers had a regular arrangement (43 percent) if their designated parent was not employed.

The numbers of regular child-care arrangements parents use for their children differ according to the children's ages; grade school-age children, for example, tend to have more arrangements, on average, than do preschoolers (Smith 2000). As children age, their needs change. A major component of the care of infants and young children is satisfying their basic needs; they must be fed, diapered, and held. Older children require supervision while they are playing and more intensive social interaction. They also benefit more from structured activities and educational programs and spend part of their day in school. These differences are likely to affect parents' child-care choices. Another major factor influencing parental choice is whether child care is used out of necessity while parents work or whether parents use child-care settings primarily to enhance their children's social and cognitive development. Certainly some parents who need child care while they are working also desire to promote the cognitive and social development of their children, but their choices in care are still likely to differ from those of nonworking parents because they need care for more hours and take different kinds of factors into account when weighing availability, cost, and quality.

For these reasons, we examine child-care arrangements separately for children ages 0 to 4 (preschoolers) and children ages 5 to 14 (grade-schoolers). We also discuss care arrangements used during the parents' working or school hours separately from those used during nonworking/nonschool hours, hereafter referred to as work and nonwork hours, respectively.

Preschool-Age Children

In 1995, three-fourths of the 19.3 million children under 5 years of age (14.4 million children) were in regular child-care arrangements during a typical week. About 44 percent were cared for in multiple arrangements (two or more arrangements per week). Of the one-quarter who had no regular child-care arrangements, the vast majority (96 percent) had a parent who was neither employed nor in school. Table 7.1 presents the percentages of preschoolers in different types of child care on a regular basis (because children may be in more than one type of arrangement, percentages do not sum to 100).

Most people think of child care as care provided by someone other than relatives, and nonrelatives play a prominent role in the case of preschoolers—49 percent of children under age 5 were cared for by nonrelatives on a regular basis. Similar proportions were cared for either in organized facilities (30 percent) or by nonrelatives in "home" settings (29 percent). Organized facilities include day-care centers, nursery schools or preschools, Head Start programs, and kindergarten. Comparable proportions of preschoolers were in day-care centers and nursery/preschools (15 percent and 14 percent, respectively). A smaller proportion of children were enrolled in federally funded Head Start programs (3 percent), reflecting the fact that most children are not eligible for these programs. Some 13 percent of preschoolers were cared for by family day-care providers, and equal proportions were cared for by other nonrelatives, either in the child's home or in the provider's home (9 percent each). Most nonrelative child care is used during parents' work hours, but about 23 percent of children receive nonrelative care during parents' nonwork hours.

TABLE 7.1   Preschoolers Using Different Types of Child-Care Arrangements: Fall 1995

Arrangement Type	Total Receiving Care[a]	Receiving Care During Work Hours[b]	Receiving Care During Nonwork Hours[c]
Children 0 to 4 years old[d] (numbers in thousands)	19,281	11,168	19,281
% using relative care	50.1	61.9	26.0
Designated parent[e]	4.9	8.5	X
Other parent[f]	18.2	31.4	X
Sibling	1.9	3.3	X
Grandparent	30.0	29.0	19.8
Other relative	14.5	9.7	10.1
% using nonrelative care	48.5	60.9	23.0
Organized facility	29.9	35.2	15.4
Day-care center	14.8	22.7	4.1
Nursery or preschool	13.5	12.3	9.0
Head Start	3.0	2.0	2.4
School[g]	1.5	1.3	0.9
Other nonrelative care	28.8	37.7	12.2
In child's home	9.1	8.0	5.8
In provider's home	21.0	30.2	6.7
Family day care	12.6	19.7	3.1
Other care arrangement	9.0	10.9	3.7
Other			
Self-care	0.1	0.1	0.1

SOURCE: Survey of Income and Program Participation, 1993 Panel, Wave 9.

NOTE: Due to multiple arrangements, children may appear in more than one arrangement type, thus percentages may exceed 100. X = category not asked for nonwork/nonschool hours.

a. If a child uses the same type of arrangement during different parental activity schedules, the arrangement type is counted only once in this column. Includes designated parent who is employed, in school, looking for work, or out of the labor force.

b. Limited to children whose parents were either employed or enrolled in school.

c. Includes care for children during nonwork/nonschool hours of employed/in-school designated parents. Also includes all care for children whose designated parents are looking for work or not in the labor force.

d. Number of children includes those children for whom no regular arrangement was used.

e. Includes care of the child by the designated parent at home or away from home while working or in school.

f. Includes care of the child by the other parent only while the designated parent works.

g. Includes kindergarten or grade school.

Table 7.1 also highlights the important role relatives play in the care of preschoolers (Casper 1996, 1997a; Presser 1989b). Half of all preschoolers were regularly cared for by relatives in 1995. Fathers and grandparents are the two most important sources of care by relatives while mothers are working (Smith 2000). As shown in Table 7.1, grandparents were the single most frequently used relatives (30 percent) in providing care for preschoolers, followed by care by the other parent, in most cases the father (18 percent), and care by other relatives, such as aunts, uncles, or cousins (15 percent). Smaller proportions of preschoolers were cared for by the parent while he or she was working (5 percent) and by older siblings (2 percent).

Research has shown that parents prefer relative care, including parental and grandparental care, to nonrelative care (Early Child Care Research Network 1997; Hofferth et al. 1991; Riley and Glass 2000). Presumably, relatives are more emotionally committed to the child and will therefore provide more loving and attentive care. Relatives are also more likely to have shared values and religious beliefs and to come from similar cultural backgrounds; research suggests that parents consider these attributes very important in selecting child-care providers. Despite the documented preference for kin care, most child-care research has neglected the important role that fathers, grandparents, and other relatives play in caring for preschoolers.

Research has also shown that substantial proportions of children have more than one regular child-care arrangement (Brown and Hagy 1997; Smith 2000) and that relatives, particularly fathers and grandparents, provide a substantial proportion of the total hours of child care in multiple care situations (Folk and Yi 1994; Smith 2000). For example, among preschoolers with two or more arrangements, almost twice as many had relatives (56 percent) as nonrelatives (31 percent) for secondary providers during the parents' work/school hours. One-fourth of preschoolers had their fathers (the other parent) and one-fifth had their grandparents as secondary providers while the parent worked. Thus relatives serve not only as a primary source of child care, but as a valuable supplemental source of child care.

Figure 7.5 shows the eight most common combinations of arrangements used for preschoolers with multiple arrangements during the designated parents' (usually mothers') work/school hours. This figure very clearly displays the importance of the supplemental role of fathers and grandparents in caring for our nation's children—seven of the eight most common combinations include either the other parent (usually the father) or a grandparent.

● **Figure 7.5.** Common Child-Care Arrangement Combinations of Preschoolers During Their Parents' Work/School Hours: Fall 1995 (percentages)

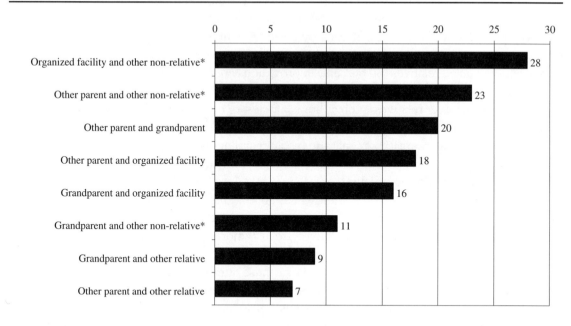

SOURCE: Survey of Income and Program Participation, 1993 Panel, Wave 9.
NOTE: Data are for preschoolers in two or more arrangements. Children may be in other arrangement types as well as these combinations.
*Includes care in the child's home or the provider's home.

Quality of care, accessibility, and affordability of provider are important factors that parents consider in choosing child care in general, and these factors also figure prominently in the selection of relatives as child-care providers. For example, having a relative nearby increases the likelihood that a parent will choose kin care (Early Child Care Research Network 1997; Floge 1985; Guzman 1998; Kuhlthau and Mason 1991). Single mothers are less likely to have their children's fathers as primary care providers because the fathers are not usually available for child care (Casper 1996). Even when fathers or other relatives are in the home or live nearby, their availability may be constrained by work schedules. Several studies have shown that the number of hours husbands and wives work and the times of day they work are related to whether or not children receive care from their fathers. For example, fathers are more likely to provide care when mothers work part-time or work shifts other than day shifts, when fathers work part-time or nonday shifts, or when mothers and fathers work shifts that don't overlap (Brayfield 1995; Casper 1996, 1997a; Casper and O'Connell

1998b; O'Connell 1993; Presser 1988, 1989a). Grandparents, too, may be constrained by their work schedules because many relatives who provide care are also employed. For example, Presser (1989b) has found that about one-third of grandmothers who care for their grandchildren are otherwise employed.

Aside from availability, the willingness of a relative to provide child care is important. Research suggests that although instrumental aid from one generation to the next is dependent in part on need (Aldous 1987), it may also be related to the quality of the relationship the relatives have (Bengtson and Roberts 1991). Aid in the form of child care appears to be no exception; women with close ties to their mothers and mothers-in-law are more likely to call upon grandparents to be primary child-care providers (Guzman 1998).

For many families, child care can be prohibitively costly, and asking relatives to serve as child-care providers may be one way to defray these costs. Poor families rely more heavily on relatives to help them out with child care during parents' working hours than do nonpoor families (Casper 1996; Smith 2000). Families with relatively high family incomes are also less like to choose fathers (Casper 1997a) or grandparents to care for their children during the mothers' working hours (Casper 1996). Single-mother families, who are more likely to be poor than married-couple families, are also more likely to choose relatives. For example, only 14 percent of children living with married parents are cared for primarily by their grandparents while their mothers are at work, compared with 21 percent of preschoolers living with divorced, widowed, or separated mothers and 28 percent who are living with never-married mothers (Casper 1996).

These studies show the connections among availability, affordability, and choice of relatives for child care, but what they don't show is the behind-the-scenes juggling act that parents and the relatives who provide care perform so that children will be cared for when parents have to work. Parents and their relatives go to considerable lengths to combine work and child-care duties, but the adaptations families make can sometimes be unsatisfactory. For example, child care by relatives is especially constraining on the number of hours mothers work (Presser 1988, 1989a, 1989b). Compared with families with part-time employed mothers who use nonrelative care, those who rely on kin care more often report that the mother would work more hours if satisfactory and affordable care were available. Grandmothers who provide child care also engage in considerable juggling of their own work schedules to provide care for their grandchildren (Presser 1989b).

School-Age Children

Sparked in part by sensationalized media accounts of tragedies that have befallen some children who have been left home alone after school, more and more parents and policy makers are beginning to ask, Who is taking care of our school-age children when they are not in school? In 1995, virtually all of the 38.2 million children in the United States ages 5 to 14 (98 percent) were in regular child-care arrangements, including school, during a typical week (Smith 2000). Three-fourths of these children were cared for in multiple arrangements. Overall, grade-schoolers were regularly using an average of 2.8 different arrangements per week. Thus they averaged about 0.8 more arrangements than preschoolers; this is as expected, given that virtually all of the children in this age group are in school.

As is the case for preschoolers, relatives are important contributors to the overall care of school-age children—43 percent of children are regularly in the care of relatives (see Table 7.2). Similar proportions of school-age children are cared for by a grandparent (17 percent) or by the other parent (16 percent). Other relatives, such as aunts, uncles, and cousins, provide regular care for 11 percent of grade-schoolers. Siblings provide care for 9 percent of school-age children.

Parents rely on nonrelative care, such as organized care facilities and other nonrelative care in the child's home or the provider's home, to a smaller degree for school-age than for preschool-age children. Only 17 percent of children 5 to 14 years old use these types of nonrelative care on a regular basis. This is due in part to the large amount of time these children spend in school, as well as to their involvement in other types of structured activities. Nearly all school-age children are in school (93 percent), and a large proportion (39 percent) participate in enrichment activities such as sports, lessons, clubs, and before- or after-school programs. In addition, many grade-schoolers care for themselves on a regular basis (18 percent) without any adult supervision.

Parents who work or who are in school on a regular basis are more likely to have to use combinations of care to be able to cover the hours their children are not in school but require care. The most common combinations of multiple care arrangements for grade school-age children, excluding school arrangements, are presented in Figure 7.6. Given that enrichment activities are important sources of care, it is not surprising that they are the most commonly combined type of care; enrichment activities are paired with other arrangements in the five most common combinations.

TABLE 7.2 School-Age Children Using Different Types of Child-Care Arrangements: Fall 1995

Arrangement Type	Total Receiving Care[a]	Receiving Care During Work Hours[b]	Receiving Care During Nonwork Hours[c]
Children 5 to 14 years old[d]			
(numbers in thousands)	38,228	24,698	38,228
% using relative care	42.6	51.5	18.0
Designated parent[e]	3.5	5.4	X
Other parent[f]	16.0	24.7	X
Sibling	9.1	14.1	X
Grandparent	17.4	15.6	11.5
Other relative	11.4	5.7	8.7
% using nonrelative care	16.8	18.4	7.0
Organized care facility	3.5	3.4	2.0
Day-care center	1.5	2.0	0.5
Nursery or preschool	1.9	1.4	1.3
Head Start	0.3	0.1	0.3
Other nonrelative care	14.1	15.9	5.9
In child's home	4.9	4.1	2.9
In provider's home	9.6	11.9	3.1
Family day care	4.5	6.3	0.8
Other care arrangement	5.2	5.7	2.3
Other			
School	92.8	87.8	59.9
Enrichment activities[g]	39.3	34.6	27.2
Self-care	18.0	20.3	8.5

SOURCE: Survey of Income and Program Participation, 1993 Panel, Wave 9.

NOTE: Due to multiple arrangements, children may appear in more than one arrangement type, thus percentages may exceed 100. X = category not asked for nonwork/nonschool hours.

a. If a child uses the same type of arrangement during different parental activity schedules, the arrangement type is counted only once in this column. Includes designated parent who is employed, in school, looking for work, or out of the labor force.

b. Limited to children whose parents were either employed or enrolled in school.

c. Includes care for children during nonwork/nonschool hours of employed/in-school designated parents. Also includes all care for children whose designated parents are looking for work or not in the labor force.

d. Number of children includes those children for whom no regular arrangement was used.

e. Includes care of the child by the designated parent at home or away from home while working or in school.

f. Includes care of the child by the other parent only while the designated parent works.

g. Includes organized sports, lessons (music, art, dance, language, computer, and so on), clubs, and before- and after-school care programs located at school or elsewhere.

● **Figure 7.6.** Common Child-Care Arrangement Combinations of Grade School-Age Children During Their Parents' Work/School Hours: Fall 1995 (percentages)

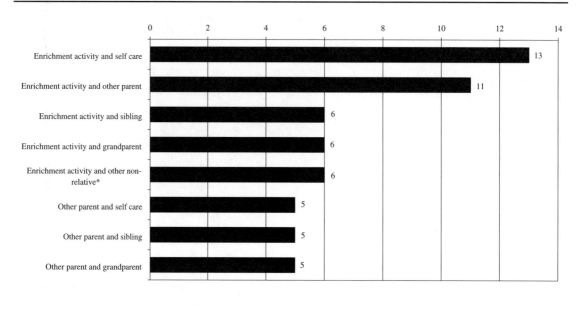

SOURCE: Survey of Income and Program Participation, 1993 Panel, Wave 9.
NOTE: Data are for grade-schoolers in two or more arrangements. Children may be in other arrangement types as well as these combinations.
*Includes care in the child's home or the provider's home.

The Importance of Enrichment Activities

Many researchers have neglected the important role that enrichment activities such as extracurricular sports, music lessons, clubs, and before- and after-school activities play in the patchwork of care parents piece together for their children (for an important exception, see Hofferth 1995). With the exception of school, more children are in enrichment activities than are in any other arrangement, and this is true regardless of whether these activities take place during or outside of the parents' working hours—35 percent during work hours and 27 percent outside of these hours (Smith 2000).

One important feature of enrichment activities stems from the secondary role these activities play in the overall mix of child-care arrangements that parents use. For example, grade school-age children spend only about 8 hours per week in enrichment activities, and only 2 percent of them are in enrichment activities as their primary arrangement. In contrast, enrichment activities are the most commonly cited secondary and tertiary arrangements: More families use enrichment activities for secondary and tertiary care than any other arrangement. And, as Figure 7.6 shows, enrichment activities are the most common arrangement paired with other arrangements to cover the time parents are working.

Evidence suggests that families use enrichment activities both for the cultural, social, and cognitive development of children and as supervision for children when parents cannot be with them. On the one hand, these activities are used in substantial proportions during nonworking hours of parents. On the other hand, the number of hours per week spent in enrichment activities during parents' working hours (14 hours) is twice the numbers spent during nonworking hours (7 hours), suggesting that parents do use enrichment activities during their working hours as supervision for their children because they enroll them for longer periods of time. The value of enrichment activities for child well-being is a topic we take up in Chapter 8.

Latchkey Kids

Many people believe that changes in women's family and work patterns have resulted in increasing numbers of children being left to care for themselves. The perceived increase in the numbers of children in self-care has been dubbed the "latchkey kid phenomenon," a label that invokes images of droves of children heading home from school sporting house keys on chains around their necks, letting themselves into empty houses where danger lurks around every corner. Indeed, these images have been concretized and sensationalized by the popular press in stories like the Schoos', mentioned at the beginning of this chapter. Concern for the well-being of children in self-care has spurred debates among policy makers and researchers, as well as among parents. Many have been worried that although self-care may be fine for some children—presumably for those who are relatively mature and live in safe neighborhoods—it may have deleterious consequences for others.

In 1995, 5.2 million (15 percent) children ages 5 to 13 were reported to be in self-care regularly during a typical week. These statistics make it seem like there may be cause for worry—after all, one in seven grade school-age children was in self-care! However, the incidence of self-care increases dramatically by age, so that very few younger children were actually caring for themselves on a regular basis. For example, 3 percent of 5- to 7-year-olds were in self-care in 1995, compared with 33 percent of 11- to 13-year-olds (see Table 7.3). Even when children were in self-care, they spent relatively little time caring for themselves—an average of less than 4 hours per week for children ages 5 to 7, 4 hours per week for those ages 8 to 10, and 6 hours a week for those ages 11 to 13. Fully half of all children ages 5 to 13 spent fewer than 5 hours per week in self-care, and only 10 percent spent more than 10 hours per week in self-care. Grade school-age children are also much more likely to have self-care as their supplemental arrangement (secondary and tertiary care) than as their primary arrangement (Smith 2000). This helps to explain why children spent relatively few hours in self-care. Even as hysteria was building about the increase in self-care, evidence suggests that self-care did not increase in the 1990s (Casper and Smith forthcoming; Smith and Casper 1999).

But how do latchkey kids fare? On the one hand, studies have generally found that children in self-care versus those in adult supervised care do not differ on several key developmental dimensions, such as independence, self-esteem, locus of control, social adjustment, and interpersonal relationships (Posner and Vandell 1994; Rodman, Pratto, and Nelson 1985; Vandell and Corasaniti 1988). These findings could result if parents select self-care for children who are relatively mature and better behaved than other children, or if self-care has no negative outcomes for children. On the other hand, research has also linked self-care to fearfulness and anxiety and to antisocial and headstrong behavior (Posner and Vandell 1994; Vandell and Ramanan 1991). Again, these findings could result if self-care causes these problems, or if children in self-care were more fearful, anxious, or antisocial than other children before they began caring for themselves. Due to the lack of longitudinal data, researchers have not been able to determine whether self-care *causes* negative outcomes for children—or, for that matter, positive ones.

Other research suggests that not all self-care is the same. Some children may have informal adult supervision, such as when they go to friends' homes or when their parents check on them by phone, and these differences can have implications for children's well-being. For example, Steinberg (1987) found that children who have more adult supervision are less likely to engage in antisocial behavior. There may also be differences in the ways in which children spend their time; Steinberg found differences in antisocial behaviors between children who stay at home while in self-care and those who "hang out" with their friends.

As suggested by prior research, the availability and cost of alternative forms of child care are related to whether or not parents choose self-care for their school-age children (Cain and Hofferth 1989; Casper, Hawkins, and O'Connell 1994; Casper and Smith forthcoming; Presser 1989a). Smith

TABLE 7.3 Hours in Self-Care per Week Among School-Age Children Who Use
Self-Care: Fall 1995

	Child's Age							
	5 to 13		5 to 7		8 to 10		11 to 13	
	No.	%	No.	%	No.	%	No.	%
Total number of children	34,618	100.0	12,253	100.0	11,584	100.0	10,781	100.0
Children in self-care	5,155	14.9	370	3.0	1,241	10.7	3,543	32.9
Fewer than 5 hours/week	2,759	53.5	253	68.2	768	63.3	1,719	48.5
5 to 10 hours/week	1,863	36.2	93	25.2	372	30.0	1,398	39.5
More than 10 hours/week	533	10.3	24	6.6	83	6.7	426	12.0
Mean hours/week	5.1		3.7		4.4		6	

SOURCE: Survey of Income and Program Participation, 1993 Panel, Wave 9.
NOTE: Numbers are in thousands, except for hours.

and Casper (1999) found that parental availability to provide care plays
perhaps the most important role in determining whether a family will
choose self-care. For example, they found that children whose parents
worked full-time were much more likely to be in self-care. In addition, the
presence of only one parent in the household was associated with a higher
likelihood that older children would be allowed to care for themselves.
Children who lived in areas where the cost of alternative child care was
high were more likely to care for themselves than were children who lived
in areas where the cost of alternative child care was low. Other factors related to the "quality" of self-care are important as well, including the responsibility or maturity level of the child and the safety of the neighborhood in which a child lives.

Child Care and Child Well-Being ●

The earliest research investigating the effects of child care on children's social, emotional, and cognitive well-being typically posed the question, Is

child care detrimental to child well-being? Most studies found the answer to this question to be a resounding no; the timing and amount of child care were found to have few consistent effects on child development (Hofferth, Phillips, and Cabrera forthcoming). With the availability of new data measuring the quality of child care, researchers instead began asking, Does the *quality* of child care affect children's development? Extensive research over the past 25 years has found significant and sometimes sizable effects of a variety of child-care quality measures on several aspects of children's developmental well-being (for excellent reviews, see Lamb 1998; Love, Schochet, and Meckstroth 1996). Several of the dimensions of quality that we have discussed are linked to child well-being. The measures most strongly correlated with positive outcomes include structural features (e.g., lower child/staff ratios, smaller group sizes, higher levels of training, lower staff turnover, and higher staff salaries) and caregiver-child interactions (e.g., caregiver sensitivity and responsiveness) (Early Child Care Research Network 1999a; Phillips 1987). Some structural features, such as provider training and the number of children in care, have also been found to affect the developmental outcomes of children in family day-care homes and other in-home arrangements indirectly by influencing caregiving technique and the likelihood of caregivers' providing developmentally appropriate activities for children (Early Child Care Research Network 1996).

But what outcomes are affected by the quality of child care? One recent study by the National Institute of Child Health and Human Development's Early Child Care Research Network (1999b) found that child-care quality was highly correlated with cognitive development and language skills, even when the researchers took into account the effects of the child's home environment; the mother's personality, sensitivity to the child, level of depression, and educational attainment; the family's income; the gender of the child; the proportion of time the child spent in center care; and the number of hours the child spent in child care overall. Specifically, children receiving high-quality care had higher scores on a school readiness measure and used more expressive and receptive language. Interestingly, child-care quality did not seem to affect children's social and emotional development as measured by problem behavior, positive social behavior, and interaction with their peers. Other research has found that child-care quality also has long-term effects on children's outcomes. For example, Peisner-Feinberg et al. (1999) found that previous child-care experiences influenced children's school performance and social skills in the second grade, even when various other factors were taken into account.

Several researchers have noted the importance of selection in the study of child care (Blau 1997; Duncan and Gibson 2000). Because parents choose child-care arrangements, the relationship between quality of care and children's well-being may not be causal if the same underlying factors responsible for the parents' selection of a specific type of child care are also responsible for a given child outcome. For example, parents who are highly motivated to seek good-quality child care are also likely to be parents who invest more in their children in terms of playing with them, educating them, and socializing them. To the extent that these parental behaviors are not adequately taken into account, the effect of child care on children's outcomes will appear greater than it really is. However, several experimental studies that have randomly assigned children to high-quality child care have shown that those who received high-quality care had better outcomes on a variety of measures than did children in control groups (Carolina Abecedarian Project 1999; Schweinhart, Barnes, and Weikart 1993). Thus, when selectivity is ruled out, some evidence still suggests that high-quality child-care programs lead to better outcomes for children, particularly those from high-risk families (Hofferth, Phillips, and Cabrera forthcoming).

The quality of child care does appear to affect various child outcomes, but what about the influence of the family? Recent studies have shown that the effects of families and mothering are much stronger than the effects of child care. Thus, although the quality of child care makes a difference, family characteristics, the home environment, and mothers' attitudes about child rearing and behaviors toward their children appear to matter much more for the positive development of children (Early Child Care Research Network 1999b).

Conclusion ●

Although the proportion of preschool-age children in organized child-care centers is growing as maternal employment increases, the data on child-care arrangements suggest the continual importance of relatives, particularly grandparents and fathers, for the care of preschool-age children in the United States. New evidence from the Survey of Income and Program Participation also points to the importance of enrichment activities in the bundles of care arrangements used for school-age children, and self-care continues to be of concern in public policy discussions regarding care of older children.

As more mothers are required to enter the labor force through welfare reform, the demand for child care will increase. The demand will be especially great for child-care centers with developmental and educational components, as recent trends indicate that more parents are choosing this type of nonrelative care. Yet even as the demand grows, other factors make it increasingly unlikely that parents will be able to place their children in the care they prefer at prices they can afford. Care in organized facilities is on the rise, yet the types of child-care organizations that are the fastest growing—for-profit centers—are also those that cost the most. And much of the new demand for extensive child care will come from poor mothers, who are the least likely to be able to afford this type of care. When they cannot afford nonrelative care, these families often turn to relatives, yet the supply of relatives available for care is also likely to decline. This decline is likely to affect child-care choices for nonpoor families as well; families generally prefer to rely on relatives, especially for the care of very young children.

The importance of child-care quality for children's positive well-being is well documented, yet a preponderance of evidence indicates that the quality of both child-care centers and family day-care homes is generally mediocre (Galinsky et al. 1994; Helburn et al. 1995) and that the care received in many is sufficiently poor as to interfere with children's emotional and intellectual development (Helburn et al. 1995). Worse yet, there is reason to believe that these studies may be painting a rosier picture than actually exists, because providers of the lowest quality are likely to refuse to participate in studies, particularly if they entail on-site observations of the quality of care and children's development (Hofferth, Phillips, and Cabrera forthcoming).

The potential for negative outcomes for children is great. We have seen that three-fourths of preschool-age children have at least one regular care arrangement, and a similar proportion of grade school-age children have at least one regular arrangement outside of school. We have also seen that many of these children have more than one regular arrangement, and some spend substantial amounts of time in the care of someone other than their parents. The increase in the demand for child care is not likely to abate any time soon. Thus, if the quality of care remains mediocre or declines, more children are apt to be negatively affected.

The amount of time parents work outside the home is also an important factor related to the time children spend in self-care. As more mothers enter the labor force and continue to increase the number of hours they work, more children will be called upon to care for themselves. These findings are particularly salient as we embark on the welfare reform journey, moving single parents with dependent children off of welfare and into jobs. Requiring single mothers to work outside the home will reduce the amount of parental time available for child care, and could therefore increase the number of children in self-care, particularly if other affordable care options are not available.

However, the possible detrimental effects of self-care may be overstated. Parents are more likely to choose unsupervised care if their children are responsible and mature and if the neighborhood is safe. Enrichment activities are important for providing alternatives to unsupervised time for older children. Participation in low-cost enrichment activities may have the added benefit of increasing children's responsibility and maturity levels. Thus in the event that parents have no alternative but to allow their children to care for themselves, enrichment activities may help to prepare the children for this responsibility. Likewise, the devotion of more resources to increasing neighborhood safety would provide more children with environments in which parents might feel comfortable leaving children unsupervised, particularly when they have no alternative but to do so.

CHAPTER **8**

CHILD WELL-BEING

Demographers have long been interested in children—indirectly. That is, the key demographic processes of fertility and mortality—how many babies are born per woman in a society and how many of them survive—are ultimately about children and their well-being. However, the traditional demographic focus has not been on how children are faring so much as it has been on how the number of births and the age pattern of mortality alter the size and age structure of society.

Demographers' interest in children broadened greatly in 1984 after Samuel Preston (1984), in his presidential address to the Population Association of America, pointed out a perplexing demographic anomaly. Beginning in the mid-1960s, as the number of births plummeted in the United States, one might have expected an increase in resources available per child and an improvement in the well-being of children. Yet many socioeconomic indicators suggested just the opposite, a deterioration in children's health and economic well-being. By contrast, the elderly, a group that grew dramatically in size throughout the latter half of the 20th century, seemed to fare quite well as their numbers increased.

The anomaly Preston noted was why trends in well-being were not the reverse—downward for the elderly as their numbers increased and competition for resources stiffened, and upward for children as their numbers decreased and pressures created by high fertility eased. Preston argued that public support and investment in dependent segments of the population actually appear to be greater when a population group is increasing in size. On the other hand, he observed that the elderly had become a potent political force, effective in lobbying for public support of programs that bene-fited them. Younger voters could also see advantages to supporting pro-grams for the elderly, both because such state support benefited those with elderly relatives and because they could foresee future benefits for them-selves from such programs. Support for programs that would benefit chil-dren, on the other hand, was being eroded because of the declining share of the population directly involved in parenting children as the population aged and fertility remained low. In addition, the growing racial and ethnic diversity of the child population tended to diminish voter support for publi-c expenditures on children, especially poor children, because members of the majority white population could more easily dismiss minority children as "other" people's children and therefore not their responsibility.

As parenthood increasingly came to be viewed as a choice individuals made, the expectation was that only those who could afford to become parents should do so. In his address Preston expressed concern that the family was being called on to bear the costs of rearing children with less-ened state assistance at the very point in time when the fragility of the fam-ily was heightened. Given the high divorce rate and the high percentage of births outside marriage, many children spend part of their childhoods in single-parent homes, usually headed by their mothers. Children living only with their mothers are much more likely to be poor than are those in two-parent families (as we have noted in Chapter 4 and will discuss further in Chapter 9). Cohabitation may create weaker ties between fathers and children than marriage because, unless paternity is established, it is harder for mothers and their children to gain access to the father's resources if the relationship ends (Manning 2000). The social and demographic trends that have changed the family lives of children are not likely to reverse any time in the near future.

The dramatic changes in the family raise important questions about pub-lic versus private support for children. Some European countries, con-cerned about low birthrates and impending population decline, offer siz-able financial incentives to encourage couples to have children and provide strong support systems and generous social insurance benefits for families with children (Bergmann 1996; Kammerman and Kahn 1988; Smeeding, Rainwater, and Danziger 1997). In the United States, aside from education and related programs, child rearing and child support have tradi-tionally been considered the responsibility of the family, not of the state. In fact, as noted in Chapter 4, the rhetoric surrounding welfare reform in the United States embodies the great ambivalence Americans have about public assistance for parents who are not capable of supporting their children financially.

How children are faring—as families change, the economy undergoes transformation, and the population ages—continues to be an important issue. In this chapter, we begin an examination of this issue with an overview of trends in the size and racial composition of the population of children, the population indicators that were the focus of Preston's argument. We briefly discuss changes in family living arrangements of children, and then devote most of our attention to an overview of the explosion of research in the past two decades on children's well-being. We pose several questions: How economically secure are children? How healthy are children? How are children doing academically? What do children do with their time? How widespread are risky behaviors in adolescence? And are children receiving what they need, in terms of time and money, from parents?

Changing Numbers of U.S. Children ●

During 1940, the year before the United States entered World War II, about 2.6 million American babies were born. As the war ended, the Baby Boom generation was launched. The number of births jumped to 3.6 million by 1950 and crested at around 4.3 million in the early 1960s. The number of U.S. births was two-thirds higher in 1960 than it was in 1940.

As public institutions, particularly schools, were beginning to adjust to the need to serve increased numbers of children, the numbers of births started a downward spiral, bottoming out at 3.1 million in 1975. Even at this low point, the number of births was 23 percent higher than in 1940. Schools built during the 1960s to handle the burgeoning number of students were closed or converted to other uses because there were not enough children to fill them.

Demographers knew that the numbers of births would again rise as the large Baby Boom cohorts reached adulthood, because there would be so many women of childbearing age. As described in Chapter 3, that rise took longer than expected, as Baby Boomers delayed having children. However, the number of births increased steadily from the mid-1970s through the 1980s and only began declining again after reaching a high point of 4.2 million births in 1990. The number of births per year remains relatively

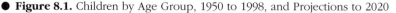

● **Figure 8.1.** Children by Age Group, 1950 to 1998, and Projections to 2020

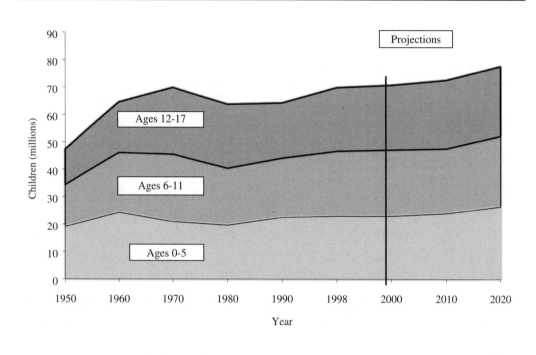

SOURCE: U.S. Bureau of the Census (1965, 1974, 1982), Day (1996), and unpublished Census Bureau tables for 1980-98 (on-line at http://www.census.gov).

high, with the National Center for Health Statistics (1999b:Table 1) reporting 3.9 million births each year in the latter 1990s.

What does all this mean in terms of the size of past, present, and future cohorts of children? Figure 8.1 shows the size of the child population beginning in 1950 and projected to 2020. The number of children in the United States rose from 47 million to almost 70 million in 1970 and then dropped back to 64 million in the 1980s. By 1999, the number of children under age 18 in the United States again stood at 70 million; this number is projected to increase to 77 million by the year 2020. However, whereas children made up 36 percent of the population in 1960 at the height of the Baby Boom, they currently account for only 26 percent of the population, a proportion that will decline slightly, to 24 percent, by 2020 (Federal Interagency Forum on Child and Family Statistics 2000).

Although the number of children is increasing, children's relative share of the population is decreasing, because the number of persons over age 65 is increasing more rapidly. Throughout the entire 1950 to 2020 period, the child population (under age 18) is losing ground, in terms of population size, to the elderly population. In the 1950s, there were 3.9 children for every elderly individual. In 1998, there were approximately 2 children per person age 65 and over, a ratio that is projected to drop to 1.4 by 2020 (Federal Interagency Forum on Child and Family Statistics 2000:66).

As Preston (1984) noted, the child population in the United States is also becoming more racially and ethnically diverse. In 1980, for example, about three-quarters of children in the United States were non-Hispanic white. By 2020, only 55 percent of children are projected to be in the non-Hispanic white category. The share of the child population identified as black, non-Hispanic (15 percent in 1999), is not projected to change much in the first two decades of the 21st century, perhaps dropping slightly, to 14 percent. By contrast, children of Hispanic background, who accounted for only 9 percent of all children in 1980, will make up almost one-fourth of the U.S. child population by 2020. The share of children who are of Asian origin will triple, from 2 percent in 1980 to 6 percent in 2020. Whereas in 1979 about 9 percent of children ages 5 to 17 in the United States spoke languages other than English at home, by the mid-1990s this proportion had increased to 14 percent (Federal Interagency Forum on Child and Family Statistics 2000: 68). The growing "otherness" of the child population remains a key indicator of the context for discussions about both the needs of the elderly and the needs of children, for increasingly the tax support required to provide programs to the mostly white elderly population will come from an increasingly nonwhite younger population.

A Transformation of Family Life ●

A sizable proportion of U.S. children see their parents divorce (or never marry) and spend much of their childhoods without fathers at home. This trend has characterized all racial and ethnic groups, but perhaps most striking are the persistent differences in living arrangements between white and black children. These two dominant facts about children's living arrangements—movement away from two-parent families and large and persistent racial differences—are illustrated in Table 8.1; however, two other facts are important. First, the most rapid decline in two-parent living, particularly among blacks, occurred between 1970 and 1980. But in the second half of the 1990s there was relative stability in children's living arrangements (Bryson and Casper 1998; Federal Interagency Forum on Child and Family

TABLE 8.1 Living Arrangements of Children Under 18 by Race and Hispanic Origin: 1960, 1970, 1980, 1990, and 1998

Living Arrangement	1960	1970	1980	1990	1998
All races					
Number (in thousands)	63,727	69,162	63,427	64,137	71,377
% living with					
Two parents	87.7	85.2	76.7	72.5	68.1
Mother only	8.0	10.8	18.0	21.6	23.3
Father only	1.1	1.1	1.7	3.1	4.4
Other	3.2	2.9	3.7	2.8	4.1
Whites					
Number (in thousands)	55,077	58,791	52,242	51,390	56,124
% living with					
Two parents	90.9	89.5	82.7	79.0	74.0
Mother only	6.1	7.8	13.5	16.2	18.2
Father only	1.0	0.9	1.6	3.0	4.6
Other	1.9	1.8	2.2	1.8	3.2
Blacks					
Number (in thousands)	8,650	9,422	9,375	10,018	11,414
% living with					
Two parents	67.0	58.5	42.2	37.7	36.2
Mother only	19.9	29.5	43.9	51.2	51.1
Father only	2.0	2.3	1.9	3.5	3.7
Other	11.1	9.8	12.0	7.5	8.9
Hispanics					
Number (in thousands)	NA	4,006	5,459	7,174	10,863
% living with					
Two parents	NA	77.7	75.4	66.8	63.6
Mother only	NA	NA	19.6	27.1	26.8
Father only	NA	NA	1.5	2.9	4.4
Other	NA	NA	3.5	3.2	5.1

SOURCE: Lugaila (1998:Table Ch-6).
NOTE: Whites and blacks may be Hispanic, and Hispanics may be of any race. NA = not available.

Statistics 2000:67; Fields 2001). Second, given the rhetoric about family demise, some may be surprised that two-thirds of children live with two parents. Among whites, almost three-fourths of children live in two-parent homes, as do 64 percent of Hispanic children; only 36 percent of black children live in two-parent homes.

One of the issues surrounding estimates of children's time in two-parent families is whether a child lives with two biological parents or a biological parent and a stepparent. The assumption is that stepparents may be less involved with children and less attentive to children's needs than biological parents. Hofferth, Pleck, et al. (forthcoming) have found that there are parenting differences between stepfathers and biological fathers: Biological fathers spend more time with their children, for example. Similarly, cohabiting partners who are the biological parents of the children in their households may be more invested in child rearing than cohabiting partners who are not the children's biological parents.

Estimates based on 1996 Survey of Income and Program Participation data can be used to determine the biological relationship of children and parents (and their partners) in the household. Table 8.2 shows, by age of child, the proportion living with both biological parents—both the small percentage with cohabiting biological parents and the much larger percentage with married biological parents (Federal Interagency Forum on Child and Family Statistics 2000). Estimates of two-biological-parent living are much lower for black children than for white or Hispanic children. In 1996, about 82 percent of preschool-age white children lived with both biological parents, with the proportion declining to 61 percent among teens ages 15 to 17. Among Hispanics, 68 percent of preschoolers lived with both biological parents, with a relatively high proportion (7 percent of all Hispanic children ages 0-4) living with two biological parents who were cohabiting. By age 15 to 17, only about half of Hispanic youth still resided with both parents. Among black children, a little more than one-third of preschoolers resided with two biological parents, with the proportion declining somewhat, to 29 percent, among teens. The low percentage of black children in two-biological-parent families, and the small decline in the proportion for older children, confirms other research that indicates that the likelihood of two-biological-parent living has been low within the black community for some time. A small proportion of children in two-parent families of all races have parents who are cohabiting, although the percentages are much higher for younger children than they are for older children.

Trends indicate that proportionately fewer children today than 10 years ago can count on growing up in households that include both their mothers and their fathers. Bumpass and Lu (2000:Table 6) estimate the propor-

TABLE 8.2   Selected Estimates of Two-Parent Living Arrangements by Race

	Total	White	Black	Hispanic
% of children living with				
two biological parents in 1996				
Child's age				
0-4	72.5	82.4	33.8	67.8
5-14	62.9	69.3	31.3	63.3
15-17	54.9	60.9	29.4	50.3
Two biological parents married				
Child's age				
0-4	68.4	79.0	30.3	60.5
5-14	61.7	68.6	29.9	60.2
15-17	54.5	60.7	29.2	48.7
Two biological parents cohabiting				
Child's age				
0-4	4.1	3.4	3.5	7.3
5-14	1.2	0.7	1.4	3.1
15-17	0.4	0.2	0.2	1.6
% of childhood years spent with married parents				
1980-84	73	83	41	80
1990-94	71	80	16	67

NOTE: Race/ethnicity categories are white, non-Hispanic; black, non-Hispanic; and Hispanic.
SOURCE: Bumpass and Lu (2000), Federal Interagency Forum on Child and Family Statistics (2000).

tion of childhood that children will spend, on average, with married parents, a parent who is cohabiting, or with a single parent not living with a partner in the mid-1980s and mid-1990s. Based on the more recent data, non-Hispanic white children are projected to spend 80 percent of childhood in households with married parents (Table 8.2). Black children, on the other hand, are estimated to spend only 16 percent of childhood with a married parent. This represents a sizable decrease from estimates based on data collected in the mid-1980s, when, on average, 41 percent of a black child's childhood was estimated to be with married parents. Hispanic children are intermediate between black and white households, with 67 percent of childhood expected to be with married parents. The Hispanic estimates are very similar to white rates in the mid-1980s, but according to these projections, Hispanic children experienced a greater shift than white children away from two-parent, married households between the mid-1980s and mid-1990s.

Bumpass and Lu (2000) also estimate very large differences by educational attainment of a child's mother (data not shown). A child born to a college-educated mother is likely to spend close to 90 percent of his or her childhood living with married parents, whereas the proportion drops to 70 percent among children with only high school-educated mothers and to 53 percent among children whose mothers did not complete high school. Part of the racial difference is attributable to average socioeconomic differences among the racial/ethnic groups, although the racial variation is larger than the socioeconomic variation, and hence differences in average educational attainment of mothers cannot explain away the race differential in children's living arrangements. Socioeconomic status may account for more of the difference than these estimates suggest because education is only a rough proxy for socioeconomic status and does not take into account income or wealth differences across racial and ethnic groups.

Foster Children and Adopted Children ●

In Tables 8.1 and 8.2, adoptive parents are considered together with two biological parents, but children who reside with foster parents are classified as living with neither parent. A child is placed in foster care when a court determines that the child's family cannot adequately feed and clothe him or her and provide a minimally safe environment. Between 1982 and 1998, the number of children in foster care more than doubled, from 262,000 to 560,000. The rate per thousand children also increased, from 4.2 to 8.0 (U.S. Department of Health and Human Services 2000a).

Adoptive children constitute a very different group of children. In 1996, an estimated 1.3 million children were living with adoptive parents (Fields 2001). The past three decades have witnessed a decline in adoption overall. On the one hand, there has been a decline in unrelated adoptions, where no preexisting blood tie or marital relationship exists between the adoptive parent and the child. On the other hand, there has been a rise in the proportion of all adoptions that are related adoptions, which may reflect increases in adoptions of stepchildren (Chandra et al. 1999). The overall decline in total adoptions since the 1970s is due to the generally lower fertility during those years, easier access to abortion to prevent unplanned births, and the growing tendency of unmarried mothers to keep their babies rather than give them up for adoption.

In 1995, 1.3 percent of women ages 18 to 44 had ever adopted a child, compared with 2.2 percent in 1982, according to survey data from the National Center for Health Statistics. In 1995, black women were slightly more likely than white women to have adopted a child, whereas in 1988 white women were slightly more likely to have adopted (1.8 percent) than were black women (1.6 percent). Hispanic women were the least likely to have adopted a child in all years of the survey (1973, 1982, 1988, and 1995) (Chandra et al. 1999).

How do adopted children fare compared with other children? The sketchy evidence available suggests that the parents who adopt unrelated children tend to be older, to be more educated, and to have higher incomes than the average couple. Because many couples adopt only after spending some years trying to have their own children and then making their way through the adoption process, adoptive parents, compared with other parents, tend to have been married longer and are more likely to have well-established careers. Also, because finances enter into adoption approval, adoptive parents tend to be better-off financially. All these factors work to the benefit of the child's well-being. Adopted children tend to live with higher-income families than the average, and an overwhelming majority are reported to be in very good health. We have little evidence about other aspects of adoptive children's well-being, but we do know that such children at least begin their new lives with certain advantages (Bachrach 1986; Bachrach et al. 1989).

● Children in Gay and Lesbian Families

Much of the research on the well-being of children in gay and lesbian families has been conducted in response to the issues some judges have raised concerning children's psychological health in custody cases (Falk 1989). Judicial concerns have generally surfaced in three main areas: children's sexual identity, children's personal development (behavioral, emotional, cognitive, and so on), and children's social relationships. In assessing the well-being of children in gay and lesbian families, it is important to consider how these families are formed.

Two of the most common ways gay and lesbian families are formed are when children start out life in gay or lesbian families, either through adoption or through donor insemination, and when children are brought into gay or lesbian families from other families that were begun by heterosexual unions. These two types of families have different sets of concerns, given that children in the latter families were born into a heterosexual context and will have experienced different sets of relationships, including perhaps with fathers, stepparents, mothers' opposite-sex partners, and the extended families of these fathers.

Most of the studies of children's well-being in lesbian families have focused on the differences between lesbian families and heterosexual families and have compared the children of custodial lesbian mothers with those of custodial heterosexual mothers, reflecting primarily the concerns of family courts. For children born into lesbian families, the referent has been either a large representative sample of American children or children born of heterosexual couples using donor insemination. Because relatively few gay families have children living with them, the majority of studies have been based on lesbian families with children (Patterson 2000). Given the low prevalence of gay and lesbian families with children in the U.S. population, most of these studies have been conducted on small, nonrepresentative samples.

Despite study design issues, and regardless of how gay and lesbian families are formed, the overwhelming majority of studies looking at children in these families have found no substantial problems in the children's development of sexual identity, the children's personal development (e.g., behavior, personality, self-concept, locus of control, moral judgment, and intelligence), the children's peer relations, the children's relationships with adults of either gender, or the children's experiencing a heightened risk of sexual abuse (Patterson 1992, 2000; Tasker and Golombok 1997).

Children's Economic Security ●

No child fares well in a situation where the available material resources are inadequate. Consequently, there has been a burgeoning literature on child outcomes focused largely on problem behaviors and children at the low end of the income distribution. Table 8.3 displays several of the most common indicators used to assess children's economic security. The most common is the poverty rate of children. During most of the past two decades,

TABLE 8.3   Indicators of Economic Security for Children: 1980, 1990, and 1998

	1980	1990	1998
% of children in poverty			
All children	18	20	18
Children in two-parent families	NA	10	9
Children in mother-only families	51	53	46
% of children in high-income families[a]	17	21	27
% of children with at least one parent employed full-time, year-round			
All children	70	72	77
Children in two-parent families	80	85	89
Children in mother-only families	33	33	44
Children in father-only families	57	64	70
% of children in two-parent families with both parents employed full-time, year-round	17	25	31
% of children with no parent in the labor force			
All children	NA	10	9
Children in two-parent families	NA	2	2
Children in mother-only families	NA	37	28
Children in father-only families	NA	12	12
Housing problems (%)[b]			
Cost burden > 30% of income	15	24	28
Inadequate physical structure	9	9	7
Crowded (< 1 person/room)	9	7	7
Food security			
Insecure without hunger	NA	NA	15
Insecure with moderate/severe hunger	NA	NA	5

SOURCE: Federal Interagency Forum on Child and Family Statistics (2000).
NOTE: NA = not available.
a. Four or more times the poverty threshold.
b. Years for housing measurement are 1978, 1989, and 1997.

this rate has hovered at or above 20 percent, dipping below 20 percent at the end of the 1990s.

Although there is little question, if one looks at official rates, that poverty has "juvenilized" (Lichter 1997), Mayer and Jencks (1989a) question how this affects children's lives. First, they note that the use of different adjustments for inflation gives a sizable range of poverty estimates for children. Second, the official definition of poverty, which excludes income from nonrelatives such as cohabiting partners of children's mothers, may underestimate the income available to children. Third, data from the Consumer Expenditure Survey indicate that consumption by households with children may not have declined. This raises the possibility that more income may go unreported now than in the past, something that is also suggested by ethnographic evidence (e.g., Edin and Lein 1997a). Finally, the official measure of poverty does not include the value of noncash assistance, such as food stamps and Medicaid, both of which have been important for poor households in the past three decades.

Measures of serious hardship suggest continued improvement in the living standards of children—especially in the most income deprived of households (Mayer 1997b). Mayer (1997a) paints a picture of poor children who are increasingly better housed over time. For example, the percentage of children in the lowest income quintile living in homes without complete bathrooms, with leaky roofs, holes in the floors, no central heat, no electric outlets, or no sewer or septic systems has declined substantially. Children have become less likely to live in crowded housing conditions, although home ownership has declined and crime in children's neighborhoods has increased. Mayer and Jencks (1989b) argue that a relatively high-quality housing stock in central cities was vacated by the middle class, increasing the ability of the poor to live in uncrowded housing with amenities such as indoor plumbing, electric lights, and even air conditioning. However, the safety and vibrancy of the neighborhoods surrounding this housing stock may have deteriorated over time.

Mayer (1997a) also finds poor children today to be more likely to receive medical attention than in the past. In terms of health, the proportion who had not visited a doctor in the previous year declined, especially in the 1970s. Poor children are more likely to be immunized against disease today than in the past. In terms of consumer durables, children at the bottom of the income distribution have become more likely to live in families that own air conditioners and have telephone service. In sum, Mayer (1997b) argues that these indicators at least raise the possibility that trends in the official poverty measure based on money income do not adequately capture trends in material hardship of children. On indicators of housing, health, and certain consumption items, children's material conditions seem to have improved over time, even among the poorest income quintile. The most dramatic improvement took place during the 1970s, but conditions have not deteriorated since then and some indicators (e.g., access to air conditioning) suggest continued improvement.

However, it is important to remember that even during the period of greatest economic expansion in U.S. history, one out of five children is poor. A vast amount of research on child poverty documents that deep and early poverty has long-lasting effects on children (Duncan et al. 1998). Assessments of welfare reform have directed attention to the plight of women and children in low-income families. There has been increased attention to the possible negative employment and marriage incentives embodied in previous welfare programs (Moffitt 1992; Murray 1984). Ethnographic work has enhanced our knowledge of how poor mothers package income and welfare in order to provide for their households (Edin and Lein 1997a, 1997b; Harris 1993).

This attention to the bottom of the income distribution and incentive effects in welfare programs has resulted in a heavy emphasis on the negative effects of single parenting in the parental investment literature. In their widely cited book *Growing Up With a Single Parent: What Hurts, What Helps,* McLanahan and Sandefur (1994) focus on the negative outcomes among young adults (lower educational achievement, early parenting, and youth "idleness") that might be attributed to growing up in single-parent families. What has received much less attention is how children are faring at the "high" end of the income distribution and whether the parenting that occurs among highly educated, high-income families is increasingly differentiated from that in households with less educated parents with low income.

Table 8.3 shows that the group of children in high-income households (here defined as children in families with income more than four times the poverty level) has grown during the past two decades, from about 17 percent of all children in 1980 to 27 percent in 1998. The robust economy of the late 1990s also meant that an increasing proportion of children lived with at least one parent who was "securely" attached to the labor force—that is, a parent who held a full-time, year-round job during the preceding year. The proportion of children living with a full-time breadwinning parent is much higher for those in two-parent families, and the proportion with a parent "securely" attached to the labor force increased from 80 percent to 89 percent between 1980 and 1998. The proportion of children in two-parent families in which both parents are employed full-time and year-round remained in the minority but increased from 17 percent in 1980 to 31 percent in 1998 as married mothers' labor force rates continued to increase (see Chapter 10 for more discussion of this topic).

Perhaps more striking is the fact that increases in full-time employment also occurred for children living with single mothers in the 1990s (from 33 percent to 44 percent) and for children living with single fathers in both the

1980s and the 1990s (from 57 percent in 1980 to 64 percent in 1990, to 70 percent in 1998). Reciprocally, for children living only with their mothers, there was a decrease in the proportion living in households where no parent was in the labor force, although this proportion remained relatively high (28 percent) in 1998. Labor force attachment does not in and of itself indicate whether parents are able to earn sufficient income to cover their families' needs, but the high poverty rates for children living only with their mothers suggest that low earnings continue to be a problem for many single mothers. Although rates of poverty declined from 1990 to 1998 (from 53 percent to 46 percent) as labor force rates of single mothers increased, a child was nonetheless almost as likely to be in poverty as not when he or she lived in a mother-only family.

Housing indicators also suggest a heightened problem for all families. As housing prices soared in many localities, the proportion of children residing in families where more than 30 percent of income went to housing almost doubled (from 15 percent to 28 percent). Other housing indicators suggest that a slightly smaller proportion of children lived in crowded dwellings or inadequate housing in 1998 (7 percent) than in 1980 (9 percent). Note that these are most likely the children at the bottom of the income distribution—the children Mayer maintains are faring better today than in the past.

Data on one more indicator of whether children are receiving the necessities of life—levels of food security and hunger—are shown in Table 8.3. We have measures of this dimension of children's lives only for the most recent time period, but we know that in 1998 approximately 15 percent of children lived in families that experienced "food insecurity," and 5 percent actually had family members who went hungry at some point. According to the Food and Nutrition Service of the U.S. Department of Agriculture (1997), in some food-insecure households no one goes hungry, but family members report anxiety about and difficulty obtaining enough food, reduced quality of diets, and use of emergency food sources and other coping behaviors. In households with moderate hunger, adults report a pattern of hunger, and adults and children both report going hungry in households with severe hunger.

One of the issues that arises for low-income and high-income children alike, as parents, especially mothers, increase their labor force participation and more children live with only one parent, is whether children gain access to better material resources but lose access to parental time as a result of their mothers' increased need (and also desire) to work outside the home. The answer to this question that is emerging from time diary research is somewhat surprising.

● Parents and Children

Reliable, responsive, and sensitive parental care plays a key role in children's growth and development, and parents have profound influence on children from the beginning of their children's lives (Cummings, Goeke-Morey, and Graham forthcoming). Regardless of whether "parents" live with their children or whether they are single parents, married-couple parents, grandparents, foster parents, or stepparents, parents' maintenance of positive relationships with their children provides those children with stable environments in which to grow and affects their well-being. For example, Hofferth recently found that parents who have warm and loving relationships with their children have children who are happier, less withdrawn, and less likely to have behavior problems compared with parents who do not have warm relationships with their children (see National Institute of Child Health and Human Development 2000).

What parents say and do, how they feel, and whether they approve or disapprove of their children's behavior affects children's well-being. Children who receive feedback and advice from their parents have higher self-esteem and self-confidence, and these traits help to prepare children to make better decisions (Cummings et al. forthcoming). Parents' behavior is also associated with children's behavior; children often imitate what their parents say and do (Radke-Yarrow, Zahn-Waxler, and Chapman 1983). Parents' thoughts, feelings, and attitudes also affect children's behavior; children sense their parents' feelings, and children's subsequent behavior has been linked to the way parents feel (Cohn and Tronick 1983). And finally, parents' approval and disapproval also affect children's behavior. On the one hand, harsh disapproval from parents can hurt children's self-esteem; on the other, parents' never expressing disapproval can hurt children's ability to deal with criticism.

Parental Time With Children

There seems to be widespread consensus among family demographers that the lack of two-parent families—because they are not formed or because, once formed, partnerships are unstable—is problematic for children (Cherlin 1999; McLanahan and Sandefur 1994). This consensus is also shared by policy makers; welfare reform specifically calls for encouraging marriage and two-parent families among the poor. The most compelling evidence to support this claim is that "father absence" harms children because child support is not paid (Furstenberg, Morgan, and Allison 1987; Garfinkel, McLanahan, and Robins 1994). Lack of father involvement may also disadvantage children in other ways, but the evidence on this is far less definitive (Amato and Gilbreth 1999; King 1994). Biblarz and Raftery (1999) express unease with the "new consensus" that the "stable 'intact' family remains the best-functioning form" (p. 327); using an evolutionary biology perspective, they develop an argument for why children may not be seriously disadvantaged (controlling for economic resources) in single-mother homes but would be at risk of underinvestment in single-father and step-parent families. Also, as we have noted above, there is a presumption (and some evidence) that stepfathers are less involved in parenting children than are biological fathers in two-parent families.

In single-mother families, most mothers must work to compensate for the reduction (or lack) of income from absent fathers. The growth in the numbers of single-parent families alters mothers' behavior primarily by inducing greater maternal employment, given that most mothers still retain physical custody of their children after divorce or when there is a child born outside of marriage who is not given up for adoption.

Because of this, more married mothers are employed today than was true in the 1950s (see Chapter 10). Given the increase in women's paid employment, many people have begun to worry about how mothers' employment affects children's well-being. This is not the first time this concern has been raised: After World War II, when women were being encouraged to leave the labor force, mothers' employment was portrayed as harmful to children; during the war, when there were labor shortages, mothers' employment was encouraged. Relatively few studies have assessed the effects of paternal employment on children's outcomes, because the vast majority of fathers have always earned money to support their families (but for an exception, see Parcel and Menaghan 1994). A number of researchers have used data from the National Longitudinal Survey of Youth to assess the effects of maternal employment on children's cognitive ability and behavioral adjustment. There may be some negative effects of maternal employment—when employment occurs early in the first year of life (Belsky and Eggebeen 1991; Blau and Grossberg 1990; Han, Waldfogel, and Brooks-Gunn 2001), and perhaps for middle-class sons (Baydar and Brooks-Gunn 1991; Desai, Chase-Lansdale, and Michael 1989; Greenstein 1995), although here the evidence is not entirely consistent (Parcel and Menaghan 1994). Negative outcomes can also occur when maternal employment is combined with other stressful conditions, such as the birth of another child or unusually long work hours of fathers (Parcel and Menaghan 1994), or if mothers feel distress due to role overload or conflict between work and family roles (Perry-Jenkins, Repetti, and Crouter 2000). But given the effort that has been devoted to searching for negative effects of maternal employment on children's academic achievement and emotional adjustment, the paucity of findings (either positive or negative) is surprising.

Two reasons for the lack of findings on maternal employment may be that mothers' time with children may not vary as much as one might think, either across time or by mothers' work status, and that fathers may be picking up some of the slack (Bianchi 2000). Time diary data suggest that we may tend to *overestimate* maternal time available for child rearing when mothers do not work outside the home and *underestimate* the adjustments mothers and fathers make to protect their time with children when they increase their work hours.

It is difficult to estimate changes in parental time with children in the United States because there has been relatively little direct measurement across time and because most surveys have focused solely on maternal time. Keith Bryant and Cathleen Zick (1996a, 1996b; Bryant 1996; Zick and Bryant 1996) have done the most extensive historical work on maternal time with children, piecing together trends from time diary studies conducted between the 1920s and the early 1980s—that is, from studies in which interviewers walk respondents through the previous day, recording all activities sequentially as they occurred (Juster and Stafford 1985; Robinson and Godbey 1999). Due to data limitations, Bryant and Zick's analyses are restricted to parental time in white, two-parent families with children, and they examine only time during which mothers and fathers report they are primarily engaged in family care.

On a per family basis, Bryant and Zick (1996a) show virtually no change between the 1920s and 1975: They estimate that mothers spent an average of 1.2 hours per day caring for family members in both the 1920s and the 1970s. On a per child basis, their estimates suggest an increase, from 0.6 to 0.9 hours per day, per child, in direct care, primarily because families were smaller by 1975. The estimates may seem low, as they capture only time during which mothers report they are directly involved in caring for children and do not include time the mother spends with children but engaged in other activities, such as housework.

Bryant and Zick acknowledge that employment outside the home reduces time spent caring for children, other things being equal. Increasing female employment rates should have reduced maternal time with children during the time period they examine. However, their findings indicate that they would have overestimated a reduction in maternal time if they had not considered changes in family size, attention to who was actually looking after children in the large families of the 1920s, and investigation of competing "unpaid" work mothers were doing instead of child care at the earlier time point. In addition, they note that over time, as mothers moved into the paid workforce, average educational attainment also rose. More highly educated mothers spend more time in direct child care, other things being equal, perhaps because they are more aware of the effects of parental involvement in children's social, cognitive, and emotional development.

How did parental time change, and what happened in more recent decades when the most dramatic changes in mothers' labor force participation occurred in the United States? Figure 8.2 compares mothers' and fathers' time with children in 1998 with comparably collected data for 1965.[1] The figure shows three measures of time with children: time when the main (or primary) activity was a child-care activity, time when child care was mentioned as a secondary use of time in response to the query "Were you doing anything else?" (e.g., cooking dinner but also helping a child with homework), and time that a parent reported doing any activity (child care or other) in the company of children, with children present (e.g., watching television).

The top panel of the figure shows that despite increased single parenting and maternal employment, when we compare mothers' reports of the hours per day they spend caring for children directly (either as a primary activity or as a secondary activity) or time with children in any activity, mothers today are spending as much, if not more, time with their children as they did during the Baby Boom. The bottom panel shows that the increases in married fathers' time with children between 1965 and 1998 were substantial—from 2.8 to 3.8 hours per day spent in any activity with children. Thus both mothers and fathers, but especially fathers, have increased the time they spend with children. If we adjust for the smaller family sizes in 1998, these estimates suggest that mothers and fathers may be spending significantly more time per child today than were mothers and fathers during the "family-oriented" 1960s.

Compared with single-earner families, mothers in dual-earner families do not substitute "quality" for "quantity" of time with children when they work long hours: Employed mothers spend substantially less time with children than do nonemployed mothers in direct "quality" time with children—less time educating/playing with preschool-age children and less time "having fun" with children of all ages on their longest work days (Nock and Kingston, 1988). But most of the time that nonemployed mothers spend with their preschoolers is not necessarily one-on-one quality

● **Figure 8.2.** Change in Parents' Daily Hours of Child Care and Time With Children

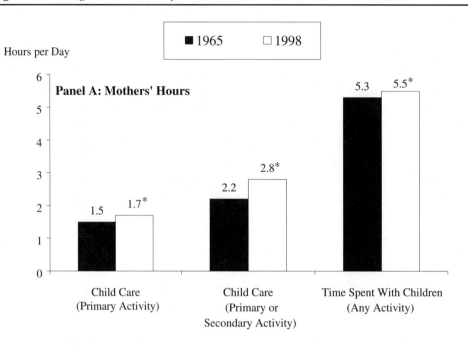

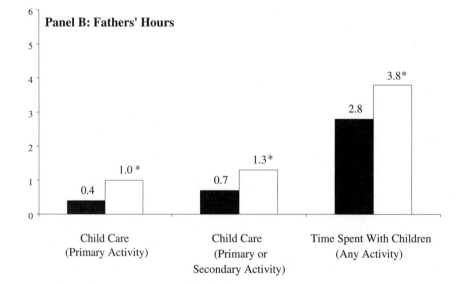

SOURCE: Bianchi (2000).
NOTE: Estimates based on one-day, "yesterday" time diaries collected from 417 mothers in 1965-66, 273 mothers in 1998-99, 326 married fathers in 1965-66, and 194 married fathers in 1998-99, all with children under age 18 at the time of the interview. Child care includes child and baby care, helping/teaching children, speaking/reading to children, indoor/outdoor play with children, and medical/travel/other child-related care.
*Test of 1965-98 difference in means is statistically significant, $p < .05$.

time. Rather, it is time during which the mothers are engaged in cooking and other household chores. Whereas nonemployed mothers spend more than twice as much time per day with their preschoolers present (9 hours compared with a little more than 4 hours for employed mothers), there is a difference of less than an hour in time in direct child care and play/education. However, there is an additional hour's difference in "having fun" with their preschoolers, which includes things like trips to museums and the movies, but these are activities that high-quality child-care settings might also provide. For school-age children, there are no differences in child-care time or play/education time between employed and nonemployed mothers, although employed mothers spend less time with their children on their longest work days: 40 minutes less time "having fun" with their children and less time doing household chores with the children present.

Nock and Kingston (1988:81) suggest that perhaps part of the reason so few negative effects have been found for children of employed mothers is that even nonemployed mothers spend a relatively small portion of their time interacting directly with their children, and this tends to minimize differences between employed and nonemployed mothers. Whether this assessment is correct or not depends on the importance to children of their mothers' (or fathers') "being there," because the large difference between employed and nonemployed mothers is in time during which mothers are available but not directly engaged in activities with their children. As technology has changed and the availability and use of cellular phones and pagers have become more widespread, working mothers (and fathers) may increasingly be able to fill their children's need to have parents "on call" without being physically present in the home; this is an area that researchers are only beginning to explore (Galinsky 1999; Waite et al. 2000).

If mothers have not reduced their time with children, on average, and fathers, at least married fathers, are increasing their time with children, isn't this good news for children? It would seem so, and U.S. trends are similar to those found in several other industrialized countries (Niemi 1988). For example, Michael Bittman (1999a, 1999b) has shown that fathers' (and mothers') time in child care rose substantially in Australia between 1974 and 1992. Interestingly, the age profile of fathers' time with children also shifted in such a way as to suggest that fathers are much more involved in infant care than in the past. Fischer, McCulloch, and Gershuny (1999) show similar trends for Britain: increased child-care time on the part of fathers (and mothers) between the mid-1970s and 1999, with increases especially sharp since 1985 for those with children under age 5. Heather Joshi (1998:Table 2) noted in her 1996 presidential address to the European Society for Population Economics that men's share of work in the home (including child care) increased from about one-fourth in the 1960s or early 1970s to 35-40 percent by the late 1980s in the United Kingdom, the Netherlands, and Denmark.

What Activities Do Parents Engage in With Children?

Of course, the more important question is, What are parents doing with and for their children when they spend time with them? Further, how do these activities vary by family type and socioeconomic status? A child well-being supplement to the Survey of Income and Program Participation ascertained for a large national sample how often parents read to preschool children and whether parents monitored TV watching for both preschool and older children.[2] As Hofferth (1999) has shown, these types of reports may be subject to "social desirability" effects, as parents tend to throw a favorable light on their involvement with and monitoring of children. Still, the variation in these parental reports is striking.

Table 8.4 shows the percentages of parents who report that their preschool-age children are never read to and, at the other end of the spectrum, the percentages who report that their children are read to daily (seven or more times per week). About 13 percent of very young children and 9 percent of children ages 3 to 5 are never read to, according to parental reports. Conversely, almost half are read to seven or more times a week. White children are read to more often than are black children, who in turn are read to more often than are Hispanic children. Children living in two-parent families are much more likely to be read to often than are children with single parents. Most striking are the differences in frequent reading to children by socioeconomic status, differences that factor into race and family-type differences. According to parental reports, more than 60 percent of children of college-educated parents are read to seven or more times a week, compared with only 40 percent of children of high school-educated parents and about 30 percent of those whose parents did not complete high school. Patterns are similar by monthly family income.

A very high proportion of children have parents who report setting rules on TV viewing. Table 8.5 shows the percentages of children in three age groups whose parents reported setting rules. Parents were asked about whether or not they had set three types of rules: rules on the types of programs their children could watch, restrictions on the times of day when children could watch television, and limits on the number of hours their children could watch. The overwhelming majority of parents reported set-

TABLE 8.4 Parental Reading to Preschool-Age Children[a]: Fall 1994

	Children 1-2 Years Old		Children 3-5 Years Old	
	% Never	% 7+ Times	% Never	% 7+Times
Total	12.8	48.2	9.1	46.5
Child's race				
White	7.6	56.2	4.2	52.9
Black	16.3	30.7	15.1	34.4
Hispanic	37.1	20.1	26.9	25.6
Family type				
Two parents	11.2	51.6	7.4	49.9
Ever-married single parent	19.9	32.8	11.2	37.1
Never-married single parent	19.6	32.9	19.7	31.2
Educational attainment of parents				
Less than high school	28.1	28.3	22.5	30.0
High school	15.1	40.0	10.0	40.1
Some college	9.1	49.3	5.0	50.1
College +	4.7	68.7	2.4	63.4
Monthly family income				
Less than $1,500	22.5	32.7	17.3	34.4
$1,500-$2,999	11.8	47.7	9.8	43.4
$3,000-$4,499	11.2	49.2	5.3	48.9
$4,500+	4.9	64.7	2.5	61.2

SOURCE: Fields et al. (2001:Tables 5 and 6).
NOTE: Race/ethnicity categories are white, non-Hispanic; black, non-Hispanic; and Hispanic.
a. Data displayed also include some reading by other family members.

ting at least one rule, and more than 50 percent of all children ages 3 to 5 and ages 6 to 11 were subject to all three types of limitations, according to parental reports. Constraints seem to ease for teenage children, but even for this group, 79 percent are subject to at least one type of rule. Again, there are variations by race, family type, and socioeconomic status, particularly by educational attainment of parents, but the variations are not as extreme as those for reading to preschoolers.

TABLE 8.5 Parental TV Rule Setting for Children Ages 3-5, 6-11, and 12-17 by Selected Characteristics: Fall 1994

	% With at Least One TV Rule			% With Three Types of Rules		
	Ages 3-5	Ages 6-11	Ages 12-17	Ages 3-5	Ages 6-11	Ages 12-17
Total	91.3	94.7	79.2	54.0	60.3	40.2
Child's race						
White	93.0	96.3	80.2	53.3	59.3	37.6
Black	93.0	94.3	80.2	57.9	67.1	47.5
Hispanic	82.5	88.1	74.6	52.7	59.7	45.6
Family type						
Two parents	91.9	95.2	80.7	54.8	61.1	41.1
Ever-married single parent	91.8	94.7	76.7	57.4	61.1	38.6
Never-married single parent	86.3	89.5	70.2	43.8	51.9	33.7
Educational attainment of parents						
Less than high school	81.3	86.1	73.7	45.5	51.2	38.5
High school	91.5	95.6	78.2	47.8	57.0	37.9
Some college	93.3	96.4	81.5	57.5	62.8	40.9
College +	96.3	98.1	83.6	65.1	70.2	45.1
Monthly family income						
Less than $1,500	89.2	91.7	78.2	50.5	57.7	43.2
$1,500-$2,999	89.8	93.5	77.8	53.4	58.8	40.0
$3,000-$4,499	93.2	96.4	80.6	58.2	60.9	38.7
$4,500+	93.9	97.1	79.9	54.9	63.6	39.2

SOURCE: Fields et al. (2001:Tables 8 and 10).
NOTE: Parents were asked whether they had rules about what programs children could watch, the times of day children could watch TV, and the number of hours children could watch TV. Race/ethnicity categories are white, non-Hispanic; black, non-Hispanic; and Hispanic.

● How Do Children Spend Their Time?

Time diary data on how children spend time and variation by parental characteristics suggest that parental education may be the strongest predictor of children's time use. Using time diary data collected from a statewide probability sample of California children ages 3-11 in 1989-90, Bianchi and

Robinson (1997) examined the amount of time children spent on activities presumed to affect their cognitive development—reading or being read to, studying, and watching TV. Children of highly educated parents studied and read more and watched TV less. Hofferth also found this relationship using a nationally representative sample (see National Institute of Child Health and Human Development 2000). In multivariate analysis, and contrary to initial expectations, net of education, children with stay-at-home mothers did not spend more time reading and studying and less time TV watching. Nor were children of single parents significantly different in their time in these activities from children living with two parents, once parental education was controlled. These results reinforce the findings of other research that suggests that parental education may be the predominant predictor of types of parental investment and monitoring of children (Hill and Stafford 1974, 1980; Leibowitz 1974, 1977).

How has children's use of time changed? Using data from the Panel Study of Income Dynamics, Hofferth and Sandberg (2001) have documented changes in children's activities for 3- to 11-year-olds from 1981 to 1997. On the one hand, they note, children spend more time in school (including day care), accompanying their parents on errands, and performing household chores than they did in 1981 (National Institute of Child Health and Human Development 2000). On the other hand, children spend less time in unstructured play.

In 1997, children spent slightly more than 29 hours per week in school, compared with only 21 hours in 1981. The amount of time they spent doing housework nearly doubled over the time period, from about 2.5 hours per week in 1981 to more than 5.5 hours in 1997. In 1997, children spent more time in school than in any other activity, yet coming in at second place was television watching. Children spent slightly more than 13 hours per week watching television. However, their television watching decreased by 2 hours from 1981 to 1997.

Children's Enrichment Activities

Studies have found that involvement in sports, lessons, clubs, and after-school programs helps children to develop positive social and psychological attributes as well as better social skills and improved math and reading skills. Specifically, research that has controlled for maternal education, race, and family income has shown that children involved in after-school programs have more advanced social skills (Howes, Olenick, and Der-Kiureghian 1987) and higher levels of math and reading achievement (Mayesky 1979) than do those not involved in such programs. Among researchers, a prevalent assumption is that sports can build character in important ways, such as developing responsibility, a strong work ethic, persistence, and a sense of fairness (Griffen 1998), as well as strengthening overall self-esteem (Kishton and Dixon 1995). Support for this assumption appears to exist, with some studies finding a positive correlation between participation in sports and good self-image among children (Kishton and Dixon 1995). Other research has found that enrichment activities play a role in children's levels of self-control, as participation in such group activities may mediate the tendency toward committing deviant acts (McNeal 1995) and provides children with networks or places where they can meet and interact (Griffen 1998).

Table 8.6 shows that in 1994 almost 13 percent of students were in classes for gifted students, with the proportion varying from a high of 21 percent for students whose parents were college educated to a low of 6 percent for those whose parents had not completed high school. White and black children were almost twice as likely as Hispanic children to be in gifted classes. Boys were three times more likely than girls to be enrolled in gifted classes.

Among children ages 6 to 11, one-third participated in sports, 39 percent belonged to clubs, and almost one-fourth took some type of lessons. Participation in sports and clubs was higher for those ages 12 to 17, but in this age group the proportion who took lessons dropped to just below one-fifth. Despite Title IX and the amazing increase it brought about in girls' opportunities to participate in sports, boys are still much more likely than girls to participate in sports. By contrast, clubs and, even more so, lessons are more the purview of girls than of boys. The incidence of participation in all types of extracurricular activities is lower among minority children, those who live with single parents, those who live with less educated parents, and those who live in families with lower incomes.

But participation in enrichment activities can also be very expensive, both in terms of finances and in terms of the time required of parents to transport children to and from the activities. In addition, costs are likely to vary by activity type. For example, a child who participates in a soccer league may be charged a registration fee as well as the cost of a uniform, including cleats and shin guards; a child who takes piano lessons has to pay for each lesson received, and the family incurs the cost of purchasing or renting a piano. In contrast, participation in school-based sports activities and clubs may be free of charge. Although research has yet to examine whether and how much families pay for these activities, we can

TABLE 8.6   Percentages of School-Age Children Enrolled in Gifted Classes and
Extracurricular Activities: Fall 1994

	Ages 6-11				Ages 12-17		
	Gifted Classes[a]	Sports	Clubs	Lessons	Sports	Clubs	Lessons
Total	12.5	34.3	38.8	23.7	42.2	42.5	19.1
Child's sex							
Female	3.7	25.5	40.8	30.9	35.1	47.1	24.7
Male	11.4	42.5	36.9	16.9	49.0	38.2	13.8
Child's race							
White	13.5	41.1	45.1	27.1	47.0	48.6	21.1
Black	13.1	17.2	28.4	15.2	35.3	33.1	14.3
Hispanic	7.9	20.2	20.6	12.6	29.0	23.8	12.3
Family type							
Two parents	13.3	38.7	42.0	26.7	45.9	46.4	21.0
Ever-married single parent	10.6	26.8	31.9	17.5	34.4	35.4	15.1
Never-married single parent	9.7	13.2	26.2	12.5	26.0	20.3	11.3
Educational attainment of parents							
Less than high school	6.0	15.5	18.0	9.5	24.7	21.3	10.0
High school	9.4	31.4	35.5	17.9	41.1	38.8	15.1
Some college	14.1	36.7	45.2	23.9	45.7	48.0	21.0
College +	20.9	51.4	53.5	45.1	57.2	63.1	33.3
Monthly family income							
Less than $1,500	9.1	16.4	25.1	12.9	25.9	28.0	11.5
$1,500-$2,999	10.0	29.6	33.4	17.4	38.2	36.4	14.9
$3,000-$4,499	12.0	40.0	46.1	25.9	45.0	46.3	19.5
$4,500+	18.7	51.3	51.0	39.0	54.8	55.1	27.8

SOURCE: Fields et al. (2001:Tables 11, 12, 13, and 14).
NOTE: Race/ethnicity categories are white, non-Hispanic; black, non-Hispanic; and Hispanic.
a. Data on attendance in gifted classes were gathered only for children ages 6-11.

explore whether participation in particular activities is related to family income levels.

Table 8.7 shows the proportion of children ages 5 to 14 participating in
each type of activity by the family's income level in 1995. Children were indeed more likely to participate in these activities if their families had more

money. For example, twice as many children living in families with monthly incomes of $4,500 or more (52 percent) participated in some type of enrichment activity, compared with those living in families with monthly incomes of less than $1,200 (24 percent). These differences by income persist regardless of the activity. The obvious explanation for this finding is that children from families with lower incomes are less able to afford the costs associated with participation in such activities. However, other possible explanations exist as well. For example, children in families with lower incomes are more likely than other children to live in poor neighborhoods, and these neighborhoods may be less likely to offer enrichment opportunities for children. In addition, children from poor families are more likely to be in single-mother families, and research has shown that children who live with their fathers are more likely to be involved in sports than are those living only with their mothers (Smith 2000).

Children and School

Preschool Enrollment

The increase in nursery school or preschool attendance is the major change in U.S. school enrollment during the past two decades. In the case of 3- to 5-year-olds, the percentage enrolled in nursery schools, pre-kindergarten or kindergarten programs, or child-care centers with "educational" curricula increased dramatically between 1965 and 1997 (see Figure 7.3 in Chapter 7). As we have discussed in Chapter 7, this change has been motivated, in part, by the increased demand for child care as more mothers of young children have joined the labor force. However, enrollment in nursery and preschool programs has been nearly as high for children of nonemployed mothers as for children of mothers employed outside the home. In October 1997, 52 percent of 3- and 4-year-old children of employed mothers attended nursery school or kindergarten, compared with 44 percent of children whose mothers did not work outside the home.

Enrollment in nursery schools is higher for black children (54 percent) than for white children (47 percent) or Hispanic children (31 percent), but a larger proportion of black and Hispanic children are enrolled in public programs. About three-fourths of black and Hispanic children attend public nursery schools, compared with only 42 percent of white children (Martinez and Day 1999).

Nursery school attendance is more common in the Northeast than in other U.S. regions (55 percent, compared with a low of 41 percent in the

TABLE 8.7 Participation in Enrichment Activities Among Children Ages 5 to 14 by Family Income: Fall 1995

| | | % Participating in Enrichment Activities | | | | |
Characteristic	Number of Children (in thousands)	Total	Sports	Lessons	Clubs	Before/ After-School Program
Children 5-14 years old	38,288	39.3	22.4	16.1	14.5	5.6
Monthly family income						
Less than $1,200	9,374	24.0	11.1	9.5	7.9	3.2
$1,200 to $2,999	9,817	37.0	21.1	13.7	12.9	5.1
$3,000 to $4,499	7,837	43.2	23.9	18.3	17.1	5.0
$4,500 or more	10,881	52.4	32.5	22.8	20.3	8.5
Missing	319	17.6	7.6	7.0	—[a]	3.0

SOURCE: Survey of Income and Program Participation, 1993 Panel, Wave 9.
a. Rounds to zero.

West) and is slightly higher among children who live outside the central cities of metropolitan areas than among those in central cities or rural areas (U.S. Bureau of the Census 1997). However, the gap between nursery school attendance in central cities and the suburbs has closed since 1988, when there was a difference of almost 9 percentage points in nursery school attendance. Thus, although the higher incidence of preprimary enrollment among suburban children could reflect the fact that families living in these areas tend to be more affluent than families living in central cities or nonmetropolitan areas, the greater similarity in the late 1990s may have to do with mothers' increased labor force participation and increased income in this period. Even so, the cost of preschool may be prohibitive for low-income parents. Except for programs such as Head Start and pre-kindergarten programs offered in some public schools, nursery school can be relatively expensive (see Chapter 7).

Well-educated families, which are probably also more affluent, are more likely than less educated families to enroll their children in preschool programs: 61 percent of young children whose mothers were college graduates (or had advanced degrees) attended nursery school in the fall of 1997, whereas only 33 percent of those whose mothers had not completed high school were enrolled.

Thirty years ago, most children's first experience with a school setting came at around age 5, when they entered kindergarten. Today, a significant minority of American 3- and 4-year-olds, the majority in affluent families with well-educated parents, have learned many of the behavioral expectations of teachers and classrooms prior to their entry into kindergarten. Kindergarten curricula have become somewhat more "academic," partially in response to this trend in prekindergarten enrollment.

Grade School and High School Enrollment

School attendance is compulsory for children between the ages of 7 and 15, and enrollment in school has been virtually universal for this age group since at least 1960. For 5- and 6-year-olds, school attendance increased from about 80 percent in 1960 to 95 percent in the mid-1970s, reflecting the general move toward school attendance at earlier ages and almost universal kindergarten attendance (U.S. Bureau of the Census 1997).

One important change in school enrollment has been an increase in the proportion of 16- and 17-year-olds who remain enrolled in school. In 1960, 85 percent of white and 76 percent of black youths in this age group were enrolled in school. In the latter 1990s, the proportions stood at about 95 percent for whites and 93 percent for blacks. Asian and Pacific Islander students have a comparable enrollment rate of 96 percent. For Hispanic youth, enrollment in school for 16-year-olds is close to the proportions found in other racial and ethnic groups, but the rate for 17-year-olds is quite low compared with the others, at 83 percent (U.S. Bureau of the Census 1997).

High school completion rates improved in the 1980s for white and black students and in both the 1980s and 1990s for Hispanic students, although Hispanic students continue to have the lowest completion rates (see Table 8.8). An increasing proportion of students are completing high school by equivalency exam than by the more traditional diploma. For example, in 1990, 81 percent received diplomas and 4 percent received equivalency degrees. In 1998, the comparable numbers were 75 percent and 10 percent, respectively (Federal Interagency Forum on Child and Family Statistics 2000:103). College completion rates have also risen, but more so for whites than for minority students.

Academic Performance

After age 5 or 6, children spend much of their day in school. The school environment and how it affects children—educationally, socially, and

TABLE 8.8 High School and College Completion of Young Adults and Education Performance of Schoolchildren

	1980	1990	1998
% of 18- to 24-year-olds who have completed high school			
Total	84	86	85
Whites	88	90	90
Blacks	75	83	81
Hispanics	57	59	63
% of high school graduates ages 25-29 with B.A. or more education			
Total	26	27	31
Whites	28	30	35
Blacks	15	16	18
Hispanics	13	14	17
Math achievement (NAEP) scores[a]			
Age 9	219	230	231
Age 13	269	270	274
Age 17	299	305	307
Reading achievement (NAEP) scores[b]			
Age 9	215	209	212
Age 13	259	257	259
Age 17	286	290	287

SOURCE: Federal Interagency Forum on Child and Family Statistics (2000).
NOTE: Race/ethnicity categories are white, non-Hispanic; black, non-Hispanic; and Hispanic. NAEP = National Assessment of Educational Progress.
a. Math assessments for 1982, 1990, 1996.
b. Reading assessments for 1980, 1990, 1996.

emotionally—are critical aspects of children's well-being. Concerns about the quality of education children are receiving in the public schools continue to command the attention of local school boards and state legislatures. Many parents also spend considerable time and energy monitoring their children's progress in school, helping with homework, and interacting with teachers and other school officials. It has been estimated that children spent about an hour more a week studying and reading in 1981 than they did in 1997 (National Institute of Child Health and Human Development 2000). Most parents want their children to do well in school, finish high school, perhaps go on to college, and move successfully into the adult world of work.

The academic competence of students as they leave high school is at least as important as the proportion of high school students who graduate. During the past three decades, considerable attention has been given to declining levels of achievement, at least among the brightest schoolchildren, and the disadvantage in math and science achievement of U.S. schoolchildren compared with schoolchildren in other advanced industrial nations. The most often cited measures of school achievement among elementary and secondary school-age children come from the congressionally mandated National Assessment of Educational Progress (NAEP), which has tested students' reading, mathematics, and science achievement at selected intervals in the 1970s, 1980s, and the 1990s. In recent years, the NAEP has assessed more than just basic skills, adding sections on children's computer literacy and high school students' knowledge of history, geography, and literature. Table 8.8 shows average reading and math scores on the NAEP over the past two decades. According to these assessments, average reading achievement scores have not changed, and math achievement scores are somewhat higher than in the early 1980s. However, over this period a substantial number of children came to the United States from other countries, most of whom did not speak English as their first language.

The most often cited evidence of the deterioration of the academic achievement of U.S. students has been the decline in average scores on college entrance examinations, particularly the Scholastic Aptitude Test (SAT), that occurred between 1963 and 1980. Research indicates that a sizable portion of the decline in the 1960s resulted from a change in the composition of the population taking the test, as college attendance rose among students of lower ability. However, this does not explain the continued decline during the 1970s. Some of the decline may have resulted from changes in high school curricula that allowed students to take more electives and a general movement away from traditional academic course work (Mare 1981, 1995). Partially in response to these findings, there was a "back to basics" movement in the schools during the 1980s, with many states increasing the courses required for high school graduation (National Center for Education Statistics 1989:Table 133).

A slight increase in verbal and mathematics scores on the SAT in 1982 halted a decade-long decline. The trend since 1982 has been decidedly mixed. Average verbal SAT scores fell from 1987 to 1994, and then a 5-point gain occurred in 1995, bringing the average verbal score to 428 points. This, however, is 50 points lower than the level in 1963, which was 478. Mathematics scores have fared differently. The gains in students' mathematics abilities on the SAT appear to be more sustained. Between 1982 and

1995 there was only a single year in which scores fell rather than holding steady or increasing. This has meant that average mathematics scores in 1995 were only 2 points below their 1972 mark of 484.

The achievement scores of minority students have improved over the past 20 years, although a wide gap remains between minority and non-minority students. The average score of black students taking the SAT rose 24 points on the verbal section and 34 points on the mathematics section between 1976 and 1995. White students' average verbal score declined 3 points over this same period, although their average mathematics score increased by 5 points (College Entrance Examination Board 1995).

Children's Health ●

In many ways, the physical health of American children has never been better. Although the infant mortality rate remains higher in the United States than in most other industrialized countries, both infant and child mortality rates have dropped significantly since 1960. When parents are asked to assess the overall health of their children, the vast majority (81 percent in 1997) rate their children's physical health as very good or excellent. But fewer poor parents (68 percent) than nonpoor parents (88 percent) rate their children's overall health this high. Many serious illnesses, such as diphtheria and polio, have been greatly reduced through widespread inoculation campaigns. Most children may not enter school unless they have been vaccinated against several major childhood diseases. Figure 8.3 indicates a significant increase in the likelihood that children received all immunizations in the latter part of the 1990s, although minority children were still less likely than white children to receive these vaccines. Poor children (74 percent) were less likely to be immunized than were higher-income children (82 percent).

As Table 8.9 indicates, infant mortality continues to decline, and the proportion of babies born who are of low birth weight has been stable or rising slightly. These two trends may be intertwined, as improvements in technology allow doctors to keep more premature babies alive today than in the past. The most striking finding displayed in this table is that the proportion of black infants who are of low birth weight is twice as large as that for white and Hispanic infants. The infant mortality rate among blacks is similarly twice as high as the rates for whites and Hispanics. One reason for the increase in numbers of low-birth-weight infants is that numbers of multiple

● **Figure 8.3.** Percentages of Children 19-35 Months Old With Complete Immunization/Vaccination: 1994 and 1998

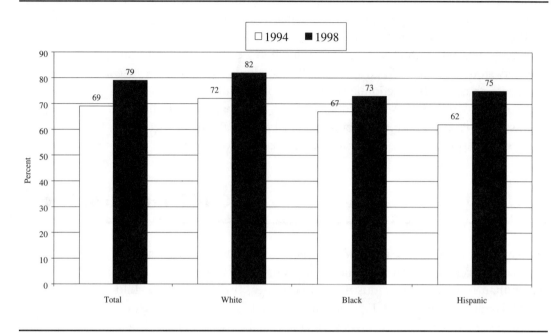

SOURCE: Federal Interagency Forum on Child and Family Statistics (2000).
NOTE: Complete immunizations include 4 doses of diptheria, pertussis, tetanus toxoids (DPT) vaccine; 3 doses of polio vaccine; 1 dose measles-containing vaccine (MCV); and 3 doses of hacmophilus influenza type b (Hib) vaccine. Race/ethnicity categories are white, non-Hispanic; black, non-Hispanic; and Hispanic.

TABLE 8.9 Low Birth Weight and Infant Mortality by Race: 1980, 1990, and 1998

	1980	1990	1998
% low birth weight			
Total	6.8	7.0	7.6
Whites	5.7	5.6	6.6
Blacks	12.7	13.3	13.2
Hispanics	6.1	6.1	6.4
Infant mortality rate (per 1,000)[a]			
Total	10.9	8.9	7.2
Whites	9.2	7.2	6.0
Blacks	19.1	16.9	13.7
Hispanics	9.5	7.5	6.0

SOURCE: Federal Interagency Forum on Child and Family Statistics (2000).
NOTE: Low birth weight is defined as weight at birth of less than 2,500 grams. Race/ethnicity categories are white, non-Hispanic; black, non-Hispanic; and Hispanic.
a. Infant mortality rates are per 1,000 live births for 1983, 1990, and 1997.

births have also been rising, and infants in multiple births (twins, triplets, and so on) are much more likely to be of low birth weight (Federal Interagency Forum on Child and Family Statistics 2000).

Teens, Mortality, and Risky Behaviors ●

Once children survive the first year of life, their risk of death decreases dramatically. However, it rises again in the teen years as youths, especially males and minority youths, are subject to heightened risk of fatal motor vehicle accidents and homicides. As Table 8.10 shows, black males are extremely likely to be victims of homicide in their teenage years. Boys' mortality rates are usually at least twice as high as those of girls for all the causes of death listed in the table. Hispanic teenage girls have the lowest mortality rates and black teenage boys have the highest rates. Car accidents account for more deaths among white adolescents than among minority adolescents for both boys and girls.

The teen years are also a time of heightened experimentation with behaviors that engender health consequences. Table 8.11 documents trends in the 1990s in four such behaviors. The risk of an adolescent birth declined, but smoking, use of alcohol, and use of illicit drugs were more prevalent at the end of the 1990s than they were at the beginning. Interestingly, the risky behaviors of smoking and alcohol and drug use are all much more likely among whites than among minority youth (see Figure 8.4). Blacks were the least likely to report engaging in any of these behaviors. Although Figure 8.4 shows data for 12th graders, the same patterns by race were evident among 8th and 10th graders (data not shown). Research with new large data sets such as that established by the National Study of Adolescent Health is just beginning to untangle the effects of peer influences, family factors, school climate, and neighborhood contexts on youth risk-taking behavior (Duncan, Harris, and Boisjoly 1999; Harris and Ryan 2000).

Conclusion ●

What is the value of children? For society, it is obvious: Children represent the next generation of workers and embody each nation's hope for a continued, perhaps improved, existence. In the United States, we tend to ig-

TABLE 8.10 Adolescent Mortality From Selected Causes (deaths per 100,000 15- to 19-year-olds)

	Total Mortality		Motor Vehicle Mortality		Firearm Mortality					
					Homicide		Suicide			
	1990	1997	1990	1997	1990	1997	1990	1997		
Total death rates	87.8	74.8	32.8	27.0	13.8	11.6	7.4	6.0		
Boys										
White	108.7	90.1	48.2	37.1	4.0	4.3	13.6	10.5		
Black	201.9	169.9	28.8	29.6	105.7	80.6	8.6	8.7		
Hispanic	132.2	107.1	41.0	27.7	40.0	33.2	8.6	8.5		
Girls										
White	45.5	43.8	23.2	22.5	1.4	1.3	2.3	1.9		
Black	54.9	50.5	9.3	10.7	10.3	7.8	—[a]	1.6		
Hispanic	35.7	33.7	10.5	12.6	4.9	3.2	—[a]	—[a]		

SOURCE: Federal Interagency Forum on Child and Family Statistics (2000).

NOTE: Race/ethnicity categories are white, non-Hispanic; black, non-Hispanic; and Hispanic.

a. Number too small to calculate a reliable rate.

TABLE 8.11 Selected Risky Behaviors of Adolescents: 1991 and 1998.

	1991	1998
Adolescent birthrate (per 1,000)		
Ages 15-17	38.7	30.4
Ages 18-19	94.4	82.0
% smoking daily		
8th grade	7.2	8.8
10th grade	12.6	15.8
12th grade	18.5	22.4
% consuming alcohol in past 2 weeks[a]		
8th grade	12.9	13.7
10th grade	22.9	24.3
12th grade	29.8	31.5
% using illicit drugs in past 30 days		
8th grade	5.7	12.1
10th grade	11.6	21.5
12th grade	16.4	25.6

SOURCE: Federal Interagency Forum on Child and Family Statistics (2000:Tables BEH1, BEH2, BEH3, BEH4.A).
a. Alcohol consumption of 5 or more drinks in a row in the past 2 weeks.

nore the role that unpaid labor plays in increasing the public good, and one of the most important jobs is that of raising children (Folbre 1994). Yet public policy and public opinion have been slow to recognize this and have shifted public resources away from children and parents raising children to the elderly. As the population ages, erosion of support for children could have devastating effects: To support the elderly population, society will need to depend on the very children it previously abandoned.

For parents, children offer fulfillment, opportunities to care for and help mold the personalities of other human beings, but children also demand from parents a great deal of time, money, attention, and self-sacrifice. Whether the costs of raising children will continue to be outweighed by children's benefits to individuals and families can be debated. The emphasis on individual fulfillment in the United States may come into conflict with the very essence of raising children: the need to place the interests of others first.

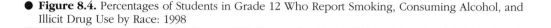

● **Figure 8.4.** Percentages of Students in Grade 12 Who Report Smoking, Consuming Alcohol, and Illicit Drug Use by Race: 1998

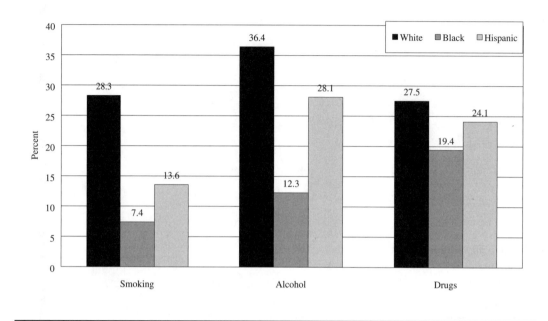

SOURCE: Federal Interagency Forum on Child and Family Statistics (2000).
NOTE: Smoking is defined as smoking cigarettes daily in the previous 30 days; consuming alcohol is defined as consuming five or more alcoholic drinks in a row during the past 2 weeks; illicit drug use is defined as using illicit drugs in the previous 30 days.

Some of the indicators of children's well-being during the past several decades are sobering, but others provide an optimistic picture and hopeful signs for the future of U.S. children. First, the Baby Boom generation is making up for some of the childbearing they put off earlier in their lives. Predictions of childlessness and large-scale abandonment of family life for this generation, a generation supposedly obsessed with individual fulfillment and achievement, will not be realized. Women and men today may be moving more slowly toward meeting their childbearing goals than their parents did, and, by choice or necessity, they may be combining family and work responsibilities in ways not envisioned 30 years ago, but they are not all giving up child rearing.

Nor are most children being shortchanged in terms of what money can buy, although there is some cause for concern in that inequality in the material well-being of children appears to be increasing. Whether children are being neglected in terms of the time parents spend with them is harder to assess, but available evidence suggests that children are not being shortchanged in this area. Despite the increase in maternal employment and father absence, there is evidence of a continued, almost surprisingly high level of family involvement in caring for young children and for school-age children when they are not in school.

The educational attainment of blacks appears to have kept pace, even improved slightly, when compared with that of whites, despite the widening racial differences in family lives of black and white children. Most of the improvement in academic skills of American children has been among low-achieving students.

On other aspects of children's well-being the evidence is mixed: Their physical health is probably better than ever, but their risk-taking behaviors may have increased. Still, most children report healthy, happy lives and satisfaction with their families. This, as much as anything, portends well for the future.

Today's children are being shaped differently from yesterday's children. By the time they are adults, they will have spent considerably more time in group settings, cared for by individuals other than their parents. They will have more frequently observed that mothers, as well as fathers, leave for work each day. More of them will see their fathers, and in some cases their mothers, move out of their households and will be forced to deal with the trauma this entails. They will have fewer siblings with whom to compete, but also fewer from whom to learn and with whom to share.

Will children today be better- or worse-off than their parents in the long run? Part of the answer rests on the commitment by the public and by parents to ensure the well-being of children. Children traditionally embody their parents' hopes for a better life and their country's wish for a more resourceful and productive citizenry. They also reflect the strengths and values of the society that produces them: Their well-being exemplifies the country's well-being; their future is the country's future. The major unanswered question is, How much will the country invest in them?

Notes

1. Typically, time diary data collections include the following under the category of child care: child and baby care, helping/teaching, speaking/reading, indoor/outdoor play, and medical/travel/other child-related care. That is, the activities are more inclusive than merely caring for a child's needs.

2. This estimate also includes children who are read to by family members other than parents.

CHAPTER 9

ECONOMIC CAUSES AND CONSEQUENCES OF CHANGING FAMILY STRUCTURE

F rank Levy (1998) opens his book on income distribution in the United States with three economic stories. The most visible story, he asserts, is the economy's robust performance in the 1990s. While inflation and unemployment were kept low, growth of the large federal government deficits of the 1980s was checked so successfully that by the end of the 1990s Congress was arguing about how to spend the "surplus." Levy's other two stories are less sanguine: He documents the stagnation of average wages after 1973, especially among the less educated, and the high level of income inequality in recent decades. Levy argues that 1973 was a watershed year for the understanding of family economic well-being:

> In the first quarter-century after World War II—from 1946 to 1973—the economy grew very rapidly and achieved most of the nation's economic goals. In the quarter-century since 1973, the economy's performance has been much weaker. . . . As a consequence, many of today's older workers have not seen significant income gains over their careers. If slow average wage growth continues, many young workers—particularly those who have not attended college—will not earn as much as their parents earned. (p. 3)

In 1949, 15 percent of children lived in the poorest 20 percent of families; by 1996, the proportion of children living in the poorest families had risen to 28 percent (Levy 1998). That is, over the years 1949 to 1996, the percentage of children in families at the bottom of the income distribution almost doubled. The increase in children at the bottom of the income distribution paralleled a notable shift in family structure and the greater concentration of disadvantage in mother-only families. Of families in the bottom fifth of the income distribution, 15 percent had female householders in 1949; this figure rose to 42 percent by 1996. Reflecting this shift toward mother-child families, 75 percent of the poorest families had at least one employed person in the household in 1949, compared with only 62 percent in 1996 (Levy 1998).

At the other end of the income distribution, in the top 40 percent of families, another revolution has been under way. The likelihood that married-couple families have earnings from both husband and wife grew tremendously. Figure 9.1 shows that the likelihood of wives' being employed outside the home rose within married-couple families in each quintile of the income distribution. However, the level of wives' employment was 80 percent for married-couple families in the top two income quintiles in 1996, a much higher proportion than at midcentury. In 1996, for example, 81 percent of married-couple families in the richest 20 percent of families had employed wives, compared with 32 percent in 1949.

In this chapter, we provide an overview of trends in family economic well-being and assess the claims that poverty in the United States has become "feminized" and "juvenilized." We also discuss the increase in income inequality among families and the role wives' earnings may be playing in this. We examine the ways in which economic factors influence family behaviors such as marriage and divorce. And finally, we discuss the economic consequences for men, women, and children of the dramatic shifts in rates of marriage and divorce.

● Trends in Household and Per Capita Income

We begin our story about the changing economic fortunes of various types of families with a look at household income and per capita income (household income divided by household size). Table 9.1 shows median household and per capita income by household type for 1977, 1987, and 1997.

● **Figure 9.1.** Percentages of Wives Who Are Employed by Income Quintiles: 1949 and 1961[a]

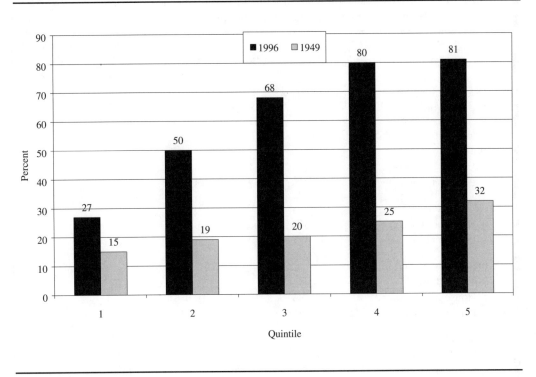

SOURCE: Levy (1998).
a. As a percentage of all wives in married-couple families.

Throughout the period, household income was highest in households that include married couples with children under age 18, but per capita income was highest for married couples without children. For married-couple households, income grew throughout the period, although the increase was greater in the 1980s than in the 1990s. Recall that during this period married-couple households with children declined from one-third to one-fourth of all households in the United States (see Figure 1.1 in Chapter 1).

In households with female householders with children, income declined in the 1980s but then rebounded substantially by the end of the 1990s. The end result was that household income in 1997 was 11 percent higher and per capita income 20 percent higher than in 1977 in mother-only family households. Women who lived alone or maintained households without children did exceptionally well in the 1980s and hence witnessed sizable (average) income growth over the entire 20-year period.

TABLE 9.1 Changes in Median Household Income and Per Capita Income by Household Type: 1977-1997 (in 1997 dollars)

	1977	1987	1997	% Change 1977-87	% Change 1987-97
Total households					
Household income	35,004	37,394	37,581	6.8	0.5
Per capita income					
Married-couple householders					
With children					
Household income	47,114	51,172	54,748	8.6	7.0
Per capita income	11,238	12,716	13,625	13.2	7.1
No children					
Household income	40,368	46,034	48,564	14.0	5.5
Per capita income	17,777	19,921	20,816	12.1	4.5
Female householders					
With children					
Household income	17,188	16,021	18,855	-6.8	17.7
Per capita income	5,169	5,110	6,216	-1.1	21.6
Living alone					
Household income	12,271	14,835	15,418	20.9	3.9
Per capita income	12,271	14,835	15,418	20.9	3.9
Other					
Household income	29,020	33,342	34,440	14.9	3.3
Per capita income	12,048	13,622	13,967	13.1	2.5
Male householders					
With children					
Household income	37,052	33,428	32,417	-9.8	-3.0
Per capita income	11,606	11,404	10,450	-1.7	-8.4
Living alone					
Household income	21,424	23,312	23,999	8.8	2.9
Per capita income	21,424	23,312	23,999	8.8	2.9
Other					
Household income	39,020	42,138	43,800	8.0	3.9
Per capita income	16,571	18,014	17,860	8.7	-0.9

SOURCE: Current Population Survey, March supplements, 1978, 1988, 1998.
NOTE: Data collected in the March 1978, 1988, and 1998 Current Population Survey reflect money income received (before taxes) by all household members in the previous year.

TABLE 9.2 Changes in Median Household Income and Per Capita Income for Families With Children by Employment Status of Parents: 1977-1997 (in 1997 dollars)

	1977	1987	1997	% Change 1977-87	% Change 1987-97
Two-parent, dual-earner family					
Household income	50,999	55,723	59,900	9.3	7.5
Per capita income	12,402	14,058	15,004	13.4	6.7
Two-parent family, father only employed					
Household income	43,680	42,959	42,040	-1.7	-2.1
Per capita income	10,190	10,158	9,930	-0.3	-2.2
Single-mother family, employed					
Household income	24,024	25,968	25,306	8.1	-2.5
Per capita income	7,619	8,229	8,005	8.0	-2.7
Single-mother family, not employed					
Household income	11,535	8,731	9,332	-24.3	6.9
Per capita income	3,223	2,422	2,621	-24.9	8.2
Single-father family, employed					
Household income	40,933	36,310	35,976	-11.3	-0.9
Per capita income	12,464	11,903	11,600	-4.5	-2.5

SOURCE: Current Population Survey, March supplements, 1978, 1988, 1998.
NOTE: Families are family groups with own children under age 18. Employment status refers to employment last year. Data are shown for all family types that accounted for at least 5 percent of families in 1998. Not shown are married-couple families with only the mother or neither parent employed and single-father families in which the father was not employed. Combined, these groups accounted for only about 3.5 percent of families in 1998: 1.8 percent were two-parent families with only a mother employed, 1.2 percent were two-parent families with neither employed, and 0.5 percent were single-father families without employed fathers.

By contrast, the very small segment of households with children living with male householders (1.8 percent of all households in 1998) witnessed considerable income erosion over the period, such that income in these households in 1997 was only about 87 percent what it was in 1977. Men who lived alone or maintained households without children tended to experience significant increases in household income especially in the 1980s.

Table 9.2 tightens the focus on families with children and displays data on income growth in families with employed and nonemployed parents. In both absolute and relative terms, married-couple families with both parents employed fared best over the period. These families had the highest average household and per capita income at each point in time, changes in income were positive in both decades, and percentage increases in income tended to outpace those in other types of households.[1]

One way to think about these numbers is to compare the per capita income levels a child would enjoy, on average, if he or she lived in different types of families. Figure 9.2 makes these comparisons, and, in fact, compares the relative statuses of the mothers and fathers living with the children as well. In 1997, a child in a two-parent family with only the father employed had a per capita income level about two-thirds as high as that of a child in a dual-earner, two-parent family. Interestingly, two decades earlier, in 1977, such a child would have had average per capita income about 82 percent that of a child in a dual-earner, two-parent family. Thus married-couple families with only the fathers employed lost ground vis-à-vis families with two earners.

Comparisons of income may overstate the gap between two-parent families with one parent employed and two-parent families with both parents employed because presumably families with one earner have more time to invest in child care and household maintenance than do dual-earner families, who commit more hours to market work. However, the trends suggest that dual earners had relatively more income at their disposal in 1997 than in 1977 to purchase household help and child care to make up for this difference. As dual earning became more common, the advantages of keeping one parent out of the labor force may have decreased, at least in terms of standard of living provided to families with children.

Similar comparisons can be made for children who lived with only one parent. Children who lived in single-parent families with employed mothers in 1997 had per capita income levels about 53 percent those of children in two-parent, dual-earner families. In 1977, the comparable proportion was 61 percent. Children who lived only with their (employed) fathers experienced per capita income levels about three-fourths as high as those of dual-earner, two-parent families in 1997. Two decades earlier, per capita income in these families equaled that in dual-earner, two-parent families.

Most disadvantaged of all were children who lived only with mothers who were not employed. The per capita income in these households averaged 17 percent the income of dual-earner, two-parent families in 1997, down from about 26 percent in 1977. In sum, the income gap separating children in the least economically advantaged families from those in the most economically advantaged families grew over the period.

Figure 9.2. Ratios of Per Capita Income of Selected Family Types Relative to Two-Parent, Dual-Earner Families

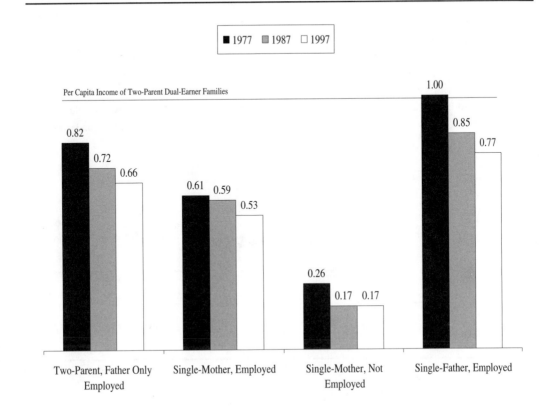

SOURCE: Current Population Survey, March supplements, 1978, 1988, 1998.
NOTE: Families are family groups with own children under age 18.

Poverty Trends ●

Data on household and per capita income are useful for assessing how families are doing, *on average,* but no assessment of family economic well-being is complete without a look at those families at the bottom of the income distribution, who experience substantial material hardship. The U.S. Bureau of the Census began calculating the poverty rate in 1959 and has tracked it annually since that time.[2] During the decade of the 1960s, there was a dramatic decline in poverty rates as the economy expanded. Rates reached their lowest point in the 1970s as the public programs developed to wage war on poverty took hold. After 1980, poverty rose and re-

● **Figure 9.3.** Poverty Rates by Age: 1959-1998

Percent

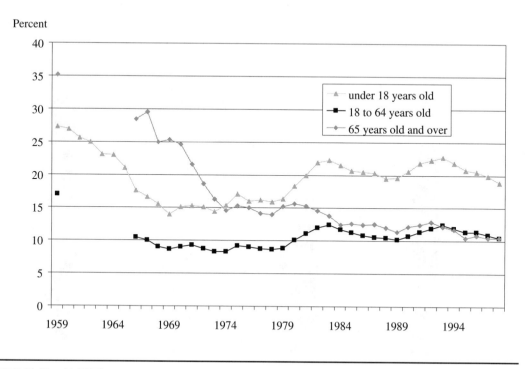

SOURCE: Bianchi (1999).

mained higher in the 1980s and 1990s than during the 1970s. Rates tended to fluctuate with recessions, reaching a peak in the early 1980s, falling off in the later 1980s, then peaking again in 1993. During the latter half of the 1990s, a period of strong economic performance in the United States, the poverty rate dropped and the number of families in poverty declined, although the low levels achieved in the 1970s were still not matched by the end of the 1990s.

Figure 9.3 shows the long-term trends in poverty rates for the elderly, children, and the working-age population. The pattern for the working-age population mirrors the overall trend just described. Rates were lowest in the 1970s, rose in the 1980s, but declined in the late 1990s. The elderly, on the other hand, experienced sustained decline throughout the period: Poverty rates dropped dramatically during the early 1970s and then continued to decline somewhat throughout the 1980s and 1990s as rates rose for other age groups. The trend that has most concerned commentators is the dramatic increase in child poverty (as we have discussed in Chapters 4 and 8) in the 1980s and its elevated level during the past two decades. In 1998, for the first time in decades, the rate of child poverty dropped below 20 percent, but it remained well above the 14-15 percent level achieved in the early 1970s.

A comparison of poverty levels across family types shows that the chances of falling into poverty vary greatly by family type and employment status of householder. For example, married-couple households with children had a poverty rate of 6.9 percent in 1997, whereas married couples without children had poverty rates only half this high. All households with unmarried men or women as householders had higher poverty rates than did households with married couples, but it was female householders with children who fared worst—42.5 percent were in poverty in 1997, a rate six times higher than that for married-couple households with children (see Table 9.3).

Two-parent families that are buffered against poverty by earnings from both mother and father have poverty rates that are extremely low (2.4 percent in two-parent, dual-earner families). If a two-parent family has only one earner, poverty rates rise considerably—to almost 15 percent if that one earner is the father and to more than 28 percent if the sole earner is the mother. Single-parent families in which the parents are employed have poverty rates similar to those of two-parent families in which the mothers are the sole earners—about 30 percent of single, employed mothers are in poverty. However, less than 2 percent of all families are two-parent families relying only on a mother's earnings, whereas 20 percent of families are single-mother families relying on her earnings. Almost 14 percent of single, employed fathers are in poverty, again similar to the 15 percent of two-parent families that rely only on the father's earnings. Families with no parents in the labor force run an extremely high risk of living in poverty—more than half of two-parent and father-only families and three-fourths of mother-only families without an employed parent were in poverty in 1997.

Racial Differences in Income and Poverty ●

The level of income in minority families is significantly lower and the likelihood of poverty much higher than in non-Hispanic white families. Table 9.4 shows per capita income and the percentages in poverty for selected types of families with children. The second (and fifth) columns of the table show the relative positions of black and Hispanic families compared with white families with similar structure and levels of parental employment.

TABLE 9.3   Changing Poverty Levels for Households and Selected Family Types: 1997

	% in Poverty 1997	Ratio 1997[a]
All households		
Married-couple householders		
With children	6.9	1.0
No children	3.7	0.5
Female householders		
With children	42.5	6.2
Living alone	20.8	3.0
Other	16.4	2.4
Male householders		
With children	18.2	2.6
Living alone	14.3	2.1
Other	11.8	1.7
All families[b]		
Two-parent families		
Dual earners	2.4	1.0
Father only employed	14.7	6.1
Mother only employed	28.3	11.8
Neither employed	57.0	23.7
Single-mother families		
Employed	30.0	12.5
Not employed	74.4	31.0
Single-father families		
Employed	13.7	5.7
Not employed	55.4	23.0

SOURCE: Current Population Survey, March supplement, 1998.

a. Ratios for households are relative to married couples with children. Ratios for family groups are relative to two-parent, dual-earner families.

b. Families are family groups with own children under age 18. Employment status refers to employment in 1997.

The third (and sixth) columns compare black and Hispanic families to the most "income-advantaged" families—white, two-parent families with both parents employed.

Minority two-parent, dual-earner families are advantaged relative to other types of minority families, but disadvantaged relative to comparable white families. Black two-parent families with two earners have per capita income levels that are only 79 percent those of white families and have poverty rates that are 44 percent higher. Hispanic families fall even further

TABLE 9.4   Economic Well-Being in White, Black, and Hispanic Families With Children: 1997

Selected Family Types	Per Capita Income			Poverty Rate		
	Median	Ratio to White Family of Same Type	Ratio to White Dual-Earner, Two-Parent Family	% in Poverty	Ratio to White Family of Same Type	Ratio to White Dual-Earner, Two-Parent Family
Two-parent, dual-earner family						
White	16,061	1.00	1.00	1.6	1.00	1.00
Black	12,750	0.79	0.79	2.3	1.44	1.44
Hispanic	9,691	0.60	0.60	8.4	5.25	5.25
Two-parent family, father only employed						
White	12,025	1.00	0.75	8.0	1.00	5.00
Black	6,615	0.55	0.41	22.7	2.84	14.19
Hispanic	5,280	0.44	0.33	34.8	4.35	21.75
Single-mother family, employed						
White	9,698	1.00	0.60	24.8	1.00	15.50
Black	6,193	0.64	0.39	35.8	1.44	22.38
Hispanic	6,387	0.66	0.40	35.6	1.44	22.25
Single-mother family, not employed						
White	3,900	1.00	0.24	65.8	1.00	41.13
Black	1,832	0.47	0.11	80.8	1.23	50.50
Hispanic	2,069	0.53	0.13	82.6	1.26	51.63
Single-father family, employed						
White	12,333	1.00	0.77	11.5	1.00	7.19
Black	9,585	0.78	0.60	15.2	1.32	9.50
Hispanic	7,333	0.59	0.46	26.1	2.27	16.31

SOURCE: Current Population Survey, March supplement, 1998.
NOTE: Families are family groups with children under age 18. Race/ethnicity categories are white, non-Hispanic; black, non-Hispanic; and Hispanic.

behind, with per capita income levels only 60 percent of those in comparable white families and poverty rates that are five times greater.

Two-parent minority families with only a father employed are even more disadvantaged. Income in black families of this type is only about 40 percent that of white dual-earner, two-parent families, and their poverty rates are 14 times as high. Hispanic two-parent families with only the father employed have income only about one-third that of the white two-parent, dual-earner families and poverty rates that are 22 times higher. Interestingly, the income position of minority single-father families is somewhat better than that of minority two-parent families in which the fathers are the sole earners.

Black and Hispanic single mothers have income about two-thirds that of comparable white families when they are employed and about half that of white mothers when they are not employed. But when minority single mothers are compared with white two-parent, dual-earner families, the inequality for children across family type becomes especially apparent. Black and Hispanic single-mother families in which the mothers are employed have incomes about 40 percent that of the most advantaged white families with children and a likelihood of poverty that is more than 20 times as great. Those with single mothers who are not employed have per capita income levels only about 10 percent those of two-parent, dual-earner white families, and their chances of falling into poverty are 50 times as great.

The trends in overall income and poverty highlighted in the foregoing discussion are parallel for white and black families, but some types of Hispanic families have experienced declines in income and increases in poverty (data not shown). Trend data also indicate that the poverty and income of black families have become more similar over time to those of similar types of white families. By contrast, Hispanics in most family types have lost ground relative to white families. For example, in 1978, Hispanics in married-couple, dual-earner families had poverty rates about twice as high as white married-couple, dual-earner families, but by 1998, Hispanic poverty rates were more than five times higher than those among white counterparts.

● The Feminization of Poverty

The term *feminization of poverty* was coined by Diana Pearce in a 1978 article in *Urban and Social Change Review,* in which she argued that poverty was "rapidly becoming a female problem" and that women accounted "for an increasingly large proportion of the economically disadvantaged" (p. 128). Pearce noted that in 1976 two out of three poor adults were women, that the number of female-headed families was increasing rapidly, and that the number of poor female-headed families had doubled between 1950 and 1974.[3] She also suggested that female-headed families were losing ground vis-à-vis families with adult males present in the household, noting that the ratio of income in female-headed families to other families had declined between 1950 and 1974. In a later piece, Pearce (1988) suggested that if such trends continued, nearly all the poor would be living in female-headed families by the year 2000.

McLanahan, Sørensen, and Watson (1989) argue that the expression *feminization of poverty* conveys the notion that the risks of poverty were rising for women *relative* to men, and that researchers needed to examine poverty rates for women and men and assess feminization by the *trend* in the ratio of women's to men's poverty rates. McLanahan et al. showed that poverty was indeed feminizing between 1950 and 1980: Among adult whites and blacks, at all ages, the ratio of women's to men's poverty rates increased during the period. Among whites, women's poverty rates were 10 percent higher than men's in 1950, but almost 50 percent higher in 1980.

Although poverty may have continued to feminize at the youngest and oldest ages, after 1980, trends were in the opposite direction for the working population (see Figure 9.4). Among those in the prime working ages, poverty actually defeminized after 1980 (Bianchi 1999; England 1997:Table 4; McLanahan and Kelly 1997:Table 1). Poverty ratios of working-age women to working-age men (age 30 to 64) were relatively stable in the 1970s and then declined from 1.60 in 1980 to 1.39 in 1996.

The interesting question is, Why did the feminization of poverty reverse after 1980 for the working-age population? To solve this puzzle, we need to examine trends in employment and earnings for women and men in the past two decades. Women's increasing ability to support themselves financially and men's decreasing access to "family wage" jobs in the 1980s coincides reasonably well with the halt in the feminization of poverty among working-age adults after 1980.

Changing Employment ● and Earnings of Women

The gains women would make in the labor force in the 1980s and 1990s were not readily apparent in the 1970s, when Pearce (1978) described the

● Figure 9.4. Women's Poverty Risks Relative to Men's by Age: 1977-1996

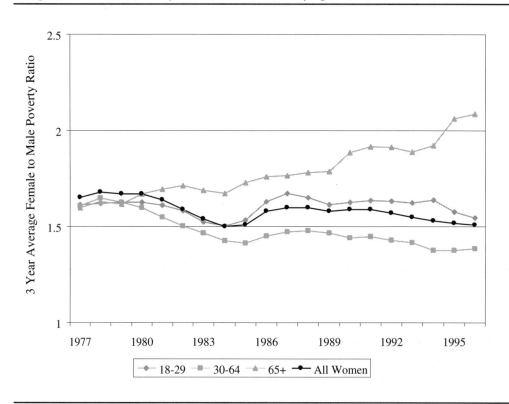

SOURCE: Current Population Survey, March supplements, 1977-1996.

feminization of poverty. Women earned less than men, and the average earnings of women who were full-time, year-round workers had remained unchanged, fluctuating for decades around 55-59 percent of men's earnings (Spain and Bianchi 1996). During the 1950s, the gender segregation of occupations actually increased and then declined only slightly in the 1960s (Blau and Hendricks 1979; Jacobs 1989). At the beginning of the 1970s, it seemed as if women's progress toward equality in areas where it really mattered—better jobs and higher wages—was permanently stalled.

Now, three decades later, it is much easier to see that women made substantial progress in narrowing the gap in both occupational attainment and average wages after 1970 (Blau 1998; Spain and Bianchi 1996). Although in 1990 job segregation was still high, and more than half of the female labor force would have had to change occupations to be distributed across categories the same as were men, the decline in segregation after 1970 was dramatic, especially when compared with the 1950s and 1960s (Bianchi 1995b; Bianchi and Rytina 1986; Cotter and DeFiore 1996). Between 1980 and 1995, women's earnings as a percentage of men's, the most commonly used barometer of gender wage inequality, rose from 60 percent to 71 percent among full-time, year-round workers (Bianchi and Spain 1996:Fig. 5, Table 8). Women's hourly wages increased from 64 percent to 79 percent of men's. The decline in occupational gender segregation and narrowing of the gender wage gap coincided with an important alteration in female labor force patterns.

Women's employment increased substantially throughout the post–World War II period, but in the 1950s and 1960s the increase was greatest among women in their 40s and 50s—women past the most intense years of child rearing (Bianchi 1995b; Goldin 1990; Smith and Ward 1989). In these decades, women worked before marriage and children, dropped out of the labor force to rear their children, and returned after their children had grown, after a long absence. Their pattern of lifetime attachment to the labor force was discontinuous.

During the 1970s and 1980s, the lifetime pattern of female labor participation shifted dramatically. The largest increases in rates of women's employment occurred among younger women, women in their 20s and 30s. Participation rates increased for those who in the past had been the least likely to be employed—married mothers with preschool-age children. The result was a change in the lifetime pattern of labor force participation of women. Recent cohorts of women are much more likely to be attached to the labor force throughout adulthood, hence their patterns of employment have become much more similar to men's. (See Chapter 10 for a more detailed account of change in women's employment.)

Because of the changing patterns in women's employment, the average work experience of women workers increased dramatically after 1970, an increase that paralleled the decline in the gender wage gap (Bianchi and Spain 1996; O'Neill and Polachek 1993; Wellington 1993). It became increasingly difficult to predict whether a woman would engage in market work based on her marital and motherhood status. With women's increase in work experience, it probably became increasingly difficult—both unprofitable and illegal—for employers to discriminate based on gender as well.

The narrowing of the gender wage gap has led to considerable debate between those who attribute the narrowing primarily to gains made by women in education, work experience, and resulting real wage gains (Cotter et al. 1997; O'Neill and Polachek 1993) and those who argue that the narrowing is much more a result of stagnation or decline in male wages than of improvement in female wages (Bernhardt, Morris, and Handcock 1995). There is ample evidence that income inequality has increased among both male and female workers (Levy 1995) and that less educated workers have been disadvantaged in the labor market during the past two decades (Levy and Murnane 1992). The question here is, To what extent are declining male wages (rather than rising female wages) the explanation for the halt in the feminization of poverty in the 1980s?

● Declining Male Wages

Levy (1995) has argued that the economic restructuring to improve productivity in manufacturing ultimately resulted in a substantially decreased demand for semiskilled workers in the United States. Manufacturing productivity was revived in the 1980s, but the losers were semiskilled workers, those who had not gone beyond high school. During the 1980s, total durable goods employment declined by 1 million workers (Levy 1995:11).

Companies facing import competition were the first to make changes. Due to large trade deficits, the globalization of trade, and the availability of cheaper labor pools outside the United States, demand for low-skill labor declined as production jobs were either automated or moved overseas (Borjas, Freeman, and Katz 1992; Murphy and Welch 1992). At first, low-skill workers (with less than a high school education) were most affected—perhaps women even more than men as textile manufacturing moved outside U.S. borders. Employment of low-skill male workers declined in the 1970s and 1980s, as wages dropped, and the duration of spells of nonemployment also lengthened (Juhn 1992).

By the 1980s, the demand for semiskilled labor also declined. Men were especially vulnerable because they were in the "family wage"-paying, unionized, manufacturing jobs that were undergoing transition. As Wetzel (1995) notes, "Before 1975, spending on domestically produced goods stimulated rapid job growth in goods-producing industries and provided 'middle class' jobs with comparatively low educational requirements for millions of Americans" (p. 76). In reality, it was American men who held these jobs—women had never gained access and hence benefited primarily by being married to workers who had these semiskilled jobs. After 1980, construction employment grew, but otherwise "employment in manufacturing and mining, where men outnumber women three to one and wages are high relative to the schooling levels of workers," declined considerably (Wetzel 1995:76, Table 2.3).

Blau and Kahn (1997) argue that, relative to men, it was high-wage rather than low-wage women workers who had to struggle more to achieve equality in the 1980s. First, the supply of college-educated women workers increased faster than the supply of less educated women workers. Second, the gap between highly educated women's and men's wages widened because of the high returns to skill in the 1980s and the lesser work experience of highly skilled women relative to men. In contrast, at lower skill levels, occupational and industry trends (e.g., the decline in durable manufacturing) and deunionization resulted in more job loss for men than women; low-wage women increased their work experience vis-à-vis low-wage men.

In sum, shifts in demand for labor benefited women relative to men at lower skill levels but men relative to women at high skill levels (Blau and Kahn 1997). Thus, among those close to the poverty level or below it, workers—men and women—faced job loss and wage erosion, but men lost more ground than women; this helps explain the end of the feminization of poverty in the early 1980s.

One of the ironies noted in the original formulation of the feminization of poverty thesis was that increased poverty for women occurred as affirmative action supposedly opened doors for women. There is now some evidence to suggest that any affirmative action benefits for women ended in the 1980s (Leonard 1989)—that is, ended at the very time poverty stopped "feminizing" among working-age adults. However, feedback effects of earlier affirmative action efforts of the 1960s and 1970s may have encouraged women to invest in their education and made employers less likely to stereotype and discriminate statistically—in effect, setting in motion actions that continued even after retrenchment in affirmative action efforts (Blau and Kahn 1997).[4]

The Juvenilization of Poverty ●

The feminization of poverty thesis was not only about women, it was also about the children that single mothers were raising. After reaching a low point in the 1970s, poverty rates increased among children in the 1980s. The elevation in poverty rates in the early 1980s captured public attention for two reasons. First, increased poverty among children was not confined

● **Figure 9.5.** Children's Relative Poverty Risks: 1966-1996

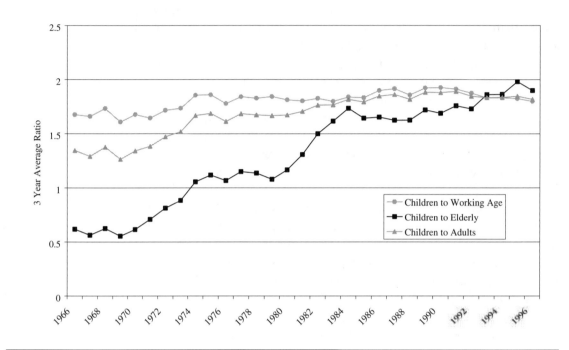

SOURCE: Current Population Survey, March supplements, 1966-1996.

to children in mother-child families, as the feminization argument suggested. In a widely cited article that appeared in *Science* in 1989, Mary Jo Bane and David Ellwood pointed out that poverty was also rising among children in two-parent families. Researchers increasingly turned their attention to declining male wages to explain these poverty trends (Bianchi 1993; Blank 1991). Second, increased child poverty in the 1980s was at odds with trends for the other "dependent" segment of the population, the elderly. Poverty rates among the elderly continued to decline in the 1980s, whereas rates among children rose.

As shown in Figure 9.5, over the past three decades poverty has "juvenilized." Children's poverty rates rose relative to adult rates during the 1970s and 1980s. Relative to the elderly, children's rates of poverty rose dramatically between the late 1960s, when children's odds of poverty were only about 60 percent those for the elderly, and the early 1990s, when children's poverty rates climbed to almost twice those of the elderly.

For children, the distinction between *absolute* poverty levels and *relative* risk of poverty is important. Rates of child poverty came down dramatically between the Great Depression of the 1930s and the mid-1970s (Bianchi 1990, 1993; Hernandez 1993; Lichter 1997). In 1959, when the official poverty figures were established, 27 percent of children were counted as poor, and the proportion declined to 14-15 percent by the 1970s. During the same period, the poverty decline for the elderly was even sharper—from 36 percent in 1959 to 14-15 percent by the mid-1970s, a rate roughly equal to children's. After the mid-1970s, trends diverged for the two groups. The elderly continued to experience declines in poverty, whereas children's poverty rates began to increase. During the 1980s and 1990s, children's rates fluctuated between 20 percent and 23 percent, never dropping below about 20 percent poor until 1998. Hence children's *relative* risks of poverty skyrocketed compared with those of the elderly. Children make up 40 percent of the poor, and this proportion has not changed much since the 1960s. But this stability does not take into account that in 1966, children accounted for 36 percent of the population, whereas in 1994 they made up only 27 percent of the population. If their *relative* risk of poverty were similar to that for adults, they should have accounted for a much smaller share of the poor than 40 percent in the 1990s.

Family Income Inequality ●
and Relative Economic Well-Being

Some would argue that the key to assessing well-being should be how well the poorest families are doing relative to those in the middle or those at the highest income levels (e.g., see Hernandez 1993:Chap. 7). The notion is that being poor when everyone around you is poor is not as bad as being poor when most can afford a much higher standard of living. Hence what is considered a "minimally acceptable" standard of living rises as the affluence of the society increases.

It is this notion of the significance of relative comparisons that requires a focus on the concentration of income and inequality in the income distribution. Increased income inequality may be destabilizing in democratic societies, creating a class of individuals who feel so left out of the mainstream that they develop extreme or deviant behaviors and eschew participation in society. To a large extent, a nation-state such as the United States functions smoothly and with minimal political unrest because the vast majority

TABLE 9.5   Changes in Household Income Inequality: 1970-1998

	1970	1980	1990	1998
Share of household income (percentage)				
Lowest quintile	4.1	4.3	3.9	3.6
Highest quintile	43.3	43.7	46.6	49.2
Ratios of household income of selected percentiles				
Top/middle				
95th/50th	2.7	2.9	3.2	3.4
80th/50th	1.7	1.8	1.8	1.9
Top/bottom				
95th/20th	6.3	6.8	7.6	8.2
80th/20th	4.0	4.2	4.4	4.7
Bottom/middle	0.4	0.4	0.4	0.4

SOURCE: DeNavas and Cleveland (1999:Table C).

of the populace see society as basically fair and as providing opportunities for a "good" life. Growing income inequality holds out the possibility of undermining the legitimacy of the system and perhaps creating an "underclass" of individuals so disenfranchised and distant from the mainstream that they come to threaten the well-being of the rest of the population. This is why analysts such as Levy (1998) are concerned about trends toward greater income inequality in U.S. society.

There are various ways to measure family income inequality. A common one is to array families from lowest to highest income and then assess how much income is controlled by the bottom 20 percent of families compared with the top 20 percent. Another is to assess the income of families at various points on the income distribution, not only the median, and take the ratio of incomes at various points. So, for example, how does the income of a family at the 20th percentile compare with the income of a family at the 50th percentile (the median), or to a family at the 80th or 95th percentile? Are families at the bottom of the income distribution "losing ground" relative to families in the middle or at the top of the distribution?

Virtually any measure suggests that income inequality has grown in recent decades in the United States. Table 9.5 shows that in 1970, the bottom 20 percent (the lowest quintile) of households controlled only 4.1 percent of all household income in the United States, whereas the top 20 percent of households (the highest quintile) controlled 43.3 percent of income. By

1998, the gap had widened as the share of the bottom 20 percent dropped to 3.6 percent and the share of the top 20 percent expanded to 49.2 percent.

Households at the top of the income distribution have increasingly pulled away from those at the middle and bottom of the income distribution. For example, households at the 95th percentile enjoyed incomes 2.7 times those of families at the median in 1970 but had incomes 3.4 times those of families at the median in 1998. In 1970, families at the very top of the distribution (the 95th percentile) had incomes 6.3 times those at the 20th percentile. By 1998, these families had incomes 8.2 times those of families at the 20th percentile (the lowest quintile). If one uses ratios for households at the 80th percentile (the highest quintile), the trends are similar but less dramatic. By contrast, the relative incomes of those at the 20th percentile remained at less than half of those at the middle of the income distribution throughout the period.

What is clear from these trends is that households at the top of the income distribution are increasing their income advantage relative to other families. Other evidence suggests that if wealth were measured rather than money income, the inequality in economic well-being would be even greater (Oliver and Shapiro 1995). Wealth is even more highly concentrated than income in the hands of those at the top of the distribution, with most American families having relatively few assets beyond the residences in which they live.

Given this picture of increased income (and wealth) inequality, one of the important questions to ask is, Why has this happened? The answer, it turns out, is complex and involves a mix of factors, some having to do with how well certain types of workers are doing in the labor force and others having to do with marriage and living arrangements. For example, it is now well established that inequality in the earnings distribution has increased with less educated workers, male and female, falling behind college-educated workers. Families relying on the earnings of householders with only high school educations or less are increasingly disadvantaged. But this is not the whole story. At the same time that earnings inequality has grown, household structure has also changed. The number of one-person households has grown, as has the proportion of families that have only one parent present. Mother-only families, as we have seen, have low income relative to two-parent families. But single-person households, in which income rose substantially in the 1980s, also have lower incomes than married-couple families with two earners. Hence the changing composition of families and the labor force participation rates of members within those families require increased scrutiny.

● Components of Rising Household Income Inequality

Several studies have documented the role that changing household structure has played in trends in income inequality. The movement away from married-couple families and the increase in dual earning within married-couple families are compositional shifts that have contributed to rising income inequality across households (Karoly and Burtless 1995; McLanahan and Casper 1995; Ryscavage 1995). Levy (1998) estimates that these compositional changes explain as much as two-fifths of the growth in inequality. Change in income and earnings account for the other three-fifths, according to Levy.

The largest wage factor is men's earnings. Cancian and Reed (1999) estimate that of these income changes, changes in husbands' earnings alone can explain more than 90 percent of the increase in family income inequality. The role of wives' earnings has also been a factor, but a much lesser one. Prior to 1970, studies of wives' earnings and their contribution to family income inequality suggested that wives' earnings were equalizing—that is, wives tended to be employed in families with lower- rather than higher-earning husbands. Hence their earnings tended to increase income in otherwise low-income families and reduce inequality across families (Maxwell 1990).

In the past two decades, however, this pattern seems to have reversed, with labor force rates rising more sharply for more highly educated wives. Better-educated men are more likely to marry, and higher-earning husbands are increasingly likely to have employed wives, wives who earn relatively high incomes themselves (Burtless 1996). Correlation between husbands' and wives' earnings grew in the 1980s, as did the share of total income from wives' earnings (Cancian and Reed 1999). Hence recent work on income inequality has returned to the question of whether wives' earnings contribute to the growing inequality among families (Cancian, Danziger, and Gottschalk 1993; Cancian and Reed 1999; Karoly and Burtless 1995).

How much have wives' employment and earnings contributed to income inequality across families in the past two decades? Cancian and Reed (1999) estimate that if wives' earnings were the only source of change, they would have accounted for about 14 percent of the increase in family income inequality. This estimate is substantially lower than Karoly and Burtless's (1995) estimate of 40 percent. Although the increased correlation between husbands' and wives' earnings was creating larger inequalities across families, wives' earnings actually became less unequal over time as more wives entered the labor force. When all of these factors are taken into account, the total effect was to decrease income inequality, although if wives' earnings had not become more highly correlated with husbands' earnings, the equalizing tendencies would have been stronger.

In sum, household compositional change and growing inequality in men's earnings were the two largest factors increasing family income inequality. The role wives played was primarily compositional: Their increased labor force participation shifted the high-income families toward dual-earning families. Across all wives, earnings became more equal as more married women worked for pay, but those families with working wives also became increasingly advantaged compared with families who did not have this source of income.

Changing Economics and ●
Family Formation and Dissolution

Both changing family structure and changing economic opportunities of men and women are interwoven in complex ways to create more inequality in family and household income. Although the two factors, family structure and economic change, are analytically separable in studies of the growth of income inequality, in reality the two factors interact and affect each other. A relatively large body of theory and empirical research assesses the ways in which economic changes may have promoted family changes such as the delay in marriage, the increase in nonmarriage (especially among the black population), and the increase in marital disruption.

In a decade review article on the effects of economic conditions on family behaviors, White and Rogers (2000) suggest that there have been two main thrusts in the literature on the economic causes of changes in marriage timing and divorce. On the one hand, there are theories that place major emphasis on male economic opportunities as causal in determining when couples marry, whether couples marry at all, and whether marriages disrupt. On the other hand, other theories emphasize the role of changes in women's labor market opportunities and see these as causally connected to the delay in first marriage and increase in marital disruption. Some argue that female labor market opportunities should be conducive to marriage in that women's high earnings may make them more "attractive" as marital partners. Others assert that women's employment inhibits marriage and erodes marital stability to the extent that women's increased opportunities for employment and enhanced earnings make them more "independent" and less inclined toward marriage.

Men's Income and Their Attractiveness in the Marriage Market

Researchers have developed a number of hypotheses that emphasize men's labor market opportunities as the key to marriage behavior. For example, Gary Becker's (1981) theory of the "gains to marriage" emphasizes the importance of men's employment and earnings in models of marriage and divorce. Marriage is viewed as a "trading relationship" that is most enduring when men are able to trade their prowess as wage earners and family breadwinners for domestic caregiving on the part of their wives. Nock (1998b) argues that, although the expectations for breadwinning and domestic caregiving change as women move into the paid labor force, there remain substantial normative pressures on men to be good financial providers. Masculinity is partly defined by the ability to provide economically; men marry when they feel they can provide for a family, and women seek husbands who will be good providers. Ethnographic work suggests that young women remain hesitant to marry men who are unemployed, even in those cases where the man is the father of the woman's children (White and Rogers 2000).

Richard Easterlin's (1978) cyclical theory of marriage and fertility emphasizes that marriage will occur earlier and more often when wage opportunities are good for men and when men's ability to provide a given standard of living for their families matches or exceeds their expectations. Valerie Oppenheimer (1997) argues that the delay in marriage during the past two decades has been greatly influenced by men's increased difficulties in securing stable employment and "family wage" jobs. Oppenheimer, Kalmijn, and Lim (1997) show that recent cohorts of young men have spent longer than earlier cohorts in "stopgap" jobs and that young men's difficulty in securing stable employment lengthens the time it takes them to marry. William Julius Wilson (1987) has argued that a major factor in the apparent increase in nonmarriage among the black population is the increasing difficulty that inner-city black males have in securing steady employment.

Research has established that men's financial breadwinning ability speeds the transition from cohabitation to marriage (Smock and Manning 1997). Men with higher earnings are more likely to marry (Lloyd and South

1996) and less likely to divorce (Hoffman and Duncan 1995; South and Lloyd 1995). Married men earn more than unmarried men, whether because higher-earning men are more likely to marry or because marriage changes the behaviors of men in ways that enhance labor market productivity (Gray 1997; Kaestner 1993; Korenman and Neumark 1991; Nock 1998b). Men's unemployment is associated with an increased likelihood of divorce (Bumpass, Martin, and Sweet 1991). All this is evidence for the importance of men's employment and earnings in facilitating marriage and enhancing marital stability.

Women's Economic Independence, Marriage, and Marital Disruption

An alternative hypothesis, that women's employment destabilizes marriage, is prominent in both sociological and economic theories of marital instability. Supposedly, women's decreased specialization in child rearing and household maintenance, coupled with their increased labor force participation, reduces the benefits of marriage for men and women (Becker 1974, 1981; Becker, Landes, and Michael 1977; Espenshade 1983). The effect of a wife's increased economic resources on marital disruption has been termed the "independence effect" (Ross and Sawhill 1975). Women who can support themselves and their children, through either their own earnings or welfare payments, may have less incentive to marry and greater ability to exit unsatisfactory marriages. Historical trend data seem to support a link between women's increased labor force participation and delayed marriage and rising divorce (Cherlin 1992; Ruggles 1997).

Oppenheimer (1997) argues, however, that the theoretical and empirical evidence of the connection between women's increased economic independence is circumstantial and unconvincing. For one thing, most of the more recent studies suggest that women who have higher earnings are actually more attractive in the marriage market (South 1991) and more likely to marry (McLaughlin and Lichter 1997; McLaughlin, Lichter, and Johnson 1993; Oppenheimer and Lew 1995; Qian 1998). Oppenheimer (1988, 1994) argues that the "independence effect" may delay marriage, as men and women take longer to search for a good match under conditions of considerable labor market uncertainty, but there is little evidence that marriage is being forgone due to women's increased economic opportunities. White and Rogers (2000), in their review of research in this area, conclude that the relationships among employment, earnings, and marriage are actually quite similar for men and women: Higher earnings and better job prospects enhance the likelihood of marriage. White and Rogers note, however, that the effects are larger and more consistent for men's than for women's earnings.

Empirical evidence relating a wife's greater economic independence to increased likelihood of divorce is also decidedly mixed. Sayer and Bianchi (2000) summarize the evidence from a number of studies of the effect of women's income on marital dissolution. Studies that find that the wife's wages or her relative contribution to family income are positively associated with increased risks of marital disruption (Cherlin 1979; D'Amico 1983; Heckert, Nowak, and Snyder 1998; Hiedemann, Suhomlinova, and O'Rand 1998; Moore and Waite 1981; Ono 1998; Ross and Sawhill 1975; Spitze and South 1985) are counterbalanced by studies that find no relationship between a wife's economic independence and marital disruption (Greenstein 1990, 1995; Hoffman and Duncan 1995; Mott and Moore 1979; South and Lloyd 1995). White and Rogers (2000) note that "perhaps the safest conclusion is that there is no consistent evidence that wives' success as co-providers reduces marital stability" (p. 1043).

● Consequences of Marital Disruption in Families With Children

Just as economic conditions are implicated in who marries and divorces, economic consequences attend decisions about whether to enter and remain in marriage. Perhaps the area that is of greatest concern is the gender inequality in economic conditions that tends to follow marital disruption. Virtually all studies report a decline in economic well-being for women (and children) in the immediate postdivorce period (Holden and Smock 1991; Smock, Manning, and Gupta 1999). The range of estimates for men is more variable than that for women. Some studies have found that men experience a sizable improvement in economic well-being after divorce (e.g., Smock 1993, 1994), whereas others suggest that men's living standards undergo modest positive change (e.g., Peterson 1996). Still others estimate that both men and women see their standard of living go down, but that women's decline is far more serious than men's (e.g., Burkhauser et al. 1990, 1991). However, Smock et al. (1999) suggest that the benefits of staying married have been somewhat overstated in previous research. They found that divorced women would not have fared as well economically as other married women had they remained married rather than divorcing.

But all studies suggest that women (and children) are worse-off than men after divorce.

The *relative* costs of marital disruption to couples seem particularly salient when the adequate support of children is at issue. Ideally, both parents provide for their children after a marriage fails, although there is now considerable empirical evidence that this often does not occur (Grall 2000; Scoon-Rogers and Lester 1995). Nonresident parents often do not pay child support (Garfinkel 1992), and loss of parental economic support is an important cause of the more negative outcomes for children in one-parent families (McLanahan and Sandefur 1994).

Sørensen (1989) has argued that the increased labor force participation of women, the declining gender segregation of occupations, and the narrowing of the wage gap all should be propelling men and women toward more equality after divorce. The evidence that women's earnings have increased relative to men's seems indisputable, although debate continues as to whether this has come about because of gains by women or because of deterioration in the labor force prospects and earnings of men (Bernhardt et al. 1995, 1997; Cotter et al. 1997).

Since the late 1960s, younger cohorts of women have increasingly delayed marriage and children in order to devote time to schooling and labor market activity, a fact that Sørensen (1989) suggests should result in more "egalitarian" divorces among young couples separating in the 1980s and 1990s. Women are also less likely than in the past to discontinue market work when they marry or have children, hence their work experience, compared with that of men, has increased (O'Neill and Polachek 1993). As women behave more like men in terms of market work, they should be buffered from some of the dire economic consequences that follow divorce.

Smock (1993, 1994), however, reports that, despite women's increased market work, more recent cohorts are as disadvantaged as earlier cohorts when they divorce. Because wives still reduce market work to care for children, women continue to be less economically self-sufficient than men when marriage ends. Marriage often leads to economic *dependence* for women, as homemaking and child-rearing responsibilities reduce hours of employment and earnings and lead women to forgo or delay education, training, and occupational mobility (Bergmann 1986; Blau and Ferber 1992; Morgan 1991; Risman, Atkinson, and Blackwelder 1999).

Time diary estimates for 1995 suggest that women allocate 75 percent more hours per week to household work than men and do 3 hours of child care for every hour men do (Bianchi 1998). According to the 1990 Census, married women ages 35 to 44 averaged 900 fewer hours of paid work per year than married men (Spain and Bianchi 1996:Table 6.6). March Current Population Survey data for the 1964-97 period show that in the 1990s children continued to depress annual hours of market work of mothers, although not to the same extent as in the 1960s (Cohen and Bianchi 1999). Goldin (1997) shows that among recent cohorts of highly educated women, a relatively small proportion (15 percent) successfully combine marriage, motherhood, and careers at midlife.

Married men, on the other hand, typically do not forgo labor market opportunities to rear children. In fact, marriage may enhance men's earnings: Korenman and Neumark (1991) note that studies have found that married men typically earn anywhere from 10 percent to 40 percent more than unmarried men. Data from the early 1990s suggest that the "marriage premium" for men may have declined (Blackburn and Korenman 1994; Gray 1997), but married men continue to earn significantly more than similar unmarried men (Waite 1995).

Men also tend to exit marriage without custody of minor children (Seltzer 1991a). Although it is becoming more difficult for men to shirk their child support obligations, the support they are required to pay is often relatively low when compared with what they would have provided to their wives and children had they remained married (Garfinkel, McLanahan, and Hanson 1997). The courts have been slow to recognize accumulated work experience and education as "marital property," hence women's claims on the rewards of their investments in their husbands' careers have not always been strong (Weitzman 1992). The movement away from "fault" divorce has resulted in less frequent award of alimony to former wives, and when alimony is awarded, the time period is more circumscribed than in the past (McLindon 1987).

Finally, women tend to marry men of equal (or higher) educational attainment, with educational similarity between spouses increasing over time (Kalmijn 1991; Mare 1991). On average, men earn more than women at the same educational level (Spain and Bianchi 1996:Fig. 5.2). Hence gender differences in income exist at the beginning of marriage and tend to increase rather than diminish over time, because children reduce women's labor market skills and earnings (as women devote time to child rearing and being "good" mothers) but enhance men's employment and earnings (as men focus on providing financially for their families and being "good" fathers). If the narrowing of the gender gap in earnings and labor force participation in the larger population is attenuated within marriage, this may explain the perplexing anomaly that although women are moving toward greater equality with men in the labor market, they remain more economically vulnerable when marriages end.

The Gender Gap in Income ●
After Marital Disruption

Just how do husbands and wives with children fare after they divorce? For couples with children who separated in the late 1980s or early 1990s, the economic well-being of mothers declined by 36 percent and the financial status of fathers improved by 28 percent. One-fifth of mothers experienced improvement in their standard of living, compared with two-thirds of fathers. Conversely, more than one-fourth of mothers experienced declines of more than 50 percent in their income relative to needs, compared with only 5 percent of fathers (Bianchi, Subaiya, and Kahn 1999).[5]

In Table 9.6, we use a sample of couples from the Survey of Income and Program Participation to estimate the gap in family income, per capita income, and income relative to needs (income relative to the poverty threshold) in fathers' and mothers' (and their children's) households in the year following separation. The average monthly dollar gap (in 1997 dollars) in family income between these mothers and their ex-husbands was more than $700: Husbands' households had average income of $2,600 per month, compared with $1,900 in wives' households. The difference in per capita income was almost $900 per month. The income/needs measure suggests that nonresident fathers have income about 3 times their needs level, on average, in the year after separation, whereas their former wives and children live on income that is only about 1.5 times their household needs level. Mothers (and children) have average levels of well-being in the year after separation that are estimated to be only about 56 percent those of fathers. Wives' well-being actually exceeds that of their former spouses in about one in five couples, but in almost half (45 percent) of the cases, the father's financial well-being is more than twice the mother's.

We also find that in poor families, divorced fathers are significantly more likely than their ex-wives to rise out of poverty. Only one-fourth of previously poor fathers remained in poverty after marital disruption, compared with almost three-fourths of poor mothers. Similarly, among couples with preseparation income above the poverty line, mothers were much more likely (19 percent) than fathers (3 percent) to fall into poverty as a result of separation (data not shown).

TABLE 9.6   Estimates of the Gender Gap in Economic Well-Being After Marital Disruption (in 1997 dollars)

	Monthly Family Income	Monthly Per Capita Income	Monthly Family Income/Needs
Mother's household	1,886	542	1.51
Father's household	2,592	1,429	2.98
Median difference (father – mother)	706	887	1.36
Median ratio (mother/father)	0.74	0.38	0.56
% of couples in which gains of			
Mother > father	35	10	19
Father > mother	65	90	81
101-150% of mother	24	12	17
151-200% of mother	9	12	20
> 200% of mother	32	66	45

NOTE: Sample size = 199 husbands and 199 wives. The ratio of family income to needs is monthly family money income (converted to 1997 dollars using the Consumer Price Index) divided by the poverty threshold for a household of given size in a given month. Child support (reported by wives) is included in wives' family income and subtracted from husbands' family income. The before measure is averaged over the 4 months preceding the month in which separation occurred. The after measure is averaged over the 12 months after the separation.
SOURCE: Data are from pooled 1984, 1985, 1986, 1987, 1988, and 1990 panels of the Survey of Income and Program Participation.

Although shared physical custody of children may be increasing (Cancian and Meyer 1998), it is still the case that in the vast majority (85 percent) of marital separations, mothers live with children (Grall 2000). These estimates suggest that gender equality in the postseparation households of these couples remains a serious problem. On average, mothers and children have income sufficient to meet their needs, but their standard of living is lower than that of fathers in four out of five cases, and substantially lower in one out of two couples.

● Conclusion

There are complex sets of interconnections among changes in family structure, decisions adults make about employment, and conditions in the labor market and the larger economy that constrain, or at least set the context for, how well families do economically. The economy sets the stage for how families are doing by either providing or not providing enough jobs of high quality for people to earn a living wage. For example, changes in the market such as the globalization of trade, large trade deficits, and the movement of many manufacturing jobs overseas have had a negative impact on the economic well-being of working- and middle-class families. But demographic changes and the attendant shifts in family structure also have important effects. Growth in the numbers of single-parent families since the 1970s has meant that more families today have only one potential earner. At the micro level, divorce, postponement of marriage, and increases in nonmarital births have economic consequences for families. At the same time, the economy affects family formation and dissolution. For example, a couple is more likely to marry and less likely to divorce when the male has a good job.

Overall, changes in the economy, employment, and family behaviors have led to income improvement over time, but improvement amid ever-growing inequality. Inequalities overlay race, age, and gender such that children and families, especially minority families, without multiple wage earners increasingly have lost ground relative to those with two (or more) earners. Income disparities have increased over time for single-mother and single-father families relative to two-parent, dual-earner families. Because more families today than in the past have only one parent and because that parent is usually the mother, children are more likely than those in the working-age population or the elderly to be in poverty, and this inequality has increased over time. Women's risk of poverty increased relative to men's for all women from 1950 to 1980 and continued to increase in the 1980s but only for young women (under 25) and elderly women (over 65). Although the economic situation for most types of white and black families improved in the 1980s and 1990s, it deteriorated for most types of Hispanic families. And whereas economic inequality grew among Hispanic and white families of similar types, it actually decreased between black and white families of similar types between 1978 and 1998.

In the United States, growing income inequality is focused at the two extremes, with the rich getting richer and the poor getting poorer. Although income inequality is growing in many countries, in the United States, unlike in most other countries, the inequalities are developing along age, gender, and race lines. The ability to identify the "haves" and the "have-nots" makes it possible for some observers to blame particular groups for others' misfortunes. During an era of economic expansion, such as the late 1990s, the problem this situation presents is relatively small. But we have yet to see what might happen in the event of an economic downturn if joblessness increases and wages decline. Given our history, it is possible that social unrest will occur, but it is equally possible that America will pull together and adopt new economic and political strategies to stem the tide of rising inequality.

Notes

1. In 1977, the per capita income of families with single fathers who were employed was actually $62 more than the per capita income of two-parent, dual-earner families.

2. For a discussion of how the poverty rate is determined, see Ruggles (1990). We focus on the "official" poverty rate, an absolute measure of income relative to a standard of "minimum need"; despite the criticisms aimed at this rate, it is widely used and there is a long time series required for assessing trends.

3. *Female-headed families* was the common term at the time Pearce (1978) described the feminization of poverty. With the 1980 Census, the U.S. Census Bureau discontinued use of the term *head* in describing household and family relationships. However, researchers outside the Census Bureau continue to use the phrase *female-headed families* when describing households that include mothers living with their dependent children and no adult males present.

4. Goldin's (1990) historical analysis of women's employment and earnings over the past two centuries illustrates the complexity of sorting out trends in the gender wage gap and increases/decreases in discriminatory treatment of women. Goldin suggests that narrowing wage gaps do not always signal declining discrimination and, reciprocally, increasing wage gaps can accompany more equal opportunities for women, at least in the short run.

5. These estimates are based on data from the Survey of Income and Program Participation and are similar to those reported for recently divorced women and their children in the Panel Study of Income Dynamics (Burkhauser et al. 1990, 1991). As noted earlier, estimates for men vary considerably from study to study. Our SIPP-based estimates for fathers (and mothers) are similar to those reported by Peterson (1996).

CHAPTER 10

COMBINING WORK AND FAMILY

More than two decades ago, Rosabeth Moss Kanter (1977) pointed out that, despite the "myth of separate worlds" of work and family, there are myriad ways in which work "spills over" into and affects family life.[1] As Kanter noted, occupations differ in the level of absorption—or commitment—they require from the persons who fill them. Some occupations require the unpaid assistance and cooperation of family members. The numbers of family members' work hours, shifts, and schedules tend to define the pace of family life and determine when family members can all be together. Work provides the income for the consumption that determines how family members allocate their time. And finally, work settings come with "cultures" that affect workers' social and psychological well-being. These work cultures and emotional states in turn can affect family life.

Becker and Moen (1999) report findings from recently conducted in-depth interviews that confirm that the influence of work on family continues to be strong, probably stronger than the influence of family on work. They found that work tends to structure family life in the dual-earner families they interviewed. Financial rewards from work define the opportunities families have, and hence men, women, and children are called upon to adapt home life to the work schedules of the adults within the home. However, families develop a number of strategies for combining work and family. During periods of particularly intense family demands, workers tend to try to "scale back" their commitment to long work hours. Couples continue to privilege one person's job over the other's, although for today's couples

282 • Continuity and Change in the American Family

that more often takes the form of two people remaining employed rather than the more extreme form of adaptation practiced in the decades after World War II, when one person, almost always the mother, dropped out of the labor force completely to meet family demands. This practice was much more common in white middle-class families than in minority and poor white families: Minority and white women in blue-collar and poor families have always had substantial levels of paid work and have not been able to separate family from paid work nearly as much as have middle-class women. Finally, Becker and Moen interviewed a number of couples who, over the course of their marriages, traded off on whose job would take precedence in order to handle work-family demands. Their research illustrates that the path from work to family is reciprocal: Work affects family life, but, over the life course, families affect individual workers' allocation of time to market work.

In thinking about changes that are affecting working families with children, it is important to place families, working families in particular, into perspective. To do this, we need to return to the distribution of all households presented in Chapter 1. Most Americans will have periods in their lives in which the competing demands of family and workplace are intense, because most Americans still marry and have children (see Chapters 1 and 3; see also Spain and Bianchi 1996). However, this child-rearing period of sustained, intense demand on time and money comes later in life as marriages are delayed and spans fewer years as families have fewer children and as parents survive longer after their children are raised.

Currently, only 34 percent of all households in the United States have children under age 18 residing in them; 25 percent of all households are two-parent families, and 9 percent are single-parent households (see the top panel of Figure 10.1). Focusing on the distribution of people, the percentages are higher, but only half of the population currently resides in households with dependent children; 39 percent of all Americans (children + adults) live in two-parent families, and an additional 11 percent are in single-parent families (see Figure 10.1).

Why is this important? Unless one is currently engaged in the day-to-day juggling involved in getting kids to the day-care center, rushing to the office, and then leaving work at the end of the day in time to make sure children are picked up by 6:00 p.m., the stress involved recedes and the memory of the difficulty of sustaining such a balancing act lessens. It is not that parents who have launched their children or now have grandchildren cannot empathize with those engaged in this balancing act; it is more that the juggling of jobs and children is not uppermost in their minds. Thus they may be aware of work-family balance issues, but these may not be at the

Figure 10.1. Distribution of Households and Persons by Household Type and Presence of Children: 1998

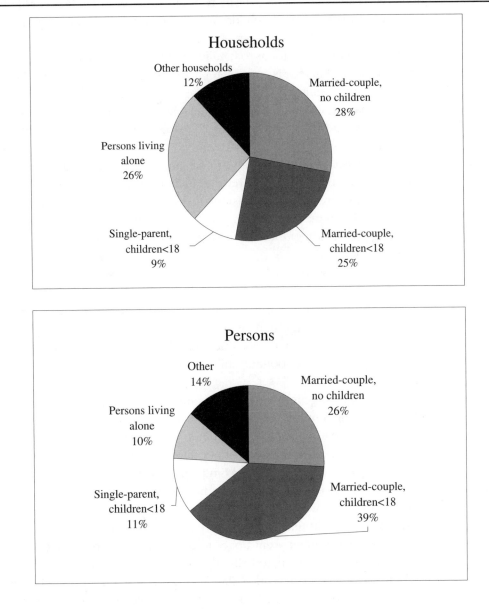

SOURCE: Current Population Survey, March supplement, 1998.

top of their agenda. Projections of households to the year 2010 suggest that the proportion of households with children under age 18 will decline by about 5 percentage points as the Baby Boom generation moves into retirement age (Day 1996). This will increase the number of married-couple households *without* minor children and the number of persons living alone.

When we narrow our focus to families with children, what we observe is that work-family balance is an issue for a growing number of parents. More married-couple families with children are dual-earner families than in the past, and many fewer include a parent, usually the mother, who is not engaged in any paid work (see Chapter 1). Also, with increases in family disruption and postponement of marriage (resulting in more births outside marriage), more children today spend time in single-parent families, where, coincident with welfare reform, increasingly the only option is for the coresident parent to work outside the home to support the family. Families with children may be shrinking as a percentage of all households, but a growing proportion of them have all parents attempting to balance work and family demands.

Perhaps the best way to illustrate this change is to focus on children. By the mid-1980s, 59 percent of children had all parents with whom they lived in the workforce (51 percent for children under age 6 and 63 percent among school-age children, ages 6-17). By 1997, this had increased by 9 percentage points, so that 68 percent of children (61 percent of preschoolers and 71 percent of school-age children) had all parents working at least some hours for pay.

Most of this change is driven by the dramatic increase in labor force participation among mothers, particularly married mothers. The increase in labor force participation has meant that more married couples commit more than 40 hours a week to market work because now both husband and wife are working for pay. Time is finite: Single parents have only 168 hours per week to commit to all activities (including sleep). Jointly, married parents have 336 hours per week. One-breadwinner families in the past might have allocated about 40 hours per week for paid work. As mothers entered the labor force, that number went up. Studies indicate that in the mid-1970s, husbands and wives averaged slightly more than 80 hours per week of combined labor market work (Clarkberg and Moen 1998; Jacobs and Gerson 2001). These estimates suggest that a sizable reallocation of time is under way in American households with children.

In this chapter, we first discuss the dramatic increase in mothers' labor force participation, particularly among married mothers, that has brought work-family issues to the forefront of national consciousness. We examine how much mothers are working—how many are part-time versus full-time workers, how many hours they commit to market work, and how this has changed over time. Then we consider the flip side, trends in women's (and men's) time spent in nonmarket work, or housework. Finally, we turn to subjective indicators of individuals' feelings about work and family. We assess trends in attitudes toward women's work outside the home and report on recent data on women's and men's satisfaction with the balance between work and family that they have achieved. We also discuss the relationship between marital satisfaction and the allocation of men's and women's time to paid work and unpaid activities.

The Increase in Mothers' • Labor Force Participation

Women's Entrance Into Paid Employment

The changed allocation of time in two-parent families is primarily a change in the allocation of women's time. Hence it will be useful for us to focus on trends in female labor force participation and show just how dramatic these changes have been. Figure 10.2 shows labor force participation rates for men and women in the "work and family" ages of 25 to 54, ages when schooling is typically complete, when individuals are most likely to be combining paid market work with child rearing, and before retirement begins to remove persons in substantial numbers from the paid workforce. The figure illustrates the dramatic increase in women's participation in the paid labor force since 1950 and the substantial narrowing of the gap between men's and women's labor force participation rates. A differential of 60 percentage points existed in the labor force rates of women and men in 1950, when 37 percent of women but 97 percent of men were in the labor force. The Bureau of Labor Statistics projects that the gap will narrow to only 12 percentage points by 2006, when 79 percent of women in the "work and family" ages and 91 percent of men will be in the paid workforce (Fullerton 1997).

There are two ways in which a society might reach such gender similarity in labor market participation in the "work and family" ages: Adults may commit much less time to alternatives to paid employment, such as caring for children, or a much higher percentage of women (as well as men) may engage in the simultaneous pursuit of rearing children and working for pay. Both changes characterize the United States: Women and men spend

● **Figure 10.2.** Gender Differences in Labor Force Participation (ages 25-54): 1950-2006

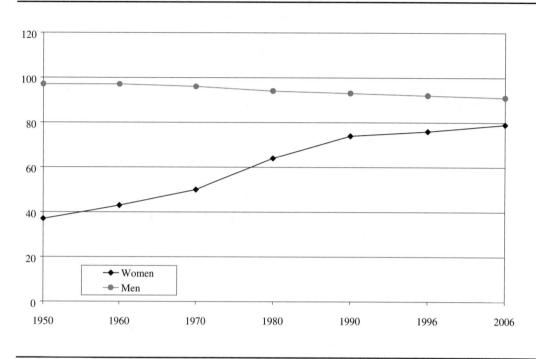

SOURCE: Current Population Survey, March supplements, 1950-96; Fullerton (1997:Table 4).

smaller percentages of their "work and family" years raising small children as fertility has declined and marriages are postponed (Watkins, Menken, and Bongaarts 1987), and many more women today than in the past work for pay while they rear small children (Cohen and Bianchi 1999; Hayghe 1997).

The rise in U.S. women's participation in market work in the 1950s and the early 1960s can be traced largely to an increase in the employment rates of older women—women in their 40s and 50s whose children were either grown or in school (Goldin 1990). During these decades, younger women (under age 40) married early, had children quickly after marriage, and remained outside the paid labor force to rear their children.

A dramatic change took place after 1970, as women born during the post-World War II Baby Boom followed a path that was very different from the one their mothers had walked (Bianchi 1995b). Baby Boomer daughters postponed marriage and children, went to college in increasing numbers, entered the labor force after finishing school, and did not leave their jobs so readily when their children were born. That is, a relatively large fraction of these women spent several years establishing themselves in the labor market prior to marriage and then remained attached to market work after they began having children. This new pattern has continued to the present.

Were it only unmarried and childless women who were increasing their paid work, the increase in female labor force participation would have limited implications for families. However, unmarried women marry and childless women become mothers—and what they do about paid work once they make these transitions has tremendous implications for families. In recent decades, more and more women have remained attached to the labor force even after making the transitions to wife and mother. The most dramatic increases in labor force attachment have been among married women, particularly those with young children.

Historically, mothers of young children who were not married (either never married or formerly married) had higher labor force participation rates than did married mothers. Not surprisingly, these women were more often compelled to combine market work with child rearing. But the truly remarkable change has been the dramatic increase in the combination of paid work and mothering among those women who might be thought to have more options—married mothers (see Figure 10.3). In 1960, only 19 percent of married mothers with children under age 6 were in the labor force; the proportion had increased to 64 percent by 1997, a rate much lower than that of formerly married mothers (74 percent) and similar to that of never-married mothers, who tended to be younger and less well educated than the other two groups (65 percent).

American women born in the late 1940s and the 1950s were the first cohorts to benefit from the affirmative action programs in the United States that followed passage of the 1964 Civil Rights Act, the "consciousness-raising" of the renewed women's movement of the 1970s, the widespread availability of the birth control pill, and the legalization of abortion (in 1972). Each of these factors tended to facilitate educational achievement, nontraditional occupational entry, and sustained labor market involvement. Women could increasingly plan when to begin childbearing and how to space their desired number of children. Affirmative action programs in education and business and (potential) sanctions on institutions that discriminated against women helped motivate women to invest in education and training to a far greater extent than earlier generations. Rising standards of living and strong economic growth during the 1950s and 1960s meant that women born after World War II were raised by parents whose ability to finance a college education for their daughters as well as their

● **Figure 10.3.** Labor Force Participation Rates for Mothers With Children under Age 6: 1960-1997

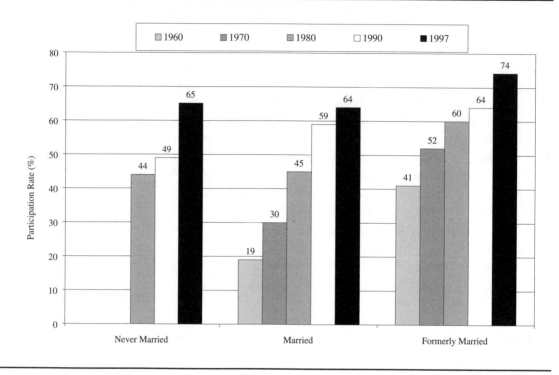

SOURCE: U.S. Bureau of the Census (1998).
NOTE: Data not available for never-married mothers in 1960, 1970.

sons was unprecedented (see Chapters 1 and 9 for a discussion of changes in the economy). The birth cohorts afforded these new opportunities, especially college-educated Baby Boom women, found they had much to give up if they left market work completely upon marriage or the birth of their first child.

We do not want to suggest that the rapid movement of younger women into the labor force in the 1970s and 1980s, and their continued market work after having children, characterized all women or was only the result of the expanded opportunities afforded women in the U.S. labor market. Baby Boomers, particularly those with less than a college education, flooded into the labor market in the 1970s, just as oil price shocks and worldwide food shortages made it increasingly difficult to find "good" jobs. The U.S. labor market had to absorb a huge number of workers in the 1970s, and this dampened job opportunities and wages for new entrants. But this too tended to increase, not decrease, women's lifetime attachment to market work.

Women whose pay and career trajectories were more similar to those of their mothers' generation—women who were segregated into lower-paying jobs that were generally known as "women's work"—also found increased incentives to remain employed after marrying and starting their families. Why? These women often married men who could not earn enough to support a family on their wages alone or at least not at a level of consumption that young families had come to appreciate and expect as a result of growing up in relatively well-off parental households in which fathers often could command a "family" wage. Across the educational spectrum in the 1970s and 1980s, there was both a demographic response to labor market entry constraints and opportunities (a decline in average family size, assisted by the postponement in marriage and first births) and an economic response to new conditions (a dramatic increase in the labor force participation of younger women, even those rearing small children).

Women's Attachment to the Labor Force

Perhaps the most striking aspect of women's labor force participation over the past 20 years is how steadily and linearly upward the trends move no matter what the universe or measure. Table 10.1 shows that, in 1978, almost 66 percent of women ages 25 to 54 worked at least some weeks during the previous year, and the proportion grew to 79 percent in 1998—an increase of nearly 14 percentage points. The increase in full-time, year-round work was almost 18 percentage points: In 1978, 32 percent of women in the prime "work and family" ages worked full-time and year-round, but this rose to 50 percent by 1998. Between 1978 and 1998, average annual hours of paid employment for all women ages 25 to 54 increased from 1,002 to 1,415, or by more than 40 percent. Most of the increase was because more women were working in 1998 rather than because working women dramatically increased the number of hours per year they worked for pay. This is shown in the bottom panel for employed women. An employed woman worked more hours per year in 1998 than in 1978 (1,830 hours compared with 1,596 hours), but this represents a 15 percent increase in work hours rather than the 40 percent figure found when all women are considered.

Is the juggling of work and family responsibilities more common today than it was two decades ago? The answer seems to be yes. Proportionately more adult women are combining these two spheres of life, and the number of weekly hours of paid work that an employed woman must balance with other commitments has increased.

TABLE 10.1 Hours and Weeks of Paid Work for All Women, Married Women, and Married Women With Young Children (all ages 25-54): 1976-1998

	All Women			Married Women			Married Women With Children Under Age 6		
	1978	1998	% Point Change	1978	1998	% Point Change	1978	1998	% Point Change
All women									
Previous week									
Average hours	19.6	26.6	7.0	17.4	25.1	7.7	11.8	19.6	7.8
% employed 1+ hours	55.5	71.0	15.5	51.4	68.8	17.4	38.1	58.2	20.1
% employed full-time	38.1	51.2	13.1	32.5	47.2	14.7	21.1	34.5	13.4
Previous year									
Average weeks	27.5	36.8	9.3	25.2	35.8	10.6	17.5	30.9	13.4
% employed 1+ weeks	65.7	79.4	13.7	62.0	77.7	15.7	50.5	70.5	20.0
% employed full-time, year-round	32.4	50.2	17.8	26.9	46.1	19.2	14.3	34.7	20.4
Annual hours	1,002	1,415	413	884	1,339	455	583	1,094	511
Employed women[a]									
Previous week									
Average hours	35.3	37.5	2.2	33.8	36.4	2.6	31.0	33.7	2.7
% employed full-time	68.6	72.2	3.6	63.2	68.6	5.4	55.4	59.3	3.9
Previous year									
Average weeks	43.5	47.3	3.8	42.4	47.2	4.8	36.0	45.4	9.4
% employed full-time, year-round	54.4	67.1	12.7	48.5	63.3	14.8	33.2	54.0	20.8
Annual hours	1,596	1,830	234	1,501	1,779	278	1,215	1,625	410

SOURCE: Current Population Survey, March supplements, 1978, 1998.
a. Women employed 1+ hours in the preceding week.

Table 10.1 also describes labor force trends for married women and married mothers with children under age 6. Again, there is no question that married mothers' attachment to market work has increased greatly since 1978. In 1998, 71 percent of married mothers of young children did some work for pay during the previous year and 35 percent worked full-time and year-round. However, the flip side of this is that 65 percent of married mothers of preschoolers were not full-time, year-round workers in 1998. This is not a picture of married mothers abandoning the rearing of their own children for paid work. Rather, there has been a ratcheting up of attachment to market work, with the norm—at least in terms of how frequently it occurs—continuing to be something other than full-time, year-round work for married mothers during their children's preschool years.

Married mothers with young children could conceivably commit *more* time to market work than single mothers because they have another parent in the household who can care for the children and perform other "household tasks." However, in the past, married mothers were the ones who more often oriented their time away from market work and toward child rearing. In 1978, single mothers with young children were working many more hours than their married counterparts, 816 hours per year compared with 583 hours per year for married mothers. By 1998, this gap narrowed substantially, such that single mothers were working 1,115 hours and married mothers were working 1,094 hours. Married mothers closed the "hours gap" by doubling their average annual hours of market work.

Figure 10.4 shows that the proportion of married and unmarried mothers who work full-time and year-round has increased but remains below 40 percent for both married and single mothers with young children. That is, it is not yet the case that the majority of mothers of young children work more than 35 hours a week throughout the year. Rather, 42 percent of the married mothers juggle work and family by not working for pay in a given year while they have preschoolers, and an additional 24 percent juggle work and family by working for pay but doing so part-time or only for part of the year (Cohen and Bianchi 1999). Hence, still in 1998, only about one-third of married mothers of children under age 6 (mothers with the most choice about employment because there were other potential earners in their households) worked full-time and year-round.

Explaining Trends in Women's Attachment to Paid Work

In the past, children curtailed women's labor market activity, as did access to other means of support, such as a husband's income. For the 1978 to

● **Figure 10.4.** Percentages Working Full-Time and Year-Round: Mothers of Children Under Age 6: 1978-1998

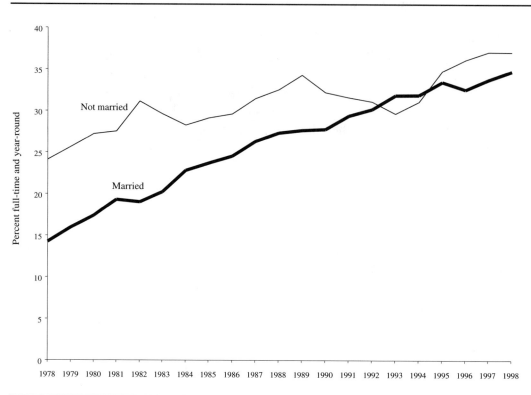

SOURCE: Cohen and Bianchi (1999).

1998 period, we estimate change in women's annual hours of market work by taking into account marital and motherhood status, access to other income (usually a husband's earnings), educational attainment, and age. We also take into account the women's race/ethnicity, given that black women historically have had higher rates of labor force participation than white women but also suffer more unemployment. Figure 10.5 plots the difference in estimated annual work hours of married women and mothers of young children relative to single women without young children. Relative to single women, marriage depressed annual hours by more than 100 hours per year in the late 1970s, and living with a child under 6 depressed a married mother's annual employment by an additional 800 hours. By the 1990s, marriage had no significant effect on those without young children, and from the mid-1980s to the mid-1990s married women with young children actually worked more than single mothers with young children, with other variables held constant. Over time, children made less of a difference

● **Figure 10.5.** Differences in Estimated Annual Hours Worked Relative to Single Women With No Children Under Age 6: 1978-1998

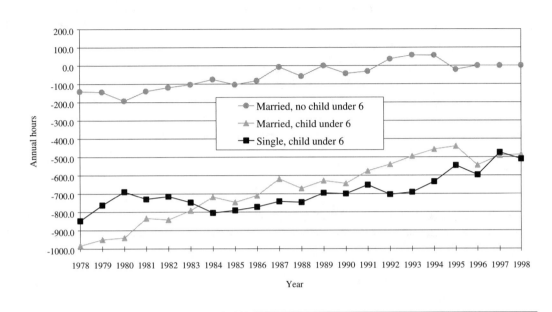

SOURCE: Cohen and Bianchi (1999).
NOTE: Estimates take into account differences in age, education, other income, and race/ethnicity. The zero line on the plot is the annual hours of single women with no children under age 6 in each year.

for both single and married women. By 1998, both single and married mothers were working about 500 fewer hours than single childless women compared with a difference of more than 800 hours in 1978.

In sum, relative to unmarried women without children, we find that mothers commit far fewer hours to market work—but this differential has declined significantly over the past two decades. In the late 1970s married women without children worked significantly fewer hours than their single counterparts, but by the late 1990s there was no longer a significant difference in labor supply attributable to marriage among these women.

Even though children affect a mother's labor supply in the 1990s less than they did in the late 1970s, the effect of having preschool-age children on annual hours continues to be substantial, cutting annual hours by about 500 (the equivalent of one-fourth of a year of full-time work). American women increasingly seem to exchange some hours of caring for their own children for hours of paid work, but married mothers remain a long way from a situation in which most commit to full-time, year-round market work.

Women have reached the point where marriage, per se, has relatively little effect on their labor supply, although access to other income, which for married women is primarily earnings from their spouses, continues to decrease women's allocation of time to paid work (Cohen and Bianchi 1999). The effect of income from other sources is diminishing, however.

Over time, educational differentials in labor supply have grown, widening the gap between more and less educated women. That is, relative to those without a high school diploma, women who are high school and college graduates increasingly work more hours. This is similar to what has occurred for men (Juhn, Murphy, and Pierce 1993).

● Attitudes About Women's Work

As women have become more equal with men in the labor market, attitudes about women's labor force participation have become increasingly liberal. Data from the General Social Survey for the period 1977-94 indicate a relatively steady increase in approval of women's labor force participation. However, disapproval of *mothers* working outside the home remains, as does a gender gap in this disapproval, particularly when young children are involved. That is, our ideas about care of children and women's place in the workforce have become much more supportive of paid work for mothers, but there is still ambivalence about the consequences for children of combining paid work and family.

Table 10.2 presents responses to items about work and family issues from the General Social Survey in 1977 and 1994. The top panel of the table shows that the proportion of Americans, men and women, who disapprove of a married woman's working even if her husband can support her has declined from one-third to less than one-fifth. A very dramatic decline has occurred in the proportion agreeing that it is more important for a wife to help her husband's career than to have one herself. In 1977, more women than men (61 percent and 53 percent, respectively) agreed with this statement, whereas by 1994 only a little more than 20 percent of both men and women agreed.

Somewhat more disagreement between men and women is evidenced by responses to the item concerning whether it is better if a man achieves outside the home and a woman cares for home and family. Both women and men were dramatically less likely to agree with this "traditional" divi-

TABLE 10.2 Changes in Attitudes About Women's Roles as Wives, Mothers, and Workers: 1977-1994

	1977		1994	
	Men	*Women*	*Men*	*Women*
Attitudes about gender roles				
% who disapprove of married woman working if her husband can support her	32.3	34.8	18.9	18.9
% who agree that it is more important for a wife to help her husband's career than to have one herself	52.7	60.7	22.2	21.1
% who agree that it is better for everyone if man achieves outside the home and woman takes care of home and family	68.9	63.2	38.4	32.6
Attitudes about mother's paid work and child rearing				
% who say a working mother cannot have as warm and secure a relationship with child as a nonworking mother	58.4	44.9	39.2	24.2
% who say a preschool child is likely to suffer if mother works	73.2	62.5	50.7	36.8

SOURCE: Authors' tabulations from the General Social Survey.

sion of labor in the home in 1994 than they were in 1977, but more men (38 percent) than women (33 percent) still agreed.

The items about combining paid work and the rearing of children appear in the bottom panel. They, too, show a dramatic change over time, with a smaller proportion of respondents in 1994 thinking that children will suffer if a mother is employed outside the home. What is interesting about these items, however, is the large gender difference and the relatively high percentage of men who still questioned whether children do as well when their mothers work for pay. Almost 40 percent of men (but about one-fourth of women) surveyed felt that a working mother cannot have as warm and secure a relationship with a child as a mother who is not employed. And half of the men and more than one-third of the women surveyed still felt that a preschool child is likely to suffer if a mother works for pay. By 1994, women and men seemed to hold similar attitudes about the desirability of women's establishing independent labor market careers but differed when it came to assessing the costs for children of women's realizing their labor market goals, with men expressing greater concern about the costs to children and family life.

● Women's and Men's Nonmarket Work

Who's Doing the Housework?

Given the striking trends in women's labor force participation and concerns about gender equality in the labor force, it is perhaps not surprising that during the past two decades much attention has focused on trends and gender differentials in unpaid household work as well (Bianchi et al. 2000). That is, the interest in women's reallocation of time toward market work has spawned attention to the flip side—women's (and men's) allocation of time to unpaid, nonmarket work. Because time is finite, as women spend more time in the labor force, they have less time available for unpaid work.

Trends over time in market work, however, are more readily measured than trends in unpaid work. Federal data-gathering surveys (most important, the Current Population Survey) monitor paid work on a monthly basis in order to produce estimates of unemployment for the system of national accounts. Work done in the home for one's family has never been included in measures of national wealth, such as the gross domestic product, hence the measurement of household work is far less systematic and frequent.

Prior research shows that regardless of demographic or life-course characteristics, women invest significantly more hours in household labor than do men, but there has been some convergence over time (Berardo, Shehan, and Leslie 1987; Brines 1993; Coverman and Sheley 1986; Gershuny and Robinson 1988; Hochschild 1989; Marini and Shelton 1993; Nock and Kingston 1988; Robinson 1988; Robinson and Godbey 1999; Shelton 1992; Shelton and John 1996). Time diary data collections at 10-year intervals since 1965 allow us to assess time spent in unpaid household work (Gershuny and Robinson 1988; Robinson and Godbey 1999).

TABLE 10.3 Trends in Average Weekly Housework Hours by Gender for Men and Women Ages 25 to 64: 1965-1995

	All Women				All Men				Ratio of Women's Time to Men's			
	1965	1975	1985	1995	1965	1975	1985	1995	1965	1975	1985	1995
Total housework	30	23.7	19.7	17.5	4.9	7.2	9.8	10	6.1	3.3	2	1.8
Core housework (total)	26.9	21	16.3	13.9	2.3	2.5	4	3.8	11.9	8.3	4	3.7
Cooking meals	9.3	8.1	7	4.6	1.1	1.5	2	1.6	8.8	5.3	3.4	2.8
Meal cleanup	4.5	2.4	1.9	0.7	0.5	0.3	0.4	0.1	9.9	9.4	4.9	5.4
Housecleaning	7.2	7.3	5	6.7	0.5	0.5	1.3	1.7	15.5	14	3.9	3.8
Laundry, ironing	5.8	3.2	2.4	1.9	0.3	0.2	0.3	0.3	22.1	13.5	7.5	6.9
Other housework (total)	3.1	2.7	3.4	3.6	2.6	4.7	5.7	6.2	1.2	0.6	0.6	0.6
Outdoor chores	0.3	0.7	0.5	0.8	0.4	1	1.3	1.9	0.7	0.7	0.4	0.4
Repairs	0.4	0.6	0.5	0.7	1	2	1.8	1.9	0.4	0.3	0.3	0.4
Garden, animal care	0.6	0.8	0.8	0.8	0.2	0.7	0.9	1	2.4	1.1	0.9	0.8
Bills, other financial	1.8	0.7	1.6	1.3	0.9	1	1.6	1.5	2	0.7	1	0.9
N	579	927	1,725	493	469	783	1,405	359				

SOURCE: Reprinted from *Social Forces* vol. 79, no. 1, 2000. "Is Anyone Doing the Housework? Trends in the Gender Division of Household Labor" by Suzanne M. Bianchi, Melissa A. Milkie, Liana C. Sayer, and John P. Robinson. Copyright © The University of North Carolina Press.

Table 10.3 displays the weekly housework hours for men and women and the ratio of women's to men's hours for all persons ages 25 to 64.[2] Housework is separated into core tasks, cooking meals, meal cleanup, housecleaning, laundry, and other tasks that are more discretionary and/or less time-consuming—outdoor chores and repairs, gardening/animal care, and bill paying.

Table 10.3 shows that women spent about 30 hours a week doing unpaid household work in 1965, more than 6 times the 4.9 hours men spent in housework. Women's housework hours dropped to 23.7 per week in 1975 and 19.7 per week in 1985 and reached a low of 17.5 hours per week by 1995. Men's hours increased to 7.2 in 1975 and 9.8 hours in 1985 and leveled off at 10.0 hours in 1995. In 1965, women averaged 6 times more hours in housework than men; by 1985, women's hours were only twice the number of men's. The ratio declined further to 1.8 in 1995, but largely because women continued to do less housework, not because men increased their hours of household work.

Almost two-thirds of total housework hours are spent doing the core housework tasks of cooking and cleaning. When we examine these tasks, all continue to be the purview of women much more so than of men. Cooking, more than any of the cleaning tasks, is the area in which women and men have shown the greatest current equality, with women's reported hours 8.8 times men's in 1965 but only 2.8 times men's in 1995. In 1995, women continued to spend about 4 to 7 times as many hours as men on cleaning and laundry tasks. For all core tasks, the ratios have become much smaller; that is, women's and men's time has become more similar, but women still do nearly 4 times as much of this work as men.

Overall, there was a marginal increase in the time men and women devoted to other kinds of housework, from 3.1 hours in 1965 to 3.6 hours in 1995. Whereas there is a linear decline across time in women's participation in core housework tasks, trends in women's hours spent in these other tasks are inconsistent. By contrast, after 1965, men increased the time they spent in noncore tasks: outdoor chores, repairs, garden/animal care, and bill paying. In 1965, the ratio of women's to men's hours in these noncore tasks taken as a whole was around unity; in later years women did about 60 percent as much of this type of work as men.

There are three broad perspectives on the process of domestic labor allocation between (married) men and women; these involve time availability, resource bargaining, and gender. The first theoretical perspective posits that women and men perform household labor to the extent that they have available time, as determined by competing demands (Coverman 1985; England and Farkas 1986; Hiller 1984). This time-availability perspective draws heavily on Becker's (1991) human capital theory on how the nature and level of competing demands are determined (Greenstein 1998). It implies that women's and men's time in household labor should be strongly related to time spent in market labor. Time constraints, as indexed by employment status, marital status, and parental status, account for a large amount of variation in household labor (Shelton and John 1996), but the association between these time constraints and household labor differs markedly by gender.

The second perspective focuses on resource bargaining, or exchange among partners. The basic idea is that the person with the most power will do the least household work. People act in their own self-interest and use their resources to strike the best bargain. Those with more resources have more power. The amount of income a person brings into the relationship influences the amount of unpleasant work he or she must do. And because women's "market work" is generally lower paid than men's, women tend to do more housework (Brines 1993). Empirical evidence suggests that men do more domestic labor when their wives earn a higher percentage of the household income, especially if they are defined as coproviders (Coltrane 1996).

The idea of housework as a symbolic enactment of gender relations is the third theoretical perspective, developed to explain why there is not a simple trade-off between time spent in unpaid labor and paid labor among men and women in either marital or cohabiting relationships (Ferree 1990; South and Spitze 1994; West and Zimmerman 1987). From this perspective, housework is a symbolic enactment of gender relations. This gender perspective emphasizes that housework does not have a neutral meaning; rather, its performance by women and men contributes to the definition and expression of gender relations within households. That is, women's performance of household tasks subjectively represents their caring for the family and displays femininity. Women and men in marital households, compared with other household types, have the greatest gap in housework time (South and Spitze 1994). When couples marry, the women's housework hours go up and the men's decline (Gupta 1999). In other words, wives and husbands are displaying their "proper" gender roles through the amount and type of housework they perform. Viewed within the framework of the gender perspective on housework, the roles of wife and mother are intimately tied to expectations for doing housework (regardless of other pressures) and displayed through outcomes such as a clean house (Robinson and Milkie 1998).

In addition, the gender perspective suggests that women are disadvantaged in the allocation of their time. Women spend their time doing the least favorite housework activities and their time is more subject to whims and demands of other family members. Whatever housework becomes necessary, such as additional work created by the needs of children, women (have to) make time for it. Husbands tend not to respond (for example, by doing more housework) to their wives' constraints or their children's demands. The gender perspective also suggests that ideology matters, too, in that those who believe in equality at home may be more likely to act in profeminist ways; however, even here husbands' power is evident, in that wives tend to be affected by husbands' preferences and ideology, more so than vice versa (Ferree 1991; Shelton and John 1996).

It has also been suggested, and some empirical literature exists to bolster the claim, that husbands may contribute relatively little to "core" housework tasks, in part, because wives are hesitant to relinquish control or they set standards that husbands consider to be unacceptably high (Allen and Hawkins 1999). To the extent that this happens in married-couple households, this too can be understood within the gender perspective. Because the cleanliness of the home is a reflection on a woman's competence as a "wife and mother" but not on a man's competence as a "husband and father," women may come to hold higher standards for household cleanliness and become more invested in the control and supervision of household work.

Explanations of Trends in Unpaid Household Work

How important are changes in relative time constraints and economic resources, as indexed by changes in employment, education, marriage, and children, to the explanation of the decline in hours spent in housework for women and the increase for men? Women's employment is negatively associated with time spent in household labor (Brines 1993; Gershuny and Robinson 1988; Robinson 1993; Robinson and Converse 1972; Sanchez 1993; Shelton 1990; Shelton and John 1996; Vanek 1974; Walker 1969). Women's education is also negatively associated with household labor time (Berardo et al. 1987; Bergen 1991; Brines 1993; Shelton and John 1996; South and Spitze 1994). Women's employment has increased dramatically over time, and women's educational attainment has also risen (Mare 1995).

This suggests that, other things being equal, women's time in unpaid work should be declining due to this increase in employment.

Unlike for women, whether or not men are employed has not been shown to alter the amount of time they invest in household labor (Coverman and Sheley 1986; Sanchez 1993; Shelton 1990; Shelton and John 1996). But how much they work does affect the hours of housework they do (Coltrane and Ishii-Kuntz 1992; Coverman 1985; Haddad 1994; Kamo 1991; South and Spitze 1994). The more hours men are employed, the more segregated the household division of chores becomes. The more hours men work, the more likely they are to engage in the more discretionary "male" tasks of outside maintenance and repairs (Blair and Lichter 1991). In recent years men have been retiring earlier than in the past, resulting in an employment decline for older men. However, there has not been much change in the average hours of work among employed men (Rones, Ilg, and Gardner 1997). Hence it is not clear whether employment changes for men have been significant enough, in and of themselves, to increase men's hours of unpaid work.

The bulk of research indicates a positive association between men's education and time spent in housework (Berardo et al. 1987; Bergen 1991; Brayfield 1992; Brines 1993; Kamo 1988; Presser 1994; Shelton and John 1996; South and Spitze 1994). However, Shelton (1992) reports a curvilinear relationship, where men with high school degrees or some college education perform more housework than either men who are high school dropouts or men with college degrees. As it has for women, educational attainment has increased for men over time (Mare 1995). To the extent that the relationship between education and doing housework is positive for men, this change may be increasing men's housework time.

Marital status also affects housework hours, and the effects differ for men and women. Married women spend more time on housework, compared with women who are not married, whereas most studies report little or no difference in men's household labor time by marital status (Shelton and John 1993; South and Spitze 1994). However, Gupta (1999), using longitudinal data, found that men who married reduced the amount of housework they did compared to when they were single.

In most studies, the presence of children in the household has been found to be positively related to time spent in household labor (in addition to child-care time) for both women and men, although the effect appears to be much stronger for women (Brines 1993; Gershuny and Robinson 1988; Haddad 1994; Presser 1994; Sanchez and Thomson 1997; Shelton and John 1996; South and Spitze 1994). A few studies have found either no effect

(Fried and Settergren 1986; Ross 1987) or a negative effect (Pleck 1983) for men. Over time, as marriages are delayed and families have fewer children (McLanahan and Casper 1995), adults (at least women) should be allocating fewer hours to household work, other things being equal.

Changes in housework time that are not accounted for by changes in American employment statuses, education, and marriage and parental statuses may indicate social and cultural change in household services and their value. For example, Oropesa (1993) found that women with full-time jobs relied more on housecleaning services (although still only a very small proportion did so) and on restaurant meals more than did part-time and nonemployed women. However, all types of women, regardless of work status, reported that their households made relatively high use of take-out foods, averaging about one meal every 2-3 weeks. National Consumer Expenditure Survey data corroborate these findings: Consumption of household cleaning services has increased, but in 1990, only 7 percent of households used such services (Gray 1992). On the other hand, almost 80 percent of consumer units spent money on meals at restaurants.

It is likely, however, that some amount of housework goes undone today, at least compared with 1965. This may be especially true if we consider that the amount of cleaning time should have *increased* over the years, all else being equal, because homes have become significantly larger over time, with more rooms to clean. If work does go undone, it may be that people generally do not care about the services "lost" compared to the time gained for other pursuits; cleanliness standards and standards for prepared foods may have declined. One of the ways people balance work and family is by doing less work in the home, especially those activities that are viewed as most discretionary or easily replaced.

For women, compositional changes are an important part of the explanation of their 12-hour-per-week decrease in household work, with about half of the decline associated with larger proportions of women who are employed and college educated and smaller proportions who are married and living with children in the household in 1995 compared with 1965. More specifically, if women in 1995 had the same characteristics as those in 1965—with the same low rates of labor force participation and higher rates of marriage and greater numbers of children—the decline would be about 6 hours per week, not 12 hours (Bianchi et al. 2000). The other half of the decline, however, can be attributed to a decreased propensity of women to do housework. For men, almost all of the 5-hour-per-week increase in housework time is related to men's increased propensity to do housework; relatively little (14 percent) is due to shifts in men's demographic characteristics.

In sum, the evidence suggests a continued decline in hours of housework by women but a stalled increase (after 1985) on the part of men. Interestingly, the decline for women is even greater across time for those who are not employed than for those who are employed. This suggests that the propensity to use time for housework declined most among the group with the most, not the least, time available for housework. So families may balance work and family demands by having employed mothers do less housework, and fathers pick up some of the slack, but this type of adjustment is being made as much by families with limited work-family conflict as it is by those with the most intense demands on their time.

When Do Men Do More Housework? ●

In his book *Family Man: Fatherhood, Housework, and Gender Equity*, Scott Coltrane (1996) describes the situations in which men do a greater share of the household labor. He found that husbands' share of housework is greater when their wives are employed more hours. When wives relinquish their control over managing the household and delegate chores, husbands are more likely to share in the housework. Sharing of household labor is also more common among couples who believe in egalitarian gender roles. Husbands who work fewer hours and value family time over their careers also do a greater share of the housework and caring for children. And finally, more tasks are shared when fathers care for their infants, take responsibility for the mundane aspects of parenting, and assume a more involved role than that of "household helper."

Families benefit when men take on more of the household chores. When husbands do more of the housework, employed wives escape the total responsibility of the "second shift" (Coltrane 1996) and women have less psychological distress and better mental health (Mirowsky and Ross 1989). Fathers also benefit when they become more involved in household work. When they take on responsibility for children, they develop "parenting" sensitivities that were previously assumed to be the sole purview of mothers (Parke 1995). And children benefit emotionally and intellectually from their fathers' involvement in parenting.

● Perceived Success at Work-Family Balance

What do we know about how married, employed men and women feel about the balance they have struck between work and family in their lives? Surprisingly, evidence suggests that men and women do not differ in their levels of felt success in these matters (Milkie and Peltola 1999). The vast majority (86 percent of women, 85 percent of men) feel at least somewhat successful in balancing work and family, with about 40 percent feeling very or totally successful.

When asked about work adjustments they have made for family, men and women are equally likely to report that they have turned down promotions (around 16 percent) and that they have refused to work overtime or cut back on work (around 30 percent each). The felt need to be the family breadwinner continues to motivate men more so than women, however, in that more men (54 percent) than women (41 percent) report taking on additional paid work because of family economic pressures (Milkie and Peltola 1999:Table 3).

What family adjustments do workers make to fulfill work responsibilities? Men report more often missing family occasions due to work (62 percent of men but only 37 percent of women report such absences). But women more often than men report that work has interfered with family by making them unable to care for a sick child (25 percent of women and 18 percent of men report this family-work conflict). Time diary data show that women do three times more child care than men, but perhaps, as with housework, this is because women feel it is their responsibility. Hence they may feel more conflict when work keeps them from caring for a sick child even though they miss work more often than men to do so.

● Dual Earning and Family Well-Being

West and Zimmerman (1987) pioneered the idea of "doing gender" and saw it as creating unnatural, inessential, and nonbiological differences between the sexes. In traditional families, roles are typically constructed with the notion that there exist appropriate tasks for women that are distinct from those appropriate for men—for example, men take out the garbage and women cook dinner. Egalitarian couples tend to disparage such ideas, viewing household tasks as the responsibility of both spouses, consciously rejecting traditional gender stereotypes and redefining what it means to be a man or a woman. Crucial to reports of marital satisfaction are the ways couples reconcile their gender ideologies and the division of labor. When the division of labor in the home is incongruent with one or both spouses' gender ideologies, it is likely that marital quality declines and perceptions of unfairness increase.

In middle-class couples where wives perceive greater equity in the division of household labor, husbands report less conflict (Perry-Jenkins and Folk 1994). But husbands' beliefs and perceptions about gender equity are more likely to affect wives' marital quality than the reverse (Wilkie, Ferree, and Ratcliff 1998). Thus perceptions of fairness are crucial, and in assessments of marital quality they may be as important as or more important than the actual distribution of housework (Blair and Johnson 1992; Thompson 1991; Wilkie et al. 1998). For example, Wilkie et al. (1998) found that wives felt the division of household work was unfair when they were responsible for performing the majority of it; however, husbands responsible for half the housework felt that such a distribution was unfair.

Others have linked increased educational attainment with more egalitarian gender roles and have found that the more educated the husband, the higher the wife's marital quality (Vannoy and Philliber 1992). Education serves to alter perceptions of gender, making it more acceptable to hold nontraditional notions about women's and men's appropriate duties and roles. The primacy of gender ideology in influencing marital satisfaction is supported by Vannoy and Philliber's (1992:397) conclusion that gender role attitudes have a greater impact on marital satisfaction than do socioeconomic and life-course variables.

One of the major changes occurring in the division of family responsibilities is a trend toward increasing dependence upon women's salaries in dual-income families. Some theorists have posited that women's employment leads to marriages of poor quality, which are then more prone to disruption. This conjecture is not supported by the literature, however. Studies done before 1970 found some association, but recent studies based on large national samples have reported no effect of wife's employment on marital satisfaction of either the wife or the husband (Spitze 1988). Additionally, in a recent analysis of panel data, Rogers (1999:131) found that a wife's employment did not increase the risk of divorce but that marital conflict led to increased labor force participation of a wife, perhaps in anticipation of the need to support herself in the event of divorce. These findings are consistent with previous research reporting that higher risks of marital dissolution were positively associated with women's employment, but women's employment was not associated with higher risks of marital dissolution (Greene and Quester 1982; Johnson and Skinner 1986).

How do the multiple roles of worker, spouse, and parent affect family interaction? Research shows that multiple roles can increase stress levels, cause problems with physical health, and reduce family well-being (O'Neil and Greenberger 1994; Perry-Jenkins, Repetti, and Crouter 2000; Repetti 1993). But multiple roles can also have a positive side—increased income, greater challenges, increased self-esteem, the power to delegate the least pleasant responsibilities, and more complex social interaction (Barnett 1999; Barnett, Marshall, and Pleck 1992).

Stressful working conditions spill over to affect family life when they cause feelings of role overload or a sense of conflict between work and family roles. Stressful conditions in the workplace affect family interaction primarily by increasing feelings of emotional distress, depression, fatigue, role overload, and work-family conflict. And this heightened emotional state results in less supportive and less responsive, as well as more negative and conflicted, family interactions (Perry-Jenkins et al. 2000; Repetti 1993).

Responses to role overload and work-family conflicts range from withdrawal from family interactions to negative interactions that include greater irritability and impatience and more domination. For example, emotional distress has been linked to anger and withdrawal in marital interactions (Barling and MacEwen 1992) and withdrawal from children (Repetti and Wood 1997). Stressful experiences due to the combination of work and family roles have also been associated with problematic parent-child relations and negative child outcomes (Barling and MacEwen 1992; Perry-Jenkins et al. 2000; Sears and Galambos 1992). Stressful interaction with co-workers and work overload can also have negative physical health consequences (Repetti 1998).

Marriages are often permanently altered upon the transition to parenthood. Children may affect marriages in ways that differ for men and women. Vannoy and Philliber (1992) found that children decrease men's marital satisfaction, a decrease that is magnified by the presence of greater numbers of children. These researchers speculate that this may be because children take up attention and time that men's wives may otherwise spend on them. By contrast, wives' marital satisfaction is unaffected by the presence of children (Vannoy and Philliber 1992:391). Other research using longitudinal data, however, suggests that children lower marital satisfaction for both spouses (Amato and Booth 1997). Interestingly, although children, especially young children, tend to lower marital satisfaction, they also reduce the probability of divorce (Heaton 1990; Waite and Lillard 1991).

Conclusion ●

The changing context surrounding working families includes changing demographics—delayed marriage, more childbearing outside marriage, high levels of divorce, and lengthening life expectancy. In this chapter, we have focused on work-family balance issues primarily as they relate to the balancing of caring for children and paid work. Obviously, there are other work-family balance issues, but the child-rearing years are a period of particularly intense work-family demands. They are also the years in which there have been very large changes in women's allocation of time in recent decades.

How are families balancing paid work and child rearing? First, as women increase their market work, they seem to be shedding unpaid work (i.e., housework) at a rapid rate. Second, despite the increase in women's employment, many mothers still do not work full-time and year-round when their children are of preschool age. Families are also more likely to purchase domestic services than in the past as more market alternatives become available and time constraints increase. More families are using child-care centers, buying take-out meals, and employing cleaning services. Although there has been a substantial shift in attitudes toward more acceptance of working women and working mothers, there continues to be concern about the effects of maternal paid work on young children.

Given that people are still concerned about how women's working outside the home affects children when they are young, women today tend to devote a significant amount of time to raising children despite their increased labor force participation. On average, for every hour men spend caring for children, women spend 3 hours (Robinson and Godbey 1999). Even today, many women spend less time in the labor force (either by taking time off or by working part-time) than men because they devote time to child rearing. The result is that women have continued to amass (albeit to a lesser and lesser extent) less labor market experience than men over their lifetimes, which retards progress toward wage and job equality with men (see Chapter 9). The likelihood of the continued movement toward gender equality in occupation and earnings may depend on men's and women's more equal participation in child rearing and domestic work.

Still, many individuals feel they have struck a reasonable balance between paid work and family—and interestingly, men and women are equally likely to report success in this juggling act. Yet there continue to be large gender differences in work-family balance, with men more likely to take on additional work in response to felt need to support a family and more likely to miss family events to fulfill work obligations. Women are far more likely than men to reduce their commitment to market work to less than full-time to give more time to child rearing. The implications of these gendered responses to work-family balance—for men's "caring" selves, for women's labor market success, and for children's lives—are the major issues to be explored in the future.

Although women's and men's work and family lives have become more similar since the 1960s, the movement toward equality seems to have stalled for two reasons. First, although women are still moving closer to men in their attachment to the labor force, men have not reciprocated as readily on the home front. Second, employers have been slow to recognize the need for new family-friendly benefits, even though more of their employees are mothers. And the new welfare-to-work policies have resulted in more single mothers, the most time-disadvantaged employees, entering the workforce.

As it stands, only 8 percent of medium and large firms provide any kind of child-care assistance to employees, and only 2 percent provide paid family leave; in addition, only 26 percent of women in these firms are on flexible work schedules. Low unemployment, growth in service sector and high-tech jobs, and a relatively greater increase in women's than men's educational levels increase the likelihood that employers will have to become more serious about providing family-friendly benefits if they hope to compete for the best employees.

Finally, the aging of the population, in particular the Baby Boom generation, is likely to alter further how men and women combine work and family in the future. This is a very important dimension of the work-family nexus, because elder care and meeting the needs of parents as well as children will grow as an issue facing tomorrow's working families (see Chapter 6). The increase in numbers of the elderly also is important for the public policy debates that will take place in the coming years, because support for work-family initiatives will have to come in part from those who no longer juggle work and family as intensely as in the past—that is, support will have to come from grandparents as well as parents.

Notes

1. People generally regard "work" as paid employment, but the shopping, cooking, cleaning, laundry, bill paying, yard work, and caring for children people do within the home to make sure families run smoothly is also work. Most demographers, sociologists, and economists still use the terms *work* and *family* to differentiate these two spheres of life. We chose the title of this chapter to reflect the terms these scholars use, but we are mindful that homemaking is also work. In this chapter, we use terms such as *paid work, market work,* and *employment* to describe activities that are done to earn money and *unpaid work, household work,* and *housework* to describe homemaking activities.

2. The table displays respondent-reported time diary data on housework that were collected in four national studies in the United States in 1965, 1975, 1985, and 1995, all of which were based on probability sampling methods. The earlier studies (1965 and 1975) were done in person and had higher response rates, but were not spread over the entire year. The later studies (1985 and 1995) were done in part or wholly over the telephone and had lower response rates, but were spread over the entire year. For a more complete discussion of the differences in samples and methodology, see Robinson and Godbey (1999). In this analysis, we weight the data at each point so that all days of the week are equally represented.

CONCLUSION

W e began this volume with a description of a wedding, an event uniting a couple and bringing together a group of kin with a complex history of relationships. Our purpose was to illustrate that family relationships are diverse and multifaceted; families are groups of individuals knit together by overlapping histories, interconnections, and obligations. We asked how families had changed in the second half of the 20th century, focusing specifically on the past two decades, and entertained notions about what might have precipitated those changes. We outlined our approach in the introduction and discussed the broad societal shifts that formed the context for family change in the first chapter of this volume. In subsequent chapters, we covered a wealth of material. Perhaps the best way to conclude a book on the American family is to revisit several of the questions that motivated us at the outset.

One topic that has captured the attention of family demographers in the past decade is that of cohabitation, the topic taken up in Chapter 2. Perhaps the most important question about cohabitation is, What does the growth in cohabitation mean for the future of marriage? We would argue that it means relatively little if cohabitation is merely becoming a phase or a "space" that people typically occupy on their way to forming a first marriage or entering a remarriage. And certainly for many individuals, particularly those at higher socioeconomic levels, this appears to be what is happening. Most still eventually marry and delay having children until they do so. Children are still most often raised in marriage. The interesting question is whether cohabitation is being used differently—and whether it increasingly means something quite different—in poor and minority families, where it may more often be a substitute for rather than a precursor to marriage. And if it is being used as a substitute for marriage among low-income, less educated groups and minorities, is it a much weaker mechanism for obligating fathers to the care and support of their children?

A related question is whether there is a decoupling of marriage and childbearing under way. There certainly seems to be less pressure to marry before the birth of a premaritally conceived child, as evidenced by trends discussed in Chapter 3. But the eschewing of marriage before childbearing in the United States is not so extreme as in some other countries, such as Sweden. Again, the interesting question is whether this decoupling is occurring with equal probability for all socioeconomic, race, and ethnic groups. For example, as college-educated women delay childbearing, they have higher nonmarital fertility than in the past, yet most of their childbearing still takes place within marriage. This seems to be less true among less educated women (Martin 2000). And black women are much more likely than other women to forgo marriage and to have nonmarital births.

As the relationship between marriage and childbearing undergoes change, what happens to intergenerational linkages and extended family members' roles in the family? There is no question, as we have shown in Chapter 4, that more women will experience single parenting while raising children than a generation ago. When single parenting occurs, grandparents often provide support, and we have documented the increase in grandparents' involvement in rearing grandchildren in Chapter 6. Bengtson (2001) has recently argued that intergenerational family obligations and support may be increasing in importance, given some of the changes that seem to be permanently altering family life. For example, although the divorce rate stopped increasing two decades ago, it did not subsequently drop back to the low levels it was at prior to its steep increase in the latter 1960s and 1970s. Nonmarital childbearing, even if stabilizing, remains high. These trends, combined with increased longevity and the important role relatives play as backup caregivers in families (as documented in Chapter 7) suggest that much more attention must be paid to the ties that bind families across households and generations.

How do families balance paid work and child rearing in the United States? The short answer is "with difficulty," yet they seem to manage to do it. U.S. fertility rates remain at replacement levels across cohorts, unlike in most European contexts, where fertility is declining and is well below replacement (Frejka and Calot 2001). In the United States, despite the increase in mothers' labor force participation, mothers still provide a large proportion of the care for young children. Only one-third of married mothers with children under age 6 work full-time and year-round. U.S. families increasingly use child-care centers, patch together care by relatives, and use enrichment activities for older children, perhaps to a far greater extent than has been acknowledged (as documented in Chapter 7). There is clearly a need for higher-quality child care, particularly if we expect all single mothers, even low-income mothers, to be employed when children are young. In the absence of much government and employer support for combining work and family—certainly less than in most Scandinavian countries—American families appear to "make do" and arrive at private, individualized solutions to the inherent time conflicts between market work and care of family (as we have discussed in Chapter 10). However, pressure may be mounting for more public recognition of the difficulties involved and for more support for parents faced with the dilemma of how to financially support their families adequately and still provide sufficient time for their children.

Are fathers' roles within families changing? Our answer is an unqualified yes. We can argue over the pace of change—whether fathers are doing enough on the home front or changing fast enough—but we have presented a variety of evidence in Chapter 5 that men's roles are changing. Again, the most important questions have to do with the pace of change and whether father involvement varies by socioeconomic status, race, and ethnic group. That is, are some fathers moving toward increased involvement with children while others are eschewing their responsibilities altogether? Do these "good dads" and "bad dads" align with race and class? We suspect not, at least not totally, although increased *feelings* that they should spend time with their children may be most characteristic of college-educated fathers. However, economic conditions (e.g., lack of resources for expensive child care) may also push lower-income, less educated men toward child rearing and, indeed, these men may always have had greater involvement in the family than we have heretofore appreciated. Black and Hispanic men face a greater challenge in being "good dads" than do white men mainly because so many more of them do not live with their children. In addition, they have more difficulty in the labor market and hence find it harder to fulfill the "good provider" role.

The question that has most concerned family scholars is, Has children's well-being been compromised by changes in the family? Much has been made of the lower level of well-being, on average, of children who grow up with one rather than two parents in the household (a topic addressed in Chapter 8). Yet some of these effects are quite small, with most children in both types of households performing well academically and exhibiting good social-psychological adjustment. Children's lives are clearly altered by the changed circumstances of families: Children today grow up differently than in the past. Yet it is unclear whether their lives are worse or better than the lives of children a generation ago. Some trends (e.g., alcohol and drug use) appear problematic, whereas others (e.g., increased parental time) suggest that children may be doing better than in the past. Again, an important and unanswered question is whether greater inequality separates the life chances of minority children and children at the bottom and the top of the income distribution more so than in the past.

What surprised us most as we reexamined family trends in preparation for writing this book was how little change was occurring in some of the standard indicators of family structure in the latter half of the 1990s (as shown in Chapter 1). So, for example, the long-discussed rise of the single-mother family and decline of the two-parent family—trends that many have argued seriously compromise children's well-being—seemed largely to have halted in the latter half of the 1990s, if only temporarily. In fact, as this book went into production in the middle of 2001, the Census Bureau had just released its latest statistics on the family, heralding a slight rise in the proportion of families with two-parents, the first such rise in decades. Nonmarital birthrates stabilized (even declined slightly) in the latter half of the 1990s, and living arrangements that continued to increase in popularity, such as cohabitation, seemed to be doing so at a decreasing rate.

This seeming "quieting" of family change interests us a great deal because it seems to have been largely ignored by much of the scientific community, and certainly in the rhetoric of policy makers. Have we merely hit a temporary lull in family change, perhaps due to the good economic conditions of the second half of the 1990s? Or have the transformations that so altered family formation and dissolution largely worked themselves out such that we can expect much more family stability in the future?

Our guess is the following: If one looks at the trends in the family that disturbed so many academics and policy makers—the increase in births outside marriage, increasing divorce, more single parenting—the large upswing happened during the 1970s, as discussed in Chapter 1. Change continued in subsequent decades, but at a slowing rate until the 1990s, when it slowed so much that it stopped. If the economy turns sour, there may be some small upswing in single parenting. Economic stress is destabilizing. However, a major change to affect the family in the latter part of the 20th century was the expansion of equal access to educational and occupational opportunity to women and minorities. The march toward equality is an ongoing project, but we have now had almost 40 years to adjust and to redefine appropriate gender relations within and outside the family.

The revolution of inclusiveness in the labor market rocked the family in the United States and elsewhere. Other factors also buffeted the family, the most important of which is perhaps the aging of society and the implications this has had for intergenerational relationships. Continued improvement in per capita material affluence of the population and increased educational upgrading also aided a revolution in expectations about how family life should work. If one returns to the notion we raised in our introduction, that the family is a complex set of gender and intergenerational relationships, one could argue that what most changed the family in the second half of the 20th century was the movement of women, especially mothers, into the paid labor force.

What is still changing in the family are behaviors related to the continued evolution of new gender relations within the family (see Chapter 10) and the intergenerational ties that result from changed gender relations in an aging society (see Chapter 6). Marriages continue to be delayed more so than forgone, at least among the majority of the population, because for many it makes sense to do so. Both women and men assume they will have labor force careers. Increasingly, those who are successful have more education. Parents' ability to provide their children with college educations as part of child rearing is increasing, and children's sense of entitlement to such education funded by their parents is also on the rise. Hence it is perhaps not surprising that financial dependency in young adulthood is extended and the period of experimentation with living arrangements, jobs, and relationships that might have ended by the late teens or early 20s for past cohorts now lasts well beyond those years for many in the population.

Women's greater access to education and jobs affected them first—they changed their behavior—and this now seems to be affecting men (see Chapter 5). Men generally seem to be changing their behavior toward families, increasing their participation in household work a little and their involvement with children a lot. But this type of change is slow and probably occurs across generations more than across individual life spans. Married fathers' time with children is increasing; the numbers of single-father families continue to rise, although they constitute only a small portion of households with children; fathers seem to be sharing custody of their children more often after divorce; and public policy is attempting to strengthen the financial and parental ties between unmarried fathers and their children.

Is family life so changed that what women do in families no longer resembles what their mothers did, and what fathers do is totally different from what their own fathers did for their families? No—women continue to devote more time to child rearing than do men, and most men continue to value and be valued for the financial support they can provide their families. But these relationships are changing toward more gender similarity, and in the process they are transforming what marriages look and feel like in contemporary society. At the same time, they circumscribe somewhat who chooses marriage for companionship, economic security, child rearing, and fulfillment of life's needs.

Our view is admittedly a rather sanguine, optimistic one. We see families as continuing to transform, sometimes with negative consequences, but usually in ways that make sense given changing contexts. For example, would a marriage system that has people entering at age 20 or 21 make sense today? Probably not, given that so many young adults have not completed their schooling or established themselves in the labor market by that age.

The most disturbing trend in the family may be that family behaviors may be bifurcating or becoming more dissimilar along economic and racial lines, but even this is not totally clear. There is some indication that there may be increasing nonmarriage and lack of involvement of both parents in raising children at the bottom of the income distribution as the economic fortunes of those at the bottom grow further from those at the top (a topic discussed in Chapter 9). However, we do not know a lot about what is causing this trend, and we know virtually nothing about the intergenerational consequences. In other ways, things have become more similar across the economic spectrum. Women's labor force behavior—the combining of motherhood and market work—has become less differentiated by economic position, as market work is increasingly defined as normative and necessary for all women regardless of class, race, or ethnicity.

In this volume we have painted with a broad brush, describing the family "on average." We view this as a necessary first step. Were we now to proceed to a second book, we would examine the race, ethnic, and class variation in each of the topics we have addressed, assess the differential effects of each of these components on family change, and place them in international context. We have done that occasionally in this volume but not systematically, because that has not been our primary focus. However, given the rise in income inequality in the past decades in the United States, the large influx of immigrants in the last quarter of the 20th century and the resulting racial and ethnic diversity of the population, and the often parallel trends but quite different contexts of immigration and public policy in support of the family in other developed countries, we will disentangle many of the most interesting questions this volume has generated only by expressly examining the variation in the patterns we have observed, both inside and outside the United States.

REFERENCES

Abma, Joyce and Linda Peterson. 1995. "Voluntary Childlessness among U.S. Women: Recent Trends and Determinants." Presented at the annual meeting of the Population Association of America, April 6-8, San Francisco.

Administration for Children and Families. 2001. "Temporary Assistance for Needy Families (TANF)" [On-line].
Available Internet: http://www.acf.dhhs.gov/programs/opa/facts/tanf.htm

Alan Guttmacher Institute. 1999. *Why Is Teenage Pregnancy Declining? The Roles of Abstinence, Sexual Activity and Contraceptive Use.* New York: Author.

Aldous, Joan. 1985. "Parent-Adult Child Relations as Affected by the Grandparents' Status." Pp. 117-32 in *Grandparenthood,* edited by Vern L. Bengtson and Joan F. Robertson. Beverly Hills, CA: Sage.

———. 1987. "New Views on the Family Life of the Elderly and the Near-Elderly." *Journal of Marriage and Family* 49:227-34.

———. 1995. "New Views of Grandparents in Intergenerational Context." *Journal of Family Issues* 16:104-22.

Allen, Katherine R., Rosemary Bleiszner, and Karen A. Roberto. 2000. "Families in the Middle and Later Years: A Review and Critique of Research in the 1990s." *Journal of Marriage and Family* 62:911-26.

Allen, Sarah M. and Alan J. Hawkins. 1999. "Maternal Gatekeeping: Mothers' Beliefs and Behaviors That Inhibit Greater Father Involvement in Family Work." *Journal of Marriage and Family* 61:199-212.

Amato, Paul R. and Alan Booth. 1997. *A Generation at Risk: Growing Up in an Era of Family Upheaval.* Cambridge, MA: Harvard University Press.

Amato, Paul R. and Joan Gilbreth. 1999. "Nonresident Fathers and Children's Well-Being." *Journal of Marriage and Family* 61:557-73.

Anderson, Michael. 1971. *Family Structure in Nineteenth-Century Lancashire.* Cambridge: Cambridge University Press.

Angel, Ronald and Marta Tienda. 1982. "Determinants of Extended Family Structure: Cultural Pattern or Economic Need?" *American Journal of Sociology* 87:1360-83.

Arendell, Terry. 1992. "After Divorce: Investigations into Father Absence." *Gender & Society* 6:562-86.

Associated Press. 1999. "Poll Reveals Another Sign of Changing U.S. Families." *Washington Post,* November 26.

Axinn, William G. and Arland T. Thornton. 1992. "The Relationship between Cohabitation and Divorce: Selectivity or Causal Influence?" *Demography* 29:357-74.

———. 1996. "The Influence of Parents' Marital Dissolutions on Children's Attitudes toward Family Formation." *Demography* 33:66-81.

———. 2000. "The Transformation in the Meaning of Marriage." Pp. 147-65 in *The Ties That Bind: Perspectives on Marriage and Cohabitation,* edited by Linda J. Waite, Christine A. Bachrach, Michelle Hinden, Elizabeth Thomson, and Arland T. Thornton. New York: Aldine de Gruyter.

Bachrach, Christine A. 1986. "Adoption Plans, Adopted Children, and Adoptive Mothers." *Journal of Marriage and Family* 48:246-53.

Bachrach, Christine A., Patricia F. Adams, Soledad Sambrano, and Kathryn A. London. 1989. *Adoption in the 1980s.* Advance Data from Vital and Health Statistics No. 181, DHHS Publication No. PHS 90-1250. Hyattsville, MD: National Center for Health Statistics.

Bachrach, Christine A. and Freya Sonenstein. 1998. "Male Fertility and Family Formation: Research and Data Needs on the Pathways to Fatherhood." Pp. 45-99 in *Nurturing Fatherhood: Improving Data and Research on Male Fertility, Family Formation, and Fatherhood,* edited by Federal Interagency Forum on Child and Family Studies. Washington, DC: Federal Interagency Forum on Child and Family Studies.

Bachu, Amara. 1999. *Trends in Premarital Childbearing: 1930 to 1994.* Current Population Reports, Series P-23, No. 197. Washington, DC: Government Printing Office.

Bachu, Amara and Martin O'Connell. 2000. *Fertility of American Women: June 1998.* Current Population Reports, Series P-20, No. 526. Washington, DC: Government Printing Office.

Bane, Mary Jo and David T. Ellwood. 1989. "One-Fifth of the Nation's Children: Why Are They Poor?" *Science* 245:1047-53.

———. 1994. *Welfare Realities: From Rhetoric to Reform.* Cambridge, MA: Harvard University Press.

Barling, Julian and Karyl E. MacEwen. 1992. "Linking Work Experiences to Facets of Marital Functioning." *Journal of Organizational Behavior* 13:573-83.

Barnett, Rosalind C. 1999. "A New Work-Life Model for the Twenty-First Century." *Annals of the American Academy of Political and Social Science* 562:143-58.

Barnett, Rosalind C., Nancy L. Marshall, and Joseph H. Pleck. 1992. "Men's Multiple Roles and Their Relationship to Men's Psychological Distress." *Journal of Marriage and Family* 54:358-67.

Baydar, Nazli and Jeanne Brooks-Gunn. 1991. "Effects of Maternal Employment and Child-Care Arrangements on Preschoolers' Cognitive and Behavioral Outcomes: Evidence from the Children of the National Longitudinal Survey of Youth." *Developmental Psychology* 27:923-45.

Becker, Gary S. 1960. "An Economic Analysis of Fertility." Pp. 209-31 in *Demographic and Economic Change in Developed Countries,* edited by the National Bureau of Economic Research. Princeton, NJ: Princeton University Press.

———. 1974. "A Theory of Marriage." Pp. 299-344 in *Economics of the Family: Marriage, Children, and Human Capital,* edited by Theodore W. Schultz. Chicago: University of Chicago Press.

———. 1981. *A Treatise on the Family.* Cambridge, MA: Harvard University Press.

———. 1991. *A Treatise on the Family.* Rev. ed. Cambridge, MA: Harvard University Press.

Becker, Gary S., Elizabeth M. Landes, and Robert T. Michael. 1977. "An Economic Analysis of Marital Instability." *Journal of Political Economy* 85:1141-87.

Becker, Penny Edgell and Phyllis Moen. 1999. "Scaling Back: Dual-Career Couples Work-Family Strategies." *Journal of Marriage and Family* 61:995-1007.

Beller, Andrea H. and John W. Graham. 1993. *Small Change: The Economics of Child Support*. New Haven, CT: Yale University Press.

Belsky, Jay and David J. Eggebeen. 1991. "Early and Extensive Maternal Employment and Young Children's Socioemotional Development: Children of the National Longitudinal Survey of Youth." *Journal of Marriage and Family* 53:1083-98.

Bengtson, Vern L. 2001. "Beyond the Nuclear Family: The Increasing Importance of Multigenerational Bonds." *Journal of Marriage and Family* 63:1-16.

Bengtson, Vern L. and Robert E. L. Roberts. 1991. "Inter-generational Solidarity in Aging Families: An Example of Formal Theory Construction." *Journal of Marriage and Family* 53:856-70.

Bengtson, Vern L. and Sandi S. Schrader. 1982. "Parent-Child Relations." Pp. 115-86 in *Research Instruments in Social Gerontology*, vol. 2, *Social Roles and Social Participation*, edited by David J. Mangen and Warren A. Peterson. Minneapolis: University of Minnesota Press.

Berardo, Donna H., Constance L. Shehan, and Gerald R. Leslie. 1987. "A Residue of Tradition: Jobs, Careers, and Spouses Time in Housework." *Journal of Marriage and Family* 49:381-90.

Bergen, Elizabeth. 1991. "The Economic Context of Labor Allocation: Implications for Gender Stratification." *Journal of Family Issues* 12:140-57.

Bergmann, Barbara. 1986. *The Economic Emergence of Women*. New York: Basic Books.

————. 1996. *Saving Our Children from Poverty*. New York: Russell Sage Foundation.

Bernhardt, Annette, Martina Morris, and Mark S. Handcock. 1995. "Women's Gains or Men's Losses? A Closer Look at the Shrinking Gender Gap in Earnings." *American Journal of Sociology* 101:302-28.

————. 1997. "Percentages, Odds, and the Meaning of Inequality: Reply to Cotter et al." *American Journal of Sociology 102:1154-62.*

Bianchi, Suzanne M. 1990. "America's Children: Mixed Prospects." *Population Bulletin* 45(1):3-42.

————. 1993. "Children of Poverty: Why Are They Poor?" Pp. 91-125 in *Child Poverty and Public Policy,* edited by Judith A. Chafel. Washington, DC: Urban Institute Press.

————. 1995a. "The Changing Demographic and Socioeconomic Characteristics of Single-Parent Families." *Marriage and Family Review* 20:71-97.

————. 1995b. "Changing Economic Roles of Women and Men." Pp. 107-54 in *State of the Union: America in the 1990s,* vol. 2, *Social Trends,* edited by Reynolds Farley. New York: Russell Sage Foundation.

————. 1998. "The Rise in Women's Paid Employment in the U.S.: Trends, Causes, Consequences, and Future Prospects." Presented at the conference "Model USA: Social Justice through More Employment?" at the John F. Kennedy Institute for North American Studies, Free University of Berlin, November 19.

————. 1999. "Feminization and Juvenilization of Poverty: Trends, Relative Risks, Causes, and Consequences." *Annual Review of Sociology* 25:307-33.

————. 2000. "Maternal Employment and Time with Children: Dramatic Change or Surprising Continuity?" *Demography* 37:401-14.

Bianchi, Suzanne M. and Lynne M. Casper. 2000. "American Families." *Population Bulletin* 55(4):3-42.

Bianchi, Suzanne M., Melissa A. Milkie, Liana C. Sayer, and John P. Robinson. 2000. "Is Anyone Doing the Housework? Trends in the Gender Division of Household Labor." *Social Forces* 79:2-39.

Bianchi, Suzanne M. and John P. Robinson. 1997. "What Did You Do Today? Children's Use of Time, Family Composition, and the Acquisition of Social Capital." *Journal of Marriage and Family* 59:332-44.

Bianchi, Suzanne M. and Nancy Rytina. 1986. "The Decline in Occupational Sex Segregation during the 1970s: Census and CPS Comparisons." *Demography* 23:79-86.

Bianchi, Suzanne M. and Daphne Spain. 1996. "Women, Work, and Family in America." *Population Bulletin* 51(3):2-46.

Bianchi, Suzanne M., Lekha Subaiya, and Joan R. Kahn. 1999. "The Gender Gap in the Economic Well-Being of Nonresident Fathers and Custodial Mothers." *Demography* 36:195-203.

Biblarz, Timothy J. and Adrian E. Raftery. 1999. "Family Structure, Educational Attainment, and Socioeconomic Success: Rethinking the Pathology of Matriarchy." *American Journal of Sociology* 105:321-65.

Bittman, Michael. 1999a. "Parenthood without Penalty: Time Use and Public Policy in Australia and Finland." *Feminist Economics* 5(3):27-42.

———. 1999b. "Recent Changes in Unpaid Work." Occasional paper, Social Policy Research Centre, University of New South Wales, Australia.

Black, Dan, Gary Gated, Seth Sanders, and Lowell Taylor. 2000. "Demographics of the Gay and Lesbian Population in the United States: Evidence from Available Systematic Data Sources." *Demography* 37:139-54.

Blackburn, McKinley and Sanders Korenman. 1994. "The Declining Marital-Status Earnings Differential." *Journal of Population Economics* 7:249-70.

Blair, Sampson Lee and Michael P. Johnson. 1992. "Wives' Perceptions of Fairness of the Division of Household Labor: The Intersection of Housework and Ideology." *Journal of Marriage and Family* 54:570-81.

Blair, Sampson Lee and Daniel T. Lichter. 1991. "Measuring the Division of Household Labor: Gender Segregation of Housework among American Couples." *Journal of Family Issues* 12:91-113.

Blake, Judith. 1968. "Are Babies Consumer Durables? A Critique of the Economic Theory of Reproductive Motivation." *Population Studies* 22:5-25.

Blank, Rebecca. 1991. "Why Were Poverty Rates So High in the 1980s?" Working Paper No. 3878, National Bureau of Economic Research, Cambridge, MA.

———. Forthcoming. "Fighting Poverty: Lessons from Recent U.S. History." *Journal of Economic Perspectives*.

Blau, David M. 1991. "The Quality of Child Care: An Economic Perspective." Pp. 145-74 in *The Economics of Child Care,* edited by David M. Blau. New York: Russell Sage Foundation.

———. 1997. "The Production of Quality in Child Care Centers." *Journal of Human Resources* 32:354-87.

Blau, David M. and Philip K. Robins. 1988. "Child Care Costs and Family Labor Supply." *Review of Economics and Statistics* 70:374-81.

———. 1991. "Child Care Demand and Labor Supply of Young Mothers over Time." *Demography* 28:333-51.

Blau, Francine D. 1998. "Trends in the Well-Being of American Women, 1970-1995." *Journal of Economic Literature* 36:112-65.

Blau, Francine D. and Marianne A. Ferber. 1992. *The Economics of Women, Men, and Work.* 2d ed. Englewood Cliffs, NJ: Prentice Hall.

Blau, Francine D. and Adam J. Grossberg. 1990. "Maternal Labor Supply and Children's Cognitive Development." Working Paper No. 3536, National Bureau of Economic Research, Cambridge, MA.

Blau, Francine D. and Wallace E. Hendricks. 1979. "Occupational Segregation by Sex: Trends and Prospects." *Journal of Human Resources* 14:197-210.

Blau, Francine D. and Lawrence M. Kahn. 1997. "Swimming Upstream: Trends in the Gender Wage Differential in the 1980s." *Journal of Labor Economics* 15:1-42.

Bloom, David E. 1982. "What's Happening to the Age at First Birth in the United States? A Study of Recent Cohorts." *Demography* 19:351-70.

Bloom, David E. and James Trussell. 1984. "What Are the Determinants of Delayed Childbearing and Permanent Childlessness in the United States?" *Demography* 21:591-611.

Borjas, George, Jr., Richard B. Freeman, and Laurence F. Katz. 1992. "On the Labor Market Effects of Immigration and Trade." Pp. 213-14 in *Immigration and the Work Force: Economic Consequences for the United States and Source Areas,* edited by George Borjas, Jr., and Richard B. Freeman. Chicago: University of Chicago Press.

Brauner, Sarah and Pamela Loprest. 1999. *Where Are They Now? What States' Studies of People Who Left Welfare Tell Us.* Assessing the New Federalism Policy Brief, Series A, No. A-32. Washington, DC: Urban Institute Press.

Brayfield, April. 1992. "Employment Resources and Housework in Canada." *Journal of Marriage and Family* 54:19-30.

———. 1995. "Juggling Jobs and Kids: The Impact of Employment Schedules on Fathers Caring for Children." *Journal of Marriage and Family* 57:321-32.

Brines, Julie. 1993. "The Exchange Value of Housework." *Rationality and Sociology* 5:302-40.

Brines, Julie and Kara Joyner. 1999. "The Ties That Bind: Principles of Cohesion in Cohabitation and Marriage." *American Sociological Review* 64:333-55.

Brown, Eleanor and Alison P. Hagy. 1997. "The Demand for Multiple Child Care Arrangements." Center for Economic Studies, U.S. Bureau of the Census. Unpublished manuscript.

Brown, Susan L. 2000. "Union Transitions among Cohabiters: The Significance of Relationship Assessment and Expectations." *Journal of Marriage and Family* 62:833-46.

Brown, Susan L. and Alan Booth. 1996. "Cohabitation versus Marriage: A Comparison of Relationship Quality." *Journal of Marriage and Family* 58:668-78.

Bryant, W. Keith. 1996. "A Comparison of the Household Work of Married Females: The Mid-1920s and the Late 1960s." *Family and Consumer Sciences Research Journal* 24:358-84.

Bryant, W. Keith and Cathleen D. Zick. 1996a. "Are We Investing Less in the Next Generation? Historical Trends in Time Spent Caring for Children." *Journal of Family and Economic Issues* 17:365-91.

———. 1996b. "An Examination of Parent-Child Shared Time." *Journal of Marriage and Family* 58:227-37.

Bryson, Ken and Lynne M. Casper. 1998. *Household and Family Characteristics: March 1997.* Current Population Reports, Series P-20, No. 509. Washington, DC: Government Printing Office.

———. 1999. *Co-resident Grandparents and Their Grandchildren.* Current Population Reports, Series P-23, No. 198. Washington, DC: Government Printing Office.

Buehler, Cheryl and Jean M. Gerard. 1995. "Divorce Law in the United States: A Focus on Child Custody." *Family Relations* 44:439-58.

Bumpass, Larry L. 1990. "What's Happening to the Family? Interactions between Demographic and Institutional Change." *Demography* 27:483-93.

Bumpass, Larry L. and Hsien-Hen Lu. 2000. "Trends in Cohabitation and Implications for Children's Family Contexts in the United States." *Population Studies* 54:29-41.

Bumpass, Larry L., Teresa Castro Martin, and James A. Sweet. 1991. "The Impact of Family Background and Early Marital Factors on Marital Disruption." *Journal of Family Issues* 12:22-42.

Bumpass, Larry L. and R. Kelly Raley. 1995. "Redefining Single-Parent Families: Cohabitation and Changing Family Reality." *Demography* 32:97-109.

Bumpass, Larry L., R. Kelly Raley, and James A. Sweet. 1995. "The Changing Character of Stepfamilies: Implications of Cohabitation and Nonmarital Childbearing." *Demography* 32:425-36.

Bumpass, Larry L. and James A. Sweet. 1989a. "Children's Experience in Single-Parent Families: Implications of Cohabitation and Marital Transitions." *Family Planning Perspectives* 21:256-60.

———. 1989b. "National Estimates of Cohabitation." *Demography* 26:615-25.

Bumpass, Larry L., James A. Sweet, and Andrew J. Cherlin. 1991. "The Role of Cohabitation in the Declining Rates of Marriage." *Journal of Marriage and Family* 53:913-27.

Burkhauser, Richard V., Greg J. Duncan, Richard Hauser, and Roland Bernsten. 1990. "Economic Burdens of Marital Disruptions: A Comparison of the United States and the Federal Republic of Germany." *Review of Income and Wealth* 36:319-33.

———. 1991. "Wife or Frau, Women Do Worse: A Comparison of Men and Women in the United States and Germany after Marital Dissolution." *Demography* 28:353-60.

Burtless, Gary. 1996. "Worsening American Income Inequality." *Brookings Review* 14(2): 16-21.

Burton, Linda M. 1992. "Black Grandparents Rearing Children of Drug-Addicted Parents: Stressors, Outcomes, and Social Service Needs." *Gerontologist* 32:744-51.

Burton, Linda M. and Vern L. Bengtson. 1985. "Black Grandmothers: Issues of Timing and Continuity of Roles." Pp. 61-77 in *Grandparenthood,* edited by Vern L. Bengtson and Joan F. Robertson. Beverly Hills, CA: Sage.

Burton, Linda M. and Peggye Dilworth-Anderson. 1991. "The Intergenerational Family Roles of Aged Black Americans." *Marriage and Family Review* 16:311-30.

Butz, William P. and Michael P. Ward. 1979a. "The Emergence of Countercyclical U.S. Fertility." *American Economic Review* 69:318-27.

———. 1979b. "Will U.S. Fertility Remain Low? A New Economic Interpretation." *Population and Development Review* 5:663-89.

Cain, Virginia and Sandra L. Hofferth. 1989. "Parental Choice of Self-Care for School-Age Children." *Journal of Marriage and Family* 51:65-77.

Cancian, Maria, Sheldon Danziger, and Peter Gottschalk. 1993. "Working Wives and Family Income Inequality among Married Couples." Pp. 195-221 in *Uneven Tides: Rising Inequality in America,* edited by Sheldon Danziger and Peter Gottschalk. New York: Russell Sage Foundation.

Cancian, Maria and Daniel R. Meyer. 1998. "Who Gets Custody?" *Demography* 35:147-58.

Cancian, Maria and Deborah Reed. 1999. "The Impact of Wives' Earnings on Income Inequality: Issues and Estimates." *Demography* 36:173-84.

Carolina Abecedarian Project. 1999. *Early Learning, Later Success: The Abecedarian Study* [On-line]. Available Internet: http://www.fpg.unc.edu/~abc/embargoed/executive_summary.htm

Casper, Lynne M. 1995. *What Does It Cost to Mind Our Preschoolers?* Current Population Reports, Series P-70, No. 52. Washington, DC: Government Printing Office.

———. 1996. *Who's Minding Our Preschoolers?* Current Population Reports, Series P-70, No. 53. Washington, DC: Government Printing Office.

———. 1997a. *My Daddy Takes Care of Me! Fathers as Care Providers*. Current Population Reports, Series P-70, No. 59. Washington, DC: Government Printing Office.

———. 1997b. *Who's Minding Our Preschoolers? Fall 1994 (Update)*. Current Population Reports, Series P-70, No. 62. Washington, DC: Government Printing Office.

Casper, Lynne M. and Ken Bryson. 1998a. "Co-resident Grandparents and Their Grandchildren: Grandparent-Maintained Families." Working Paper No. 26, Population Division, U.S. Bureau of the Census, Washington, DC.

———. 1998b. *Household and Family Characteristics: March 1998 (Update)*. Current Population Reports, Series P-20, No. 515. Washington, DC: Government Printing Office.

Casper, Lynne M. and Philip N. Cohen. 2000. "How Does POSSLQ Measure Up? Historical Estimates of Cohabitation." *Demography* 37:237-45.

Casper, Lynne M., Mary Hawkins, and Martin O'Connell. 1994. *Who's Minding the Kids? Child Care Arrangements: Fall 1991*. Current Population Reports, Series P-70, No. 36. Washington, DC: Government Printing Office.

Casper, Lynne M., Sara S. McLanahan, and Irwin Garfinkel. 1994. "The Gender-Poverty Gap: What We Can Learn from Other Countries." *American Sociological Review* 59:594-60.

Casper, Lynne M. and Martin O'Connell. 1998a. "State Estimates of Organized Child Care Facilities." Working Paper No. 21, Population Division, U.S. Bureau of the Census, Washington, DC.

———. 1998b. "Work, Income, the Economy, and Married Fathers as Child-Care Providers." *Demography* 35:243-50.

Casper, Lynne M. and Liana C. Sayer. 2000. "Cohabitation Transitions: Different Attitudes and Purposes, Different Paths." Presented at the annual meeting of the Population Association of America, March, Los Angeles.

Casper, Lynne M. and Kristin E. Smith. Forthcoming. "Dispelling the Myths: Self-Care, Class, and Race." *Journal of Family Issues*.

Chalfie, Deborah. 1994. *Going It Alone: A Closer Look at Grandparents Rearing Grandchildren*. Washington, DC: American Association of Retired Persons.

Chandra, Anjani, Joyce Abma, Penelope Maza, and Christine A. Bachrach. 1999. *Adoption, Adoption Seeking, and Relinquishment for Adoption in the United States*. Advance Data from Vital and Health Statistics No. 306, DHHS Publication No. PHS 99-1250. Hyattsville, MD: National Center for Health Statistics.

Charles, Enid. 1934. *The Twilight of Parenthood*. London: Watts.

Chen, Renbao and S. Philip Morgan. 1991. "Recent Trends in the Timing of First Births in the United States." *Demography* 28:513-33.

Cherlin, Andrew J. 1978. "Remarriage as an Incomplete Institution." *American Journal of Sociology* 84:634-50.

———. 1979. "A Work Life and Marital Dissolution." Pp. 151-66 in *Divorce and Separation: Context, Causes and Consequences,* edited by George Levinger and Oliver C. Moles. New York: Basic Books.

———. 1992. *Marriage, Divorce, Remarriage*. Rev. ed. Cambridge, MA: Harvard University Press.

———. 1999. "Going to Extremes: Family Structure, Children's Well-Being, and Social Science." *Demography* 36:421-28.

———. 2000. "How Is the 1996 Welfare Reform Law Affecting Poor Families?" In *Public and Private Families: A Reader,* 2d ed., edited by Andrew J. Cherlin. New York: McGraw-Hill.

Cherlin, Andrew J. and Frank F. Furstenberg, Jr. 1985. "Styles and Strategies of Grandparenting." Pp. 97-116 in *Grandparenthood,* edited by Vern L. Bengtson and Joan F. Robertson. Beverly Hills, CA: Sage.

———. 1986. *The New American Grandparent: A Place in the Family, a Life Apart.* New York: Basic Books.

Cherlin, Andrew J., Kathleen E. Kiernan, and P. Lindsay Chase-Lansdale. 1995. "Parental Divorce in Childhood and Demographic Outcomes in Young Adulthood." *Demography* 32:299-318.

Cherlin, Andrew J., Pamela Winston, Ronald Angel, Linda Burton, P. Lindsay Chase-Lansdale, Robert A. Moffitt, William Julius Wilson, Rebekah Levine Coley, and James Quane. 2000. *What Welfare Recipients Know about the New Rules and What They Have to Say about Them.* Welfare, Children and Families: A Three-City Study, Policy Brief 00-1. Baltimore: Johns Hopkins University Press.

Clarkberg, Marin and Phyllis Moen. 1998. "Working Families in Transition: Husbands' and Wives' Hours on the Job." Presented at the annual meeting of the American Sociological Association, August, San Francisco.

Clarkberg, Marin, Ross M. Stolzenberg, and Linda J. Waite. 1995. "Attitudes, Values, and Entrance into Cohabitational versus Marital Unions." *Social Forces* 74:609-34.

Coale, Ansley J. and Melvin Zelnik. 1963. *New Estimates of Fertility and Population in the United States.* Princeton, NJ: Princeton University Press.

Cohen, Philip N. and Suzanne M. Bianchi. 1999. "Marriage, Children, and Women's Employment: What Do We Know?" *Monthly Labor Review* 122(December):22-31.

Cohen, Philip N. and Lynne M. Casper. 2000. "In Whose Home? Multigenerational Families in the United States, 1997-1999." Presented at the annual meeting of the American Sociological Association, August, Washington, DC.

Cohen, Philip N. and Lynne M. Casper. Forthcoming. "In Whose Home? Multigenerational Families in the United States, 1997-1999." *Sociological Perspectives, 45*(1).

Cohn, Jeffrey F. and Edward Z. Tronick. 1983. "Three-Month-Old Infants' Reaction to Simulated Maternal Depression." *Child Development* 54:185-93.

Coleman, James S. 1990. *Foundations in Social Theory.* London: Belknap.

College Entrance Examination Board. 1995. *National Report: College Bound Seniors, 1972-1995.* New York: Author.

Coltrane, Scott. 1996. *Family Man: Fatherhood, Housework, and Gender Equity.* New York: Oxford University Press.

Coltrane, Scott and Masako Ishii-Kuntz. 1992. "Men's Housework: A Lifecourse Perspective." *Journal of Marriage and Family* 54:43-57.

Commission on Population Growth and the American Future. 1972. *Population and the American Future: Final Report.* Washington, DC: Government Printing Office.

Committee for Economic Development. 1993. *Why Child Care Matters: Preparing Young Children for a More Productive America.* New York: Author.

Connelly, Rachel. 1992. "The Effect of Child Care Costs on Married Women's Labor Force Participation." *Review of Economics and Statistics* 74:83-90.

"Considering Alternative Lifestyles: A Roper Center Data Review." 2000. *Public Perspective,* January/February, pp. 24-32.

Cooksey, Elizabeth C. and Patricia H. Craig. 1998. "Parenting from a Distance: The Effects of Paternal Characteristics on Contact between Nonresidential Fathers and Their Children." *Demography* 35:187-200.

Cotter, David A. and JoAnn DeFiore. 1996. "Gender Inequality in Non-metropolitan and Metropolitan Areas." *Rural Sociology* 61:272-88.

Cotter, David A., JoAnn DeFiore, Joan M. Hermsen, Brenda Marstellar Kowalewski, and Reeve Vanneman. 1997. "Same Data, Different Conclusions: Comment on Bernhardt et al." *American Journal of Sociology* 102:1143-53.

Coverman, Shelly. 1985. "Explaining Husband's Participation in Domestic Labor." *Sociological Quarterly* 26:81-97.

Coverman, Shelly and Joseph F. Sheley 1986. "Changes in Men's Housework and Child-Care Time, 1965-1975." *Journal of Marriage and Family* 48:413-22.

Cowan, Philip. 1993. "The Sky Is Falling, but Popenoe's Analysis Won't Help Us Do Anything about It." *Journal of Marriage and Family* 55:548-53.

Crimmins, Eileen M. 1981. "The Changing Pattern of American Mortality Decline, 1940-1977, and Its Implications for the Future." *Population and Development Review* 7:229-54.

Crimmins, Eileen M. and Dominique G. Ingegneri. 1990. "Interaction and Living Arrangements of Older Parents and Their Children." *Research on Aging* 12:3-35.

Culter, Lawrence. 1991. "More and More, Grandparents Raise Grandchildren." *New York Times* April 7, p. C12.

Cummings, E. M., M. C. Goeke-Morey, and M. A. Graham. Forthcoming. "Interparental Relations as a Dimension of Parenting." In *Parenting and the Child's World: Multiple Influences on Intellectual and Socioemotional Development,* edited by John G. Borkowski, Sharon Landesman Ramey, and Marie Bristol-Power. Mahwah, NJ: Lawrence Erlbaum.

D'Amico, Robert. 1983. "Status Maintenance or Status Competition? Wife's Relative Wages as a Determinant of Labor Supply and Marital Instability." *Social Forces* 61:1186-1205.

DaVanzo, Julie and M. Omar Rahman. 1993. "American Families: Trends and Correlates." *Population Index* 59:350-86.

Day, Jennifer Cheeseman. 1996. *Population Projections of the United States by Age, Sex, Race, and Hispanic Origin: 1995 to 2050.* Current Population Reports, Series P-25, No. 1130. Washington, DC: Government Printing Office.

DeMaris, Alfred and William MacDonald. 1993. "Premarital Cohabitation and Marital Instability: A Test of the Unconventionality Hypothesis." *Journal of Marriage and Family* 55:399-407.

DeMaris, Alfred and K. Vannadha Rao. 1992. "Premarital Cohabitation and Subsequent Marital Stability in the United States: A Reassessment." *Journal of Marriage and Family* 54:178-90.

Demos, John. 1982. "The Changing Faces of Fatherhood." Pp. 425-45 in *Father and Child Developmental and Clinical Perspectives,* edited by Stanley H. Cath, Alan R. Gurwitt, and John M. Ross. Boston: Little, Brown.

DeNavas, Carmen and Robert W. Cleveland. 1999. *Money Income in the United States: 1998.* Current Population Reports, Series P-60, No. 206. Washington, DC: Government Printing Office.

Desai, Sonalde, P. Lindsay Chase-Lansdale, and Robert T. Michael. 1989. "Mother or Market? Effects of Maternal Employment on the Intellectual Ability of 4-Year-Old Children." *Demography* 26:547-57.

Deutsch, Francine M., Jennifer L. Lozy, and Susan Saxon. 1993. "Taking Credit: Couples' Reports of Contributions to Child Care." *Journal of Family Issues* 14:421-37.

Dowdell, Elizabeth B. 1995. "Caregiver Burden: Grandparents Raising Their High Risk Children." *Journal of Psychosocial Nursing* 33(3):27-30.

Dressel, Paula L. 1996. "Grandparenting at Century's End: An Introduction to the Issue." *Generations* 20:5-6.

Dressel, Paula L. and Sandra K. Barnhill. 1994. "Reframing Gerontological Thought and Practice: The Case of Grandmothers with Daughters in Prison." *Gerontologist* 34:685-90.

Duncan, Greg J. and Christina Gibson. 2000. "Selection and Attrition in the NICHD Child Care Study's Analyses of the Impacts of Child Care Quality on Child Outcomes." Unpublished manuscript.

Duncan, Greg J., Kathleen Mullan Harris, and Johanne Boisjoly. 1999. "Sibling, Peer, Neighbor, and Schoolmate Correlations as Indicators of the Importance of Context for Adolescent Development." Unpublished manuscript.

Duncan, Greg J., W. Jean Yeung, Jeanne Brooks-Gunn, and Judith R. Smith. 1998. "How Much Does Childhood Poverty Affect the Life Chances of Children?" *American Sociological Review* 63:406-23.

Dwyer, Jeffrey W. and Raymond T. Coward. 1991. "A Multivariate Comparison of the Involvement of Adult Sons versus Daughters in the Care of Impaired Parents." *Journal of Gerontology: Social Sciences* 46:S259-69.

Early Child Care Research Network, National Institute of Child Health and Human Development. 1996. "Characteristics of Infant Child Care: Factors Contributing to Positive Caregiving." *Early Childhood Research Quarterly* 11:269-306.

———. 1997. "Familial Factors Associated with the Characteristics of Nonmaternal Care for Infants." *Journal of Marriage and Family* 59:389-408.

———. 1999a. "Child Outcomes When Child Care Center Classes Meet Recommended Standards for Quality." *American Journal of Public Health* 89:1072-77.

———. 1999b. "Effect Sizes from the NICHD Study of Early Child Care." Presented at the annual meeting of the American Psychological Association, Boston.

East, Edward M. 1923. *Mankind at the Crossroads*. New York: Scribners.

Easterlin, Richard A. 1973. "Relative Economic Status and the American Fertility Swing." In *Family Economic Behavior,* edited by Eleanor Sheldon. Philadelphia: J. B. Lippincott.

———. 1978. "What Will 1984 Be Like? Socioeconomic Implications of Recent Twists in Age Structure." *Demography* 15:397-432.

———. 1980. *Birth and Fortune: The Impact of Numbers on Personal Welfare*. New York: Basic Books.

Edelman, Peter. 1997. "The Worst Thing Bill Clinton Has Done." *Atlantic Monthly,* March, pp. 43-56.

Edin, Kathryn and Laura Lein. 1997a. *Making Ends Meet: How Single Mothers Survive Welfare and Low-Wage Work*. New York: Russell Sage Foundation.

———. 1997b. "Work, Welfare, and Single Mothers' Economic Survival Strategies." *American Sociological Review* 62:253-66.

Eggebeen, David J. 1999. "The Changing Course of Fatherhood: Men's Experience with Children in Demographic Perspective." Presented at the annual meeting of the Population Association of America, March, New York.

Eggebeen, David J. and Dennis P. Hogan. 1990. "Giving between Generations in American Families." *Human Nature* 1:211-32.

Eggebeen, David J. and Peter Uhlenberg. 1985. "Changes in the Organization of Men's Lives: 1960-1980." *Family Relations* 34:251-57.

Ehrlich, Paul. 1968. *The Population Bomb*. New York: Sierra Club-Ballantine.

Eisenberg, Anne R. 1988. "Grandchildren's Perspectives on Relationships with Grandparents: The Influence of Gender across Generations." *Sex Roles* 19:205-17.

Elder, Glen H., Jr. 1985. *Life Course Dynamics: Trajectories and Transition: 1968-80*. Ithaca, NY: Cornell University Press.

El Nasser, Haya. 1999. "Raising Grandkids: No Day at the Beach." *USA Today,* July 1, p. A1.

England, Paula. 1997. "Gender and Access to Money: What Do Trends in Earnings and Household Poverty Tell Us?" Prepared for the Conference on Reconfigurations of Class and Gender, August, Canberra.

England, Paula and George Farkas. 1986. *Households, Employment and Gender: A Social, Economic and Demographic View*. New York: Aldine.

Espenshade, Thomas. 1983. "Marriage Trends in America: Estimates, Implications, and Underlying Causes." *Population and Development Review* 9:193-245.

Falk, Patricia J. 1989. "Lesbian Mothers: Psychological Assumptions in Family Law." *American Psychologist* 44:941-47.

Farley, Reynolds. 1996. *The New American Reality: Who We Are, How We Got Here, Where We Are Going*. New York: Russell Sage Foundation.

Federal Interagency Forum on Child and Family Statistics. 2000. *America's Children: Key National Indicators of Well-Being*. Washington, DC: Government Printing Office.

Ferree, Myra Marx. 1990. "Beyond Separate Spheres: Feminism and Family Research." *Journal of Marriage and Family* 52:866-84.

———. 1991. "The Gender Division of Labor in Two-Earner Marriages: Dimensions of Variability and Change." *Journal of Family Issues* 12:158-80.

Fields, Jason M. 2001. *Living Arrangements of Children: 1996*. Current Population Reports, Series P-70, No. 74. Washington, DC: Government Printing Office.

Fields, Jason M. and Rose Kreider. 2000. "Marriage and Divorce Rates in the U.S.: A Multistate Life Table Analysis, Fall 1996 SIPP." Presented at the annual meeting of the Southern Demographic Association, New Orleans.

Fields, Jason M., Kristin Smith, Loretta E. Bass, and Terry Lugaila. 2001. *A Child's Day: Home, School, and Play (Selected Indicators of Child Well-Being)*. Current Population Reports, Series P-70, No. 68. Washington, DC: Government Printing Office.

Fischer, Kimberly, Andrew McCulloch, and Jonathan Gershuny. 1999. "British Fathers and Children." Working paper, Institute for Social and Economic Research, Essex University.

Floge, Liliane. 1985. "The Dynamics of Child Care Use and Some Implications for Women's Employment." *Journal of Marriage and Family* 47:143-54.

Folbre, Nancy. 1994. "Children as Public Goods." *American Economic Review* 84:86-90.

Folk, Karen Fox and Yunae Yi. 1994. "Piecing Together Child Care with Multiple Arrangements: Crazy Quilt or Preferred Pattern for Employed Parents of Preschool Children." *Journal of Marriage and Family* 56:669-80.

Freedman, Ronald, Pascal K. Whelpton, and Arthur A. Campbell. 1959. *Family Planning, Sterility, and Population Growth*. New York: McGraw-Hill.

Frejka, Tomas and Gerard Calot. 2001. "Cohort Reproductive Patterns in Low-Fertility Countries." *Population and Development Review* 27:103-32.

Fried, Ellen S. and Susan Settergren. 1986. "The Effects of Children on Wives' and Husbands' Allocation of Time." Presented at the annual meeting of the Population Association of America, March, San Francisco.

Fuller-Thomson, Esme, Meredith Minkler, and Diane Driver. 1997. "A Profile of Grandparents Raising Grandchildren in the United States." *Gerontologist* 37:406-11.

Fullerton, Howard N., Jr. 1997. "Labor Force 2006: Slowing Down and Changing Composition." *Monthly Labor Review* 120(November):23-38.

Furstenberg, Frank F., Jr. 1988. "Good Dads–Bad Dads: Two Faces of Fatherhood." Pp. 193-218 in *The Changing American Family and Public Policy,* edited by Andrew J. Cherlin. Washington, DC: Urban Institute Press.

———. 1995. "Changing Roles of Fathers." Pp. 189-210 in *Escape from Poverty: What Makes a Difference for Children?* edited by P. Lindsay Chase-Lansdale and Jeanne Brooks-Gunn. New York: Cambridge University Press.

Furstenberg, Frank F., Jr., Jeanne Brooks-Gunn, and S. Philip Morgan. 1987. *Adolescent Mothers in Later Life*. Cambridge: Cambridge University Press.

Furstenberg, Frank F., Jr., Richard Lincoln, and Jane Menken. 1981. *Teenage Sexuality, Pregnancy, and Childbearing*. Philadelphia: University of Pennsylvania Press.

Furstenberg, Frank F., Jr., S. Philip Morgan, and Paul D. Allison. 1987. "Paternal Participation and Children's Well-Being after Marital Dissolution." *American Sociological Review* 48:695-701.

Furstenberg, Frank F., Jr., Christine Winquist, James L. Peterson, and Nicholas Zill. 1983. "The Life Course of Children of Divorce: Marital Disruption and Parental Context." *American Sociological Review* 48:656-68.

Galinsky, Ellen. 1999. *Ask the Children*. New York: Morrow.

Galinsky, Ellen, Carollee Howes, Susan Kontos, and Marybeth Shinn. 1994. *The Study of Children in Family Child Care and Relative Care: Highlights of Findings*. New York: Families and Work Institute.

Garasky, Steven and Daniel R. Meyer. 1996. "Reconsidering the Increase in Father-Only Families." *Demography* 33:385-93.

Garfinkel, Irwin. 1992. *Assuring Child Support: An Extension of Social Security*. New York: Russell Sage Foundation.

Garfinkel Irwin and Sara S. McLanahan. 1995. "The Effects of Child Support Reform on Child Well-Being." Pp. 211-38 in *Escape from Poverty: What Makes a Difference for Children?* edited by P. Lindsay Chase-Lansdale and Jeanne Brooks-Gunn. New York: Cambridge University Press.

———. 2000. "The Future of the Family: Fragile Families in the 21st Century." Presented at the annual meeting of the Population Association of America, March, Los Angeles.

Garfinkel, Irwin, Sara S. McLanahan, and Thomas L. Hanson. 1997. "A Patchwork Portrait of Nonresident Fathers." Unpublished manuscript.

Garfinkel, Irwin, Sara S. McLanahan, Daniel R. Meyer, and Judith A. Seltzer, eds. 1998. *Fathers under Fire: The Revolution in Child Support Enforcement*. New York: Russell Sage Foundation.

Garfinkel, Irwin, Sara S. McLanahan, and Philip K. Robins, eds. 1994. *Child Support and Child Well-Being*. Washington, DC: Urban Institute.

Garfinkel, Irwin, Daniel R. Meyer, and Sara S. McLanahan. 1998. "A Brief History of Child Support Policies in the United States." Pp. 14-30 in *Fathers under Fire: The Revolution in Child Support Enforcement,* edited by Irwin Garfinkel, Sara S. McLanahan, Daniel R. Meyer, and Judith A. Seltzer. New York: Russell Sage Foundation.

Garfinkel, Irwin and Donald Oellerich. 1989. "Non-custodial Fathers; Ability to Pay Child Support." *Demography* 26:219-33.

Garrett, Bowen and John Holahan. 2000. *Welfare Leavers, Medicaid Coverage, and Private Health Insurance*. Assessing the New Federalism Policy Brief No. B-13. Washington, DC: Urban Institute.

Gershuny, Jonathan and John P. Robinson. 1988. "Historical Shifts in the Household Division of Labor." *Demography* 25:537-53.

Ghosh, Susmita, Richard A. Easterlin, and Diane J. Macunovich. 1993. "How Badly Have Single Parents Done? Trends in the Economic Status of Single Parents since 1964." Presented at the annual meeting of the Population Association of America, March, Cincinnati.

Glick, Paul C. 1975. "A Demographer Looks at American Families." *Journal of Marriage and Family* 37:15-26.

———. 1979. "Children of Divorced Parents in Demographic Perspective." *Journal of Social Issues* 35:170-82.

Glick, Paul C. and Arthur J. Norton. 1977. "Marrying, Divorcing, and Living Together in the U.S. Today." *Population Bulletin* 32(1):3-41.

Goldin, Claudia. 1990. *Understanding the Gender Gap.* New York: Oxford University Press.

———. 1997. "Career and Family: College Women Look to the Past." Pp. 20-58 in *Gender and Family Issues in the Workplace,* edited by Francine D. Blau and Ronald G. Ehrenberg. New York: Russell Sage Foundation.

Goldscheider, Calvin and Mali B. Jones. 1989. "Living Arrangements among the Older Population." Pp. 75-91 in *Ethnicity and the New Family Economy,* edited by Frances K. Goldscheider and Calvin Goldscheider. Boulder, CO: Westview.

Goldscheider, Frances K. 1995. "Interpolating Demography with Families and Households." *Demography* 32:471-80.

———. 1997. "Family Relationships and Life Course Strategies for the 21st Century." Pp. 73-85 in *The Family on the Threshold of the 21st Century,* edited by Solly Dreman. Mahwah, NJ: Lawrence Erlbaum.

Goldscheider, Frances K. and Calvin Goldscheider. 1994. "Leaving and Returning Home in 20th-Century America." *Population Bulletin* 48(4):2-33.

Goldscheider, Frances K. and Linda J. Waite. 1991. *New Families, No Families?* Berkeley: University of California Press.

Goldstein, Joshua R. 1999. "The Leveling of Divorce in the United States." *Demography* 36:409-14.

Grabill, Wilson H., Clyde V. Kiser, and Pascal K. Whelpton. 1958. *The Fertility of American Women.* New York: John Wiley.

Graham, John W. 1995. "Why Did Child Support Award Levels Decline from 1978 to 1985? A Comment." *Journal of Human Resources* 30:622-32.

Grall, Timothy. 2000. *Child Support for Custodial Mothers and Fathers.* Current Population Reports, Series P-60, No. 212. Washington, DC: Government Printing Office.

Gray, Jeffrey S. 1997. "The Fall in Men's Return to Marriage: Declining Productivity Effects or Changing Selection." *Journal of Human Resources* 32:481-504.

Gray, Maureen Boyle. 1992. "Consumer Spending on Durables and Services in the 1980s." *Monthly Labor Review* 115(May):18-26.

Greenberg, Mark. 1999. "Welfare Restructuring and Working-Poor Family Policy: The New Context." In *Hard Labor: Women and Work in the Post-welfare Era,* edited by Joel F. Handler and Lucie White. Armonk, NY: M. E. Sharpe.

Greene, William H. and Aline O. Quester. 1982. "Divorce Risk and Wives' Labor Supply Behavior." *Social Science Quarterly* 63:16-27.

Greenstein, Theodore N. 1990. "Marital Disruption and the Employment of Married Women." *Journal of Marriage and Family* 52:657-76.

———. 1995. "Gender Ideology, Marital Disruption, and the Employment of Married Women." *Journal of Marriage and Family* 57:31-42.

———. 1998. "Does Housework Cause Divorce? Effects of the Division of Household Labor and Gender Ideology on Marital Stability." Presented at the annual meeting of the American Sociological Association, August, San Francisco.

Griffen, Robert. 1998. "Play Ball? The Role of Sports in Children's Lives." *Vermont Quarterly* 12:16-17.

Grimsley, Kirsten Downey. 2000. "Family a Priority for Young Workers." *Washington Post,* May 3, pp. E1-2.

Gupta, Sanjiv. 1999. "The Effects of Marital Status Transitions on Men's Housework Performance." *Journal of Marriage and Family* 61:700-711.

Guzman, Lina. 1998. "The Use of Grandparents as Child Care Providers." Working Paper No. 84, National Survey of Families and Households, Center for Demography and Ecology, University of Wisconsin, Madison.

Haddad, Tony. 1994. "Men's Contribution to Family Work: A Re-examination of Time Availability." *International Journal of Sociology of the Family* 24:87-111.

Hagestad, Gunhild O. 1985. "Continuity and Connectedness." Pp. 31-48 in *Grandparenthood,* edited by Vern L. Bengtson and Joan F. Robertson. Beverly Hills, CA: Sage.

———. 1996. "On-Time, Off-Time, Out of Time? Reflections of Continuity and Discontinuity from an Illness Process." Pp. 204-22 in *Adulthood and Aging: Research on Continuities and Discontinuities,* edited by Vern L. Bengtson. New York: Springer.

Hamilton, Gayle, with Stephan Freedman and Sharon M. McGroder. 2000. "Do Mandatory Welfare-to-Work Programs Affect the Well-Being of Children? A Synthesis of Child Research Conducted as Part of the National Evaluation of Welfare-to-Work Strategies." [On-line]. http://aspe.hhs.gov/hsp/newws/child-synthesis/index.htm

Han, Wen-Jui, Jane Waldfogel, and Jeanne Brooks-Gunn. 2001. "The Effects of Early Maternal Employment on Later Cognitive and Behavioral Outcomes." *Journal of Marriage and Family* 63:336-54.

Hanson, Thomas L., Irwin Garfinkel, Sara S. McLanahan, and Cynthia K. Miller. 1996. "Trends in Child Support Outcomes." *Demography* 33:483-96.

Harris, Kathleen Mullan and Suzanne Ryan. 2000. "Family Processes, Neighborhood Context, and Adolescent Risk Behavior." Unpublished manuscript.

Hayes, Cheryl, John Palmer, and Martha Zaslow. 1990. *Who Cares for America's Children? Child Care Policy for the 1990s.* Washington, DC: National Academy of Sciences Press.

Hayghe, Howard V. 1997. "Developments in Women's Labor Force Participation." *Monthly Labor Review* 120(September):41-46.

He, Wan. 2000. "Choice and Constraint: Fertility Patterns of Chinese American Women." Ph.D. dissertation.

Head Start Bureau. 1998. "1998 Fact Sheet." [on-line]. http://www2.acf.dhhs.gov/programs/hsb/html/1998_fact_sheet.html

Heaton, Timothy B. 1990. "Marital Stability throughout the Childrearing Years." *Demography* 27:55-63.

———. 1998. "Factors Contributing to Increasing Marital Stability in the United States." Presented at the Conference on the National Survey of Family Growth, National Center for Health Statistics, October.

Heckert, D. Alex, Thomas C. Nowak, and Kay A. Snyder. 1998. "The Impact of Husbands and Wives' Relative Earnings on Marital Disruption." *Journal of Marriage and Family* 60:690-703.

Helburn, Suzanne, Mary L. Culkin, Carollee Howes, M. Cryer, and Ellen Peisner-Feinberg. 1995. *Cost, Quality, and Child Outcomes in Child Care Centers.* Denver: University of Colorado.

Henshaw, Stanley K. 1998. "Abortion Incidence and Services in the United States, 1995-1996." *Family Planning Perspectives* 30:263-70, 287.

Hernandez, Donald J. 1993. *America's Children: Resources from Family, Government, and the Economy*. New York: Russell Sage Foundation.

Heuser, Robert L. 1976. *Fertility Tables for Birth Cohorts by Color*. DHEW Publication No. HRA 76-1152. Washington, DC: Government Printing Office.

Hiedemann, Bridget, Olga Suhomlinova, and Angela M. O'Rand. 1998. "Economic Independence: Economic Status and Empty Nest in Midlife Marital Disruption." *Journal of Marriage and Family* 60:219-31.

Hill, C. Russell and Frank P. Stafford. 1974. "Allocation of Time to Pre-school Children and Educational Opportunity." *Journal of Human Resources* 9:323-41.

———. 1980. "Parental Care of Children: Time Diary Estimates of Quantity, Predictability, and Variety." *Journal of Human Resources* 15:219-39.

Hiller, Dana V. 1984. "Power Dependence and Division of Family Work." *Sex Roles* 10:1003-19.

Hilton, Jeanne M. and Daniel P. Macari. 1997. "Grandparent Involvement following Divorce: A Comparison in Single-Mother and Single-Father Families." *Journal of Divorce and Remarriage* 28:203-24.

Himes, Norman E. 1936. *Medical History of Contraception*. Baltimore: Williams & Wilkins.

Hirshorn, Barbara A. 1998. "Grandparents as Caregivers." Pp. 200-14 in *Handbook on Grandparenthood*, edited by Maximiliane E. Szinovacz. Westport, CT: Greenwood.

Hochschild, A. R., with A. MacHung. 1989. *The Second Shift: Working Parents and the Revolution at Home*. New York: Viking.

Hofferth, Sandra L. 1992. "The Demand for and Supply of Child Care in the 1990s." Pp. 3-25 in *Child Care in the 1990s: Trends and Consequences*, edited by Alan Booth. Hillsdale, NJ: Lawrence Erlbaum.

———. 1995. "Out-of-School Time: Risk and Opportunity." Pp. 123-53 in *America's Working Poor*, edited by Thomas R. Swartz and Kathleen M. Weigert. Notre Dame, IN: University of Notre Dame Press.

———. 1999. "Family Reading to Young Children: Social Desirability and Cultural Biases in Reporting." Presented at the Workshop on Measurement and Research on Time Use, sponsored by the Committee on National Statistics, National Research Council, May, Washington, DC.

Hofferth, Sandra L., April Brayfield, Sharon Deich, and Pamela Holcomb. 1991. *National Child Care Survey, 1990*. Washington, DC: Urban Institute Press.

Hofferth, Sandra L. and Duncan Chaplin. 1994. *Child Care Quality versus Availability: Do We Have to Trade One for the Other?* Washington, DC: Urban Institute Press.

Hofferth, Sandra L. and Ellen Eliason Kisker. 1994. "Comprehensive Services in Child Care Settings: Prevalence and Correlates." *Pediatrics* 94:1088-91.

Hofferth, Sandra L. and Deborah Phillips. 1991. "Child Care in the United States Today." *Journal of Social Issues* 47(2):1-13.

Hofferth, Sandra L., Deborah Phillips, and Natasha Cabrera. Forthcoming. "Public Policy and Family and Child Well-Being." In *The Well-Being of Children and Families*, edited by Arland T. Thornton. Ann Arbor: University of Michigan Press.

Hofferth, Sandra L., Joseph H. Pleck, Jeffrey L. Stueve, Suzanne M. Bianchi, and Liana C. Sayer. Forthcoming. "The Demography of Fathers: What Fathers Do." In *Handbook of Father Involvement: Multidisciplinary Perspectives*, edited by C. Tamis-LeMonda and Natasha Cabrera. Mahwah, NJ: Lawrence Erlbaum.

Hofferth, Sandra L. and John F. Sandberg. 2001. "How American Children Spend Their Time." *Journal of Marriage and Family* 63:295-308.

Hofferth, Sandra L. and Douglas A. Wissoker. 1992. "Price, Quality, and Income in Child Care Choice." *Journal of Human Resources* 27:71-111.

Hoffman, Saul D. and Greg J. Duncan. 1995. "The Effect of Income, Wages, and AFDC Benefits on Marital Disruption." *Journal of Human Resources* 30:19-41.

Hogan, Dennis P., David J. Eggebeen, and Clifford C. Clogg. 1993. "The Structure of Intergenerational Exchanges in American Families." *American Journal of Sociology* 98:1428-58.

Hogan, Dennis P. and Frances Goldscheider. 2000. "Men's Flight from Children in the U.S.? A Historical Perspective." Presented at the annual meeting of the Population Association of America, March, Los Angeles.

Holden, Karen C. 1988. "Poverty and Living Arrangements among Older Women: Are Changes in Economic Well-Being Underestimated?" *Journal of Gerontology: Social Sciences* 43:S22-27.

Holden, Karen C. and Pamela J. Smock. 1991. "The Economic Cost of Marital Disruption: Why Do Women Bear Disproportionate Cost?" *American Review of Sociology* 17:51-78.

Horowitz, Amy. 1985. "Family Caregiving to the Frail Elderly." Pp. 194-246 in *Annual Review of Gerontology and Geriatrics,* vol. 5, edited by Carl Eisdorfer. New York: Springer.

Howes, Carollee, Michael Olenick, and Tagoush Der-Kiureghian. 1987. "After School Child Care in an Elementary School: Social Development and Continuity and Complementarity of Programs." *Elementary School Journal* 88:93-103.

Inkeles, Alex and David H. Smith. 1974. *Becoming Modern: Individual Change in Six Developing Countries.* Cambridge, MA: Harvard University Press.

Jacobs, Jerry A. 1989. "Long-Term Trends in Occupational Segregation by Sex." *American Journal of Sociology* 95:160-73.

Jacobs, Jerry A. and Kathleen Gerson. 2001. "Overworked Individuals or Overworked Families? Explaining Trends in Work, Leisure and Family Time." *Work and Occupations* 28:40-63.

Jendrek, Margaret P. 1994. "Grandparents Who Parent Their Grandchildren: Circumstances and Decisions." *Gerontologist* 34:206-16.

Johansen, Anne S., Arleen Leibowitz, and Linda J. Waite. 1996. "The Importance of Child Care Characteristics to Choice of Care." *Journal of Marriage and Family* 58:759-72.

Johnson, William R. and Jonathan Skinner. 1986. "Labor Supply and Marital Separation." *American Economic Review* 76:455-69.

Joshi, Heather. 1998. "The Opportunity Costs of Childbearing: More Than Mothers' Business." *Journal of Population Economics* 11:161-83.

Joslin, Daphne and Anne Brouard. 1995. "The Prevalence of Grandmothers as Primary Caregivers in a Poor Pediatric Population." *Journal of Community Health* 20:383-401.

Juhn, Chinhui. 1992. "Decline of Male Labor Market Participation: The Role of Declining Market Opportunities." *Quarterly Journal of Economics* 107:79-121.

Juhn, Chinhui, Kevin M. Murphy, and Brooks Pierce. 1993. "Wage Inequality and the Rise in Returns to Skill." *Journal of Political Economy* 101:410-42.

Juster, Thomas F. and Frank P. Stafford. 1985. *Time, Goods, and Well-Being.* Ann Arbor: Institute for Social Research, University of Michigan.

Kaestner, Robert. 1993. "Recent Changes in the Labor Supply Behavior of Married Couples." *Eastern Economic Journal* 19(2):185-208.

Kalmijn, Matthijs. 1991. "Status Homogamy in the United States." *American Journal of Sociology* 97:496-523.

———. 1999. "Father Involvement in Childrearing and the Perceived Stability of Marriage." *Journal of Marriage and Family* 61:409-21.

Kammerman, Sheila B. and Alfred J. Kahn 1988. "Social Policy and Children in the United States and Europe." In *The Vulnerable,* edited by John L. Palmer, Timothy Smeeding, and Barbara Boyle Torrey. Washington, DC: Urban Institute Press.

Kamo, Yoshinori. 1988. "Determinants of Household Division of Labor: Resources, Power, and Ideology." *Journal of Family Issues* 9:177-200.

———. 1991. "A Nonlinear Effect of the Number of Children on the Division of Household Labor." *Sociological Perspectives* 34:205-18.

———. 1998. "Asian Grandparents." Pp. 97-112 in *Handbook on Grandparenthood,* edited by Maximiliane E. Szinovacz. Westport, CT: Greenwood.

Kanter, Rosabeth Moss. 1977. *Work and Family in the United States: A Critical Review and Agenda for Research and Policy.* New York: Russell Sage Foundation.

Karoly, Lynn A. and Gary Burtless. 1995. "Demographic Change, Rising Earnings Inequality, and the Distribution of Personal Well-being." *Demography* 32:379-406.

Kasindorf, Martin. 1999. "Three Generations, One Happy Family." *USA Today,* July 1, p. D8.

Kennedy, Gregory E. 1990. "College Students' Expectations of Grandparent and Grandchild Role Behaviors." *Gerontologist* 30:43-48.

Kiecolt, K. Jill and Mark A Fossett. 1995. "Mate Availability and Marriage among African Americans: Aggregated and Individual-Level Analyses." Pp. 121-35 in *The Decline in Marriage among African Americans: Causes, Consequences, and Policy Implications,* edited by M. Belinda Tucker and Claudia Mitchell-Kernan. New York: Russell Sage Foundation.

King, Rosalind Berkowitz. 1999. "Time Spent in Parenthood Status among Adults in the United States." *Demography* 36:377-85.

King, Valerie. 1994. "Variation in the Consequences of Nonresident Father Involvement for Children's Well-Being." *Journal of Marriage and Family* 56:963-72.

King, Valerie and Glen H. Elder, Jr. 1995. "American Children View Their Grandparents: Linked Lives across Three Rural Generations." *Journal of Marriage and Family* 57:165-78.

———. 1997. "The Legacy of Grandparenting: Childhood Experiences with Grandparents and Current Involvement with Grandchildren." *Journal of Marriage and Family* 59:848-59.

King, Valerie, Steven T. Russell, and Glen H. Elder, Jr. 1998. "Grandparenting in Family Systems: An Ecological Perspective." Pp. 53-69 in *Handbook on Grandparenthood,* edited by Maximiliane E. Szinovacz. Westport, CT: Greenwood.

Kishton, Joseph and Ashley Dixon. 1995. "Self-Perception Changes among Sports Camp Participants." *Journal of Social Psychology* 135:135-41.

Kisker, Ellen and Rebecca Maynard. 1991. "Quality, Cost, and Parental Choice of Child Care." Pp. 127-43 in *The Economics of Child Care,* edited by David M. Blau. New York: Russell Sage Foundation.

Kivnick, Helen Q. 1982. "Grandparenthood: An Overview of Meaning and Mental Health." *Gerontologist* 22:59-66.

Klerman, Jacob Alex and Arleen Leibowitz. 1999. "Job Continuity among New Mothers." *Demography* 36:145-55.

Kobrin, Francis E. 1981. "Family Extension and the Elderly: Economic, Demographic, and Family Cycle Factors." *Journal of Gerontology* 36:370-77.

Korenman, Sanders and David Neumark. 1991. "Does Marriage Really Make Men More Productive?" *Journal of Human Resources* 26:282-307.

Kramarow, Ellen. 1995. "Living Alone among the Elderly in the United States: Historical Perspectives on Household Change" *Demography* 32:335-52.

Ku, Leighton, Freya Sonenstein, and Joseph H. Pleck. 1994. "The Dynamics of Young Men's Condom Use during and across Relationships." *Family Planning Perspectives* 26:246-51.

Kuhlthau, Karen and Karen Oppenheim Mason. 1991. "Type of Child Care: Determinants of Use among Working and Non-working Mothers." Working Paper No. 91-218, Population Studies Center, University of Michigan.

Lamb, Michael E. 1998. "Nonparental Child Care: Contexts, Quality, Correlates, and Consequences." Pp. 73-144 in *Handbook of Child Psychology,* 5th ed., vol. 4, *Child Psychology in Practice,* edited by Irving E. Sigel and K. Anne Renninger. New York: John Wiley.

LaRossa, Ralph. 1988. "Fatherhood and Social Change." *Family Relations* 37:451-57.

———. 1997. *The Modernization of Fatherhood: A Social and Political History.* Chicago: University of Chicago Press.

LaRossa, Ralph and Donald C. Reitzes. 1995. "Gendered Perceptions of Father Involvement in Early 20th Century America." *Journal of Marriage and Family* 57:223-29.

Lasch, Christopher. 1979. *The Culture of Narcissism: American Life in an Age of Diminishing Expectations.* New York: W. W. Norton.

Leibowitz, Arlene. 1974. "Home Investments in Children." *Journal of Political Economy* 82:111-31.

———. 1977. "Parental Inputs and Children's Achievement." *Journal of Human Resources* 12:243-51.

Leibowitz, Arlene, Linda J. Waite, and Christina Witsberger. 1988. "Child Care for Preschoolers: Differences by Child's Age." *Demography* 25:205-20.

Leonard, Jonathan S. 1989. "Women and Affirmative Action." *Journal of Economic Perspectives* 3:61-75.

Lesthaeghe, Ron. 1995. "The Second Demographic Transition in Western Countries: An Interpretation." Pp. 17-62 in *Gender and Family Change in Industrialized Countries,* edited by Karen Oppenheim Mason and An-Magritt Jensen. Oxford: Clarendon.

Lesthaeghe, Ron and John Surkyn. 1988. "Cultural Dynamics and Economic Theories of Fertility Change." *Population and Development Review* 14:1-45.

Levy, Frank. 1995. "Incomes and Income Inequality." Pp. 1-58 in *State of the Union: America in the 1990s,* vol. 1, *Economic Trends,* edited by Reynolds Farley. New York: Russell Sage Foundation.

———. 1998. *The New Dollars and Dreams.* New York: Russell Sage Foundation.

Levy, Frank and Richard J. Murnane. 1992. "U.S. Earnings Levels and Earnings Inequality: A Review of Recent Trends and Proposed Explanations." *Journal of Economic Literature* 30:1333-81.

Lichter, Daniel T. 1997. "Poverty and Inequality Among Children." *Annual Review of Sociology* 23:121-45.

Lillard, Lee A., Michael J. Brien, and Linda J. Waite. 1995. "Premarital Cohabitation and Subsequent Marital Dissolution: A Matter of Self-Selection?" *Demography* 32:437-57.

Lloyd, Kim M. and Scott J. South. 1996. "Contextual Influences on Young Men's Transitions to First Marriages." *Social Forces* 74:1097-1119.

London, Rebecca A. 1998. "Trends in Single Mothers' Living Arrangements from 1970 to 1995: Correcting the Current Population Survey." *Demography* 35:125-31.

Loprest, Pamela. 1999. *How Families That Left Welfare Are Doing: A National Picture?* Assessing the New Federalism Policy Brief No. B-1. Washington, DC: Urban Institute.

Love, John M., Peter Z. Schochet, and Alicia L. Meckstroth. 1996. *Are They in Any Real Danger? What Research Does—and Doesn't—Tell Us about Child Care Quality and Children's Well-Being.* Princeton, NJ: Mathematica Policy Research.

Lugaila, Terry. 1998. *Marital Status and Living Arrangements: March 1998.* Current Population Reports, Series P-20, No. 514. Washington, DC: Government Printing Office.

Lundberg, Shelly and Robert A. Pollak. 1996. "Bargaining and Distribution in Marriage." *Journal of Economic Perspectives* 10:139-58.

Mancini, Jay and Rosemary Bleiszner. 1989. "Aging Parents and Adult Children: Research Themes in Intergenerational Relations." *Journal of Marriage and Family* 51:275-90.

Mangen, David J., Vern L. Bengtson, and Pierre H. Landry. 1988. *Measurement of Intergenerational Relations.* Newbury Park, CA: Sage.

Manning, Wendy D. 1993. "Marriage and Cohabitation following Premarital Conception." *Journal of Marriage and Family* 55:839-50.

———. 2000. "The Implications of Cohabitation for Children's Well-Being." Presented at the National Symposium "Just Living Together: Implications of Cohabitation for Children, Families, and Social Policy," Pennsylvania State University, October.

Manning, Wendy D. and Nancy S. Landale. 1996. "Racial and Ethnic Differences in the Role of Cohabitation in Premarital Childbearing." *Journal of Marriage and Family* 58:63-77.

Manning, Wendy D. and Pamela J. Smock. 1995. "Why Marry? Race and the Transition to Marriage among Cohabitors." *Demography* 32:509-20.

———. 1999. "New Families and Nonresident Father-Child Visitation." *Social Forces* 78:87-116.

———. 2000. "Serial Parenting and Economic Support for Children. *Journal of Marriage and Family* 62:111-122.

Mare, Robert D. 1981. "Trends in Schooling: Demography, Performance, and Organization." *Annals of the American Academy of Political and Social Science* 453:107-9.

———. 1991. "Five Decades of Educational Assortive Mating." *American Sociological Review* 56:15-32.

———. 1995. "Changes in Educational Attainment and School Enrollment." Pp. 155-214 in *State of the Union: America in the 1990s,* vol. 1, *Economic Trends,* edited by Reynolds Farley. New York: Russell Sage Foundation.

Marini, Margaret M. and Beth Anne Shelton. 1993. "Measuring Household Work: Recent Experience in the United States." *Social Science Research* 22:361-82.

Marsiglio, William. 1995. "Young Nonresident Biological Fathers." Pp. 325-48 in *Single Parent Families: Diversity, Myths, and Realities,* edited by Shirley M. H. Hanson, Marsha L. Heims, Doris J. Julian, and Marvin B. Sussman. Binghamton, NY: Haworth.

Martin, Joyce A., Betty Smith, T. J. Mathews, and Stephanie J. Ventura. 1999. "Births and Deaths: Preliminary Data for 1998." *National Vital Statistics Reports* 47(25).

Martin, Steven. 2000. "Diverging Fertility among U.S. Women Who Delay Childbearing." *Demography* 37:415-26.

Martinez, Gladys M. and Jennifer C. Day. 1999. *School Enrollment—Social and Economic Characteristics of Students.* Current Population Reports, Series P-20, No. 516. Washington, DC: Government Printing Office.

Mason, Karen Oppenheim and Karen Kuhlthau. 1989. "Determinants of Child Care Ideals among Mothers of Preschool-Aged Children." *Journal of Marriage and Family* 51:593-603.

Masumura, Wilfred and Paul Ryscavage. 1994. *Dynamics of Economic Well-Being: Labor Force and Income: 1990 to 1992.* Current Population Reports, Series P-70, 40. Washington, DC: Government Printing Office.

Maxwell, Nan. 1990. "Changing Female Labor Force Participation: Influence on Income Inequality and Distribution." *Social Forces* 68:1251-66.

Mayer, Susan E. 1997a. "Trends in the Economic Well-Being and Life Chances of America's Children." Pp. 49-69 in *Consequences of Growing Up Poor,* edited by Greg J. Duncan and Jeanne Brooks-Gunn. New York: Russell Sage Foundation.

———. 1997b. *What Money Can't Buy: Family Income and Children's Life Chances.* Cambridge, MA: Harvard University Press.

Mayer, Susan E. and Christopher Jencks. 1989a. "Growing Up in Poor Neighborhoods: How Much Does It Matter?" *Science* 243:1441-45.

———. 1989b. "Poverty and the Distribution of Material Hardship." *Journal of Human Resources* 24:88-114.

Mayesky, Mary E. 1979. "Extended Day Program in a Public Elementary School." *Children Today* 8(3):6-9.

McDaniel, Antonio and S. Philip Morgan. 1996. "Racial Differences in Mother-Child Coresidence in the Past." *Journal of Marriage and Family* 58:1011-17.

McFalls, Joseph and Marguerite McFalls. 1984. *Disease and Fertility.* Orlando, FL: Academic Press.

McGarry, Kathleen and Robert F. Schoeni. 2000. "Social Security, Economic Growth, and the Rise in Elderly Widows' Independence in the Twentieth Century." *Demography* 37:221-36.

McLanahan Sara S., and Lynne M. Casper. 1995. "Growing Diversity and Inequality in the American Family." Pp. 1-45 in *State of the Union: America in the 1990s,* vol. 2, *Social Trends,* edited by Reynolds Farley. New York: Russell Sage Foundation.

McLanahan, Sara S, Lynne M. Casper, and Annemette Sørensen. 1995. "Women's Roles and Women's Poverty in Eight Industrialized Countries." Pp. 258-78 in *Gender and Family Change in Industrialized Countries,* edited by Karen Oppenheim Mason and An-Magritt Jensen. Oxford: Clarendon.

McLanahan, Sara S. and Erin L. Kelly. 1997. "The Feminization of Poverty: Past and Future." Unpublished manuscript.

McLanahan, Sara S. and Gary Sandefur. 1994. *Growing Up with a Single Parent: What Hurts, What Helps.* Cambridge, MA: Harvard University Press.

McLanahan, Sara S., Annemette Sørensen, and Dorothy Watson. 1989. "Sex Differences in Poverty, 1950-1980." *Signs* 15:102-22.

McLaughlin, Diane K. and Daniel T. Lichter. 1997. "Poverty and the Marital Behavior of Young Women." *Journal of Marriage and Family* 59:582-94.

McLaughlin, Diane K., Daniel T. Lichter, and Gail M. Johnson. 1993. "Some Women Marry Young: Transitions to First Marriage in Metropolitan and Non-metropolitan Areas." *Journal of Marriage and Family* 55:827-38.

McLaughlin, Steven D. 1982. "Differential Patterns of Female Labor Force Participation Surrounding the First Birth." *Journal of Marriage and Family* 44:407-20.

McLindon, J. 1987. "Separate but Unequal: The Economic Disaster of Divorce for Women and Children." *Family Law Quarterly* 21:351-409.

McNeal, Ralph. 1995. "Extracurricular Activities and High School Dropouts." *Sociology of Education* 68:62-81.

Meyer, David R. 1998. "The Effect of Child Support on the Economic Status of Nonresidents." Pp. 67-93 in *Fathers under Fire: The Revolution in Child Support Enforcement,* edited by Irwin Garfinkel, Sara S. McLanahan, Daniel R. Meyer, and Judith A. Seltzer. New York: Russell Sage Foundation.

Milkie, Melissa A., Suzanne M. Bianchi, Marybeth J. Mattingly, and John P. Robinson. 2000. "How Involved Are Fathers? Ideals, Realities, and the Relationship to Parental Well-Being." Presented at the annual meeting of the American Association for Public Opinion Research, May, Portland, OR.

Milkie, Melissa A. and Pia Peltola. 1999. "Playing All the Roles: Gender and the Work-Family Balancing Act." *Journal of Marriage and Family* 61:476-90.

Mincer, Jacob and Solomon Polachek. 1974. "Family Investments in Human Capital: Earnings of Women." Pp. 397-429 in *Economics of the Family,* edited by Theodore W. Schultz. Chicago: University of Chicago Press.

Mincy, Ronald B. 1994. *Nurturing Young Black Males: Challenges to Agencies, Programs, and Social Policy.* Washington, DC: Urban Institute Press.

Minkler, Meredith. 1998. "Intergenerational Households Headed by Grandparents: Demographic and Sociological Contexts." Pp. 3-18 in *Grandparents and Other Relatives Raising Children: Background Papers from Generations United's Expert Symposium,* edited by Generations United. Washington, DC: Generations United.

Minkler, Meredith, Esme Fuller-Thomson, Doriane Miller, and Diane Driver. 1997. "Depression in Grandparents Raising Grandchildren: Results of a National Longitudinal Study." *Archives of Family Medicine* 6:445-52.

Minkler, Meredith and Kathleen M. Roe. 1993. *Grandmothers as Caregivers: Raising Children of the Crack Cocaine Epidemic.* Newbury Park, CA: Sage.

———. 1996. "Grandparents as Surrogate Parents." *Generations* 20:34-38.

Mintz, Steven. 1998. "From Patriarchy to Androgamy and Other Myths: Placing Man's Family Roles in Historical Perspective." Pp. 3-30 in *Men in Families: When Do They Get Involved? What Difference Does it Make?* edited by Alan Booth and Ann C. Crouter. Mahwah, NJ: Lawrence Erlbaum.

Mirowsky, John and Catherine E. Ross. 1989. *Social Consequences of Psychological Distress.* New York: Aldine de Gruyter.

Moen, Phyllis, Donna Dempster-McClain, and Robin M. Williams, Jr. 1992. "Successful Aging: A Life Course Perspective on Women's Multiple Roles and Health." *American Journal of Sociology* 97:1612-38.

Moffitt, Robert A. 1992. "Incentive Effects of the U.S. Welfare System: A Review." *Journal of Economic Literature* 30:1-61.

Moffitt, Robert A. and Michael S. Rendall. 1995. "Cohort Trends in the Lifetime Distribution of Female Family Headship in the U.S., 1968-85." *Demography* 32:407-24.

Moffitt, Robert A. and Jennifer Roff. 2000. *The Diversity of Welfare Leavers.* Welfare, Children and Families: A Three-City Study, Policy Brief 00-2. Baltimore: Johns Hopkins University.

Moore, John C. 1982. "Parents' Choice of Day Care Services." *Annals of the American Academy of Political and Social Science* 461:125-34.

Moore, Kristen A. and Linda J. Waite. 1981. "Marital Dissolution, Early Motherhood and Early Marriage." *Social Forces* 60:20-40.

Morgan, Leslie. 1991. *After Marriage Ends: Economic Consequences for Midlife Women.* Newbury Park, CA: Sage.

Morgan, S. Philip. 1996. "Characteristic Features of Modern American Fertility." Pp. 19-66 in *Fertility in the United States: New Patterns, New Theories,* edited by J. B. Casterline, Ronald D. Lee, and Karen A. Foote. New York: Population Council.

Mosher, William D. and Christine A. Bachrach. 1982. "Childlessness in the United States: Estimates from the National Survey of Family Growth." *Journal of Family Issues* 3:517-43.

Mott, Frank L. and S. F. Moore. 1979. "The Causes of Marital Disruption among Young American Women: An Interdisciplinary Perspective." *Journal of Marriage and Family* 41:355-65.

Mott, Frank L. and David Shapiro. 1983. "Complementarity of Work and Fertility among Young Mothers." *Population Studies* 37:239-52.

Moynihan, Daniel P. 1965. *The Negro Family: The Case for National Action.* Washington, DC: Office of Policy Planning and Research, U.S. Department of Labor.

Murphy, Kevin M. and Finis Welch. 1992. "Wage Differentials in the 1980s: The Role of International Trade." Pp. 39-69 in *Workers and Their Wages: Changing Patterns in the United States,* edited by Marvin K. Kosters. Washington, DC: American Enterprise Institute.

Murray, Charles. 1984. *Losing Ground: American Social Policy 1950-1980.* New York: Basic Books.

Mutchler, Jan. 1992. "Living Arrangements and Household Transitions among the Unmarried in Later Life." *Social Science Quarterly* 73:565-80.

Mutchler, Jan and W. Parker Frisbie. 1987. "Household Structure among the Elderly: Race/Ethnic Differences." *National Journal of Sociology* 1:3-23.

Myrdal, Gunnar and Alva Myrdal. 1934. *Ris i befolkningsfragan.* Stockholm: Bonniers.

Nathan, Richard P. and Thomas L. Gais. 1999. *Implementing the Personal Responsibility Act of 1996: A First Look.* Albany, NY: Nelson A. Rockefeller Institute of Government.

National Center for Education Statistics. 1989. *Digest of Education Statistics 1989.* Washington, DC: Government Printing Office.

National Center for Health Statistics. 1995. "Advance Report of Final Divorce Statistics, 1989 and 1990." *Monthly Vital Statistics Report* 43(9S).

———. 1999a. "United States Life Tables, 1997." *National Vital Statistics Reports* 47(28).

———. 1999b. "United States Life Tables, 1998." *National Vital Statistics Reports* 48(18).

———. 2000a. "Births: Final Data for 1998." *National Vital Statistics Reports* 48(3).

———. 2000b. "Deaths: Final Data for 1998." *National Vital Statistics Reports* 48(11).

National Institute of Child Health and Human Development. 2000. *How Do Children Spend Their Time? Children's Activities, School Achievement, and Well-Being.* Research on Today's Issues No. 11. Washington, DC: Author.

National Research Council. 1987. *Risking the Future: Adolescent Sexuality, Pregnancy, and Childbearing.* Washington, DC: National Academy Press.

National Women's Conference Committee. 1986. *National Plan of Action Update.* Washington, DC: Author.

Neugarten, Bernice L. and Karol K. Weinstein. 1964. "The Changing American Grandparent." *Journal of Marriage and Family* 26:199-204.

Niemi, Iiris. 1988. "Main Trends in Time Use from the 1920s to the 1980s." Presented at the meeting of the International Research Group on Time Budgets and Social Activities, June, Budapest.

Nock, Steven L. 1995. "A Comparison of Marriages and Cohabiting Relationships." *Journal of Family Issues* 16:53-76.

———. 1998a. "The Consequences of Premarital Fatherhood." *American Sociological Review* 63:250-63.

———. 1998b. *Marriage in Men's Lives.* New York: Oxford University Press.

Nock, Steven L. and Paul William Kingston. 1988. "Time with Children: The Impact of Couples' Work-Time Commitments." *Social Forces* 67:59-85.

Nord, Christine W. and Nicholas Zill. 1996. *Non-custodial Parents' Participation in Their Children's Lives: Evidence from the Survey of Income and Program Participation.* Vol. 1. Final report prepared for the Office of Human Services Policy, Office of the Assistant Secretary for Planning and Evaluation, U.S. Department of Health and Human Services. Washington, DC: Government Printing Office.

Norris, Michele. 1991. "Grandmothers Who Fill Void Carved by Drugs." *Washington Post,* August 30, p. C12.

O'Connell, Martin. 1977. *Fertility of American Women: June 1976.* Current Population Reports, Series P-20, No. 308. Washington, DC: Government Printing Office.

———. 1990. "Maternity Leave Arrangements: 1961-85." Pp. 11-52 in *Work and Family Patterns of American Women.* Current Population Reports, Series P-23, No. 165. Washington, DC: Government Printing Office.

———. 1991. "Late Expectations: Childbearing Patterns of American Women for the 1990's." Pp. 1-18 in *Studies in American Fertility.* Current Population Reports, Series P-23, No. 176. Washington, DC: Government Printing Office.

———. 1993. *Where's Papa? Father's Role in Child Care.* Population Trends and Public Policy No. 20. Washington, DC: Population Reference Bureau.

O'Connell, Martin and David E. Bloom. 1987. *Juggling Jobs and Babies: America's Child Care Challenge.* Population Trends and Public Policy No. 12. Washington, DC: Population Reference Bureau.

O'Connell, Martin and Maurice J. Moore. 1977. "New Evidence on the Value of Birth Expectations." *Demography* 14:255-64.

Oliver, Melvin L. and Thomas M. Shapiro. 1995. *Black Wealth/White Wealth: A New Perspective on Racial Inequality.* New York: Routledge.

O'Neil, Robin and Ellen Greenberger. 1994. "Patterns of Commitment to Work and Parenting: Implication for Role Strain." *Journal of Marriage and Family* 56:101-18.

O'Neill, June and Solomon Polachek. 1993. "Why the Gender Gap in Wages Narrowed in the 1980s." *Journal of Labor Economics* 11:205-28.

Ono, Hiromi. 1998. "Husbands' and Wives' Resources and Marital Dissolution." *Journal of Marriage and Family* 60:674-89.

Oppenheimer, Valerie Kincade. 1988. "A Theory of Marriage Timing." *American Journal of Sociology* 94:563-91.

———. 1994. "Women's Rising Employment and the Future of the Family in Industrial Societies." *Population and Development Review* 20:293-342.

———. 1997. "Women's Employment and the Gain to Marriage: The Specialization and Trading Model." *Annual Review of Sociology* 23:431-53.

Oppenheimer, Valerie Kincade, Matthijs Kalmijn, and Nelson Lim. 1997. "Men's Career Development and Marriage Timing during a Period of Rising Inequality." *Demography* 34:311-30.

Oppenheimer, Valerie Kincade and Vivien Lew. 1995. "American Marriage Formation in the Eighties: How Important Was Women's Economic Independence?" Pp. 105-38 in *Gender and Family Change in Industrialized Countries,* edited by Karen Oppenheim Mason and An-Magritt Jensen. Oxford: Clarendon.

Oropesa, Ralph Salvatore. 1993. "Using the Service Economy to Relieve the Double Burden: Female Labor Force Participation and Service Purchases." *Journal of Family Issues* 14:438-73.

———. 1996. "Normative Beliefs about Marriage and Cohabitation: A Comparison of Non-Latino Whites, Mexican Americans, and Puerto Ricans." *Journal of Marriage and Family* 58:49-62.

Pampel, Fred C. 1983. "Changes in the Propensity to Live Alone: Evidence from Consecutive Cross-Sectional Surveys, 1960-1976." *Demography* 20:433-47.

Parcel, Toby L. and Elizabeth G. Menaghan. 1994. *Parents' Jobs and Children's Lives.* New York: Aldine.

Parke, Ross D. 1995. "Fathers and Families." Pp. 27-63 in *Handbook of Parenting,* vol. 3, *Status and Social Conditions of Parenting,* edited by Marc H. Bornstein. Hillsdale, NJ: Lawrence Erlbaum.

Parsons, Talcott. 1943. "The Kinship System of the Contemporary United States." *American Anthropologist* 45:22-38.

Patterson, Charlotte J. 1992. "Children of Lesbian and Gay Parents." *Child Development* 63:1025-42.

———. 2000. "Family Relationships of Lesbians and Gay Men." *Journal of Marriage and Family* 62:1052-69.

Pearce, Diana M. 1978. "The Feminization of Poverty: Women, Work, and Welfare." *Urban and Social Change Review* 11:128-36.

———. 1988. "Farewell to Alms: Women's Fare under Welfare." Pp. 493-506 in *Women: A Feminist Perspective,* 3d ed., edited by Jo Freeman. Mountain View, CA: Mayfield.

Peisner-Feinberg, Ellen S., Margaret R. Burchinal, Richard M. Clifford, Mary L. Culkin, Carollee Howes, and Sharon L. Kagan. 1999. "The Children of the Cost, Quality, and Outcomes Study Go to School" [On-line].
Available Internet: http://www.fpg.unc.edu/~ncedl/pages/cqes.htm

Perry-Jenkins, Maureen and Karen Fox Folk. 1994. "Class, Couples, and Conflict: Effects of the Division of Labor on Assessments of Marriage in Dual-Earner Families." *Journal of Marriage and Family* 56:165-80.

Perry-Jenkins, Maureen, Rena L. Repetti, and Ann C. Crouter. 2000. "Work and Family in the 1990s." *Journal of Marriage and Family* 62:981-98.

Peterson, Richard. 1996. "The Economic Consequences of Divorce: A Re-evaluation of Lenore Weitzman's *The Divorce Revolution.*" *American Sociological Review* 61:347-67.

Phillips, Deborah. 1987. *Quality of Child Care: What Does Research Tell Us?* Washington, DC: National Association for the Education of Young Children.

Pleck, Elizabeth A. and Joseph H. Pleck. 1997. "Fatherhood Ideals in the United States: Historical Dimensions." Pp. 33-48 in *The Role of the Father in Child Development,* 3d ed., edited by Michael E. Lamb. New York: John Wiley.

Pleck, Joseph H. 1983. "Husbands' Paid Work and Family Roles: Current Research Issues." Pp. 231-333 in *Research in the Interweave of Social Roles,* vol. 3, *Families and Jobs,* edited by Helena Z. Lopata and Joseph H. Pleck. Greenwich, CT: JAI.

———. 1997. "Paternal Involvement: Levels, Sources, and Consequences." Pp. 66-103 in *The Role of the Father in Child Development,* 3d ed., edited by Michael E. Lamb. New York: John Wiley.

Popenoe, David. 1988. *Disturbing the Nest: Family Change and Decline in Modern Societies.* New York: Aldine de Gruyter.

———. 1993. "American Family Decline, 1960-1990: A Review and Appraisal." *Journal of Marriage and Family* 55:527-55.

———. 1996. *Life without Father.* New York: Free Press.

Popenoe, David and Barbara Dafoe Whitehead. 1999. *Should We Live Together? What Young Adults Need to Know About Cohabitation Before Marriage.* New Brunswick, NJ: National Marriage Project.

Posner, Jill K. and Deborah Lowe Vandell. 1994. "Low Income Children's After-School Care: Are There Beneficial Effects of After-School Programs?" *Child Development* 65:440-56.

Presser, Harriet B. 1988. "Shift Work and Child Care among Young Dual-Earner American Parents." *Journal of Marriage and Family* 50:133-48.

———. 1989a. "Can We Make Time for Children? The Economy, Work Schedules, and Child Care." *Demography* 26:523-43.

———. 1989b. "Some Economic Complexities of Child Care Provided by Grandmothers." *Journal of Marriage and Family* 51:581-91.

———. 1994. "Employment Schedules among Dual-Earner Spouses and the Division of Household Labor by Gender." *American Sociological Review* 59:348-64.

Presser, Harriet B. and Amy G. Cox. 1997. "The Work Schedules of Low-Educated American Women and Welfare Reform." *Monthly Labor Review* 120(April):25-34.

Preston, Samuel H. 1984. "Children and the Elderly: Divergent Paths for America's Dependents." *Demography* 21:435-58.

———. 1993. "Demographic Change in the United States, 1970-2050." Pp. 51-77 in *Forecasting the Health of Elderly Populations,* edited by Kenneth G. Manton, Burton H. Singer, and Richard M. Suzman. New York: Springer-Verlag.

Qian, Zhenchao. 1998. "Changes in Assortative Mating: The Impact of Age and Education, 1970-1990." *Demography* 35:279-92.

Radke-Yarrow, Marian, Carolyn Zahn-Waxler, and M. Chapman. 1983. "Children's Prosocial Dispositions and Behaviors." Pp. 469-545 in *Handbook of Child Psychology,* vol. 4, *Socialization, Personality, and Social Development,* edited by Paul H. Mussen and E. Mavis Hetherington. New York: John Wiley.

Raley, R. Kelly. 1996. "A Shortage of Marriageable Men? A Note on the Role of Cohabitation in Black-White Differences in Marriage Rates." *American Sociological Review* 61:973-83.

———. 2000. "Recent Trends and Differentials in Marriage and Cohabitation: The United States." Pp. 19-39 in *The Ties That Bind: Perspectives on Marriage and Cohabitation,* edited by Linda J. Waite, Christine A. Bachrach, Michelle Hinden, Elizabeth Thomson, and Arland T. Thornton. New York: Aldine de Gruyter.

———. 2001. "Increasing Fertility in Cohabiting Unions: Evidence for the Second Demographic Transition in the United States?" *Demography* 38:59-66.

Repetti, Rena L. 1993. "Short-Term Effects of Occupational Stressors on Daily Mood and Health Complaints." *Health Psychology* 12:126-31.

———. 1998. "The Promise of a Multiple Roles Paradigm for Women's Health Research." *Women's Health: Research on Gender, Behavior, and Policy* 4:273-80.

Repetti, Rena L. and Jenifer Wood. 1997. "Effects of Daily Stress at Work on Mothers' Interactions with Preschoolers." *Journal of Family Psychology* 11:90-108.

Riley, Lisa A. and Jennifer L. Glass. 2000. "You Can't Always Get What You Want: Infant Care Preferences and Use among Employed Mothers." Presented at the annual meeting of the Population Association of America, March, Los Angeles.

Riley, Matilda W. and John W. Riley. 1993. "Connections: Kin and Cohort." In *The Changing Contract across Generations,* edited by Vern L. Bengtson and W. Andrew Achenbaum. New York: Aldine de Gruyter.

Rindfuss, Ronald R. 1991. "The Young Adult Years: Diversity, Structural Change, and Fertility." *Demography* 28:493-512.

Rindfuss, Ronald R. and Larry L. Bumpass. 1976. "How Old Is Too Old? Age and the Sociology of Fertility." *Family Planning Perspectives* 8:226-30.

Rindfuss, Ronald R. and Allan M. Parnell. 1989. "The Varying Connection between Marital Status and Childbearing in the United States." *Population and Development Review* 15:447-70.

Rindfuss, Ronald R. and Audrey VandenHeuvel. 1990. "Cohabitation: A Precursor to Marriage or an Alternative to Being Single?" *Population and Development Review* 16:703-26.

Risman, Barbara J., Maxine P. Atkinson, and Stephen P. Blackwelder. 1999. "Understanding the Juggling Act: Gendered Preferences and Social Structural Constraints." *Sociological Forum* 14:319-44.

Robertson, Joan F. 1977. "Grandparenthood: A Study of Role Conceptions." *Journal of Marriage and Family* 39:165-74.

Robins, Philip K. 1992. "Why Did Child Support Award Levels Decline from 1978 to 1985?" *Journal of Human Resources* 27:362-79.

Robinson, John P. 1988. "Who's Doing the Housework?" *American Demographics* 10:24-63.

———. 1993. *The Demographics of Time Use.* Ithaca, NY: American Demographics.

Robinson, John P. and Philip E. Converse. 1972. "Social Change as Reflected in the Use of Time." Pp. 17-86 in *The Human Meaning of Social Change,* edited by Angus Campbell and Philip E. Converse. New York: Russell Sage Foundation.

Robinson, John P. and Geoffrey Godbey. 1999. *Time for Life: The Surprising Ways Americans Use Their Time.* 2d ed. State College: Pennsylvania State University Press.

Robinson, John P. and Melissa A. Milkie. 1998. "Back to the Basics: Trends in and Role Determinants of Women's Attitudes toward Housework." *Journal of Marriage and Family* 60:205-18.

Rodman, Hyman, David J. Pratto, and Rosemary Smith Nelson. 1985. "Child Care Arrangements and Children's Functioning: A Comparison of Self-Care and Adult-Care Children." *Developmental Psychology* 21:413-18.

Rogers, Stacy J. 1999. "Wives' Income and Marital Quality: Are There Reciprocal Effects?" *Journal of Marriage and Family* 61:123-32.

Rones, Philip L., Randy E. Ilg, and Jennifer M. Gardner. 1997. "Trends in Hours of Work since the Mid-1970s." *Monthly Labor Review* 120(April):3-14.

Ross, Catherine E. 1987. "The Division of Labor at Home." *Social Forces* 65:816-33.

Ross, Edward Alsworth. 1927. *Standing Room Only.* New York: Century.

Ross, Heather L. and Isabel V. Sawhill. 1975. *Time of Transition: The Growth of Families Headed by Women.* Washington, DC: Urban Institute Press.

Rossi, Alice S. and Peter H. Rossi. 1990. *Of Human Bonding: Parent-Child Relations across the Life Course.* New York: Aldine de Gruyter.

Ruggles, Patricia. 1990. *Drawing the Line: Alternative Poverty Measures and Their Implications for Public Policy.* Washington, DC: Urban Institute Press.

Ruggles, Steven. 1987. *Prolonged Connections: The Rise of the Extended Family in Nineteenth-Century England and America.* Madison: University of Wisconsin Press.

———. 1994. "The Transformation of American Family Structure." *American Historical Review* 99:103-27.

———. 1995. "Living Arrangements of the Elderly in America: 1880-1990." Pp. 254-63 in *Aging and Generational Relations over the Life Course: A Historical and Cross-Cultural Perspective,* edited by Tamara K. Hareven. New York: Aldine de Gruyter.

———. 1997. "The Rise of Divorce and Separation in the United States, 1880-1990." *Demography* 34:455-66.

Ruggles, Steven and Ronald Goeken. 1992. "Race and Multigenerational Family Structure in the United States, 1900-1980." Pp. 15-42 in *The American Family: Patterns and Prospects* edited by Scott J. South and Stuart E. Tolnay. Boulder, CO: West Wind.

Rutrough, Thyne S. and Mary Beth Ofstedal. 1997. "Grandparents Living with Grandchildren: A Metropolitan-Nonmetropolitan Comparison." Presented at the annual meeting of the Population Association of America, March.

Ryder, Norman B. 1982. "Fertility Trends." Pp. 286-92 in *International Encyclopedia of Population,* vol. 1, edited by John A. Ross. New York: Free Press.

———. 1987. "Reconsideration of a Model of Family Demography." Pp. 102-22 in *Family Demography: Methods and Their Applications,* edited by John Bongaarts, Thomas K. Burch, and Kenneth Wachter. Oxford: Clarendon.

———. 1990. "What Is Going to Happen to American Fertility?" *Population and Development Review* 16:433-54.

———. 1992. "The Centrality of Time in the Study of the Family." Pp. 161-75 in *Family Systems and Cultural Change,* edited by Elza Berquo and Peter Xenos. Oxford: Clarendon.

Ryder, Norman B. and Charles F. Westoff. 1971. *Reproduction in the United States 1965.* Princeton, NJ: Princeton University Press.

Ryscavage, Paul. 1995. "A Surge in Growing Income Inequality?" *Monthly Labor Review* 118(August):51-61.

Salmon, Jacqueline L. 2000. "Man of the House." *Washington Post Magazine,* May 7, pp. 6-11.

Sanchez, Laura. 1993. "Women's Power and the Gendered Division of Domestic Labor in the Third World." *Gender & Society* 7:434-59.

Sanchez, Laura, Wendy D. Manning, and Pamela J. Smock. 1998. "Sex-Specialized or Collaborative Mate Selection: Union Transitions among Cohabiting Couples." *Social Science Research* 27:280-304.

Sanchez, Laura and Elizabeth Thomson. 1997. "Becoming Mothers and Fathers: Parenthood, Gender, and the Division of Labor." *Gender & Society* 11:747-72.

Sandberg, John F. and Sandra L. Hofferth. 1999. "Changes in Parental Time with Children, U.S. 1981-1997." Presented at the annual meeting of the International Association for Time Use Research, University of Essex, October 6-8, Colchester, England.

Sayer, Liana C. and Suzanne M. Bianchi. 2000. "Women's Economic Independence and Divorce: A Review and Reexamination." *Journal of Family Issues* 21:906-43.

Schoen, Robert. 1992. "First Unions and the Stability of First Marriages." *Journal of Marriage and Family* 54:281-84.

Schoen, Robert and Robin M. Weinick. 1993. "Partner Choice in Marriages and Cohabitations." *Journal of Marriage and Family* 55:408-14.

Schweinhart, Lawrence, Helen Barnes, and David Weikart. 1993. *Significant Benefits: The High/Scope Perry Preschool Study through Age 27.* Ypsilanti, MI: High/Scope.

Scoon-Rogers, Lydia and Gordon Lester. 1995. *Child Support for Custodial Mothers and Fathers: 1991.* Current Population Reports, Series P-60, No. 187. Washington, DC: Government Printing Office.

Sears, Heather A. and Nancy L. Galambos. 1992. "Women's Work Conditions and Marital Adjustment in Two-Earner Couples: A Structural Model." *Journal of Marriage and Family* 54:789-97.

Seltzer, Judith A. 1991a. "Legal and Physical Custody Arrangements in Recent Divorces." *Social Science Quarterly* 71:250-66.

———. 1991b. "Relationships between Fathers and Children Who Live Apart: The Father's Role After Separation." *Journal of Marriage and Family* 53:79-101.

———. 1998. "Father by Law: Effects of Joint Legal Custody on Nonresident Fathers' Involvement with Children." *Demography* 35:135-46.

———. 2000. "Families Formed outside Marriage." *Journal of Marriage and Family* 62:1247-68.

Seltzer, Judith A. and Suzanne M. Bianchi. 1988. "Children's Contact with Absent Parents." *Journal of Marriage and Family* 50:663-77.

Semple, Shirley J. 1992. "Conflict in Alzheimer's Caregiving Families: Its Dimensions and Consequences." *Gerontologist* 32:648-55.

Sharp, Deborah. 1999. "After a Lifetime of Work, a Second Family to Raise." *USA Today,* July 1, p. D8.

Shelton, Beth Anne. 1990. "The Distribution of Household Tasks: Does Wife's Employment Status Make a Difference?" *Journal of Family Issues* 11:115-53.

———. 1992. *Women, Men, and Time: Gender Differences in Paid Work, Housework, and Leisure.* Westport, CT: Greenwood.

Shelton, Beth Anne and Daphne John. 1993. "Does Marital Status Make a Difference? *Journal of Family Issues* 14:401-20.

———. 1996. "The Division of Household Labor." *Annual Review of Sociology* 22:299-322.

Shore, Ron J. and Bert Hayslip, Jr. 1994. "Custodial Grandparenting: Implications for Children's Development." Pp. 171-218 in *Redefining Families: Implications for Children's Development,* edited by Adele Eskeles Gottfried and Allen W. Gottfried. New York: Plenum.

Silverstein, Merril. 1995. "Stability and Change in Temporal Distance between the Elderly and Their Children." *Demography* 32:29-46.

Silverstein, Merril and Vern L. Bengtson. 1997. "Intergenerational Solidarity and the Structure of Adult Child-Parent Relationships in American Families." *American Journal of Sociology* 103:429-60.

Silverstein, Merril, Roseann Giarrusso, and Vern L. Bengtson. 1998. "Intergenerational Solidarity and the Grandparent Role." Pp. 144-58 in *Handbook on Grandparenthood,* edited by Maximiliane E. Szinovacz. Westport, CT: Greenwood.

Singh, Susheela and Jacqueline E. Darroch. 1999. "Trends in Sexual Activity among Adolescent American Women: 1982-1995." *Family Planning Perspectives* 31:212-19.

Smeeding, Timothy M., Lee Rainwater, and Sheldon Danziger. 1997. "Child Poverty in Advanced Economies: The Economy, the Family, and the State." Presented at the annual meeting of the American Sociological Association, August, Toronto.

Smelser, Neil J., William Julius Wilson, and Faith Mitchell, eds. 2001. *America Becoming: Racial Trends and Their Consequences.* Washington, DC: National Academy Press.

Smith, Herbert L., S. Philip Morgan, and Tanya Koropeckyj-Cox. 1996. "A Decomposition of Trends in the Nonmarital Fertility Ratios of Blacks and Whites in the United States, 1960-1992." *Demography* 33:141-51.

Smith, Kristin E. 2000. *Who's Minding the Kids? Child Care Arrangements: Fall 1995.* Current Population Reports, Series P-70, No. 70. Washington, DC: Government Printing Office.

Smith, Kristin E. and Lynne M. Casper. 1999. "Home Alone: Reasons Parents Leave Their Children Unsupervised." Presented at the annual meeting of the Population Association of America, March, New York.

Smith, James P. and Michael Ward. 1989. "Women in the Labor Market and the Family." *Journal of Economic Perspectives* 3:9-23.

Smock, Pamela J. 1993. "The Economic Costs of Marital Disruption for Young Women over the Past Two Decades." *Demography* 30:353-71.

———. 1994. "Gender and the Short-Run Economic Consequences of Marital Disruption." *Social Forces* 73:243-62.

———. 2000. "Cohabitation in the United States: An Appraisal of Research Themes, Findings and Implications." *Annual Review of Sociology* 26:1-20.

Smock, Pamela J. and Wendy D. Manning. 1997. "Cohabiting Partners' Economic Circumstances and Marriage." *Demography* 34:331-41.

Smock, Pamela J., Wendy D. Manning, and Sanjiv Gupta. 1999. "Marriage, Divorce, and Women's Economic Well-Being." *American Sociological Review* 64:794-812.

Sonenstein, Freya L. 1991. "The Child Care Preferences of Parents with Young Children: How Little Is Known." Pp. 337-53 in *Parental Leave and Child Care: Setting a Research and Policy Agenda,* edited by Janet S. Hyde and Marilyn J. Essex. Philadelphia: Temple University Press.

Sørensen, Annemette. 1989. "Divorce and Its Consequences: The Distribution of Risk between Women and Men." Presented at the International Symposium on Status Passages and Social Risks in the Life Course, Sonderforschungsbereich 186, University of Bremen, October 2-5.

Sotomayor, M. 1989. "The Hispanic Elderly and the Intergenerational Family." *Journal of Children in Contemporary Society* 20:55-65.

South, Scott J. 1991. "Sociodemographic Differentials in Mate Selection Preferences." *Journal of Marriage and Family* 53:928-40.

South, Scott J. and Kim M. Lloyd. 1995. "Spousal Alternatives and Marital Dissolution." *American Sociological Review* 60:21-35.

South, Scott J. and Glenna Spitze. 1994. "Housework in Marital and Non-marital Households." *American Sociological Review* 59:327-47.

Spain, Daphne and Suzanne M. Bianchi. 1996. *Balancing Act: Motherhood, Marriage and Employment among American Women.* New York: Russell Sage Foundation.

Speare, Alden, Jr. and Roger Avery. 1993. "Who Helps Whom in Older Parent-Child Families." *Journal of Gerontology: Social Sciences* 48(2):S64-73.

Spitze, Glenna. 1988. "Women's Employment and Family Relations: A Review." *Journal of Marriage and Family* 50:595-618.

Spitze, Glenna and John R. Logan. 1990. "Sons, Daughters, and Intergenerational Social Support." *Journal of Marriage and Family* 52:420-30.

Spitze, Glenna and Scott J. South. 1985. "Women's Employment, Time Expenditure, and Divorce." *Journal of Family Issues* 6:307-9.

Stacey, Judith. 1990. *Brave New Families: Stories of Domestic Upheaval in the Late 20th Century.* New York: Basic Books.

———. 1993. "Good Riddance to the Family: A Response to David Popenoe." *Journal of Marriage and Family* 55:545-47.

———. 1996. *In the Name of the Family: Rethinking Family Values in the Postmodern Age.* Boston: Beacon.

Steinberg, Laurence. 1987. "Single Parents, Stepparents, and the Susceptibility of Adolescents to Antisocial Peer Pressure." *Child Development* 58:269-75.

Stommel, Manfred, Barbara A. Given, Charles W. Given, and Clare Collins. 1995. "The Impact of the Frequency of Care Activities on the Division of Labor between Primary Caregivers and Other Care Providers." *Research on Aging* 17:412-33.

Stone, Robyn, Gail Lee Cafferata, and Judith Sangl. 1987. "Caregivers of the Frail Elderly: A National Profile." *Gerontologist* 27:616-26.

Sweet, James A. and Larry L. Bumpass. 1987. *American Families and Households.* New York: Russell Sage Foundation.

———. 1990a. "Disruption of Marital and Cohabitation Relationships: A Social-Demographic Perspective." Working Paper No. 32, National Survey of Families and Households, University of Wisconsin, Madison.

———. 1990b. "Young Adults' Views of Marriage, Cohabitation, and Family." Working Paper No. 33, National Survey of Families and Households, University of Wisconsin, Madison.

Szinovacz, Maximiliane E. 1998. "Grandparent Research: Past, Present, and Future." Pp. 1-22 in *Handbook on Grandparenthood,* edited by Maximiliane E. Szinovacz. Westport, CT: Greenwood.

Tasker, Fiona L. and Susan Golombok. 1997. *Growing Up in a Lesbian Family: Effects on Child Development.* New York: Guilford.

Teachman, Jay D. 1993. "Family and Household Research: Life Course Events." Pp. 15.1-5.14 in *Readings in Population Research Methodology,* vol. 4, *Nuptiality, Migration, Household, and Family Research,* edited by Donald Bogue, Eduardo Arriaga, and Douglas Anderton. New York: United Nations Population Fund.

Teachman, Jay D. and Karen A. Polonko. 1990. "Cohabitation and Marital Stability in the United States." *Social Forces* 69:207-20.

Teachman, Jay D., Karen A. Polonko, and John Scanzoni. 1987. "Demography of the Family." Pp. 2-26 in *Handbook of Marriage and the Family,* edited by Marvin B. Sussman and Suzanne K. Steinmetz. New York: Plenum.

Thomas, Jeanne L. 1989. "Gender and Perceptions of Grandparenthood." *International Journal of Aging and Human Development* 29:269-82.

Thompson, Linda. 1991. "Family Work: Women's Sense of Fairness." *Journal of Family Issues* 12:181-96.

Thompson, Linda and Alexis J. Walker. 1989. "Women and Men in Marriage, Work, and Parenthood." *Journal of Marriage and Family* 51:845-72.

Thompson, Tracy. 1998. "A War Inside Your Head." *Washington Post Magazine,* February 15, p. W12.

Thomson, Elizabeth and Ugo Colella. 1992. "Cohabitation and Marital Stability: Quality or Commitment?" *Journal of Marriage and Family* 54:259-67.

Thornton, Arland T. 1989. "Changing Attitudes toward Family Issues in the United States." *Journal of Marriage and Family* 51:873-93.

Thornton, Arland T. and Deborah Freedman. 1983. "The Changing American Family." *Population Bulletin* 38(4).

Treas, Judith and Ramon Torrecilha. 1995. "The Older Population." Pp. 47-92 in *State of the Union: America in the 1990s,* vol. 2, *Social Trends,* edited by Reynolds Farley. New York: Russell Sage Foundation.

Troll, Lillian E. 1983. "Grandparents: The Family Watchdogs." Pp. 63-74 in *Family Relationships in Later Life,* edited by Timothy H. Brubaker. New York: Free Press.

———. 1985. "The Contingencies of Grandparenting." Pp. 135-49 in *Grandparenthood,* edited by Vern L. Bengtson and Joan F. Robertson. Beverly Hills, CA: Sage.

Uhlenberg, Peter. 1980. "Death and the Family." *Journal of Family History* 5:313-20.

———. 1996. "Mortality Decline in the Twentieth Century and Supply of Kin over the Lifecourse." *Gerontologist* 36:681-85.

Uhlenberg, Peter and James B. Kirby. 1998. "Grandparenthood over Time: Historical and Demographic Trends." Pp. 23-39 in *Handbook on Grandparenthood,* edited by Maximiliane E. Szinovacz. Westport, CT: Greenwood.

U.S. Bureau of the Census. 1965. *Estimates of the Population of the United States, by Single Years of Age, Color, and Sex: 1900-1959.* Current Population Reports, Series P-25, No. 311. Washington, DC: Government Printing Office.

———. 1970. *Projections of the Population of the United States, by Age and Sex, 1970 to 2020.* Current Population Reports, Series P-25, No. 470. Washington, DC: Government Printing Office.

———. 1972. *Projections of the Population of the United States, by Age and Sex, 1972 to 2020.* Current Population Reports, Series P-25, No. 493. Washington, DC: Government Printing Office.

———. 1974. *Estimates of the Population of the United States, by Age, Sex, and Race: April 1, 1960 to July 1, 1973.* Current Population Reports, Series P-25, No. 519. Washington, DC: Government Printing Office.

———. 1982. *Preliminary Estimates of the Population of the United States by Age, Sex, and Race*. Current Population Reports, Series P-25, No. 917. Washington, DC: Government Printing Office.

———. 1989. *Child Support and Alimony: 1985*. Current Population Reports, Series P-23, No. 154. Washington, DC: Government Printing Office.

———. 1997. *School Enrollment—Social and Economic Characteristics of Students: October 1997*. Current Population Reports, Series PPL, No. 102. Washington, DC: Government Printing Office.

———. 1998. *Statistical Abstract of the United States: 1998*. Washington, DC: Government Printing Office.

U.S. Council of Economic Advisors. 1999. "The Effects of Welfare Policy and Economic Expansion on Welfare Caseloads: An Update." Washington, DC: Government Printing Office.

U.S. Department of Agriculture, Food and Nutrition Service. 1997. "Household Food Security in the United States in 1995 and 2000: Guide to Measuring Household Food Security." Alexandria, VA: Author.

U.S. Department of Health and Human Services. 2000a. "Children in Foster Care" [On-line]. Available Internet: http://www.acf.dhhs.gov/news/stats/fc.htm

———. 2000b. "New Statistics Show Only Small Percentage of Eligible Families Receive Child Care Help." *HHS News* [On-line]. Available Internet: http://www.acf.dhhs.gov/news/press/2000/ccstudy.htm

U.S. House of Representatives. 1986. *Teen Pregnancy: What Is Being Done? A State-by-State Look*. Report of the Select Committee on Children, Youth and Families, House of Representatives, 99th Congress. Washington, DC: Government Printing Office.

———. 1992. *Grandparents: New Roles and Responsibilities*. Select Committee on Aging Publication No. 102-876. Washington, DC: Government Printing Office.

U.S. Senate. 1992. *Grandparents as Parents: Raising a Second Generation*. Special Committee on Aging Serial No. 102-24. Washington, DC: Government Printing Office.

———. 1998. *Teen Pregnancy: State and Federal Efforts to Implement Prevention Programs and Measure Their Effectiveness*. Report prepared by the General Accounting Office for the Chairman of the Committee on Labor and Human Resources, GAO/HEHS-99-4. Washington, DC: General Accounting Office.

van de Kaa, D. J. 1987. "Europe's Second Demographic Transition." *Population Bulletin* 42(1).

Van Dijk, Liset and Jacques J. Siegers. 1996. "The Division of Child Care among Mothers, Fathers, and Nonparental Care Providers in Dutch Two-Parent Families." *Journal of Marriage and Family* 58:1018-28.

Vandell, Deborah Lowe and Mary Anne Corasaniti. 1988. "The Relationship between Third Graders' After School Care and Social, Academic, and Emotional Functioning." *Child Development* 59:868-75.

Vandell, Deborah Lowe and Janaki Ramanan. 1991. "Children of the National Longitudinal Survey of Youth: Choices in After-School Care and Child Development." *Developmental Psychology* 27:637-43.

Vanek, Joann. 1974. "Time Spent in Housework." *Scientific American,* November, pp. 116-20.

Vannoy, Dana and William W. Philliber. 1992. "Wife's Employment and Quality of Marriage." *Journal of Marriage and Family* 54:387-98.

Ventura, Stephanie J., Joyce A. Martin, Sally C. Curtin, T. J. Mathews, and Melissa M. Park. 2000. "Births: Final Data for 1998." *National Vital Statistics Reports* 48(3).

Ventura, Stephanie J., T. J. Mathews, and Sally C. Curtin. 1999. "Declines in Teenage Birth Rates, 1991-98: Update of National and State Trends." *National Vital Statistics Reports* 47(26).

Vickery, Clair. 1977. "The Time-Poor: A New Look at Poverty." *Journal of Human Resources* 12:27-48.

Vobejda, Barbara. 1991. "Steep Increase Reported in U.S. Births." *Washington Post,* January 20, p. A1.

———. 1998. "Traditional Families Hold On." *Washington Post,* May 28, p. A2.

Waite, Linda J. 1995. "Does Marriage Matter?" *Demography* 32:483-507.

Waite, Linda J., Christine A. Bachrach, Michelle Hinden, Elizabeth Thomson, and Arland T. Thornton, eds. 2000. *The Ties That Bind: Perspectives on Marriage and Cohabitation.* New York: Aldine de Gruyter.

Waite, Linda J. and Maggie Gallagher. 2000. *The Case for Marriage: Why Married People Are Happier, Healthier and Better Off Financially.* Garden City, NY: Doubleday.

Waite, Linda J., Arlene Leibowitz, and Christina Witsberger. 1991. "What Parents Pay For: Child Care Characteristics, Quality and Cost." *Journal of Social Issues* 47:33-48.

Waite, Linda J. and Lee A. Lillard. 1991. "Children and Marital Disruption." *American Journal of Sociology* 96:930-53.

Walker, Kathryn E. 1969. "Homemaking Still Takes Time." *Journal of Home Economics* 61:621-24.

Warren, Charles W., John S. Santelli, Sherry A. Everett, Laura Kann, Janet L. Collins, Carol Cassell, Leo Morris, and Lloyd J. Kolbe. 1998. "Sexual Behavior among U.S. High School Students, 1990-1995." *Family Planning Perspectives* 30:170-72, 200.

Watkins, Susan Cott, Jane Menken, and John Bongaarts. 1987. "Demographic Foundations of Family Change." *American Sociological Review* 52:346-58.

Watson, Jeffrey A. and Sally A. Koblinsky. 1997. "Strengths and Needs of Working Class African-American and Anglo-American Grandparents." *International Journal of Aging and Human Development* 44:149-65.

Wattenberg, Benjamin J. 1987. *The Birth Dearth.* New York: Pharos.

Weinick, Robin M. 1995. "Sharing a Home: The Experiences of American Women and Their Parents over the Twentieth Century." *Demography* 32:281-97.

Weitzman, Lenore J. 1992. "Marital Property: Its Transformation and Division in the United States." Pp. 85-192 in *Economic Consequences of Divorce: The International Perspective,* edited by Lenore J. Weitzman and Mavis Maclean. New York: Oxford University Press.

Wellington, Alison. 1993. "Changes in the Male/Female Wage Gap, 1976-85." *Journal of Human Resources* 28:383-411.

West, Candace and Don H. Zimmerman. 1987. "Doing Gender." *Gender & Society* 1:125-51.

Westoff, Charles F. 1978. "Some Speculations on the Future of Marriage and Fertility." *Family Planning Perspectives* 10:79-83.

———. 1981. "The Validity of Birth Intentions: Evidence from U.S. Longitudinal Studies." Pp. 51-59 in *Predicting Fertility: Demographic Studies of Birth Expectations,* edited by Gerry E. Hendershot and Paul J. Placek. Lexington, MA: D. C. Heath.

Wetzel, James R. 1995. "Labor Force, Unemployment, and Earnings." Pp. 59-105 in *State of the Union: America in the 1990s,* vol. 1, *Economic Trends,* edited by Reynolds Farley. New York: Russell Sage Foundation.

Whelpton, Pascal K. 1954. *Cohort Fertility: Native White Women in the United States.* Princeton, NJ: Princeton University Press.

Whelpton, Pascal K., Arthur A. Campbell, and John E. Patterson. 1966. *Fertility and Family Planning in the United States.* Princeton, NJ: Princeton University Press.

White, Lynn and Stacy J. Rogers. 2000. "Economic Circumstances and Family Outcomes: A Review of the 1990s." *Journal of Marriage and Family* 62:1035-51.

Whitehead, Barbara Dafoe. 1993. "Dan Quayle Was Right." *Atlantic Monthly,* April, pp. 47 ff.

Wilkie, Jane Riblett, Myra Marx Ferree, and Kathryn Strother Ratcliff. 1998. "Gender and Fairness: Marital Satisfaction in Two-Earner Couples." *Journal of Marriage and Family* 60:577-94.

Willer, Barbara, Sandra L. Hofferth, Ellen Eliason Kisker, Patricia Divine-Hawkins, Elizabeth Farquhar, and Frederic B. Glantz. 1991. *The Demand and Supply of Child Care in 1990: Joint Findings from the National Child Care Survey 1990 and a Profile of Child Care Settings.* Washington, DC: National Association for the Education of Young Children.

Williams, Lindy, Joyce Abma, and Linda J. Piccinino. 1999. "The Correspondence between Intention to Avoid Childbearing and Subsequent Fertility: A Prospective Analysis." *Family Planning Perspectives* 31:220-27.

Willis, Robert J. 1973. "A New Approach to the Economic Theory of Fertility Behavior." *Journal of Political Economy* 81:514-64.

———. 1987. "What Have We Learned from the Economics of the Family?" *American Economic Review* 77:68-71.

Willis, Robert J. and Robert T. Michael. 1994. "Innovation in Family Formation: Evidence on Cohabitation in the U.S." Pp. 9-45 in *The Family, the Market, and the State in Aging Societies,* edited by John Ermisch and Naohiro Ogawa. Oxford: Clarendon.

Wilson, William Julius. 1987. *The Truly Disadvantaged: The Inner City, the Underclass, and Public Policy.* Chicago: University of Chicago Press.

———. 1996. *When Work Disappears: The World of the New Urban Poor.* New York: Alfred A. Knopf.

Wilson, William Julius and Katherine Neckerman. 1986. "Poverty and Family Structure: The Widening Gap between Evidence and Public Policy Issues." In *Fighting Poverty: What Works and What Doesn't,* edited by Sheldon H. Danziger and Daniel H. Weinberg. Cambridge, MA: Harvard University Press.

Wister, Andrew V. 1984. "Living Arrangement Choices of the Elderly: A Decision-Making Approach." Ph.D. dissertation, University of Western Ontario.

Wister, Andrew V. and Thomas K. Burch. 1987. "Values, Perceptions, and Choice in Living Arrangements of the Elderly." Pp. 180-98 in *Critical Issues in Aging Policy: Linking Research and Values,* edited by Edgar F. Borgatta and Rhonda J. V. Montgomery. Newbury Park, CA: Sage.

Wolf, Douglas A. and Beth J. Soldo. 1988. "Household Composition Choices of Older Unmarried Women." *Demography* 25:387-403.

Wood, Vivian and Joan F. Robertson. 1976. "The Significance of Grandparenthood." Pp. 278-304 in *Time, Roles and Self in Old Age,* edited by Jaber F. Gubrium. New York: Human Sciences Press.

Woroby, Jacqueline Lowe and Ronald J. Angel. 1990. "Functional Capacity and Living Arrangements of Unmarried Elderly Persons." *Journal of Gerontology: Social Sciences* 45(3):S95-101.

Yeung, W. Jean, Greg J. Duncan, and Martha S. Hill. 2000. "Putting Fathers Back in the Picture: Parental Activities and Children's Adult Outcomes." Pp. 97-114 in *Fatherhood: Research, Interventions, and Policies,* edited by H. Elizabeth Peters, Gary W. Peterson, Suzanne K. Steinmetz, and Randall D. Day. Binghamton, NY: Haworth.

Yeung, W. Jean, John F. Sandberg, Pamela E. David-Kean, and Sandra L. Hofferth. 2001. "Children's Time with Fathers in Intact Families." *Journal of Marriage and Family* 63:136-54.

Zedlewski, Sheila and Sarah Brauner. 1999. *Are the Steep Declines in Food Stamp Participation Linked to Falling Welfare Caseloads?* Assessing the New Federalism Policy Brief No. B-3. Washington, DC: Urban Institute.

Zick, Cathleen D. and W. Keith Bryant. 1996. "A New Look at Parents' Time Spent in Child Care: Primary and Secondary Time Use." *Social Science Research* 25:260-80.

INDEX

ABOUT THE AUTHORS

Lynne M. Casper received her PhD in demography and sociology from Pennsylvania State University in 1992. She is currently Health Scientist Administrator and Demographer in the Demographic and Behavioral Sciences Branch at the National Institute of Child Health and Human Development (NICHD). She has primary responsibility for research portfolios in the areas of family and households, cohabitation, child care, and fatherhood. She is also director of NICHD's training program in population studies and is program officer for many national data collection efforts. Her current research focuses on the meaning of cohabitation and how cohabitors view themselves. She has published numerous scholarly articles in the areas of families and households, cohabitation, fatherhood, child care, voting, and demographic methods. She previously spent 7 years as a Demographer and Statistician in the Fertility and Family Statistics Branch at the U.S. Bureau of the Census, where she was senior analyst for the families and households, child care, and voting programs. She has authored nearly a dozen Census Bureau Current Population Reports. She was awarded former Vice President Al Gore's Hammer Award for her work on fatherhood with the Interagency Forum on Child and Family Statistics. She is currently a member of the NICHD Family and Child Well-Being Research Network and the Federal Interagency Forum on Child and Family Statistics.

Suzanne M. Bianchi received her PhD in sociology from the University of Michigan in 1978. She is currently Professor of Sociology and Director of the Center on Population, Gender, and Social Inequality at the University of Maryland and also an affiliate faculty member of the Women's Studies Department and the School of Public Affairs. Prior to taking her current position, she was a Demographer with the U.S. Bureau of the Census for 15 years and served as Assistant Chief for Social and Demographic Statistics in the Bureau's Population Division in 1993-94. She is currently directing research projects on American families' use of time and investigating inequality in parental investments in children. She is a noted expert on changing gender roles and has published two books on American women's work and family lives. Her recent publications explore the interrelationship between maternal employment and time with children; women's financial status and the probability of divorce; the gender division of housework; the relationships among marriage, children, and women's employment; the feminization and juvenilization of poverty; the economic well-being of nonresident fathers and custodial mothers; and children's use of time. She was guest editor of a special volume of *Demography* devoted to men in families in 1998. She served as President of the Population Association of America in 2000 and has chaired the Population and Family Sections of the American Sociological Association.

Martin O'Connell received his PhD in demography from the University of Pennsylvania in 1975. Since 1976, he has worked for the U.S. Bureau of the Census and is currently Chief of the Fertility and Family Statistics Branch. In this position, he directs all Census Bureau data collection, processing, analysis, and dissemination of data related to families and households, fertility, child well-being, and child care. These data are collected primarily in the Census Bureau's demographic surveys: the Current Population Survey, the Survey of Income and Program Participation, the American Community Survey, the Survey of Program Dynamics, and the decennial censuses. His current research concentrates on child-care and maternity leave issues and their relationship to labor force participation. Among his other continuing research interests are birth expectations, fertility projections, and out-of-wedlock childbearing. In the areas of child care and the labor force, he has published articles on the effects of employment cycles on parental child-care roles, maternity leave arrangements, child-care arrangements, and the consequential balancing acts in which working parents must engage. His research regarding out-of-wedlock births includes both methodological problems of demographic estimation and the relationship of such births to family formation and dissolution. He has also published several studies on the validity of birth expectations data for long- and short-term population projections.